FUNDAMENTAL TEXTS ON EUROPEAN PRIVATE LAW

OLIVER RADLEY-GARDNER,
HUGH BEALE,
REINHARD ZIMMERMANN
AND
REINER SCHULZE

·HART·
PUBLISHING

HART PUBLISHING
OXFORD AND PORTLAND, OREGON
2003

Published in North America (US and Canada) by
Hart Publishing
c/o International Specialized Book Services
5804 NE Hassalo Street
Portland, Oregon
97213–3644
USA

Hart Publishing is a specialist legal publisher based in Oxford, England. To order
further copies of this book or to request a list of other publications please write to:

Hart Publishing, Salters Boatyard, Folly Bridge, Abingdon Rd, Oxford, OX1 4LB
Telephone: +44 (0)1865 245533 Fax: +44 (0) 1865 794882
email: mail@hartpub.co.uk
WEBSITE: http//:www.hartpub.co.uk

British Library Cataloguing in Publication Data
Data Available

ISBN 1–84113–378–7 (paperback)

Typeset by Olympus Infotech Pvt, India, in Minion 10/12 pt.
Printed and bound in Great Britain

Fundamental Texts on European Private Law

Among the most significant legal developments of our time is the emergence of a European private law. The European Union enacts directives which profoundly affect the practice, teaching and study of core areas of 'classical' private law. Internationally commissions have formulated principles of European trusts, contract and commercial law. Furthermore, uniform private law can be found in a number of international conventions.

This book gathers together fundamental texlts from these three sources into one convenient volume. Its emphasis is on general civil and commercial law, particularly on the obligations and property aspects of these. Fully updated, it contains the recent directives in the areas of E-Commerce, Electronic Signatures and Late Payments. It also makes available for the first time English language versions of a number of texts by international commissions.

This book is a sister volume to the original German and the subsequent Spanish version. With full references to the implementation of the directives in Denmark, EIRE, Finland, Sweden and the United Kingdom, this book will be a useful resource for practitioners, students and teachers working in the field of European private law.

Preface

Among the most significant legal developments of our time is the emergence of a European private law. The European Union enacts directives which profoundly affect the core areas of 'classical' private law. The European Court fashions concepts, rules and principles which are relevant for the law of the Union and, to an increasing degree, also for the laws of its member states. Several international commissions and groups of experts are competing to develop or to 'find' (by means of a type of restatement) common principles of a European law of contract, tort or even trusts. Ambitious research projects strive to establish the 'common core' of the systems of European private law. The European Parliament has repeatedly even called for a codification of European private law, and the European Commission has proposed the creation of a 'common frame of reference' for the drafting of European legislation on private law and possibly to be the basis of an 'optional instrument'.[1] Since then, not only have academic publications taken up the issue, but a number of research organisations have made considerable funds available for the development of a European code on the law of obligations. In legal education, too, there are signs of a change of perspective. The mobility of law students within the European Union is promoted by the extraordinarily successful Erasmus (now Socrates) programme. More and more law faculties are trying to give themselves a 'European' profile by offering integrated study programmes. Institutes, graduate study programmes and chairs of European private law, European commercial law and European legal history have been established. Models of legal harmonisation from Europe's past and from other parts of the world are receiving increasing attention. Moreover, the national isolation of law and legal scholarship is being overcome by the uniform private law laid down in international conventions. Of central importance for the change in consciousness taking place at the moment is the success story of the UN (Vienna) Convention on Contracts for the International Sale of Goods (CISG).

The development sketched only in the roughest outline above can also be seen in the emergence of a legal literature with a European focus. This began in the fields of comparative law and legal history. Since then, we have seen the publication of textbooks on the European law of contract and delict, of comparative casebooks, of series of monographs dealing with European legal history and European private law and of at least three legal journals which are devoted to European private law. What has been lacking so far, however, is a convenient collection which makes available, for research as well as teaching purposes, the foundational texts of European private law.

---

[1] 'An action plan on a More Coherent European Contract Law' COM [2003] 68 FINAL, OJC 63/1, available at http://europa.eu.int/eur-lex/en/com/cnc/en_cnc_number_2003_02.html

The present collection, which was first published in Germany, is intended to fill this gap. It differs from collections of texts already in existence in that country mainly in two respects: (i) It is limited to core areas of private law (ie, in particular, contract, delict/tort and property); (ii) Within those areas, however it includes not only the directives of the European Union, but also the international uniform law and the common legal principles elaborated and published by international groups of experts. Thus, we have excluded fields of law which are usually dealt with separately in legal curricula and in the general legal literature, ie in particular company law, labour law, immaterial property law and competition law. On the other hand, room has been made for texts relating to merchants and to commercial transactions; texts, in other words, which would have their place within the law of obligations in countries which have a 'code unique'. Even in countries which have a sharp distinction between private law and commercial law, a complete exclusion of the latter would, in our opinion, be just as indefensible as, for example, neglecting consumer protection.

However, the texts included in this collection are not only connected by a common thematic thread (the law of obligations and property law, admittedly, at present, with a clear emphasis on the former). They are also linked by the fact that they all aim at harmonising or unifying the law and, therefore, claim to be applicable beyond the confines of any one national legal system. The directives printed in Part I apply within the European Union and may be taken to constitute the legislative core of a specifically European Community private law. The uniform laws in Part II even go a step further by aiming at legal unification on a pan-European, or even global, level. The texts in Part III have been drafted either for the European Union (1), or for the whole of Europe (3), or with an eye to world-wide application. Taking account of initiatives which aim at legal unification beyond the boundaries of the European Union may be justified on two grounds: on the one hand, this would, implicitly, also bring about legal unification in Europe; on the other hand, European and international legal unification often go hand in hand (this is particularly clear with regard to the Principles drafted by Unidroit and by the European Contract Law Commission) and influence each other (cf, for example, the model role played by the CISG for the unification of the European law of contract). It must, of course, be borne in mind that not all of the texts in this collection constitute law which is applicable in a Member State. The uniform laws in Part II require ratification by the respective national legislatures, which has not occurred in every case. The elaboration and publication of common legal principles (Part III), on the other hand, is based on private initiative; these principles, therefore, only have the kind of persuasive authority which any academic effort may have. At the same time, however, they already occupy such an important position in current discussion that they may one day become the point of departure for far-reaching measures of legal unification. The directives of the European Union, too, have to be implemented by the national legislatures. The most important information regarding their implementation in Denmark, EIRE, Finland, Sweden and the United Kingdom is included at the end of the relevant directives in this collection, insofar as has been practically possible.

This collection reflects the law as at 16 August 2003. Obviously, like European private law itself, it is destined for growth. Further directives concerning the law of obligations and property law will be enacted. Unidroit and Uncitral will continue with their work; and in the not too distant future we may expect texts from the Tilburg/Vienna group on European tort law or even the results of the European Civil Code project. We hope to be able to include these texts in future editions of this collection. At the same time, we would like to ask the users of this collection for constructive criticism as to the choice of the texts included here. We welcome any feedback. In particular, we would be pleased if this volume could make a contribution to the teaching of a private law which extends beyond the borders of a given national legal system. The project was supported by funds provided by the TMR Programme of the European Commission within the framework of the 'Common Principles of European Private Law' network and by the Leibniz Programme of the *Deutsche Forschungsgemeinschaft*. For their help with the preparation of the original German version of this volume we would sincerely like to thank Sonja Kohtes (Meerbusch), Stefan Vogenauer and Dirk Schulz (both Regensburg). We are grateful to Jean Meiring and Catherine Maxwell for assistance with regard to the English version.

The work of the English editorial team was carried out almost entirely by Oliver Radley-Gardner, and his fellow editors wish to express gratitude for this. Responsibility for the contents is shared by all the editors, and them alone. Oliver Radley-Gardner would like additionally to thank Colleen Hanley, who gave guidance on some of the more specialist aspects of the EUROPA website.

The Editors, London, 16 August 2003

Contents

Part 2: Unitary Law

Part 3: Common Principles

PART 1

EUROPEAN UNION LEGISLATION

DIRECTIVE 2000/31/EC OF THE EUROPEAN PARLIAMENT AND OF THE COUNCIL

of 8 June 2000

on certain legal aspects of information society services, in particular electronic commerce, in the Internal Market

(Official Journal, L178/00, p 1)

THE EUROPEAN PARLIAMENT AND THE COUNCIL OF THE EUROPEAN UNION –

Having regard to the Treaty establishing the European Community, and in particular Articles 47(2), 55 and 95 thereof,

Having regard to the proposal from the Commission,[1]

Having regard to the opinion of the Economic and Social Committee,[2]

Acting in accordance with the procedure laid down in Article 251 of the Treaty,[3]

Whereas:

(1) The European Union is seeking to forge ever closer links between the States and peoples of Europe, to ensure economic and social progress; in accordance with Article 14(2) of the Treaty, the internal market comprises an area without internal frontiers in which the free movements of goods, services and the freedom of establishment are ensured; the development of information society services within the area without internal frontiers is vital to eliminating the barriers which divide the European peoples.

(2) The development of electronic commerce within the information society offers significant employment opportunities in the Community, particularly in small and medium-sized enterprises, and will stimulate economic growth and investment in innovation by European

---

[1] OJ C 30, 5.2.1999, p 4.

[2] OJ C 169, 16.6.1999, p 36.

[3] Opinion of the European Parliament of 6 May 1999 (OJ C 279, 1.10.1999, p 389), Council common position of 28 February 2000 (OJ C 128, 8.5.2000, p 32) and Decision of the European Parliament of 4 May 2000 (not yet published in the Official Journal).

companies, and can also enhance the competitiveness of European industry, provided that everyone has access to the Internet.

(3)   Community law and the characteristics of the Community legal order are a vital asset to enable European citizens and operators to take full advantage, without consideration of borders, of the opportunities afforded by electronic commerce; this Directive therefore has the purpose of ensuring a high level of Community legal integration in order to establish a real area without internal borders for information society services.

(4)   It is important to ensure that electronic commerce could fully benefit from the internal market and therefore that, as with Council Directive 89/552/EEC of 3 October 1989 on the coordination of certain provisions laid down by law, regulation or administrative action in Member States concerning the pursuit of television broadcasting activities,[4] a high level of Community integration is achieved.

(5)   The development of information society services within the Community is hampered by a number of legal obstacles to the proper functioning of the internal market which make less attractive the exercise of the freedom of establishment and the freedom to provide services; these obstacles arise from divergences in legislation and from the legal uncertainty as to which national rules apply to such services; in the absence of coordination and adjustment of legislation in the relevant areas, obstacles might be justified in the light of the case-law of the Court of Justice of the European Communities; legal uncertainty exists with regard to the extent to which Member States may control services originating from another Member State.

(6)   In the light of Community objectives, of Articles 43 and 49 of the Treaty and of secondary Community law, these obstacles should be eliminated by coordinating certain national laws and by clarifying certain legal concepts at Community level to the extent necessary for the proper functioning of the internal market; by dealing only with certain specific matters which give rise to problems for the internal market, this Directive is fully consistent with the need to respect the principle of subsidiarity as set out in Article 5 of the Treaty.

(7)   In order to ensure legal certainty and consumer confidence, this Directive must lay down a clear and general framework to cover certain legal aspects of electronic commerce in the internal market.

(8)   The objective of this Directive is to create a legal framework to ensure the free movement of information society services between Member States and not to harmonise the field of criminal law as such.

---

[4] OJ L 298, 17.10.1989, p 23. Directive as amended by Directive 97/36/EC of the European Parliament and of the Council (OJ L 202, 30.7.1997, p 60).

(9) The free movement of information society services can in many cases be a specific reflection in Community law of a more general principle, namely freedom of expression as enshrined in Article 10(1) of the Convention for the Protection of Human Rights and Fundamental Freedoms, which has been ratified by all the Member States; for this reason, directives covering the supply of information society services must ensure that this activity may be engaged in freely in the light of that Article, subject only to the restrictions laid down in paragraph 2 of that Article and in Article 46(1) of the Treaty; this Directive is not intended to affect national fundamental rules and principles relating to freedom of expression.

(10) In accordance with the principle of proportionality, the measures provided for in this Directive are strictly limited to the minimum needed to achieve the objective of the proper functioning of the internal market; where action at Community level is necessary, and in order to guarantee an area which is truly without internal frontiers as far as electronic commerce is concerned, the Directive must ensure a high level of protection of objectives of general interest, in particular the protection of minors and human dignity, consumer protection and the protection of public health; according to Article 152 of the Treaty, the protection of public health is an essential component of other Community policies.

(11) This Directive is without prejudice to the level of protection for, in particular, public health and consumer interests, as established by Community acts; amongst others, Council Directive 93/13/EEC of 5 April 1993 on unfair terms in consumer contracts[5] and Directive 97/7/EC of the European Parliament and of the Council of 20 May 1997 on the protection of consumers in respect of distance contracts[6] form a vital element for protecting consumers in contractual matters; those Directives also apply in their entirety to information society services; that same Community acquis, which is fully applicable to information society services, also embraces in particular Council Directive 84/450/EEC of 10 September 1984 concerning misleading and comparative advertising,[7] Council Directive 87/102/EEC of 22 December 1986 for the approximation of the laws, regulations and administrative provisions of the Member States concerning consumer credit,[8] Council Directive 93/22/EEC of 10 May 1993 on investment

---

[5] OJ L 95, 21.4.1993, p 29.
[6] OJ L 144, 4.6.1999, p 19.
[7] OJ L 250, 19.9.1984, p 17. Directive as amended by Directive 97/55/EC of the European Parliament and of the Council (OJ L 290, 23.10.1997, p 18).
[8] OJ L 42, 12.2.1987, p 48. Directive as last amended by Directive 98/7/EC of the European Parliament and of the Council (OJ L 101, 1.4.1998, p 17).

services in the securities field,[9] Council Directive 90/314/EEC of 13 June 1990 on package travel, package holidays and package tours,[10] Directive 98/6/EC of the European Parliament and of the Council of 16 February 1998 on consumer production in the indication of prices of products offered to consumers,[11] Council Directive 92/59/EEC of 29 June 1992 on general product safety,[12] Directive 94/47/EC of the European Parliament and of the Council of 26 October 1994 on the protection of purchasers in respect of certain aspects on contracts relating to the purchase of the right to use immovable properties on a timeshare basis,[13] Directive 98/27/EC of the European Parliament and of the Council of 19 May 1998 on injunctions for the protection of consumers' interests,[14] Council Directive 85/374/EEC of 25 July 1985 on the approximation of the laws, regulations and administrative provisions concerning liability for defective products,[15] Directive 1999/44/EC of the European Parliament and of the Council of 25 May 1999 on certain aspects of the sale of consumer goods and associated guarantees,[16] the future Directive of the European Parliament and of the Council concerning the distance marketing of consumer financial services and Council Directive 92/28/EEC of 31 March 1992 on the advertising of medicinal products,[17] this Directive should be without prejudice to Directive 98/43/EC of the European Parliament and of the Council of 6 July 1998 on the approximation of the laws, regulations and administrative provisions of the Member States relating to the advertising and sponsorship of tobacco products[18] adopted within the framework of the internal market, or to directives on the protection of public health; this Directive complements information requirements established by the abovementioned Directives and in particular Directive 97/7/EC.

(12)   It is necessary to exclude certain activities from the scope of this Directive, on the grounds that the freedom to provide services in these fields cannot, at this stage, be guaranteed under the Treaty or existing secondary legislation; excluding these activities does not preclude any instruments which might prove necessary for the proper functioning of the internal market; taxation, particularly value added

[9] OJ L 141, 11.6.1993, p 27. Directive as last amended by Directive 97/9/EC of the European Parliament and of the Council (OJ L 84, 26.3.1997, p 22).
[10] OJ L 158, 23.6.1990, p 59.
[11] OJ L 80, 18.3.1998, p 27.
[12] OJ L 228, 11.8.1992, p 24.
[13] OJ L 280, 29.10.1994, p 83.
[14] OJ L 166, 11.6.1998, p 51. Directive as amended by Directive 1999/44/EC (OJ L 171, 7.7.1999, p 12).
[15] OJ L 210, 7.8.1985, p 29. Directive as amended by Directive 1999/34/EC (OJ L 141, 4.6.1999, p 20).
[16] OJ L 171, 7.7.1999, p 12.
[17] OJ L 113, 30.4.1992, p 13.
[18] OJ L 213, 30.7.1998, p 9.

tax imposed on a large number of the services covered by this Directive, must be excluded form the scope of this Directive.

(13) This Directive does not aim to establish rules on fiscal obligations nor does it pre-empt the drawing up of Community instruments concerning fiscal aspects of electronic commerce.

(14) The protection of individuals with regard to the processing of personal data is solely governed by Directive 95/46/EC of the European Parliament and of the Council of 24 October 1995 on the protection of individuals with regard to the processing of personal data and on the free movement of such data[19] and Directive 97/66/EC of the European Parliament and of the Council of 15 December 1997 concerning the processing of personal data and the protection of privacy in the telecommunications sector[20] which are fully applicable to information society services; these Directives already establish a Community legal framework in the field of personal data and therefore it is not necessary to cover this issue in this Directive in order to ensure the smooth functioning of the internal market, in particular the free movement of personal data between Member States; the implementation and application of this Directive should be made in full compliance with the principles relating to the protection of personal data, in particular as regards unsolicited commercial communication and the liability of intermediaries; this Directive cannot prevent the anonymous use of open networks such as the Internet.

(15) The confidentiality of communications is guaranteed by Article 5 Directive 97/66/EC; in accordance with that Directive, Member States must prohibit any kind of interception or surveillance of such communications by others than the senders and receivers, except when legally authorised.

(16) The exclusion of gambling activities from the scope of application of this Directive covers only games of chance, lotteries and betting transactions, which involve wagering a stake with monetary value; this does not cover promotional competitions or games where the purpose is to encourage the sale of goods or services and where payments, if they arise, serve only to acquire the promoted goods or services.

(17) The definition of information society services already exists in Community law in Directive 98/34/EC of the European Parliament and of the Council of 22 June 1998 laying down a procedure for the provision of information in the field of technical standards and regulations and of rules on information society services[21] and in Directive 98/84/EC of the European Parliament and of the Council

---

[19] OJ L 281, 23.11.1995, p 31.
[20] OJ L 24, 30.1.1998, p 1.
[21] OJ L 204, 21.7.1998, p 37. Directive as amended by Directive 98/48/EC (OJ L 217, 5.8.1998, p 18).

of 20 November 1998 on the legal protection of services based on, or consisting of, conditional access;[22] this definition covers any service normally provided for remuneration, at a distance, by means of electronic equipment for the processing (including digital compression) and storage of data, and at the individual request of a recipient of a service; those services referred to in the indicative list in Annex V to Directive 98/34/EC which do not imply data processing and storage are not covered by this definition.

(18)   Information society services span a wide range of economic activities which take place on-line; these activities can, in particular, consist of selling goods on-line; activities such as the delivery of goods as such or the provision of services off-line are not covered; information society services are not solely restricted to services giving rise to on-line contracting but also, in so far as they represent an economic activity, extend to services which are not remunerated by those who receive them, such as those offering on-line information or commercial communications, or those providing tools allowing for search, access and retrieval of data; information society services also include services consisting of the transmission of information via a communication network, in providing access to a communication network or in hosting information provided by a recipient of the service; television broadcasting within the meaning of Directive EEC/89/552 and radio broadcasting are not information society services because they are not provided at individual request; by contrast, services which are transmitted point to point, such as video-on-demand or the provision of commercial communications by electronic mail are information society services; the use of electronic mail or equivalent individual communications for instance by natural persons acting outside their trade, business or profession including their use for the conclusion of contracts between such persons is not an information society service; the contractual relationship between an employee and his employer is not an information society service; activities which by their very nature cannot be carried out at a distance and by electronic means, such as the statutory auditing of company accounts or medical advice requiring the physical examination of a patient are not information society services.

(19)   The place at which a service provider is established should be determined in conformity with the case-law of the Court of Justice according to which the concept of establishment involves the actual pursuit of an economic activity through a fixed establishment for an indefinite period; this requirement is also fulfilled where a company

[22] OJ L 320, 28.11.1998, p 54.

is constituted for a given period; the place of establishment of a company providing services via an Internet website is not the place at which the technology supporting its website is located or the place at which its website is accessible but the place where it pursues its economic activity; in cases where a provider has several places of establishment it is important to determine from which place of establishment the service concerned is provided; in cases where it is difficult to determine from which of several places of establishment a given service is provided, this is the place where the provider has the centre of his activities relating to this particular service.

(20) The definition of 'recipient of a service' covers all types of usage of information society services, both by persons who provide information on open networks such as the Internet and by persons who seek information on the Internet for private or professional reasons.

(21) The scope of the coordinated field is without prejudice to future Community harmonisation relating to information society services and to future legislation adopted at national level in accordance with Community law; the coordinated field covers only requirements relating to on-line activities such as on-line information, on-line advertising, on-line shopping, on-line contracting and does not concern Member States' legal requirements relating to goods such as safety standards, labelling obligations, or liability for goods, or Member States' requirements relating to the delivery or the transport of goods, including the distribution of medicinal products; the coordinated field does not cover the exercise of rights of pre-emption by public authorities concerning certain goods such as works of art.

(22) Information society services should be supervised at the source of the activity, in order to ensure an effective protection of public interest objectives; to that end, it is necessary to ensure that the competent authority provides such protection not only for the citizens of its own country but for all Community citizens; in order to improve mutual trust between Member States, it is essential to state clearly this responsibility on the part of the Member State where the services originate; moreover, in order to effectively guarantee freedom to provide services and legal certainty for suppliers and recipients of services, such information society services should in principle be subject to the law of the Member State in which the service provider is established.

(23) This Directive neither aims to establish additional rules on private international law relating to conflicts of law nor does it deal with the jurisdiction of Courts; provisions of the applicable law designated by rules of private international law must not restrict the freedom to provide information society services as established in this Directive.

(24) In the context of this Directive, notwithstanding the rule on the control at source of information society services, it is legitimate under the conditions established in this Directive for Member States to take measures to restrict the free movement of information society services.

(25) National courts, including civil courts, dealing with private law disputes can take measures to derogate from the freedom to provide information society services in conformity with conditions established in this Directive.

(26) Member States, in conformity with conditions established in this Directive, may apply their national rules on criminal law and criminal proceedings with a view to taking all investigative and other measures necessary for the detection and prosecution of criminal offences, without there being a need to notify such measures to the Commission.

(27) This Directive, together with the future Directive of the European Parliament and of the Council concerning the distance marketing of consumer financial services, contributes to the creating of a legal framework for the on-line provision of financial services; this Directive does not pre-empt future initiatives in the area of financial services in particular with regard to the harmonisation of rules of conduct in this field; the possibility for Member States, established in this Directive, under certain circumstances of restricting the freedom to provide information society services in order to protect consumers also covers measures in the area of financial services in particular measures aiming at protecting investors.

(28) The Member States' obligation not to subject access to the activity of an information society service provider to prior authorisation does not concern postal services covered by Directive 97/67/EC of the European Parliament and of the Council of 15 December 1997 on common rules for the development of the internal market of Community postal services and the improvement of quality of service[23] consisting of the physical delivery of a printed electronic mail message and does not affect voluntary accreditation systems, in particular for providers of electronic signature certification service.

(29) Commercial communications are essential for the financing of information society services and for developing a wide variety of new, charge-free services; in the interests of consumer protection and fair trading, commercial communications, including discounts, promotional offers and promotional competitions or games, must meet a number of transparency requirements; these requirements are without prejudice to Directive 97/7/EC; this Directive should not

[23] OJ L 15, 21.1.1998, p 14.

affect existing Directives on commercial communications, in particular Directive 98/43/EC.

(30) The sending of unsolicited commercial communications by electronic mail may be undesirable for consumers and information society service providers and may disrupt the smooth functioning of interactive networks; the question of consent by recipient of certain forms of unsolicited commercial communications is not addressed by this Directive, but has already been addressed, in particular, by Directive 97/7/EC and by Directive 97/66/EC; in Member States which authorise unsolicited commercial communications by electronic mail, the setting up of appropriate industry filtering initiatives should be encouraged and facilitated; in addition it is necessary that in any event unsolicited commercial communities are clearly identifiable as such in order to improve transparency and to facilitate the functioning of such industry initiatives; unsolicited commercial communications by electronic mail should not result in additional communication costs for the recipient.

(31) Member States which allow the sending of unsolicited commercial communications by electronic mail without prior consent of the recipient by service providers established in their territory have to ensure that the service providers consult regularly and respect the opt-out registers in which natural persons not wishing to receive such commercial communications can register themselves.

(32) In order to remove barriers to the development of cross-border services within the Community which members of the regulated professions might offer on the Internet, it is necessary that compliance be guaranteed at Community level with professional rules aiming, in particular, to protect consumers or public health; codes of conduct at Community level would be the best means of determining the rules on professional ethics applicable to commercial communication; the drawing-up or, where appropriate, the adaptation of such rules should be encouraged without prejudice to the autonomy of professional bodies and associations.

(33) This Directive complements Community law and national law relating to regulated professions maintaining a coherent set of applicable rules in this field.

(34) Each Member State is to amend its legislation containing requirements, and in particular requirements as to form, which are likely to curb the use of contracts by electronic means; the examination of the legislation requiring such adjustment should be systematic and should cover all the necessary stages and acts of the contractual process, including the filing of the contract; the result of this amendment should be to make contracts concluded electronically workable; the legal effect of electronic signatures is dealt with by

Directive 1999/93/EC of the European Parliament and of the Council of 13 December 1999 on a Community framework for electronic signatures;[24] the acknowledgement of receipt by a service provider may take the form of the on-line provision of the service paid for.

(35) This Directive does not affect Member States' possibility of maintaining or establishing general or specific legal requirements for contracts which can be fulfilled by electronic means, in particular requirements concerning secure electronic signatures.

(36) Member States may maintain restrictions for the use of electronic contracts with regard to contracts requiring by law the involvement of courts, public authorities, or professions exercising public authority; this possibility also covers contracts which require the involvement of courts, public authorities, or professions exercising public authority in order to have an effect with regard to third parties as well as contracts requiring by law certification or attestation by a notary.

(37) Member States' obligation to remove obstacles to the use of electronic contracts concerns only obstacles resulting from legal requirements and not practical obstacles resulting from the impossibility of using electronic means in certain cases.

(38) Member States' obligation to remove obstacles to the use of electronic contracts is to be implemented in conformity with legal requirements for contracts enshrined in Community law.

(39) The exceptions to the provisions concerning the contracts concluded exclusively by electronic mail or by equivalent individual communications provided for by this Directive, in relation to information to be provided and the placing of orders, should not enable, as a result, the by-passing of those provisions by providers of information society services.

(40) Both existing and emerging disparities in Member States' legislation and case-law concerning liability of service providers acting as intermediaries prevent the smooth functioning of the internal market, in particular by impairing the development of cross-border services and producing distortions of competition; service providers have a duty to act, under certain circumstances, with a view to preventing or stopping illegal activities; this Directive should constitute the appropriate basis for the development of rapid and reliable procedures for removing and disabling access to illegal information; such mechanisms could be developed on the basis of voluntary agreements between all parties concerned and should be encouraged by

[24] OJ L 13, 19.1.2000, p 12.

Member States; it is in the interest of all parties involved in the provision of information society services to adopt and implement such procedures; the provisions of this Directive relating to liability should not preclude the development and effective operation, by the different interested parties, of technical systems of protection and identification and of technical surveillance instruments made possible by digital technology within the limits laid down by Directives 95/46/EC and 97/66/EC.

(41) This Directive strikes a balance between the different interests at stake and establishes principles upon which industry agreements and standards can be based.

(42) The exemptions from liability established in this Directive cover only cases where the activity of the information society service provider is limited to the technical process of operating and giving access to a communication network over which information made available by third parties is transmitted or temporarily stored, for the sole purpose of making the transmission more efficient; this activity is of a mere technical, automatic and passive nature, which implies that the information society service provider has neither knowledge of nor control over the information which is transmitted or stored.

(43) A service provider can benefit from the exemptions for 'mere conduit' and for 'caching' when he is in no way involved with the information transmitted; this requires among other things that he does not modify the information that he transmits; this requirement does not cover manipulations of a technical nature which take place in the course of the transmission as they do not alter the integrity of the information contained in the transmission.

(44) A service provider who deliberately collaborates with one of the recipients of his service in order to undertake illegal acts goes beyond the activities of 'mere conduit' or 'caching' and as a result cannot benefit from the liability exemptions established for these activities.

(45) The limitations of the liability of intermediary service providers established in this Directive do not affect the possibility of injunctions of different kinds; such injunctions can in particular consist of orders by courts or administrative authorities requiring the termination or prevention of any infringement, including the removal of illegal information or the disabling of access to it.

(46) In order to benefit from a limitation of liability, the provider of an information society service, consisting of the storage of information, upon obtaining actual knowledge or awareness of illegal activities has to act expeditiously to remove or to disable access to the information concerned; the removal or disabling of access has to be undertaken in the observance of the principle of freedom of expression and of procedures established for this purpose at national level; this

Directive does not affect Member States' possibility of establishing specific requirements which must be fulfilled expeditiously prior to the removal or disabling of information.

(47) Member States are prevented from imposing a monitoring obligation on service providers only with respect to obligations of a general nature; this does not concern monitoring obligations in a specific case and, in particular, does not affect orders by national authorities in accordance with national legislation.

(48) This Directive does not affect the possibility for Member States of requiring service providers, who host information provided by recipients of their service, to apply duties of care, which can reasonably be expected from them and which are specified by national law, in order to detect and prevent certain types of illegal activities.

(49) Member States and the Commission are to encourage the drawing-up of codes of conduct; this is not to impair the voluntary nature of such codes and the possibility for interested parties of deciding freely whether to adhere to such codes.

(50) It is important that the proposed directive on the harmonisation of certain aspects of copyright and related rights in the information society and this Directive come into force within a similar time scale with a view to establishing a clear framework of rules relevant to the issue of liability of intermediaries for copyright and relating rights infringements at Community level.

(51) Each Member State should be required, where necessary, to amend any legislation which is liable to hamper the use of schemes for the out-of-court settlement of disputes through electronic channels; the result of this amendment must be to make the functioning of such schemes genuinely and effectively possible in law and in practice, even across borders.

(52) The effective exercise of the freedoms of the internal market makes it necessary to guarantee victims effective access to means of settling disputes; damage which may arise in connection with information society services is characterised both by its rapidity and by its geographical extent; in view of this specific character and the need to ensure that national authorities do not endanger the mutual confidence which they should have in one another, this Directive requests Member States to ensure that appropriate court actions are available; Member States should examine the need to provide access to judicial procedures by appropriate electronic means.

(53) Directive 98/27/EC, which is applicable to information society services, provides a mechanism relating to actions for an injunction aimed at the protection of the collective interests of consumers; this mechanism will contribute to the free movement of information society services by ensuring a high level of consumer protection.

(54) The sanctions provided for under this Directive are without prejudice to any other sanction or remedy provided under national law; Member

States are not obliged to provide criminal sanctions for infringement of national provisions adopted pursuant to this Directive.

(55) This Directive does not affect the law applicable to contractual obligations relating to consumer contracts; accordingly, this Directive cannot have the result of depriving the consumer of the protection afforded to him by the mandatory rules relating to contractual obligations of the law of the Member State in which he has his habitual residence.

(56) As regards the derogation contained in this Directive regarding contractual obligations concerning contracts concluded by consumers, those obligations should be interpreted as including information on the essential elements of the content of the contract, including consumer rights, which have a determining influence on the decision to contract.

(57) The Court of Justice has consistently held that a Member State retains the right to take measures against a service provider that is established in another Member State but directs all or most of his activity to the territory of the first Member State if the choice of establishment was made with a view to evading the legislation that would have applied to the provider had he been established on the territory of the first Member State.

(58) This Directive should not apply to services supplied by service providers established in a third country; in view of the global dimension of electronic commerce, it is, however, appropriate to ensure that the Community rules are consistent with international rules; this Directive is without prejudice to the results of discussions within international organisations (amongst others WTO, OECD, Uncitral) on legal issues.

(59) Despite the global nature of electronic communications, coordination of national regulatory measures at European Union level is necessary in order to avoid fragmentation of the internal market, and for the establishment of an appropriate European regulatory framework; such coordination should also contribute to the establishment of a common and strong negotiating position in international forums.

(60) In order to allow the unhampered development of electronic commerce, the legal framework must be clear and simple, predictable and consistent with the rules applicable at international level so that it does not adversely affect the competitiveness of European industry or impede innovation in that sector.

(61) If the market is actually to operate by electronic means in the context of globalisation, the European Union and the major non-European areas need to consult each other with a view to making laws and procedures compatible.

(62) Cooperation with third countries should be strengthened in the area of electronic commerce, in particular with applicant countries, the developing countries and the European Union's other trading partners.

(63) The adoption of this Directive will not prevent the Member States from taking into account the various social, societal and cultural implications which are inherent in the advent of the information society; in particular it should not hinder measures which Member States might adopt in conformity with Community law to achieve social, cultural and democratic goals taking into account their linguistic diversity, national and regional specificities as well as their cultural heritage, and to ensure and maintain public access to the widest possible range of information society services; in any case, the development of the information society is to ensure that Community citizens can have access to the cultural European heritage provided in the digital environment.

(64) Electronic communication offers the Member States an excellent means of providing public services in the cultural, educational and linguistic fields.

(65) The Council, in its resolution of 19 January 1999 on the consumer dimension of the information society,[25] stressed that the protection of consumers deserved special attention in this field; the Commission will examine the degree to which existing consumer protection rules provide insufficient protection in the context of the information society and will identify, where necessary, the deficiencies of this legislation and those issues which could require additional measures; if need be, the Commission should make specific additional proposals to resolve such deficiencies that will thereby have been identified,n

HAVE ADOPTED THIS DIRECTIVE:

CHAPTER I

General Provisions

Article 1

Objective and scope

(1) This Directive seeks to contribute to the proper functioning of the internal market by ensuring the free movement of information society services between the Member States.

(2) This Directive approximates, to the extent necessary for the achievement of the objective set out in paragraph 1, certain national provisions on information society services relating to the internal market, the establishment of service providers, commercial communications,

---

[25] OJ C 23, 28.1.1999, p 1.

electronic contracts, the liability of intermediaries, codes of conduct, out-of-court dispute settlements, court actions and cooperation between Member States.

(3)   This Directive complements Community law applicable to information society services without prejudice to the level of protection for, in particular, public health and consumer interests, as established by Community acts and national legislation implementing them in so far as this does not restrict the freedom to provide information society services.

(4)   This Directive does not establish additional rules on private international law nor does it deal with the jurisdiction of Courts.

(5)   This Directive shall not apply to:
a)   the field of taxation;
b)   questions relating to information society services covered by Directives 95/46/EC and 97/66/EC;
c)   questions relating to agreements or practices governed by cartel law;
d)   the following activities of information society services:
   –   the activities of notaries or equivalent professions to the extent that they involve a direct and specific connection with the exercise of public authority,
   –   the representation of a client and defence of his interests before the courts,
   –   gambling activities which involve wagering a stake with monetary value in games of chance, including lotteries and betting transactions.

(6)   This Directive does not affect measures taken at Community or national level, in the respect of Community law, in order to promote cultural and linguistic diversity and to ensure the defence of pluralism.

Article 2

Definitions

For the purpose of this Directive, the following terms shall bear the following meanings:

a)   'information society services': services within the meaning of Article 1(2) of Directive 98/34/EC as amended by Directive 98/48/EC;
b)   'service provider': any natural or legal person providing an information society service;
c)   'established service provider': a service provider who effectively pursues an economic activity using a fixed establishment for an

indefinite period. The presence and use of the technical means and technologies required to provide the service do not, in themselves, constitute an establishment of the provider;

d)   'recipient of the service': any natural or legal person who, for professional ends or otherwise, uses an information society service, in particular for the purposes of seeking information or making it accessible;

e)   'consumer': any natural person who is acting for purposes which are outside his or her trade, business or profession;

f)   'commercial communication': any form of communication designed to promote, directly or indirectly, the goods, services or image of a company, organisation or person pursuing a commercial, industrial or craft activity or exercising a regulated profession. The following do not in themselves constitute commercial communications:

  − information allowing direct access to the activity of the company, organisation or person, in particular a domain name or an electronic-mail address,

  − communications relating to the goods, services or image of the company, organisation or person compiled in an independent manner, particularly when this is without financial consideration;

g)   'regulated profession': any profession within the meaning of either Article 1(d) of Council Directive 89/48/EEC of 21 December 1988 on a general system for the recognition of higher-education diplomas awarded on completion of professional education and training of at least three-years' duration[26] or of Article 1(f) of Council Directive 92/51/EEC of 18 June 1992 on a second general system for the recognition of professional education and training to supplement Directive 89/48/EEC;[27]

(h)   'coordinated field': requirements laid down in Member States' legal systems applicable to information society service providers or information society services, regardless of whether they are of a general nature or specifically designed for them.

  i)   The coordinated field concerns requirements with which the service provider has to comply in respect of:

    − the taking up of the activity of an information society service, such as requirements concerning qualifications, authorisation or notification,

    − the pursuit of the activity of an information society service, such as requirements concerning the behaviour of the service provider, requirements regarding the quality or content of the service including those applicable to advertising and

---

[26] OJ L 19, 24.1.1989, p 16.
[27] OJ L 209, 24.7.1992, p 25. Directive as last amended by Commission Directive 97/38/EC (OJ L 184, 12.7.1997, p 31).

contracts, or requirements concerning the liability of the service provider;

ii)   The coordinated field does not cover requirements such as:
   - requirements applicable to goods as such,-
   - requirements applicable to the delivery of goods,
   - requirements applicable to services not provided by electronic means.

Article 3

Internal market

(1)   Each Member State shall ensure that the information society services provided by a service provider established on its territory comply with the national provisions applicable in the Member State in question which fall within the coordinated field.

(2)   Member States may not, for reasons falling within the coordinated field, restrict the freedom to provide information society services from another Member State.

(3)   Paragraphs 1 and 2 shall not apply to the fields referred to in the Annex.

(4)   Member States may take measures to derogate from paragraph 2 in respect of a given information society service if the following conditions are fulfilled:

a)   the measures shall be:
   i)   necessary for one of the following reasons:
      - public policy, in particular the prevention, investigation, detection and prosecution of criminal offences, including the protection of minors and the fight against any incitement to hatred on grounds of race, sex, religion or nationality, and violations of human dignity concerning individual persons,
      - the protection of public health,
      - public security, including the safeguarding of national security and defence,
      - the protection of consumers, including investors;
   ii)   taken against a given information society service which prejudices the objectives referred to in point (i) or which presents a serious and grave risk of prejudice to those objectives;
   iii)   proportionate to those objectives;

b)   before taking the measures in question and without prejudice to court proceedings, including preliminary proceedings and acts carried out in the framework of a criminal investigation, the Member State has:

     – asked the Member State referred to in paragraph 1 to take measures and the latter did not take such measures, or they were inadequate,

     – notified the Commission and the Member State referred to in paragraph 1 of its intention to take such measures.

(5)   Member States may, in the case of urgency, derogate from the conditions stipulated in paragraph 4(b). Where this is the case, the measures shall be notified in the shortest possible time to the Commission and to the Member State referred to in paragraph 1, indicating the reasons for which the Member State considers that there is urgency.

(6)   Without prejudice to the Member State's possibility of proceeding with the measures in question, the Commission shall examine the compatibility of the notified measures with Community law in the shortest possible time; where it comes to the conclusion that the measure is incompatible with Community law, the Commission shall ask the Member State in question to refrain from taking any proposed measures or urgently to put an end to the measures in question.

CHAPTER II

Principles

Section 1: Establishment and information requirements

Article 4

Principle excluding prior authorisation

(1)   Member States shall ensure that the taking up and pursuit of the activity of an information society service provider may not be made subject to prior authorisation or any other requirement having equivalent effect.

(2)   Paragraph 1 shall be without prejudice to authorisation schemes which are not specifically and exclusively targeted at information society services, or which are covered by Directive 97/13/EC of the European Parliament and of the Council of 10 April 1997 on a common framework for general authorisations and individual licences in the field of telecommunications services.[28]

---

[28] OJ L 117, 7.5.1997, p 15.

Article 5

General information to be provided

(1) In addition to other information requirements established by Community law, Member States shall ensure that the service provider shall render easily, directly and permanently accessible to the recipients of the service and competent authorities, at least the following information:

a) the name of the service provider;

b) the geographic address at which the service provider is established;

c) the details of the service provider, including his electronic mail address, which allow him to be contacted rapidly and communicated with in a direct and effective manner;

d) where the service provider is registered in a trade or similar public register, the trade register in which the service provider is entered and his registration number, or equivalent means of identification in that register;

e) where the activity is subject to an authorisation scheme, the particulars of the relevant supervisory authority;

f) as concerns the regulated professions:

– any professional body or similar institution with which the service provider is registered,

– the professional title and the Member State where it has been granted,

– a reference to the applicable professional rules in the Member State of establishment and the means to access them;

g) where the service provider undertakes an activity that is subject to VAT, the identification number referred to in Article 22(1) of the sixth Council Directive 77/388/EEC of 17 May 1977 on the harmonisation of the laws of the Member States relating to turnover taxes – Common system of value added tax: uniform basis of assessment.[29]

(2) In addition to other information requirements established by Community law, Member States shall at least ensure that, where information society services refer to prices, these are to be indicated clearly and unambiguously and, in particular, must indicate whether they are inclusive of tax and delivery costs.

[29] OJ L 145, 13.6.1977, p 1. Directive as last amended by Directive 1999/85/EC (OJ L 277, 28.10.1999, p 34).

Section 2: Commercial communications

Article 6

Information to be provided

In addition to other information requirements established by Community law, Member States shall ensure that commercial communications which are part of, or constitute, an information society service comply at least with the following conditions:

a)   the commercial communication shall be clearly identifiable as such;

b)   the natural or legal person on whose behalf the commercial communication is made shall be clearly identifiable;

c)   promotional offers, such as discounts, premiums and gifts, where permitted in the Member State where the service provider is established, shall be clearly identifiable as such, and the conditions which are to be met to qualify for them shall be easily accessible and be presented clearly and unambiguously;

d)   promotional competitions or games, where permitted in the Member State where the service provider is established, shall be clearly identifiable as such, and the conditions for participation shall be easily accessible and be presented clearly and unambiguously.

Article 7

Unsolicited commercial communication

(1)   In addition to other requirements established by Community law, Member States which permit unsolicited commercial communication by electronic mail shall ensure that such commercial communication by a service provider established in their territory shall be identifiable clearly and unambiguously as such as soon as it is received by the recipient.

(2)   Without prejudice to Directive 97/7/EC and Directive 97/66/EC, Member States shall take measures to ensure that service providers undertaking unsolicited commercial communications by electronic mail consult regularly and respect the opt-out registers in which natural persons not wishing to receive such commercial communications can register themselves.

Article 8

Regulated professions

(1)   Member States shall ensure that the use of commercial communications which are part of, or constitute, an information society service provided by a member of a regulated profession is permitted subject to compliance with the professional rules regarding, in particular, the independence, dignity and honour of the profession, professional secrecy and fairness towards clients and other members of the profession.

(2)   Without prejudice to the autonomy of professional bodies and associations, Member States and the Commission shall encourage professional associations and bodies to establish codes of conduct at Community level in order to determine the types of information that can be given for the purposes of commercial communication in conformity with the rules referred to in paragraph 1.

(3)   When drawing up proposals for Community initiatives which may become necessary to ensure the proper functioning of the Internal Market with regard to the information referred to in paragraph 2, the Commission shall take due account of codes of conduct applicable at Community level and shall act in close cooperation with the relevant professional associations and bodies.

(4)   This Directive shall apply in addition to Community Directives concerning access to, and the exercise of, activities of the regulated professions.

Section 3: Contracts concluded by electronic means

Article 9

Treatment of contracts

(1)   Member States shall ensure that their legal system allows contracts to be concluded by electronic means. Member States shall in particular ensure that the legal requirements applicable to the contractual process neither create obstacles for the use of electronic contracts nor result in such contracts being deprived of legal effectiveness and validity on account of their having been made by electronic means.

(2)   Member States may lay down that paragraph 1 shall not apply to all or certain contracts falling into one of the following categories:

   a)   contracts that create or transfer rights in real estate, except for rental rights;

   b)   contracts requiring by law the involvement of courts, public authorities or professions exercising public authority;

c) contracts of suretyship granted and on collateral securities furnished by persons acting for purposes outside their trade, business or profession;

d) contracts governed by family law or by the law of succession.

(3) Member States shall indicate to the Commission the categories referred to in paragraph 2 to which they do not apply paragraph 1.Member States shall submit to the Commission every five years a report on the application of paragraph 2 explaining the reasons why they consider it necessary to maintain the category referred to in paragraph 2(b) to which they do not apply paragraph 1.

Article 10

Information to be provided

(1) In addition to other information requirements established by Community law, Member States shall ensure, except when otherwise agreed by parties who are not consumers, that at least the following information is given by the service provider clearly, comprehensibly and unambiguously and prior to the order being placed by the recipient of the service:

a) the different technical steps to follow to conclude the contract;

b) whether or not the concluded contract will be filed by the service provider and whether it will be accessible;

c) the technical means for identifying and correcting input errors prior to the placing of the order;

d) the languages offered for the conclusion of the contract.

(2) Member States shall ensure that, except when otherwise agreed by parties who are not consumers, the service provider indicates any relevant codes of conduct to which he subscribes and information on how those codes can be consulted electronically.

(3) Contract terms and general conditions provided to the recipient must be made available in a way that allows him to store and reproduce them.

(4) Paragraphs 1 and 2 shall not apply to contracts concluded exclusively by exchange of electronic mail or by equivalent individual communications.

Article 11

Placing of the order

(1) Member States shall ensure, except when otherwise agreed by parties who are not consumers, that in cases where the recipient of the

service places his order through technological means, the following principles apply:

- the service provider has to acknowledge the receipt of the recipient's order without undue delay and by electronic means,
- the order and the acknowledgement of receipt are deemed to be received when the parties to whom they are addressed are able to access them.

(2) Member States shall ensure that, except when otherwise agreed by parties who are not consumers, the service provider makes available to the recipient of the service appropriate, effective and accessible technical means allowing him to identify and correct input errors, prior to the placing of the order.

(3) Paragraph 1, first indent, and paragraph 2 shall not apply to contracts concluded exclusively by exchange of electronic mail or by equivalent individual communications.

Section 4: Liability of intermediary service providers

Article 12

'Mere conduit'

(1) Where an information society service is provided that consists of the transmission in a communication network of information provided by a recipient of the service, or the provision of access to a communication network, Member States shall ensure that the service provider is not liable for the information transmitted, on condition that the provider:

a) does not initiate the transmission;

b) does not select the receiver of the transmission; and

c) does not select or modify the information contained in the transmission.

(2) The acts of transmission and of provision of access referred to in paragraph 1 include the automatic, intermediate and transient storage of the information transmitted in so far as this takes place for the sole purpose of carrying out the transmission in the communication network, and provided that the information is not stored for any period longer than is reasonably necessary for the transmission.

(3) This Article shall not affect the possibility for a court or administrative authority, in accordance with Member States' legal systems, of requiring the service provider to terminate or prevent an infringement.

Article 13

'Caching'

(1)   Where an information society service is provided that consists of the transmission in a communication network of information provided by a recipient of the service, Member States shall ensure that the service provider is not liable for the automatic, intermediate and temporary storage of that information, performed for the sole purpose of making more efficient the information's onward transmission to other recipients of the service upon their request, on condition that:

    a)   the provider does not modify the information;

    b)   the provider complies with conditions on access to the information;

    c)   the provider complies with rules regarding the updating of the information, specified in a manner widely recognised and used by industry;

    d)   the provider does not interfere with the lawful use of technology, widely recognised and used by industry, to obtain data on the use of the information; and

    e)   the provider acts expeditiously to remove or to disable access to the information it has stored upon obtaining actual knowledge of the fact that the information at the initial sourcef of the transmission has been removed from the network, or access to it has been disabled, or that a court or an administrative authority has ordered such removal or disablement.

(2)   This Article shall not affect the possibility for a court or administrative authority, in accordance with Member States' legal systems, of requiring the service provider to terminate or prevent an infringement.

Article 14

Hosting

(1)   Where an information society service is provided that consists of the storage of information provided by a recipient of the service, Member States shall ensure that the service provider is not liable for the information stored at the request of a recipient of the service, on condition that:

    a)   the provider does not have actual knowledge of illegal activity or information and, as regards claims for damages, is not aware of facts or circumstances from which the illegal activity or information is apparent; or

b) the provider, upon obtaining such knowledge or awareness, acts expeditiously to remove or to disable access to the information.

(2) Paragraph 1 shall not apply when the recipient of the service is acting under the authority or the control of the provider.

(3) This Article shall not affect the possibility for a court or administrative authority, in accordance with Member States' legal systems, of requiring the service provider to terminate or prevent an infringement, nor does it affect the possibility for Member States of establishing procedures governing the removal or disabling of access to information.

Article 15

No general obligation to monitor

(1) Member States shall not impose a general obligation on providers, when providing the services covered by Articles 12, 13 and 14, to monitor the information which they transmit or store, nor a general obligation actively to seek facts or circumstances indicating illegal activity.

(2) Member States may establish obligations for information society service providers promptly to inform the competent public authorities of alleged illegal activities undertaken or information provided by recipients of their service or obligations to communicate to the competent authorities, at their request, information enabling the identification of recipients of their service with whom they have storage agreements.

CHAPTER III

Implementation

Article 16

Codes of conduct

(1) Member States and the Commission shall encourage:
a) the drawing up of codes of conduct at Community level, by trade, professional and consumer associations ororganisations, designed to contribute to the proper implementation of Articles 5 to 15;
b) the voluntary transmission of draft codes of conduct at national or Community level to the Commission;

c) the accessibility of these codes of conduct in the Community languages by electronic means;

d) the communication to the Member States and the Commission, by trade, professional and consumer associations or organisations, of their assessment of the application of their codes of conduct and their impact upon practices, habits or customs relating to electronic commerce;

e) the drawing up of codes of conduct regarding the protection of minors and human dignity.

(2) Member States and the Commission shall encourage the involvement of associations or organisations representing consumers in the drafting and implementation of codes of conduct affecting their interests and drawn up in accordance with paragraph 1(a). Where appropriate, to take account of their specific needs, associations representing the visually impaired and disabled should be consulted.

Article 17

Out-of-court dispute settlement

(1) Member States shall ensure that, in the event of disagreement between an information society service provider and the recipient of the service, their legislation does not hamper the use of out-of-court schemes, available under national law, for dispute settlement, including appropriate electronic means.

(2) Member States shall encourage bodies responsible for the out-of-court settlement of, in particular, consumer disputes to operate in a way which provides adequate procedural guarantees for the parties concerned.

(3) Member States shall encourage bodies responsible for out-of-court dispute settlement to inform the Commission of the significant decisions they take regarding information society services and to transmit any other information on the practices, usages or customs relating to electronic commerce.

Article 18

Court actions

(1) Member States shall ensure that court actions available under national law concerning information society services' activities allow for the rapid adoption of measures, including interim measures, designed to terminate any alleged infringement and to prevent any further impairment of the interests involved.

(2)   The Annex to Directive 98/27/EC shall be supplemented as follows:
        '11. Directive 2000/31/EC of the European Parliament and of the
        Council of 8 June 2000 on certain legal aspects on information
        society services, in particular electronic commerce, in the
        internal market (Directive on electronic commerce) (OJ L 178,
        17.7.2000, p. 1).'

Article 19

Cooperation

(1)   Member States shall have adequate means of supervision and investi-
        gation necessary to implement this Directive effectively and
        shall ensure that service providers supply them with the requisite
        information.

(2)   Member States shall cooperate with other Member States; they shall,
        to that end, appoint one or several contact points, whose details they
        shall communicate to the other Member States and to the
        Commission.

(3)   Member States shall, as quickly as possible, and in conformity with
        national law, provide the assistance and information requested by
        other Member States or by the Commission, including by appropri-
        ate electronic means.

(4)   Member States shall establish contact points which shall be accessible
        at least by electronic means and from which recipients and service
        providers may:

        a)   obtain general information on contractual rights and
             obligations as well as on the complaint and redress mechanisms
             available in the event of disputes, including practical aspects
             involved in the use of such mechanisms;

        b)   obtain the details of authorities, associations or organisations from
             which they may obtain further information or practical assistance.

(5)   Member States shall encourage the communication to the
        Commission of any significant administrative or judicial decisions
        taken in their territory regarding disputes relating to information
        society services and practices, usages and customs relating to
        electronic commerce. The Commission shall communicate these
        decisions to the other Member States.

Article 20

Sanctions

Member States shall determine the sanctions applicable to infringements of
national provisions adopted pursuant to this Directive and shall take all measures

necessary to ensure that they are enforced. The sanctions they provide for shall be effective, proportionate and dissuasive.

CHAPTER IV

Final Provisions

Article 21

Re-examination

(1)   Before 17 July 2003, and thereafter every two years, the Commission shall submit to the European Parliament, the Council and the Economic and Social Committee a report on the application of this Directive, accompanied, where necessary, by proposals for adapting it to legal, technical and economic developments in the field of information society services, in particular with respect to crime prevention, the protection of minors, consumer protection and to the proper functioning of the internal market.

(2)   In examining the need for an adaptation of this Directive, the report shall in particular analyse the need for proposals concerning the liability of providers of hyperlinks and location tool services, 'notice and take down' procedures and the attribution of liability following the taking down of content. The report shall also analyse the need for additional conditions for the exemption from liability, provided for in Articles 12 and 13, in the light of technical developments, and the possibility of applying the internal market principles to unsolicited commercial communications by electronic mail.

Arti cle 22

Transposition

(1)   Member States shall bring into force the laws, regulations and administrative provisions necessary to comply with this Directive before 17 January 2002. They shall forthwith inform the Commission thereof.

(2)   When Member States adopt the measures referred to in paragraph 1, these shall contain a reference to this Directive or shall be accompanied

[30] OJ L 24, 27.1.1987, p 36.
[31] OJ L 77, 27.3.1996, p 20.

by such reference at the time of their official publication. The methods of making such reference shall be laid down by Member States.

Article 23

Entry into force

This Directive shall enter into force on the day of its publication in the Official Journal of the European Communities.

Article 24

Addressees

This Directive is addressed to the Member States.

ANNEX

Derogations from Article 3

As provided for in Article 3(3), Article 3(1) and (2) do not apply to:

–   copyright, neighbouring rights, rights referred to in Directive 87/54/EEC[30] and Directive 96/9/EC[31] as well as industrial property rights,
–   the emission of electronic money by institutions in respect of which Member States have applied one of the derogations provided for in Article 8(1) of Directive 2000/46/EC,[32]
–   Article 44(2) of Directive 85/611/EEC,[33]
–   Article 30 and Title IV of Directive 92/49/EEC,[34] Title IV of Directive 92/96/EEC,[35] Articles 7 and 8 of Directive 88/357/EEC[36] and Article 4 of Directive 90/619/EEC,[37]
–   the freedom of the parties to choose the law applicable to their contract,
–   contractual obligations concerning consumer contacts,

[32] Not yet published in the Official Journal.
[33] OJ L 375, 31.12.1985, p 3. Directive as last amended by Directive 95/26/EC (OJ L 168, 18.7.1995, p 7).
[34] OJ L 228, 11.8.1992, p 1. Directive as last amended by Directive 95/26/EC.
[35] OJ L 360, 9.12.1992, p 2. Directive as last amended by Directive 95/26/EC.
[36] OJ L 172, 4.7.1988, p 1. Directive as last amended by Directive 92/49/EC.
[37] OJ L 330, 29.11.1990, p 50. Directive as last amended by Directive 92/96/EC.

- formal validity of contracts creating or transferring rights in real estate where such contracts are subject to mandatory formal requirements of the law of the Member State where the real estate is situated,
- the permissibility of unsolicited commercial communications by electronic mail.

Denmark	Lov om tjenester i informationssamfundet, herunder visse aspekter af elektronisk handel, Lov Nr 227 af 22/04/2002
EIRE	1. – Partially implemented by the Electronic Commerce Act 2000
	2. – European Communities (Directive 2000/31/EC) Regulations, S.I. No. 68/2003
Finland	1. – Laki tietoyhteiskunnan palvelujen tarjoamisesta ref: Suomen Säädöskokoelma n 458 du 11/06/2002 p. 3039
	2. – Laki yksityisyyden suojasta televiestinnässä ja teletoiminnan tieto-turvasta annetun lain muuttamisesta ref: Suomen Säädöskokoelma n 459 du 11/06/2002 p. 3047
	3. – Laki kuluttajansuojalain 2 luvun muuttamisesta ref: Suomen Säädöskokoelma n 460 du 11/06/2002 p. 3048
	4. – Laki sopimattomasta menettelystä elinkeinotoiminnassa annetun lain muuttamisesta ref: Suomen Säädöskokoelma n 461 du 11/06/2002 p. 3049
Sweden	Lag om elektronisk handel och andra informationssamhällets tjänster, SFS 2002:562
United Kingdom	1. – The Electronic Commerce Directive (Financial Services and Markets) Regulations 2002, S.I. No. 2002/1775.
	2. – The Financial Services and Markets Act 2002 (Regulated Activities) (Amendment) (No. 2) Order 2002, S.I. No. 2002/1776
	3. – Electronic Commerce (EC Directive) Regulations 2002, S.I. No. 2002/2013.
	4. – The Electronic Commerce Directive (Financial Services and Markets) (Amendment) Regulations 2002, S.I. No. 2002/ 2015.
	5. – The Financial Services and Markets Act 2000 (Financial Promotion) (Amendment) (Electronic Commerce Directive) Order 2002, S.I. No. 2002/2157.
	6. – The Electronic Commerce (EC Directive) (Extension) Regulations 2003, S.I. No. 2003/115.

DIRECTIVE 1999/93/EC OF THE EUROPEAN PARLIAMENT AND OF THE COUNCIL

of 13 December 1999

on a Community framework for electronic signatures

(Official Journal, L13/00, p 12)

THE EUROPEAN PARLIAMENT AND THE COUNCIL OF THE EUROPEAN UNION –

Having regard to the Treaty establishing the European Community, and in particular Articles 47(2), 55 and 95 thereof,

Having regard to the proposal from the Commission,[1]

Having regard to the opinion of the Economic and Social Committee,[2]

Having regard to the opinion of the Committee of the Regions,[3]

Acting in accordance with the procedure laid down in Article 251 of the Treaty,[4]

Whereas:

(1) On 16 April 1997 the Commission presented to the European Parliament, the Council, the Economic and Social Committee and the Committee of the Regions a Communication on a European Initiative in Electronic Commerce;

(2) On 8 October 1997 the Commission presented to the European Parliament, the Council, the Economic and Social Committee and the Committee of the Regions a Communication on ensuring security and trust in electronic communication – towards a European framework for digital signatures and encryption;

(3) On 1 December 1997 the Council invited the Commission to submit as soon as possible a proposal for a Directive of the European Parliament and of the Council on digital signatures;

(4) Electronic communication and commerce necessitate 'electronic signatures' and related services allowing data authentication; divergent

---

[1] OJ C325/98, p 5.

[2] OJ C40/99, p 29.

[3] OJ C93/99, p 33.

[4] Opinion of the European Parliament of 13 January 1999 (OJ C104/99, p 49); Council Common Position of 28 June 1999 (OJ C243/99, p 33) and Decision of the European Parliament of 27 October 1999 (not yet published in the Official Journal); Council Decision of 30 November 1999.

rules with respect to legal recognition of electronic signatures and the accreditation of certification-service providers in the Member States may create a significant barrier to the use of electronic communications and electronic commerce; on the other hand, a clear Community framework regarding the conditions applying to electronic signatures will strengthen confidence in, and general acceptance of, the new technologies; legislation in the Member States should not hinder the free movement of goods and services in the internal market;

(5)   The interoperability of electronic-signature products should be promoted; in accordance with Article 14 of the Treaty, the internal market comprises an area without internal frontiers in which the free movement of goods is ensured; essential requirements specific to electronic-signature products must be met in order to ensure free movement within the internal market and to build trust in electronic signatures, without prejudice to Council Regulation (EC) No 3381/94 of 19 December 1994 setting up a Community regime for the control of exports of dual-use goods[5] and Council Decision 94/942/CFSP of 19 December 1994 on the joint action adopted by the Council concerning the control of exports of dual-use goods;[6]

(6)   This Directive does not harmonise the provision of services with respect to the confidentiality of information where they are covered by national provisions concerned with public policy or public security;

(7)   The internal market ensures the free movement of persons, as a result of which citizens and residents of the European Union increasingly need to deal with authorities in Member States other than the one in which they reside; the availability of electronic communication could be of great service in this respect;

(8)   Rapid technological development and the global character of the Internet necessitate an approach which is open to various technologies and services capable of authenticating data electronically;

(9)   Electronic signatures will be used in a large variety of circumstances and applications, resulting in a wide range of new services and products related to or using electronic signatures; the definition of such products and services should not be limited to the issuance and management of certificates, but should also encompass any other service and product using, or ancillary to, electronic signatures, such as registration services, time-stamping services, directory services, computing services or consultancy services related to electronic signatures;

(10) The internal market enables certification-service-providers to develop their cross-border activities with a view to increasing their

[5] OJ L367/94, p 1. Regulation as amended by Regulation (EC) No. 837/95 (OJ L90/95, p 1).
[6] OJ L367/94, p 8. Decision as last amended by Decision 99/193/CFSP (OJ L73/99, p 1).

competitiveness, and thus to offer consumers and businesses new opportunities to exchange information and trade electronically in a secure way, regardless of frontiers; in order to stimulate the Community-wide provision of certification services over open networks, certification-service-providers should be free to provide their services without prior authorisation; prior authorisation means not only any permission whereby the certification-service-provider concerned has to obtain a decision by national authorities before being allowed to provide its certification services, but also any other measures having the same effect;

(11) Voluntary accreditation schemes aiming at an enhanced level of service-provision may offer certification-service-providers the appropriate framework for developing further their services towards the levels of trust, security and quality demanded by the evolving market; such schemes should encourage the development of best practice among certification-service-providers; certification-service-providers should be left free to adhere to and benefit from such accreditation schemes;

(12) Certification services can be offered either by a public entity or a legal or natural person, when it is established in accordance with the national law; whereas Member States should not prohibit certification-service-providers from operating outside voluntary accreditation schemes; it should be ensured that such accreditation schemes do not reduce competition for certification services;

(13) Member States may decide how they ensure the supervision of compliance with the provisions laid down in this Directive; this Directive does not preclude the establishment of private-sector-based supervision systems; this Directive does not oblige certification-service-providers to apply to be supervised under any applicable accreditation scheme;

(14) It is important to strike a balance between consumer and business needs;

(15) Annex III covers requirements for secure signature-creation devices to ensure the functionality of advanced electronic signatures; it does not cover the entire system environment in which such devices operate; the functioning of the internal market requires the Commission and the Member States to act swiftly to enable the bodies charged with the conformity assessment of secure signature devices with Annex III to be designated; in order to meet market needs conformity assessment must be timely and efficient;

(16) This Directive contributes to the use and legal recognition of electronic signatures within the Community; a regulatory framework is not needed for electronic signatures exclusively used within systems, which are based on voluntary agreements under private law between a specified number of participants; the freedom of parties to agree among themselves the terms and conditions under which they accept

electronically signed data should be respected to the extent allowed by national law; the legal effectiveness of electronic signatures used in such systems and their admissibility as evidence in legal proceedings should be recognised;

(17) This Directive does not seek to harmonise national rules concerning contract law, particularly the formation and performance of contracts, or other formalities of a non-contractual nature concerning signatures; for this reason the provisions concerning the legal effect of electronic signatures should be without prejudice to requirements regarding form laid down in national law with regard to the conclusion of contracts or the rules determining where a contract is concluded;

(18) The storage and copying of signature-creation data could cause a threat to the legal validity of electronic signatures;

(19) Electronic signatures will be used in the public sector within national and Community administrations and in communications between such administrations and with citizens and economic operators, for example in the public procurement, taxation, social security, health and justice systems;

(20) Harmonised criteria relating to the legal effects of electronic signatures will preserve a coherent legal framework across the Community; national law lays down different requirements for the legal validity of hand-written signatures; whereas certificates can be used to confirm the identity of a person signing electronically; advanced electronic signatures based on qualified certificates aim at a higher level of security; advanced electronic signatures which are based on a qualified certificate and which are created by a secure-signature-creation device can be regarded as legally equivalent to hand-written signatures only if the requirements for hand-written signatures are fulfilled;

(21) In order to contribute to the general acceptance of electronic authentication methods it has to be ensured that electronic signatures can be used as evidence in legal proceedings in all Member States; the legal recognition of electronic signatures should be based upon objective criteria and not be linked to authorisation of the certification-service-provider involved; national law governs the legal spheres in which electronic documents and electronic signatures may be used; this Directive is without prejudice to the power of a national court to make a ruling regarding conformity with the requirements of this Directive and does not affect national rules regarding the unfettered judicial consideration of evidence;

(22) Certification-service-providers providing certification-services to the public are subject to national rules regarding liability;

(23) The development of international electronic commerce requires cross-border arrangements involving third countries; in order to ensure interoperability at a global level, agreements on multilateral

rules with third countries on mutual recognition of certification services could be beneficial;

(24) In order to increase user confidence in electronic communication and electronic commerce, certification-service-providers must observe data protection legislation and individual privacy;

(25) Provisions on the use of pseudonyms in certificates should not prevent Member States from requiring identification of persons pursuant to Community or national law;

(26) The measures necessary for the implementation of this Directive are to be adopted in accordance with Council Decision 1999/468/EC of 28 June 1999 laying down the procedures for the exercise of implementing powers conferred on the Commission;[7]

(27) Two years after its implementation the Commission will carry out a review of this Directive so as, inter alia, to ensure that the advance of technology or changes in the legal environment have not created barriers to achieving the aims stated in this Directive; it should examine the implications of associated technical areas and submit a report to the European Parliament and the Council on this subject;

(28) In accordance with the principles of subsidiarity and proportionality as set out in Article 5 of the Treaty, the objective of creating a harmonised legal framework for the provision of electronic signatures and related services cannot be sufficiently achieved by the Member States and can therefore be better achieved by the Community; this Directive does not go beyond what is necessary to achieve that objective,

HAVE ADOPTED THIS DIRECTIVE:

Article 1

Scope

The purpose of this Directive is to facilitate the use of electronic signatures and to contribute to their legal recognition. It establishes a legal framework for electronic signatures and certain certification-services in order to ensure the proper functioning of the internal market.

It does not cover aspects related to the conclusion and validity of contracts or other legal obligations where there are requirements as regards form prescribed by national or Community law nor does it affect rules and limits, contained in national or Community law, governing the use of documents.

---

[7] OJ L184/99, p 23.

Article 2

Definitions

For the purpose of this Directive:

1. 'electronic signature' means data in electronic form which are attached to or logically associated with other electronic data and which serve as a method of authentication;
2. 'advanced electronic signature' means an electronic signature which meets the following requirements:
    a) it is uniquely linked to the signatory;
    b) it is capable of identifying the signatory;
    c) it is created using means that the signatory can maintain under his sole control; and
    d) it is linked to the data to which it relates in such a manner that any subsequent change of the data is detectable;
3. 'signatory' means a person who holds a signature-creation device and acts either on his own behalf or on behalf of the natural or legal person or entity he represents;
4. 'signature-creation data' means unique data, such as codes or private cryptographic keys, which are used by the signatory to create an electronic signature;
5. 'signature-creation device' means configured software or hardware used to implement the signature-creation data;
6. 'secure-signature-creation device' means a signature-creation device which meets the requirements laid down in Annex III;
7. 'signature-verification-data' means data, such as codes or public cryptographic keys, which are used for the purpose of verifying an electronic signature;
8. 'signature-verification device' means configured software or hardware used to implement the signature-verification-data;
9. 'certificate' means an electronic attestation which links signature-verification data to a person and confirms the identity of that person;
10. 'qualified certificate' means a certificate which meets the requirements laid down in Annex I and is provided by a certification-service-provider who fulfils the requirements laid down in Annex II;
11. 'certification-service-provider' means an entity or a legal or natural person who issues certificates or provides other services related to electronic signatures;
12. 'electronic-signature product' means hardware or software, or relevant components thereof, which are intended to be used by a certification-service-provider for the provision of electronic-signature services or are intended to be used for the creation or verification of electronic signatures;

13. 'voluntary accreditation' means any permission, setting out rights and obligations specific to the provision of certification services, to be granted upon request by the certification-service-provider concerned, by the public or private body charged with the elaboration of, and supervision of compliance with, such rights and obligations, where the certification-service-provider is not entitled to exercise the rights stemming from the permission until it has received the decision by the body.

Article 3

Market access

(1) Member States shall not make the provision of certification services subject to prior authorisation.

(2) Without prejudice to the provisions of paragraph 1, Member States may introduce or maintain voluntary accreditation schemes aiming at enhanced levels of certification-service provision. All conditions related to such schemes must be objective, transparent, proportionate and non-discriminatory. Member States may not limit the number of accredited certification-service-providers for reasons which fall within the scope of this Directive.

(3) Each Member State shall ensure the establishment of an appropriate system that allows for supervision of certification-service-providers which are established on its territory and issue qualified certificates to the public.

(4) The conformity of secure signature-creation-devices with the requirements laid down in Annex III shall be determined by appropriate public or private bodies designated by Member States. The Commission shall, pursuant to the procedure laid down in Article 9, establish criteria for Member States to determine whether a body should be designated.

A determination of conformity with the requirements laid down in Annex III made by the bodies referred to in the first subparagraph shall be recognised by all Member States.

(5) The Commission may, in accordance with the procedure laid down in Article 9, establish and publish reference numbers of generally recognised standards for electronic-signature products in the Official Journal of the European Communities. Member States shall presume that there is compliance with the requirements laid down in Annex II, point (f), and Annex III when an electronic signature product meets those standards.

(6) Member States and the Commission shall work together to promote the development and use of signature-verification devices in the light of the recommendations for secure signature-verification laid down in Annex IV and in the interests of the consumer.

(7) Member States may make the use of electronic signatures in the public sector subject to possible additional requirements. Such requirements shall be objective, transparent, proportionate and non-discriminatory and shall relate only to the specific characteristics of the application concerned. Such requirements may not constitute an obstacle to cross-border services for citizens.

Article 4

Internal market principles

(1) Each Member State shall apply the national provisions which it adopts pursuant to this Directive to certification-service-providers established on its territory and to the services which they provide. Member States may not restrict the provision of certification-services originating in another Member State in the fields covered by this Directive.

(2) Member States shall ensure that electronic-signature products which comply with this Directive are permitted to circulate freely in the internal market.

Article 5

Legal effects of electronic signatures

(1) Member States shall ensure that advanced electronic signatures which are based on a qualified certificate and which are created by a secure-signature-creation device:
   a) satisfy the legal requirements of a signature in relation to data in electronic form in the same manner as a handwritten signature satisfies those requirements in relation to paper-based data; and
   b) are admissible as evidence in legal proceedings.

(2) Member States shall ensure that an electronic signature is not denied legal effectiveness and admissibility as evidence in legal proceedings solely on the grounds that it is:
   – in electronic form, or
   – not based upon a qualified certificate, or
   – not based upon a qualified certificate issued by an accredited certification-service-provider, or
   – not created by a secure signature-creation device.

Article 6

Liability

(1) As a minimum, Member States shall ensure that by issuing a certificate as a qualified certificate to the public or by guaranteeing such a

certificate to the public a certification-service-provider is liable for damage caused to any entity or legal or natural person who reasonably relies on that certificate:

a) as regards the accuracy at the time of issuance of all information contained in the qualified certificate and as regards the fact that the certificate contains all the details prescribed for a qualified certificate;

b) for assurance that at the time of the issuance of the certificate, the signatory identified in the qualified certificate held the signature-creation data corresponding to the signature-verification data given or identified in the certificate;

c) for assurance that the signature-creation data and the signature-verification data can be used in a complementary manner in cases where the certification-service-provider generates them both; unless the certification-service-provider proves that he has not acted negligently.

(2) As a minimum Member States shall ensure that a certification-service-provider who has issued a certificate as a qualified certificate to the public is liable for damage caused to any entity or legal or natural person who reasonably relies on the certificate for failure to register revocation of the certificate unless the certification-service-provider proves that he has not acted negligently.

(3) Member States shall ensure that a certification-service-provider may indicate in a qualified certificate limitations on the use of that certificate provided that the limitations are recognisable to third parties. The certification-service-provider shall not be liable for damage arising from use of a qualified certificate which exceeds the limitations placed on it.

(4) Member States shall ensure that a certification-service-provider may indicate in the qualified certificate a limit on the value of transactions for which the certificate can be used, provided that the limit is recognisable to third parties.

The certification-service-provider shall not be liable for damage resulting from this maximum limit being exceeded.

(5) The provisions of paragraphs 1 to 4 shall be without prejudice to Council Directive 93/13/EEC of 5 April 1993 on unfair terms in consumer contracts.8

Article 7

International aspects

(1) Member States shall ensure that certificates which are issued as qualified certificates to the public by a certification-service-provider

---

8 OJ L95/93, p 29.

established in a third country are recognised as legally equivalent to certificates issued by a certification-service-provider established within the Community if:

a) the certification-service-provider fulfils the requirements laid down in this Directive and has been accredited under a voluntary accreditation scheme established in a Member State; or

b) a certification-service-provider established within the Community which fulfils the requirements laid down in this Directive guarantees the certificate; or

c) the certificate or the certification-service-provider is recognised under a bilateral or multilateral agreement between the Community and third countries or international organisations.

(2) In order to facilitate cross-border certification services with third countries and legal recognition of advanced electronic signatures originating in third countries, the Commission shall make proposals, where appropriate, to achieve the effective implementation of standards and international agreements applicable to certification services. In particular, and where necessary, it shall submit proposals to the Council for appropriate mandates for the negotiation of bilateral and multilateral agreements with third countries and international organisations. The Council shall decide by qualified majority.

(3) Whenever the Commission is informed of any difficulties encountered by Community undertakings with respect to market access in third countries, it may, if necessary, submit proposals to the Council for an appropriate mandate for the negotiation of comparable rights for Community undertakings in these third countries. The Council shall decide by qualified majority.

Measures taken pursuant to this paragraph shall be without prejudice to the obligations of the Community and of the Member States under relevant international agreements.

Article 8

Data protection

(1) Member States shall ensure that certification-service-providers and national bodies responsible for accreditation or supervision comply with the requirements laid down in Directive 95/46/EC of the European Parliament and of the Council of 24 October 1995 on tile protection of individuals with regard to the processing of personal data and on the free movement of such data.[9]

---

[9] OJ L281/95, p 31.

(2)   Member States shall ensure that a certification-service-provider which issues certificates to the public may collect personal data only directly from the data subject, or after the explicit consent of the data subject, and only insofar as it is necessary for the purposes of issuing and maintaining the certificate. The data may not be collected or processed for any other purposes without the explicit consent of the data subject.

(3)   Without prejudice to the legal effect given to pseudonyms under national law, Member States shall not prevent certification service providers from indicating in the certificate a pseudonym instead of the signatory's name.

Article 9

Committee

(1)   The Commission shall be assisted by an 'Electronic-Signature Committee', hereinafter referred to as 'the committee'.

(2)   Where reference is made to this paragraph, Articles 4 and 7 of Decision 1999/468/EC shall apply, having regard to the provisions of Article 8 thereof.

The period laid down in Article 4(3) of Decision 1999/468/EC shall be set at three months.

(3)   The Committee shall adopt its own rules of procedure.

Article 10

Tasks of the committee

The committee shall clarify the requirements laid down in the Annexes of this Directive, the criteria referred to in Article 3(4) and the generally recognised standards for electronic signature products established and published pursuant to Article 3(5), in accordance with the procedure laid down in Article 9(2).

Article 11

Notification

(1)   Member States shall notify to the Commission and the other Member States the following:

a)   information on national voluntary accreditation schemes, including any additional requirements pursuant to Article 3(7);

b)   the names and addresses of the national bodies responsible for accreditation and supervision as well as of the bodies referred to in Article 3(4);

c)   the names and addresses of all accredited national certification service providers.

(2)   Any information supplied under paragraph 1 and changes in respect of that information shall be notified by the Member States as soon as possible.

Article 12

Review

(1)   The Commission shall review the operation of this Directive and report thereon to the European Parliament and to the Council by 19 July 2003 at the latest.

(2)   The review shall inter alia assess whether the scope of this Directive should be modified, taking account of technological, market and legal developments. The report shall in particular include an assessment, on the basis of experience gained, of aspects of harmonisation. The report shall be accompanied, where appropriate, by legislative proposals.

Article 13

Implementation

(1)   Member States shall bring into force the laws, regulations and administrative provisions necessary to comply with this Directive before 19 July 2001. They shall forthwith inform the Commission thereof.

When Member States adopt these measures, they shall contain a reference to this Directive or shall be accompanied by such a reference on the occasion of their official publication. The methods of making such reference shall be laid down by the Member States.

(2)   Member States shall communicate to the Commission the text of the main provisions of domestic law which they adopt in the field governed by this Directive.

Article 14

Entry into force

This Directive shall enter into force on the day of its publication in the Official Journal of the European Communities.

Article 15

Addressees

This Directive is addressed to the Member States.

ANNEX I

Requirements for qualified certificates

Qualified certificates must contain:

a)   an indication that the certificate is issued as a qualified certificate;
b)   the identification of the certification-service-provider and the State in which it is established;
c)   the name of the signatory or a pseudonym, which shall be identified as such;
d)   provision for a specific attribute of the signatory to be included if relevant, depending on the purpose for which the certificate is intended;
e)   signature-verification data which correspond to signature-creation data under the control of the signatory;
f)   an indication of the beginning and end of the period of validity of the certificate;
g)   the identity code of the certificate;
h)   the advanced electronic signature of the certification-service-provider issuing it;
i)   limitations on the scope of use of the certificate, if applicable; and
j)   limits on the value of transactions for which the certificate can be used, if applicable.

ANNEX II

Requirements for certification-service-providers issuing qualified certificates

Certification-service-providers must:

a)   demonstrate the reliability necessary for providing certification services;
b)   ensure the operation of a prompt and secure directory and a secure and immediate revocation service;

c) ensure that the date and time when a certificate is issued or revoked can be determined precisely;

d) verify, by appropriate means in accordance with national law, the identity and, if applicable, any specific attributes of the person to which a qualified certificate is issued;

e) employ personnel who possess the expert knowledge, experience, and qualifications necessary for the services provided, in particular competence at managerial level, expertise in electronic signature technology and familiarity with proper security procedures; they must also apply administrative and management procedures which are adequate and correspond to recognised standards;

f) use trustworthy systems and products which are protected against modification and ensure the technical and cryptographic security of the process supported by them;

g) take measures against forgery of certificates, and, in cases where the certification-service-provider generates signature-creation data, guarantee confidentiality during the process of generating such data;

h) maintain sufficient financial resources to operate in conformity with the requirements laid down in the Directive, in particular to bear the risk of liability for damages, for example, by obtaining appropriate insurance;

i) record all relevant information concerning a qualified certificate for an appropriate period of time, in particular for the purpose of providing evidence of certification for the purposes of legal proceedings. Such recording may be done electronically;

j) not store or copy signature-creation data of the person to whom the certification-service-provider provided key management services;

k) before entering into a contractual relationship with a person seeking a certificate to support his electronic signature inform that person by a durable means of communication of the precise terms and conditions regarding the use of the certificate, including any limitations on its use, the existence of a voluntary accreditation scheme and procedures for complaints and dispute settlement. Such information, which may be transmitted electronically, must be in writing and in readily understandable language. Relevant parts of this information must also be made available on request to third-parties relying on the certificate;

l) use trustworthy systems to store certificates in a verifiable form so that:
- only authorised persons can make entries and changes,
- information can be checked for authenticity,
- certificates are publicly available for retrieval in only those cases for which the certificate-holder's consent has been obtained, and
- any technical changes compromising these security requirements are apparent to the operator.

ANNEX III

Requirements for secure signature-creation devices

(1) Secure signature-creation devices must, by appropriate technical and procedural means, ensure at the least that:

a) the signature-creation-data used for signature generation can practically occur only once, and that their secrecy is reasonably assured;

b) the signature-creation-data used for signature generation cannot, with reasonable assurance, be derived and the signature is protected against forgery using currently available technology;

c) the signature-creation-data used for signature generation can be reliably protected by the legitimate signatory against the use of others.

(2) Secure signature-creation devices must not alter the data to be signed or prevent such data from being presented to the signatory prior to the signature process.

ANNEX IV

Recommendations for secure signature verification

During the signature-verification process it should be ensured with reasonable certainty that:

a) the data used for verifying the signature correspond to the data displayed to the verifier;

b) the signature is reliably verified and the result of that verification is correctly displayed;

c) the verifier can, as necessary, reliably establish the contents of the signed data;

d) the authenticity and validity of the certificate required at the time of signature verification are reliably verified;

e) the result of verification and the signatory's identity are correctly displayed;

f) the use of a pseudonym is clearly indicated; and

g) any security-relevant changes can be detected.

Denmark	1. – Lov om elektroniske signaturer, Lov Nr 417 af 31/05/2001
	2. – Bekendtgørelse Nr 922 af 05/10/2000 om noglecentres og systemrevisionens indberetning af oplysninger til Telestryrelsen
	3. – Bekendtgørelse Nr 923 af 05/10/2000 om sikkerhedskrav m.v. til noglecentre
EIRE	Electronic Commerce Act 2000
Finland	1. – Laki sähköisistä allekirjoituksista, Laki du 24/01/2003
	2. – Laki viestintähallinnosta annetun lain 2 muuttamisesta, Laki du 24/01/2003
Sweden	1. – Lag om kvalificerade elektroniska signaturer, SFS 2000:832
	2. – Lagen om teknisk kontroll, SFS 1992:1119
	3. – Förordningen om vissa skyldigheter för myndigheter vid ett medlemskap i Europeiska unionen, SFS 1994:2035
United Kingdom	1. – Electronic Communications Act 2000
	2. – Electronic Signatures Regulations 2002, S.I. No. 2002/318

COUNCIL DIRECTIVE 93/13/EEC

of 5 April 1993

on unfair terms in consumer contracts

(Official Journal, L95/93, p 29)

THE COUNCIL OF THE EUROPEAN COMMUNITIES –

Having regard to the Treaty establishing the European Economic Community, and in particular Article 100a thereof,

Having regard to the proposal from the Commission,[1]

In cooperation with the European Parliament,[2]

Having regard to the opinion of the Economic and Social Committee,[3]

Whereas it is necessary to adopt measures with the aim of progressively establishing the internal market before 31 December 1992; whereas the internal market comprises an area without internal frontiers in which goods, persons, services and capital move freely;

Whereas the laws of Member States relating to the terms of contract between the seller of goods or supplier of services, on the one hand, and the consumer of them, on the other hand, show many disparities, with the result that the national markets for the sale of goods and services to consumers differ from each other and that distortions of competition may arise amongst the sellers and suppliers, notably when they sell and supply in other Member States;

Whereas, in particular, the laws of Member States relating to unfair terms in consumer contracts show marked divergences;

Whereas it is the responsibility of the Member States to ensure that contracts concluded with consumers do not contain unfair terms;

Whereas, generally speaking, consumers do not know the rules of law which, in Member States other than their own, govern contracts for the sale of goods or services; whereas this lack of awareness may deter them from direct transactions for the purchase of goods or services in another Member State;

Whereas, in order to facilitate the establishment of the internal market and to safeguard the citizen in his role as consumer when acquiring goods and services under contracts which are governed by the laws of Member States other than his own, it is essential to remove unfair terms from those contracts;

Whereas sellers of goods and suppliers of services will thereby be helped in their task of selling goods and supplying services, both at home and throughout the

---

[1] OJ C73/92, p 7.
[2] OJ C326/91, p 108, and OJ C21/93.
[3] OJ C159/91, p 34.

internal market; whereas competition will thus be stimulated, so contributing to increased choice for Community citizens as consumers;

Whereas the two Community programmes for a consumer protection and information policy[4] underlined the importance of safeguarding consumers in the matter of unfair terms of contract; whereas this protection ought to be provided by laws and regulations which are either harmonized at Community level or adopted directly at that level;

Whereas in accordance with the principle laid down under the heading 'Protection of the economic interests of the consumers', as stated in those programmes: 'acquirers of goods and services should be protected against the abuse of power by the seller or supplier, in particular against one-sided standard contracts and the unfair exclusion of essential rights in contracts';

Whereas more effective protection of the consumer can be achieved by adopting uniform rules of law in the matter of unfair terms; whereas those rules should apply to all contracts concluded between sellers or suppliers and consumers; whereas as a result inter alia contracts relating to employment, contracts relating to succession rights, contracts relating to rights under family law and contracts relating to the incorporation and organization of companies or partnership agreements must be excluded from this Directive;

Whereas the consumer must receive equal protection under contracts concluded by word of mouth and written contracts regardless, in the latter case, of whether the terms of the contract are contained in one or more documents;

Whereas, however, as they now stand, national laws allow only partial harmonization to be envisaged; whereas, in particular, only contractual terms which have not been individually negotiated are covered by this Directive; whereas Member States should have the option, with due regard for the Treaty, to afford consumers a higher level of protection through national provisions that are more stringent than those of this Directive;

Whereas the statutory or regulatory provisions of the Member States which directly or indirectly determine the terms of consumer contracts are presumed not to contain unfair terms; whereas, therefore, it does not appear to be necessary to subject the terms which reflect mandatory statutory or regulatory provisions and the principles or provisions of international conventions to which the Member States or the Community are party; whereas in that respect the wording 'mandatory statutory or regulatory provisions' in Article 1(2) also covers rules which, according to the law, shall apply between the contracting parties provided that no other arrangements have been established;

Whereas Member States must however ensure that unfair terms are not included, particularly because this Directive also applies to trades, business or professions of a public nature;

Whereas it is necessary to fix in a general way the criteria for assessing the unfair character of contract terms;

Whereas the assessment, according to the general criteria chosen, of the unfair character of terms, in particular in sale or supply activities of a public nature providing collective services which take account of solidarity among users, must be

---

[4] OJ C92/75, p 1, and OJ C133/81, p 1.

supplemented by a means of making an overall evaluation of the different interests involved; whereas this constitutes the requirement of good faith; whereas, in making an assessment of good faith, particular regard shall be had to the strength of the bargaining positions of the parties, whether the consumer had an inducement to agree to the term and whether the goods or services were sold or supplied to the special order of the consumer; whereas the requirement of good faith may be satisfied by the seller or supplier where he deals fairly and equitably with the other party whose legitimate interests he has to take into account;

Whereas, for the purposes of this Directive, the annexed list of terms can be of indicative value only and, because of the cause of the minimal character of the Directive, the scope of these terms may be the subject of amplification or more restrictive editing by the Member States in their national laws;

Whereas the nature of goods or services should have an influence on assessing the unfairness of contractual terms;

Whereas, for the purposes of this Directive, assessment of unfair character shall not be made of terms which describe the main subject matter of the contract nor the quality/price ratio of the goods or services supplied; whereas the main subject matter of the contract and the price/quality ratio may nevertheless be taken into account in assessing the fairness of other terms; whereas it follows, inter alia, that in insurance contracts, the terms which clearly define or circumscribe the insured risk and the insurer's liability shall not be subject to such assessment since these restrictions are taken into account in calculating the premium paid by the consumer;

Whereas contracts should be drafted in plain, intelligible language, the consumer should actually be given an opportunity to examine all the terms and, if in doubt, the interpretation most favourable to the consumer should prevail;

Whereas Member States should ensure that unfair terms are not used in contracts concluded with consumers by a seller or supplier and that if, nevertheless, such terms are so used, they will not bind the consumer, and the contract will continue to bind the parties upon those terms if it is capable of continuing in existence without the unfair provisions;

Whereas there is a risk that, in certain cases, the consumer may be deprived of protection under this Directive by designating the law of a non-Member country as the law applicable to the contract; whereas provisions should therefore be included in this Directive designed to avert this risk;

Whereas persons or organizations, if regarded under the law of a Member State as having a legitimate interest in the matter, must have facilities for initiating proceedings concerning terms of contract drawn up for general use in contracts concluded with consumers, and in particular unfair terms, either before a court or before an administrative authority competent to decide upon complaints or to initiate appropriate legal proceedings; whereas this possibility does not, however, entail prior verification of the general conditions obtaining in individual economic sectors;

Whereas the courts or administrative authorities of the Member States must have at their disposal adequate and effective means of preventing the continued application of unfair terms in consumer contracts.

HAS ADOPTED THIS DIRECTIVE:

Article 1

(1) The purpose of this Directive is to approximate the laws, regulations and administrative provisions of the Member States relating to unfair terms in contracts concluded between a seller or supplier and a consumer.

(2) The contractual terms which reflect mandatory statutory or regulatory provisions and the provisions or principles of international conventions to which the Member States. or the Community are party, particularly in the transport area, shall not be subject to the provisions of this Directive.

Article 2

For the purposes of this Directive:

(a) 'unfair terms' means the contractual terms defined in Article 3;

(b) 'consumer' means any natural person who, in contracts covered by this Directive, is acting for purposes which are outside his trade, business or profession;

(c) 'seller or supplier' means any natural or legal person who, in contracts covered by this Directive, is acting for purposes relating to his trade, business or profession, whether publicly owned or privately owned.

Article 3

(1) A contractual term which has not been individually negotiated shall be regarded as unfair if, contrary to the requirement of good faith, it causes a significant imbalance in the parties' rights and obligations arising under the contract, to the detriment of the consumer.

(2) A term shall always be regarded as not individually negotiated where it has been drafted in advance and the consumer has therefore not been able to influence the substance of the term, particularly in the context of a pre-formulated standard contract.

The fact that certain aspects of a term or one specific term have been individually negotiated shall not exclude the application of this Article to the rest of a contract if an overall assessment of the contract indicates that it is nevertheless a pre-formulated standard contract.

Where any seller or supplier claims that a standard term has been individually negotiated, the burden of proof in this respect shall be incumbent on him.

(3) The Annex shall contain an indicative and non-exhaustive list of the terms which may be regarded as unfair.

Article 4

(1) Without prejudice to Article 7, the unfairness of a contractual term shall be assessed, taking into account the nature of the goods or services for which the contract was concluded and by referring, at the time of conclusion of the contract, to all the circumstances attending the conclusion of the contract and to all the other terms of the contract or of another contract on which it is dependent.

(2) Assessment of the unfair nature of the terms shall relate neither to the definition of the main subject matter of the contract nor to the adequacy of the price and remuneration, on the one hand, as against the services or goods supplies in exchange, on the other, in so far as these terms are in plain intelligible language.

Article 5

In the case of contracts where all or certain terms offered to the consumer are in writing, these terms must always be drafted in plain, intelligible language. Where there is doubt about the meaning of a term, the interpretation most favourable to the consumer shall prevail. This rule on interpretation shall not apply in the context of the procedures laid down in Article 7(2).

Article 6

(1) Member States shall lay down that unfair terms used in a contract concluded with a consumer by a seller or supplier shall, as provided for under their national law, not be binding on the consumer and that the contract shall continue to bind the parties upon those terms if it is capable of continuing in existence without the unfair terms.

(2) Member States shall take the necessary measures to ensure that the consumer does not lose the protection granted by this Directive by virtue of the choice of the law of a non-Member country as the law applicable to the contract if the latter has a close connection with the territory of the Member States.

Article 7

(1) Member States shall ensure that, in the interests of consumers and of competitors, adequate and effective means exist to prevent the continued

use of unfair terms in contracts concluded with consumers by sellers or suppliers.

(2) The means referred to in paragraph 1 shall include provisions whereby persons or organizations, having a legitimate interest under national law in protecting consumers, may take action according to the national law concerned before the courts or before competent administrative bodies for a decision as to whether contractual terms drawn up for general use are unfair, so that they can apply appropriate and effective means to prevent the continued use of such terms.

(3) With due regard for national laws, the legal remedies referred to in paragraph 2 may be directed separately or jointly against a number of sellers or suppliers from the same economic sector or their associations which use or recommend the use of the same general contractual terms or similar terms.

Article 8

Member States may adopt or retain the most stringent provisions compatible with the Treaty in the area covered by this Directive, to ensure a maximum degree of protection for the consumer.

Article 9

The Commission shall present a report to the European Parliament and to the Council concerning the application of this Directive five years at the latest after the date in Article 10(1).

Article 10

(1) Member States shall bring into force the laws, regulations and administrative provisions necessary to comply with this Directive no later than 31 December 1994. They shall forthwith inform the Commission thereof. These provisions shall be applicable to all contracts concluded after 31 December 1994.

(2) When Member States adopt these measures, they shall contain a reference to this Directive or shall be accompanied by such reference on the occasion of their official publication. The methods of making such a reference shall be laid down by the Member States.

(3) Member States shall communicate the main provisions of national law which they adopt in the field covered by this Directive to the Commission.

Article 11

This Directive is addressed to the Member States.

ANNEX

TERMS REFERRED TO IN ARTICLE 3(3)

1. Terms which have the object or effect of:
    a) excluding or limiting the legal liability of a seller or supplier in the event of the death of a consumer or personal injury to the latter resulting from an act or omission of that seller or supplier;
    b) inappropriately excluding or limiting the legal rights of the consumer vis-à-vis the seller or supplier or another party in the event of total or partial non-performance or inadequate performance by the seller or supplier of any of the contractual obligations, including the option of offsetting a debt owed to the seller or supplier against any claim which the consumer may have against him;
    c) making an agreement binding on the consumer whereas provision of services by the seller or supplier is subject to a condition whose realization depends on his own will alone;
    d) permitting the seller or supplier to retain sums paid by the consumer where the latter decides not to conclude or perform the contract, without providing for the consumer to receive compensation of an equivalent amount from the seller or supplier where the latter is the party cancelling the contract;
    e) requiring any consumer who fails to fulfil his obligation to pay a disproportionately high sum in compensation;
    f) authorizing the seller or supplier to dissolve the contract on a discretionary basis where the same facility is not granted to the consumer, or permitting the seller or supplier to retain the sums paid for services not yet supplied by him where it is the seller or supplier himself who dissolves the contract;
    g) enabling the seller or supplier to terminate a contract of indeterminate duration without reasonable notice except where there are serious grounds for doing so;
    h) automatically extending a contract of fixed duration where the consumer does not indicate otherwise, when the deadline fixed for the consumer to express this desire not to extend the contract is unreasonably early;
    i) irrevocably binding the consumer to terms with which he had no real opportunity of becoming acquainted before the conclusion of the contract;

j) enabling the seller or supplier to alter the terms of the contract unilaterally without a valid reason which is specified in the contract;

k) enabling the seller or supplier to alter unilaterally without a valid reason any characteristics of the product or service to be provided;

l) providing for the price of goods to be determined at the time of delivery or allowing a seller of goods or supplier of services to increase their price without in both cases giving the consumer the corresponding right to cancel the contract if the final price is too high in relation to the price agreed when the contract was concluded;

m) giving the seller or supplier the right to determine whether the goods or services supplied are in conformity with the contract, or giving him the exclusive right to interpret any term of the contract;

n) limiting the seller's or supplier's obligation to respect commitments undertaken by his agents or making his commitments subject to compliance with a particular formality;

o) obliging the consumer to fulfil all his obligations where the seller or supplier does not perform his;

p) giving the seller or supplier the possibility of transferring his rights and obligations under the contract, where this may serve to reduce the guarantees for the consumer, without the latter's agreement;

q) excluding or hindering the consumer's right to take legal action or exercise any other legal remedy, particularly by requiring the consumer to take disputes exclusively to arbitration not covered by legal provisions, unduly restricting the evidence available to him or imposing on him a burden of proof which, according to the applicable law, should lie with another party to the contract.

2. Scope of subparagraphs (g), (j) and (l)

a) Subparagraph (g) is without hindrance to terms by which a supplier of financial services reserves the right to terminate unilaterally a contract of indeterminate duration without notice where there is a valid reason, provided that the supplier is required to inform the other contracting party or parties thereof immediately.

b) Subparagraph (j) is without hindrance to terms under which a supplier of financial services reserves the right to alter the rate of interest payable by the consumer or due to the latter, or the amount of other charges for financial services without notice where there is a valid reason, provided that the supplier is required to inform the other contracting party or parties thereof at the earliest opportunity and that the latter are free to dissolve the contract immediately.

Subparagraph (j) is also without hindrance to terms under which a seller or supplier reserves the right to alter unilaterally the conditions of a contract of indeterminate duration, provided that he is required to inform the consumer with reasonable notice and that the consumer is free to dissolve the contract.

c) Subparagraphs (g), (j) and (l) do not apply to:
   – transactions in transferable securities, financial instruments and other products or services where the price is linked to fluctuations in a stock exchange quotation or index or a financial market rate that the seller or supplier does not control;
   – contracts for the purchase or sale of foreign curren cy, traveller's cheques or international money orders denominated in foreign currency;

d) Subparagraph (l) is without hindrance to price-indexation clauses, where lawful, provided that the method by which prices vary is explicitly described.

Denmark	1. – Lov Nr 1098 af 21/12/1994
	2. – Lov Nr 428 af 01/06/1994 om markedforing
	3. – Lov om aftaler og andrer retshandler pa formurettens omrade, Lov Nr 781 af 26/08/1996.
EIRE	1. – European Communities (Unfair Terms in Consumer Contracts) Regulations, 1995, S.I. No. 27/1995
	2. – European Communities (Unfair Terms in Consumer Contracts) (Amendment) Regulations 2000, S.I. No. 307/2000.
Finland	1. – Laki terveydenhuollon ammattihenkilöistä (559/94) 28/06/1994
	2. – Asetus terveydenhuollon ammattihenkilöistä (564/94) 28/06/1994
	3. – Laki kuluttajansuojalain muuttamisesta ref. 391/2002 Suomen säädöskokoelma 29/05/2002
	4. – Laki takauksesta ja vieravelkapanttauksesta annetun lain muuttamisesta ref. 392/2002 Suomen säädöskokoelma 29/05/2002
	5. – Laki kuluttajansuojalain 3 ja 4 luvun muuttamisesta 16.12.1994/1259
Sweden	1. – Lag om avtalsvillkor i konsumentförhållanden, Svensk författningssamling, SFS 1994:1512
	2. – Lag om ändring i lagen (1915:218) om avtal och andra rättshandlingar på förmögenhetsrättens område, SFS 1994:1513.
United Kingdom	1. – The Unfair Terms in Consumer Contracts Regulations 1994, S.I. No. 1994/3159
	2. – The Unfair Arbitration Agreements (Specified Amount) Order 1996, S.I. No. 1996/3211
	3. – The Unfair Terms in Consumer Contracts Regulations 1999, S.I. No.1999/2083
	4. – The Unfair Terms in Consumer Contracts Regulations 2001, S.I. 2001 No. 1186.

DIRECTIVE 2000/35/EC OF THE EUROPEAN PARLIAMENT AND OF THE COUNCIL

of 29 June 2000

on combating late payment in commercial transactions

(Official Journal L200/35, p 35)

THE EUROPEAN PARLIAMENT AND THE COUNCIL OF THE EUROPEAN UNION –

Having regard to the Treaty establishing the European Community, and in particular Article 95 thereof,

Having regard to the proposal from the Commission,[1]

Having regard to the opinion of the Economic and Social Committee,[2]

Acting in accordance with the procedure laid down in Article 251 of the Treaty,[3] in the light of the joint text approved by the Conciliation Committee on 4 May 2000.

Whereas:

(1) In its resolution on the integrated programme in favour of SMEs and the craft sector,[4] the European Parliament urged the Commission to submit proposals to deal with the problem of late payment.

(2) On 12 May 1995 the Commission adopted a recommendation on payment periods in commercial transactions.[5]

(3) In its resolution on the Commission recommendation on payment periods in commercial transactions,[6] the European Parliament called on the Commission to consider transforming its recommendation into a proposal for a Council directive to be submitted as soon as possible.

(4) On 29 May 1997 the Economic and Social Committee adopted an opinion on the Commission's Green Paper on Public procurement in the European Union: Exploring the way forward.[7]

---

[1] OJ C 168, 3.6.1998, p 13, and OJ C 374, 3.12.1998, p 4.

[2] OJ C 407, 28.12.1998, p 50.

[3] Opinion of the European Parliament of 17 September 1998 (OJ C 313, 12.10.1998, p 142), Council Common Position of 29 July 1999 (OJ C 284, 6.10.1999, p 1) and decision of the European Parliament of 16 December 1999 (not yet published in the Official Journal). Decision of the European Parliament of 15 June 2000 and Decision of the Council of 18 May 2000.

[4] OJ C 323, 21.11.1994, p 19.

[5] OJ L 127, 10.6.1995, p 19.

[6] OJ C 211, 22.7.1996, p 43.

[7] OJ C 287, 22.9.1997, p 92.

(5)   On 4 June 1997 the Commission published an action plan for the single market, which underlined that late payment represents an increasingly serious obstacle for the success of the single market.

(6)   On 17 July 1997 the Commission published a report on late payments in commercial transactions,[8] summarising the results of an evaluation of the effects of the Commission's recommendation of 12 May 1995.

(7)   Heavy administrative and financial burdens are placed on businesses, particularly small and medium-sized ones, as a result of excessive payment periods and late payment. Moreover, these problems are a major cause of insolvencies threatening the survival of businesses and result in numerous job losses.

(8)   In some Member States contractual payment periods differ significantly from the Community average.

(9)   The differences between payment rules and practices in the Member States constitute an obstacle to the proper functioning of the internal market.

(10)   This has the effect of considerably limiting commercial transactions between Member States. This is in contradiction with Article 14 of the Treaty as entrepreneurs should be able to trade throughout the internal market under conditions which ensure that transborder operations do not entail greater risks than domestic sales. Distortions of competition would ensue if substantially different rules applied to domestic and transborder operations.

(11)   The most recent statistics indicate that there has been, at best, no improvement in late payments in many Member States since the adoption of the recommendation of 12 May 1995.

(12)   The objective of combating late payments in the internal market cannot be sufficiently achieved by the Member States acting individually and can, therefore, be better achieved by the Community. This Directive does not go beyond what is necessary to achieve that objective. This Directive complies therefore, in its entirety, with the requirements of the principles of subsidiarity and proportionality as laid down in Article 5 of the Treaty.

(13)   This Directive should be limited to payments made as remuneration for commercial transactions and does not regulate transactions with consumers, interest in connection with other payments, e.g. payments under the laws on cheques and bills of exchange, payments made as compensation for damages including payments from insurance companies.

---

[8] OJ C 216, 17.7.1997, p 10.

(14) The fact that the liberal professions are covered by this Directive does not mean that Member States have to treat them as undertakings or merchants for purposes not covered by this Directive.

(15) This Directive only defines the term 'enforceable title' but does not regulate the various procedures of forced execution of such a title and the conditions under which forced execution of such a title can be stopped or suspended.

(16) Late payment constitutes a breach of contract which has been made financially attractive to debtors in most Member States by low interest rates on late payments and/or slow procedures for redress. A decisive shift, including compensation of creditors for the costs incurred, is necessary to reverse this trend and to ensure that the consequences of late payments are such as to discourage late payment.

(17) The reasonable compensation for the recovery costs has to be considered without prejudice to national provisions according to which a national judge can award to the creditor any additional damage caused by the debtor's late payment, taking also into account that such incurred costs may be already compensated for by the interest for late payment.

(18) This Directive takes into account the issue of long contractual payment periods and, in particular, the existence of certain categories of contracts where a longer payment period in combination with a restriction of freedom of contract or a higher interest rate can be justified.

(19) This Directive should prohibit abuse of freedom of contract to the disadvantage of the creditor. Where an agreement mainly serves the purpose of procuring the debtor additional liquidity at the expense of the creditor, or where the main contractor imposes on his suppliers and subcontractors terms of payment which are not justified on the grounds of the terms granted to himself, these may be considered to be factors constituting such an abuse. This Directive does not affect national provisions relating to the way contracts are concluded or regulating the validity of contractual terms which are unfair to the debtor.

(20) The consequences of late payment can be dissuasive only if they are accompanied by procedures for redress which are rapid and effective for the creditor. In conformity with the principle of non-discrimination contained in Article 12 of the Treaty, those procedures should be available to all creditors who are established in the Community.

(21) It is desirable to ensure that creditors are in a position to exercise a retention of title on a non-discriminatory basis throughout the Community, if the retention of title clause is valid under the applicable national provisions designated by private international law.

(22) This Directive should regulate all commercial transactions irrespective of whether they are carried out between private or public undertakings or between undertakings and public authorities, having regard to the fact that the latter handle a considerable volume of payments to business. It should therefore also regulate all commercial transactions between main contractors and their suppliers and subcontractors.

(23) Article 5 of this Directive requires that the recovery procedure for unchallenged claims be completed within a short period of time in conformity with national legislation, but does not require Member States to adopt a specific procedure or to amend their existing legal procedures in a specific way.

HAVE ADOPTED THIS DIRECTIVE:

Article 1

Scope

This Directive shall apply to all payments made as remuneration for commercial transactions.

Article 2

Definitions

For the purposes of this Directive:

1. 'commercial transactions' means transactions between undertakings or between undertakings and public authorities which lead to the delivery of goods or the provision of services for remuneration,

    'public authority' means any contracting authority or entity, as defined by the Public Procurement Directives (92/50/EEC,[9] 93/36/EEC,[10] 93/37/EEC[11] and 93/38/EEC[12]),

    'undertaking' means any organisation acting in the course of its independent economic or professional activity, even where it is carried on by a single person;

2. 'late payment' means exceeding the contractual or statutory period of payment;

[9] OJ L 209, 24.7.1992, p 1.
[10] OJ L 199, 9.8.1993, p 1.
[11] OJ L 199, 9.8.1993, p 54.
[12] OJ L 199, 9.8.1993, p 84.

3.   'retention of title' means the contractual agreement according to which the seller retains title to the goods in question until the price has been paid in full;

4.   'interest rate applied by the European Central Bank to its main refinancing operations' means the interest rate applied to such operations in the case of fixed-rate tenders. In the event that a main refinancing operation was conducted according to a variable-rate tender procedure, this interest rate refers to the marginal interest rate which resulted from that tender. This applies both in the case of single-rate and variable-rate auctions;

5.   'enforceable title' means any decision, judgment or order for payment issued by a court or other competent authority, whether for immediate payment or payment by instalments, which permits the creditor to have his claim against the debtor collected by means of forced execution; it shall include a decision, judgment or order for payment that is provisionally enforceable and remains so even if the debtor appeals against it.

Article 3

Interest in case of late payment

(1)   Member States shall ensure that:

a)   interest in accordance with point (d) shall become payable from the day following the date or the end of the period for payment fixed in the contract;

b)   if the date or period for payment is not fixed in the contract, interest shall become payable automatically without the necessity of a reminder:

    i)   30 days following the date of receipt by the debtor of the invoice or an equivalent request for payment; or

    ii)   if the date of the receipt of the invoice or the equivalent request for payment is uncertain, 30 days after the date of receipt of the goods or services; or

    iii) if the debtor receives the invoice or the equivalent request for payment earlier than the goods or the services, 30 days after the receipt of the goods or services; or

    iv)   if a procedure of acceptance or verification, by which the conformity of the goods or services with the contract is to be ascertained, is provided for by statute or in the contract and if the debtor receives the invoice or the equivalent request for payment earlier or on the date on which such acceptance or verification takes place, 30 days after this latter date;

c) the creditor shall be entitled to interest for late payment to the extent that:

   i) he has fulfilled his contractual and legal obligations; and

   ii) he has not received the amount due on time, unless the debtor is not responsible for the delay;

d) the level of interest for late payment ('the statutory rate'), which the debtor is obliged to pay, shall be the sum of the interest rate applied by the European Central Bank to its most recent main refinancing operation carried out before the first calendar day of the half-year in question ('the reference rate'), plus at least seven percentage points ('the margin'), unless otherwise specified in the contract. For a Member State which is not participating in the third stage of economic and monetary union, the reference rate referred to above shall be the equivalent rate set by its national central bank. In both cases, the reference rate in force on the first calendar day of the half-year in question shall apply for the following six months;

e) unless the debtor is not responsible for the delay, the creditor shall be entitled to claim reasonable compensation from the debtor for all relevant recovery costs incurred through the latter's late payment. Such recovery costs shall respect the principles of transparency and proportionality as regards the debt in question. Member States may, while respecting the principles referred to above, fix maximum amounts as regards the recovery costs for different levels of debt.

(2) For certain categories of contracts to be defined by national law, Member States may fix the period after which interest becomes payable to a maximum of 60 days provided that they either restrain the parties to the contract from exceeding this period or fix a mandatory interest rate that substantially exceeds the statutory rate.

(3) Member States shall provide that an agreement on the date for payment or on the consequences of late payment which is not in line with the provisions of paragraphs 1(b) to (d) and 2 either shall not be enforceable or shall give rise to a claim for damages if, when all circumstances of the case, including good commercial practice and the nature of the product, are considered, it is grossly unfair to the creditor. In determining whether an agreement is grossly unfair to the creditor, it will be taken, *inter alia*, into account whether the debtor has any objective reason to deviate from the provisions of paragraphs 1(b) to (d) and 2. If such an agreement is determined to be grossly unfair, the statutory terms will apply, unless the national courts determine different conditions which are fair.

Member States shall ensure that, in the interests of creditors and of competitors, adequate and effective means exist to prevent the continued use of terms which are grossly unfair within the meaning of paragraph 3.

(5) The means referred to in paragraph 4 shall include provisions whereby organisations officially recognised as, or having a legitimate interest in, representing small and medium-sized enterprises may take action according to the national law concerned before the courts or before competent administrative bodies on the grounds that contractual terms drawn up for general use are grossly unfair within the meaning of paragraph 3, so that they can apply appropriate and effective means to prevent the continued use of such terms.

Article 4

Retention of title

(1) Member States shall provide in conformity with the applicable national provisions designated by private international law that the seller retains title to goods until they are fully paid for if a retention of title clause has been expressly agreed between the buyer and the seller before the delivery of the goods.

(2) Member States may adopt or retain provisions dealing with down payments already made by the debtor.

Article 5

Recovery procedures for unchallenged claims

(1) Member States shall ensure that an enforceable title can be obtained, irrespective of the amount of the debt, normally within 90 calendar days of the lodging of the creditor's action or application at the court or other competent authority, provided that the debt or aspects of the procedure are not disputed. This duty shall be carried out by Member States in conformity with their respective national legislation, regulations and administrative provisions.

(2) The respective national legislation, regulations and administrative provisions shall apply the same conditions for all creditors who are established in the European Community.

(3) The 90 calendar day period referred to in paragraph 1 shall not include the following:
   a) periods for service of documents;
   b) any delays caused by the creditor, such as periods devoted to correcting applications.

(4)   This Article shall be without prejudice to the provisions of the Brussels Convention on jurisdiction and enforcement of judgments in civil and commercial matters.[13]

Article 6

Transposition

(1)   Member States shall bring into force the laws, regulations and administrative provisions necessary to comply with this Directive before 8 August 2002. They shall forthwith inform the Commission thereof. When Member States adopt these measures, they shall contain a reference to this Directive or shall be accompanied by such reference on the occasion of their official publication. The methods of making such reference shall be laid down by Member States.

(2)   Member States may maintain or bring into force provisions which are more favourable to the creditor than the provisions necessary to comply with this Directive.

(3)   In transposing this Directive, Member States may exclude:
     a)   debts that are subject to insolvency proceedings instituted against the debtor;
     b)   contracts that have been concluded prior to 8 August 2002; and
     c)   laims for interest of less than EUR 5.

(4)   Member States shall communicate to the Commission the text of the main provisions of national law which they adopt in the field covered by this Directive.

(5)   The Commission shall undertake two years after 8 August 2002 a review of, inter alia, the statutory rate, contractual payment periods and late payments, to assess the impact on commercial transactions and the operation of the legislation in practice. The results of this review and of other reviews will be made known to the European Parliament and the Council, accompanied where appropriate by proposals for improvement of this Directive.

Article 7

Entry into force

This Directive shall enter into force on the day of its publication in the Official Journal of the European Communities.

---

[13] Consolidated version in OJ C 27, 26.1.1998, p 3.

Article 8

Addressees

This Directive is addressed to the Member States.

Denmark	1. – Lov om aendring af lov om renter ved forsinket betaling m.v., Lov Nr 379 af 06/06/2002
	2. – Lov om aendring af lov om renter ved forsinket betaling m.v., Lovforslag n L 74 af 30/01/2002
	3. – Bekendtgorelse om udenretlige inddrivelsesomkostninger i anledning af forsinket betaling BEK no. 601 af 12/07/2002
EIRE	European Communities (Late Payment in Commercial Transactions) Regulations 2002, S.I. No. 388/2002.
Finland	1. – Laki korkolain muuttamisesta ref: Suomen Säädöskokoelma n 340 du 10/05/2002 p. 2739
	2. – Laki elinkeinonharjoittajien välisten sopimusehtojen säntelystä 3.12.1993/1062 ref: Suomen Säädöskokoelma n 341 du 10/05/2002
Sweden	1. – Lag om ändring i räntelagen 1975:635), SFS 2002:352
	2. – Lag om ändrig i lagen (1984: 292) om avtalsvillkur mellan näringsidkare, SFS 2002/354.
United Kingdom	1. – The Late Payment of Commercial Debts (Interest) Act 1998 (Commencement No.5) Order 2002, S.I. No 2002/1673
	2. – The Late Payment of Commercial Debts Regulations 2002, S.I. No. 2002/1674.
	3. – The Late Payment of Commercial Debts (Rate of Interest) (No. 3) Order 2002, S.I. No. 2002/1675
	4. – The Late Payment of Commercial Debts (Scotland) Regulations 2002 ref: Scottish S.I. No. 2002/335
	5. – The Late Payment of Commercial Debts (Rate of Interest) (Scotland) Order 2002 ref: Scottish S.I. No. 2002/336
	6. – The Late Payment of Commercial Debts (Interest) Act 1998 (Commencement No. 6) (Scotland) Order 2002, Scottish S.I. No. 2002/337

COUNCIL DIRECTIVE 85/577/EEC

of 20 December 1985

to protect the consumer in respect of contracts negotiated away from business premises

(Official Journal, L372/85, p 31)

THE COUNCIL OF THE EUROPEAN COMMUNITIES –

Having regard to the Treaty establishing the European Economic Community, and in particular Article 100 thereof,

Having regard to the proposal from the Commission,[1]

Having regard to the opinion of the European Parliament,[2]

Having regard to the opinion of the Economic and Social Committee,[3]

Whereas it is a common form of commercial practice in the Member States for the conclusion of a contract or a unilateral engagement between a trader and consumer to be made away from the business premises of the trader, and whereas such contracts and engagements are the subject of legislation which differs from one Member State to another;

Whereas any disparity between such legislation may directly affect the functioning of the common market; whereas it is therefore necessary to approximate laws in this field;

Whereas the preliminary programme of the European Economic Community for a consumer protection and information policy[4] provides inter alia, under paragraphs 24 and 25, that appropriate measures be taken to protect consumers against unfair commercial practices in respect of doorstep selling; whereas the second programme of the European Economic Community for a consumer protection and information policy[5] confirmed that the action and priorities defined in the preliminary programme would be pursued;

Whereas the special feature of contracts concluded away from the business premises of the trader is that as a rule it is the trader who initiates the contract negotiations, for which the consumer is unprepared or which he does not except; whereas the consumer is often unable to compare the quality and price of the offer with other offers; whereas this surprise element generally exists not only in contracts made at the doorstep but also in other forms of contract concluded by the trader away from his business premises;

[1] OJ C22/77, p 6, and OJ C127/78, p 6.
[2] OJ C241/77, p 26.
[3] OJ C180/77, p 39.
[4] OJ C92/75, p 2.
[5] OJ C133/81, p 1.

Whereas the consumer should be given a right of cancellation over a period of at least seven days in order to enable him to assess the obligations arising under the contract;

Whereas appropriate measures should be taken to ensure that the consumer is informed in writing of this period for reflection; Whereas the freedom of Member States to maintain or introduce a total or partial prohibition on the conclusion of contracts away from business premises, inasmuch as they consider this to be in the interest of consumers, must not be affected;

HAS ADOPTED THIS DIRECTIVE:

Article 1

(1)   This Directive shall apply to contracts under which a trader supplies goods or services to a consumer and which are concluded:
   – during an excursion organized by the trader away from his business premises, or
   – during a visit by a trader
      i)   to the consumer's home or to that of another consumer;
      ii) to the consumer's place of work;
            where the visit does not take place at the express request of the consum er.

(2)   This Directive shall also apply to contracts for the supply of goods or services other than those concerning which the consumer requested the visit of the trader, provided that when he requested the visit the consumer did not know, or could not reasonably have known, that the supply of those other goods or services formed part of the trader's commercial or professional activities.

(3)   This Directive shall also apply to contracts in respect of which an offer was made by the consumer under conditions similar to those described in paragraph 1 or paragraph 2 although the consumer was not bound by that offer before its acceptance by the trader.

(4)   This Directive shall also apply to offers made contractually by the consumer under conditions similar to those described in paragraph 1 or paragraph 2 where the consumer is bound by his offer.

Article 2

For the purposes of this Directive:

'consumer' means a natural person who, in transactions covered by this Directive, is acting for purposes which can be regarded as outside his trade or profession;

'trader' means a natural or legal person who, for the transaction in question, acts in his commercial or professional capacity, and anyone acting in the name or on behalf of a trader.

Article 3

(1)   The Member States may decide that this Directive shall apply only to contracts for which the payment to be made by the consumer exceeds a specified amount. This amount may not exceed 60 ECU.

The Council, acting on a proposal from the Commission, shall examine and, if necessary, revise this amount for the first time no later than four years after notification of the Directive and thereafter every two years, taking into account economic and monetary developments in the Community.

(2)   This Directive shall not apply to:

a)   contracts for the construction, sale and rental of immovable property or contracts concerning other rights relating to immovable property. Contracts for the supply of goods and for their incorporation in immovable property or contracts for repairing immovable property shall fall within the scope of this Directive;

b)   contracts for the supply of foodstuffs or beverages or other goods intended for current consumption in the household and supplied by regular roundsmen;

c)   contracts for the supply of goods or services, provided that all three of the following conditions are met:

i)   the contract is concluded on the basis of a trader's catalogue which the consumer has a proper opportunity of reading in the absence of the trader's representative,

ii)   there is intended to be continuity of contact between the trader's representative and the consumer in relation to that or any subsequent transaction,

iii)   both the catalogue and the contract clearly inform the consumer of his right to return goods to the supplier within a period of not less than seven days of receipt or otherwise to cancel the contract within that period without obligation of any kind other than to take reasonable care of the goods;

d)   insurance contracts;

e)   contracts for securities.

(3)   By way of derogation from Article 1(2), Member States may refrain from applying this Directive to contracts for the supply of goods or services having a direct connection with the goods or services concerning which the consumer requested the visit of the trader.

Article 4

In the case of transactions within the scope of Article 1, traders shall be required to give consumers written notice of their right of cancellation within the period laid down in Article 5, together with the name and address of a person against whom that right may be exercised.

Such notice shall be dated and shall state particulars enabling the contract to be identified. It shall be given to the consumer:

a) in the case of Article 1(1), at the time of conclusion of the contract;
b) in the case of Article 1(2), not later than the time of conclusion of the contract;
c) in the case of Article 1(3) and 1(4), when the offer is made by the consumer. Member States shall ensure that their national legislation lays down appropriate consumer protection measures in cases where the information referred to in this Article is not supplied.

Article 5

(1) The consumer shall have the right to renounce the effects of his undertaking by sending notice within a period of not less than seven days from receipt by the consumer of the notice referred to in Article 4, in accordance with the procedure laid down by national law. It shall be sufficient if the notice is dispatched before the end of such period.
(2) The giving of the notice shall have the effect of releasing the consumer from any obligations under the cancelled contract.

Article 6

The consumer may not waive the rights conferred on him by this Directive.

Article 7

If the consumer exercises his right of renunciation, the legal effects of such renunciation shall be governed by national laws, particularly regarding the reimbursement of payments for goods or services provided and the return of goods received.

Article 8

This Directive shall not prevent Member States from adopting or maintaining more favourable provisions to protect consumers in the field which it covers.

Article 9

(1) Member States shall take the measures necessary to comply with this Directive within 24 months of its notification.[6] They shall forthwith inform the Commission thereof.

(2) Member States shall ensure that the texts of the main provisions of national law which they adopt in the field covered by this Directive are communicated to the Commission.

Article 10

This Directive is addressed to the Member States.

Denmark	1. – Lov om aendring af lov om visse forbruger aftaler (dørsalg m.v., postordresalg og løbende tjenesteydelser), Lov Nr 886 af 23/12/1987 2. – Lov Nr 262 af 06/04/93 3. – Bekendtgørelse Nr 599 af 12/7/1993 verdrørende frotrydelsesret i henhold til lov om visse forbrugeraftaler. 4. Lov Nr 1098 af 21/12/1994.
EIRE	European Communities (Cancellation of Contracts Negotiated Away from Business Premises) Regulations 1989, S.I. No. 224/1989
Finland	1. – Kuluttajansuojalaki (38/78) 20/01/1978, muutos (84/93) 08/01/1993 2. – Asetus koti- ja postimyynnistä (1601/93) 30/12/1993 3. – Kauppa- ja teollisuusministeriön päätös kotimyyntiasiakirjan kaavasta 4. – Laki kuluttajansuojalain muuttamisesta réf. Suomen säädöskokoelma nr. 391/2002 du 29/05/2002, page 2911
Sweden	1. – Hemförsäljningslag, SFS 1981:1361 2. – Lag om ändring i hemförsäljningslag, SFS 1992:1111
United Kingdom	The Consumer Protection (Cancellation of Contracts Concluded away from Business Premises) Regulations 1987, S.I. No. 1987/2117.

---

[6] This Directive was made known to Member States on 23 December 1985.

COUNCIL DIRECTIVE 87/102/EEC

of 22 December 1986

for the approximation of the laws, regulations and administrative provisions of the Member States concerning consumer credit

(Official Journal L42/87 p 48)

Amendments

Article	Nature of Amendment	Effected by	Date	Source
— 1, 2, 4	Amended	Regulation 90/88/EEC	22 February 1990	
Annexure I 1a, Annexures II, III	Inserted	of the Council		
5	Repealed	Regulation 98/7/EC of the EP and of the	16 February 1998	
1a, 3 Annexures II, III		Council		

THE COUNCIL OF THE EUROPEAN COMMUNITIES –

Having regard to the Treaty establishing the European Economic Community, and in particular Article 100 thereof,

Having regard to the proposal from the Commission,[1]

Having regard to the opinion of the European Parliament,[2]

Having regard to the opinion of the Economic and Social Committee,[3]

Whereas wide differences exist in the laws of the Member States in the field of consumer credit;

Whereas these differences of law can lead to distortions of competition between grantors of credit in the common market;

Whereas these differences limit the opportunities the consumer has to obtain credit in other Member States; whereas they affect the volume and the nature of the credit sought, and also the purchase of goods and services;

[1] OJ C80/79, p 4, and OJ C183/84, p 4.
[2] OJ C242/83, p 10.
[3] OJ C113/80, p22.

Whereas, as a result, these differences have an influence on the free movement of goods and services obtainable by consumers on credit and thus directly affect the functioning of the common market;

Whereas, given the increasing volume of credit granted in the Community to consumers, the establishment of a common market in consumer credit would benefit alike consumers, grantors of credit, manufacturers, wholesalers and retailers of goods and providers of services;

Whereas the programmes of the European Economic Community for a consumer protection and information policy[4] provide, inter alia, that the consumer should be protected against unfair credit terms and that a harmonization of the general conditions governing consumer credit should be undertaken as a priority;

Whereas differences of law and practice result in unequal consumer protection in the field of consumer credit from one Member State to another;

Whereas there has been much change in recent years in the types of credit available to and used by consumers; whereas new forms of consumer credit have emerged and continue to develop;

Whereas the consumer should receive adequate information on the conditions and cost of credit and on his obligations; whereas this information should include, inter alia, the annual percentage rate of charge for credit, or, failing that, the total amount that the consumer must pay for credit; whereas, pending a decision on a Community method or methods of calculating the annual percentage rate of charge, Member States should be able to retain existing methods or practices for calculating this rate, or failing that, should establish provisions for indicating the total cost of the credit to the consumer;

Whereas the terms of credit may be disadvantageous to the consumer; whereas better protection of consumers can be achieved by adopting certain requirements which are to apply to all forms of credit;

Whereas, having regard to the character of certain credit agreements or types of transaction, these agreements or transactions should be partially or entirely excluded from the field of application of this Directive;

Whereas it should be possible for Member States, in consultation with the Commission, to exempt from the Directive certain forms of credit of a non-commercial character granted under particular conditions;

Whereas the practices existing in some Member States in respect of authentic acts drawn up before a notary or judge are such as to render the application of certain provisions of this Directive unnecessary in the case of such acts; whereas it should therefore be possible for Member States to exempt such acts from those provisions;

Whereas credit agreements for very large financial amounts tend to differ from the usual consumer credit agreements; whereas the application of the provisions of this Directive to agreements for very small amounts could create unnecessary administrative burdens both for consumers and grantors of credit; whereas therefore, agreements above or below specified financial limits should be excluded from the Directive;

Whereas the provision of information on the cost of credit in advertising and at the business premises of the creditor or credit broker can make it easier for the consumer to compare different offers;

[4] OJ C92/75, p 1, and OJ C133/81, p 1.

Whereas consumer protection is further improved if credit agreements are made in writing and contain certain minimum particulars concerning the contractual terms;

Whereas, in the case of credit granted for the acquisition of goods, Member States should lay down the conditions in which goods may be repossessed, particularly if the consumer has not given his consent; whereas the account between the parties should upon repossession be made up in such manner as to ensure that the repossession does not entail any unjustified enrichment;

Whereas the consumer should be allowed to discharge his obligations before the due date; whereas the consumer should then be entitled to an equitable reduction in the total cost of the credit;

Whereas the assignment of the creditor's rights arising under a credit agreement should not be allowed to weaken the position of the consumer;

Whereas those Member States which permit consumers to use bills of exchange, promissory notes or cheques in connection with credit agreements should ensure that the consumer is suitably protected when so using such instruments;

Whereas, as regards goods or services which the consumer has contracted to acquire on credit, the consumer should, at least in the circumstances defined below, have rights vis-à-vis the grantor of credit which are in addition to his normal contractual rights against him and against the supplier of the goods or services; whereas the circumstances referred to above are those where the grantor of credit and the supplier of goods or services have a pre-existing agreement whereunder credit is made available exclusively by that grantor of credit to customers of that supplier for the purpose of enabling the consumer to acquire goods or services from the latter;

Whereas the ECU is as defined in Council Regulation (EEC) No 3180/78,[5] as last amended by Regulation (EEC) No 2626/84;[6] whereas Member States should to a limited extent be at liberty to round off the amounts in national currency resulting from the conversion of amounts of this Directive expressed in ECU; whereas the amounts in this Directive should be periodically re-examined in the light of economic and monetary trends in the Community, and, if need be, revised;

Whereas suitable measures should be adopted by Member States for authorizing persons offering credit or offering to arrange credit agreements or for inspecting or monitoring the activities of persons granting credit or arranging for credit to be granted or for enabling consumers to complain about credit agreements or credit conditions;

Whereas credit agreements should not derogate, to the detriment of the consumer, from the provisions adopted in implementation of this Directive or corresponding to its provisions; whereas those provisions should not be circumvented as a result of the way in which agreements are formulated;

Whereas, since this Directive provides for a certain degree of approximation of the laws, regulations and administrative provisions of the Member States concerning consumer credit and for a certain level of consumer protection, Member States should not be prevented from retaining or adopting more stringent measures to protect the consumer, with due regard for their obligations under the Treaty;

[5] OJ L379/78, p 1.
[6] OJ L247/84, p 1.

Whereas, not later than 1 January 1995, the Commission should present to the Council a report concerning the operation of this Directive,
– *Considerations underpinning Regulation 90/88/EEC:*

THE COUNCIL OF THE EUROPEAN COMMUNITIES –

Having regard to the Treaty establishing the European Economic Community, and in particular Article 100a thereof,
 Having regard to the proposal from the Commission,[7]
 In cooperation with the European Parliament,[8]
 Having regard to the opinion of the Economic and Social Committee,[9]
 Whereas Article 5 of Council Directive 87/102/EEC provides for the introduction of a Community method or methods of calculating the annual percentage rate of charge for consumer credit;
(…)
 Whereas it is desirable, with a view to introducing such a method and in accordance with the definition of the total cost of credit to the consumer, to draw up a single mathematical formula for calculating the annual percentage rate of charge and for determining credit cost items to be used in the calculation by indicating those costs which must not be taken into account;
 Whereas, during a transitional period, Member States which prior to the date of notification of this Directive, apply laws which permit the use of another mathematical formula for calculating the annual percentage rate of charge may continue to apply such laws;
 Whereas, before expiry of the transitional period and in the light of experience, the Council will, on the basis of a proposal from the Commission, take a decision which will make it possible to apply a single Community mathematical formula;
 Whereas it is desirable, whenever necessary, to adopt certain hypotheses for calculating the annual percentage rate of charge;
 Whereas by virtue of the special nature of loans guaranteed by a mortgage secured on immovable property it is desirable that such credit should continue to be partially excluded from this Directive;
 Whereas the information which must be communicated to the consumer in the written contract should be amplified –
 – *Considerations underpinning Regulation 98/7/EC:*

THE EUROPEAN PARLIAMENT AND THE COUNCIL OF THE EUROPEAN UNION,

Having regard to the Treaty establishing the European Community, and in particular Article 100a thereof,
 Having regard to the proposal of the Commission,[10]
 Having regard to the opinion of the Economic and Social Committee,[11]

---

[7] OJ C155/88, p 10.
[8] OJ C96/89, p 87, and OJ C291/89, p 50.
[9] OJ C337/88, p 1.
[10] OJ C235/96, p 8, and OJ C137/97, p 9.
[11] OJ C30/97, p 94.

Acting in accordance with the procedure laid down in Article 189b of the Treaty,[12]

Whereas it is desirable, in order to promote the establishment and functioning of the internal market and to ensure that consumers benefit from a high level of protection, that a single method of calculating the annual percentage rate of charge for consumer credit should be used throughout the Community;

Whereas Article 5 of Directive 87/102/EEC (4) provides for the introduction of a Community method or methods of calculating the annual percentage rate of charge;

Whereas, in order to introduce this single method, it is desirable to draw up a single mathematical formula for calculating the annual percentage rate of charge and for determining the credit cost items to be used in the calculation by indicating those costs which must not be taken into account;

Whereas Annex II of Directive 87/102/EEC introduced a mathematical formula for the calculation of the annual percentage rate of charge and Article 1a(2) of that Directive provided for the charges to be excluded from the calculation of the 'total cost of credit to the consumer';

Whereas during a transitional period of three years from 1 January 1993, Member States which prior to 1 March 1990 applied laws which permitted the use of another mathematical formula for calculating the annual percentage rate of charge, were permitted to continue to apply such laws;

Whereas the Commission has submitted a Report to the Council which makes it possible, in the light of experience, to apply a single Community mathematical formula for calculating the annual percentage rate of charge;

Whereas, since no Member State has made use of Article 1a(3) of Directive 87/102/EEC by which certain costs were excluded from the calculation of the annual percentage rate of charge in certain Member States, it has become obsolete;

Whereas accuracy to at least one decimal place is necessary;

Whereas a year is presumed to have 365 days or 365,25 days or (for leap years) 366 days, 52 weeks or 12 equal months; whereas an equal month is presumed to have 30,41666 days;

Whereas it is desirable that consumers should be able to recognize the terms used by different Member States to indicate the 'annual percentage rate of charge';

Whereas it is appropriate to study without delay to what extent a further degree of harmonization of the cost elements of consumer credit is necessary in order to put the European consumer in a position to make a better comparison between the actual percentage rates of charges offered by institutions in the various Member States, thereby ensuring harmonious functioning of the internal market –

HAS ADOPTED THIS DIRECTIVE:

Article 1

(1)   This Directive applies to credit agreements.

(2)   For the purpose of this Directive:

---

[12] Opinion of the European Parliament of 20 February 1997 (OJ C85/97, p 108); Common Position of the Council of 7 July 1997 (OJ C284/97, p 1), and Decision of the European Parliament of 19 November 1997. Decision of the Council of 18 December 1997.

a) 'consumer' means a natural person who, in transactions covered by this Directive, is acting for purposes which can be regarded as outside his trade or profession;

b) 'creditor' means a natural or legal person who grants credit in the course of his trade, business or profession, or a group of such persons;

c) 'credit agreement' means an agreement whereby a creditor grants or promises to grant to a consumer a credit in the form of a deferred payment, a loan or other similar financial accommodation.

Agreements for the provision on a continuing basis of a service or a utility, where the consumer has the right to pay for them, for the duration of their provision, by means of instalments, are not deemed to be credit agreements for the purpose of this Directive;

d) 'total cost of the credit to the consumer' means all the costs, including interest and other charges, which the consumer has to pay for the credit.

e) 'annual percentage rate of charge' means the total cost of the credit to the consumer, expressed as an annual percentage of the amount of the credit granted and calculated in accordance with Article 1a.

Article 1a

(1) a) The annual percentage rate of charge, which shall be that equivalent, on an annual basis, to the present value of all commitments (loans, repayments and charges), future or existing, agreed by the creditor and the borrower, shall be calculated in accordance with the mathematical formula set out in Annex II.

b) Four examples of the method of calculation are given in Annex III, by way of illustration.

(2) For the purpose of calculating the annual percentage rate of charge, the 'total cost of the credit to the consumer' as defined in Article 1 (2) (d) shall be determined, with the exception of the following charges:

i) charges payable by the borrower for non-compliance with any of his commitments laid down in the credit agreement;

ii) charges other than the purchase price which, in purchases of goods or services, the consumer is obliged to pay whether the transaction is paid in cash or by credit;

iii) charges for the transfer of funds and charges for keeping an account intended to receive payments towards the reimbursement of the credit the payment of interest and other charges except where the consumer does not have reasonable freedom of choice in the matter and where such charges are abnormally high; this provision shall not, however, apply to charges for collection of such reimbursements or payments, whether made in cash or otherwise;

iv) membership subscriptions to associations or groups and arising from agreements separate from the credit agreement, even though such subscriptions have an effect on the credit terms;

v) charges for insurance or guarantees; included are, however, those designed to ensure payment to the creditor, in the event of the death, invalidity, illness or unemployment of the consumer, of a sum equal to or less than the total amount of the credit together with relevant interest and other charges which have to be imposed by the creditor as a condition for credit being granted.

(3) (repealed)

(4) a) The annual percentage rate of charge shall be calculated at the time the credit contract is concluded, without prejudice to the provisions of Article 3 concerning advertisements and special offers.

b) The calculation shall be made on the assumption that the credit contract is valid for the period agreed and that the creditor and the consumer fulfil their obligations under the terms and by the dates agreed.

(5) (repealed)

(6) In the case of credit contracts containing clauses allowing variations in the rate of interest and the amount or level of other charges contained in the annual percentage rate of charge but unquantifiable at the time when it is calculated, the annual percentage rate of charge shall be calculated on the assumption that interest and other charges remain fixed and will apply until the end of the credit contract.

(7) Where necessary, the following assumptions may be made in calculating the annual percentage rate of charge:

– if the contract does not specify a credit limit, the amount of credit granted shall be equal to the amount fixed by the relevant Member State, without exceeding a figure equivalent to ECU 2 000;

– if there is no fixed timetable for repayment, and one cannot be deduced from the terms of the agreement and the means for repaying the credit granted, the duration of the credit shall be deemed to be one year;

– unless otherwise specified, where the contract provides for more than one repayment date, the credit will be made available and the repayments made at the earliest time provided for in the agreement'.

Article 2

(1) This Directive shall not apply to:
    a)   credit agreements or agreements promising to grant credit:
       – intended primarily for the purpose of acquiring or retaining property rights in land or in an existing or projected building,
       – intended for the purpose of renovating or improving a building as such;
    b)   hiring agreements except where these provide that the title will pass ultimately to the hirer;
    c)   credit granted or made available without payment of interest or any other charge;
    d)   credit agreements under which no interest is charged provided the consumer agrees to repay the credit in a single payment;
    e)   credit in the form of advances on a current account granted by a credit institution or financial institution other than on credit card accounts.
       Nevertheless, the provisions of Article 6 shall apply to such credits;
    f)   credit agreements involving amounts less than 200 ECU or more than 20 000 ECU;
    g)   credit agreements under which the consumer is required to repay the credit:
       – either, within a period not exceeding three months,
       – or, by a maximum number of four payments within a period not exceeding 12 months.
(2) A Member State may, in consultation with the Commission, exempt from the application of this Directive certain types of credit which fulfil the following conditions:
       – they are granted at rates of charge below those prevailing in the market, and
       – they are not offered to the public generally.
(3) The provisions of Article 1a and of Articles 4 to 12 shall not apply to credit agreements or agreements promising to grant credit, secured by mortgage on immovable property, insofar as these are not already excluded from the Directive under paragraph 1(a).
(4) Member States may exempt from the provisions of Articles 6 to 12 credit agreements in the form of an authentic act signed before a notary or judge.

Article 3

Without prejudice to Council Directive 84/450/EEC of 10 September 1984 relating to the approximation of the laws, regulations and administrative provisions of the Member States concerning misleading advertising,[13] and to the rules and principles applicable to unfair advertising, any advertisement, or any offer which is displayed at business premises, in which a person offers credit or offers to arrange a credit agreement and in which a rate of interest or any figures relating to the cost of the credit are indicated, shall also include a statement of the annual percentage rate of charge, by means of a representative example if no other means is practicable.

Article 4

(1) Credit agreements shall be made in writing. The consumer shall receive a copy of the written agreement.

(2) The written agreement shall include:
   a) a statement of the annual percentage rate of charge;
   b) a statement of the conditions under which the annual percentage rate of charge may be amended.
      In cases where it is not possible to state the annual percentage rate of charge, the consumer shall be provided with adequate information in the written agreement. This information shall at least include the information provided for in the second indent of Article 6 (1).
   c) a statement of the amount, number and frequency or dates of the payments which the consumer must make to repay the credit, as well as of the payments for interest and other charges; the total amount of these payments should also be indicated where possible;
   d) a statement of the cost items referred to in Article 1a(2) with the exception of expenditure related to the breach of contractual obligations which were not included in the calculation of the annual percentage rate of charge but which have to be paid by the consumer in given circumstances, together with a statement identifying such circumstances. Where the exact amount of those items is known, that sum is to be indicated; if that is not the case, either a method of calculation or as accurate an estimate as possible is to be provided where possible.

(3) The written agreement shall further include the other essential terms of the contract. By way of illustration, the Annex to this Directive contains a list of terms which Member States may require to be included in the written agreement as being essential.

---

[13] OJ L250/84, p 17. Directive as last amended by Directive 97/55/EC (OJ L280/97, p 18).

Article 5

(repealed)

Article 6

(1) Notwithstanding the exclusion provided for in Article 2 (1) (e), where there is an agreement between a credit institution or financial institution and a consumer for the granting of credit in the form of an advance on a current account, other than on credit card accounts, the consumer shall be informed at the time or before the agreement is concluded:
    –   of the credit limit, if any,
    –   of the annual rate of interest and the charges applicable from the time the agreement is concluded and the conditions under which these may be amended,
    –   of the procedure for terminating the agreement.
    This information shall be confirmed in writing.
(2) Furthermore, during the period of the agreement, the consumer shall be informed of any change in the annual rate of interest or in the relevant charges at the time it occurs. Such information may be given in a statement of account or in any other manner acceptable to Member States.
(3) In Member States where tacitly accepted overdrafts are permissible, the Member States concerned shall ensure that the consumer is informed of the annual rate of interest and the charges applicable, and of any amendment thereof, where the overdraft extends beyond a period of three months.

Article 7

In the case of credit granted for the acquisition of goods, Member States shall lay down the conditions under which goods may be repossessed, in particular if the consumer has not given his consent. They shall further ensure that where the creditor recovers possession of the goods the account between the parties shall be made up so as to ensure that the repossession does not entail any unjustified enrichment.

Article 8

The consumer shall be entitled to discharge his obligations under a credit agreement before the time fixed by the agreement. In this event, in accordance with the rules laid down by the Member States, the consumer shall be entitled to an equitable reduction in the total cost of the credit.

Article 9

Where the creditor's rights under a credit agreement are assigned to a third person, the consumer shall be entitled to plead against that third person any defence which was available to him against the original creditor, including set-off where the latter is permitted in the Member State concerned.

Article 10

The Member States which, in connection with credit agreements, permit the consumer:

a)   to make payment by means of bills of exchange including promissory notes;
b)   to give security by means of bills of exchange including promissory notes and cheques,

shall ensure that the consumer is suitably protected when using these instruments in those ways.

Article 11

(1)   Member States shall ensure that the existence of a credit agreement shall not in any way affect the rights of the consumer against the supplier of goods or services purchased by means of such an agreement in cases where the goods or services are not supplied or are otherwise not in conformity with the contract for their supply.
(2)   Where:
   a)   in order to buy goods or obtain services the consumer enters into a credit agreement with a person other than the supplier of them; and
   b)   the grantor of the credit and the supplier of the goods or services have a pre-existing agreement whereunder credit is made available exclusively by that grantor of credit to customers of that supplier for the acquisition of goods or services from that supplier; and
   c)   the consumer referred to in subparagraph (a) obtains his credit pursuant to that pre-existing agreement; and
   d)   the goods or services covered by the credit agreement are not supplied, or are supplied only in part, or are not in conformity with the contract for supply of them; and
   e)   the consumer has pursued his remedies against the supplier but has failed to obtain the satisfaction to which he is entitled,
        the consumer shall have the right to pursue remedies against the grantor of credit. Member States shall determine to what

extent and under what conditions these remedies shall be exercisable.

(3) Paragraph 2 shall not apply where the individual transaction in question is for an amount less than the equivalent of 200 ECU.

Article 12

(1) Member States shall:
   a) ensure that persons offering credit or offering to arrange credit agreements shall obtain official authorization to do so, either specifically or as suppliers of goods and services; or
   b) ensure that persons granting credit or arranging for credit to be granted shall be subject to inspection or monitoring of their activities by an institution or official body; or
   c) promote the establishment of appropriate bodies to receive complaints concerning credit agreements or credit conditions and to provide relevant information or advice to consumers regarding them.

(2) Member States may provide that the authorization referred to in paragraph 1 (a) shall not be required where persons offering to conclude or arrange credit agreements satisfy the definition in Article 1 of the first Council Directive of 12 December 1977 on the coordination of laws, regulations and administrative provisions relating to the taking up and pursuit of the business of credit institutions[14] and are authorized in accordance with the provisions of that Directive.

Where persons granting credit or arranging for credit to be granted have been authorized both specifically, under the provisions of paragraph 1(a) and also under the provisions of the aforementioned Directive, but the latter authorization is subsequently withdrawn, the competent authority responsible for issuing the specific authorization to grant credit under paragraph 1(a) shall be informed and shall decide whether the persons concerned may continue to grant credit, or arrange for credit to be granted, or whether the specific authorization granted under paragraph 1(a) should be withdrawn.

Article 13

(1) For the purposes of this Directive, the ECU shall be that defined by Regulation (EEC) No 3180/78, as amended by Regulation (EEC) No 2626/84. The equivalent in national currency shall initially be calculated at the rate obtaining on the date of adoption of this Directive.

---

[14] OJ L322/77, p 30.

Member States may round off the amounts in national currency resulting from the conversion of the amounts in ECU provided such rounding off does not exceed 10 ECU.

(2) Every five years, and for the first time in 1995, the Council, acting on a proposal from the Commission, shall examine and, if need be, revise the amounts in this Directive, in the light of economic and monetary trends in the Community.

Article 14

(1) Member States shall ensure that credit agreements shall not derogate, to the detriment of the consumer, from the provisions of national law implementing or corresponding to this Directive.

(2) Member States shall further ensure that the provisions which they adopt in implementation of this directive are not circumvented as a result of the way in which agreements are formulated, in particular by the device of distributing the amount of credit over several agreements.

Article 15

This Directive shall not preclude Member States from retaining or adopting more stringent provisions to protect consumers consistent with their obligations under the Treaty.

Article 16

(1) Member States shall bring into force the measures necessary to comply with this Directive not later than 1 January 1990 and shall forthwith inform the Commission thereof.

(2) Member States shall communicate to the Commission the texts of the main provisions of national law which they adopt in the field covered by this Directive.

Article 17

Not later than 1 January 1995 the Commission shall present a report to the Council concerning the operation of this Directive.

Article 18

This Directive is addressed to the Member States.

ANNEX 1

List of terms referred to in Article 4(3)

1. **Credit agreements for financing the supply of particular goods or services:**
   i)   a description of the goods or services covered by the agreement;
   ii)   the cash price and the price payable under the credit agreement;
   iii) the amount of the deposit, if any, the number and amount of instalments and the dates on which they fall due, or the method of ascertaining any of the same if unknown at the time the agreement is concluded;
   iv)   an indication that the consumer will be entitled, as provided in Article 8, to a reduction if he repays early;
   v)   who owns the goods (if ownership does not pass immediately to the consumer) and the terms on which the consumer becomes the owner of them;
   vi)   a description of the security required, if any;
   vii) the cooling-off period, if any;
   viii) an indication of the insurance (s) required, if any, and, when the choice of insurer is not left to the consumer, an indication of the cost thereof.

2. **Credit agreements operated by credit cards:**
   i)   the amount of the credit limit, if any;
   ii)   the terms of repayment or the means of determining them;
   iii) the cooling-off period, if any.

3. **Credit agreements operated by running account which are not otherwise covered by the Directive:**
   i)   the amount of the credit limit, if any, or the method of determining it;
   ii)   the terms of use and repayment;
   iii) the cooling-off period, if any.

4. **Other credit agreements covered by the Directive:**
   i)   the amount of the credit limit, if any;
   ii)   an indication of the security required, if any;
   iii) the terms of repayment;
   iv)   the cooling-off period, if any;
   v)   an indication that the consumer will be entitled, as provided in Article 8, to a reduction if he repays early.

ANNEX II

(not reprinted)

ANNEX III

(not reprinted)

Denmark	1. – Lov Nr 395 af 13/06/1990
	2. – Lov om kreditaftaler, Lov Nr 398 af 13/06/1990
	3. – Bekendtgørelse Nr 902 af 12/11/1992
	4. – Bekendtgørelse Nr 1228 af 21/12/1992
	5. – Bekendtgørelse Nr 871 af 14/10/1994 om Forbrugerklagenaevnets virksomhedsomrade
	6. – Lov Nr 328 af 31/05/1999
	7. – Lov Nr 391 30/05/2000
EIRE	1. – Consumer Credit Act 1995
	2. – The Consumer Credit Act, 1995 (Commencement) Order 1996, S.I. No. 121/1996
	3. – The Consumer Credit Act, 1995 (Section 2) Regulations 1996 S.I. No. 127/1996
	5. – The Consumer Credit Act, 1995 (Section 36) Regulations 1996, S.I. No. 128/1996
	6. – The Consumer Credit Act, 1995 (Section 37) Regulations 1996, S.I. No. 129/1996
	7. – The Consumer Credit Act, 1995 (Section 60) Regulations 1996, S.I. No. 130/1996
	8. – The Consumer Credit Act, 1995 (Section 86) Regulations 1996, S.I. No. 131/1996
	9. – The Consumer Credit Act, 1995 (Section 129) Regulations 1996, S.I. No. 132/1996
	10. – The Consumer Credit Act, 1995 (Section 28) Regulations 1996, S.I. No. 245/1996
	11. – The Consumer Credit Act, 1995 (Section 129) (No. 2) Regulations 1996, S.I. No. 246/1996
	12. – The Consumer Credit Act, 1995 (Section 120) Regulations 1996, S.I. No. 247/1996
	13. – The Consumer Credit Act, 1995 (Section 3) Regulations, 1997, S.I. No. 186/1997
	14. – The European Communities (Consumer Credit Act 1995) (Amendment) Regulations 1996
	15. – The European Communities (Consumer Credit) Regulations 2000, S.I. No. 294/2000
Finland	1 – Laki kuluttajansuojalain 7 luvun muuttamisesta 8.1.1993/85
	2. – Kuluttajansuojalaki (38/78) 20/01/1978, muutos (85/93) 08/01/1993
	3. – Asetus eraiden kuluttajansuojalain 7 luvun saannosten soveltamista koskevista poikkeuksista (1602/93) 30/12/1993
	4. – Kauppa- ja teollisuusministerion paatos kuluttajansuojalain 7 luvun eraiden saannosten soveltamisesta (874/86) 28/11/1986

Sweden	1. – Konsumentkreditlag, SFS 1992:830 2. – Förordning om effectiv ränta vid konsumentkrediter, SFS 1992:1010
United Kingdom	1. – Consumer Credit Act 1974 2. – The Consumer Credit (Total Charge for Credit and Rebate on Early Settlement) (Amendment) Regulations 1989, S.I. No. 1989/596. 3. – The Consumer Credit (Exempt Agreements) Order 1989, S.I. No. 1989/869 4. – The Consumer Credit (Total Charge for Credit, Agreements and Advertisements) (Amendment) Regulations, S.I. No. 1999/3177.

DIRECTIVE 97/7/EC OF THE EUROPEAN PARLIAMENT AND OF THE COUNCIL

of 20 May 1997

on the protection of consumers in respect of distance contracts

(Official Journal L144/97 p 19)

THE EUROPEAN PARLIAMENT AND THE COUNCIL OF THE EUROPEAN UNION –

Having regard to the Treaty establishing the European Community, and in particular Article 100a thereof,

Having regard to the proposal from the Commission,[1]

Having regard to the opinion of the Economic and Social Committee,[2]

Acting in accordance with the procedure laid down in Article 189b of the Treaty,[3] in the light of the joint text approved by the Conciliation Committee on 27 November 1996,

(1) Whereas, in connection with the attainment of the aims of the internal market, measures must be taken for the gradual consolidation of that market;

(2) Whereas the free movement of goods and services affects not only the business sector but also private individuals; whereas it means that consumers should be able to have access to the goods and services of another Member State on the same terms as the population of that State;

(3) Whereas, for consumers, cross-border distance selling could be one of the main tangible results of the completion of the internal market, as noted, inter alia, in the communication from the Commission to the Council entitled 'Towards a single market in distribution'; whereas it is essential to the smooth operation of the internal market for consumers to be able to have dealings with a

---

[1] OJ C156/92, p 14, and OJ C308/93, p 18.

[2] OJ C19/93, p 111.

[3] Opinion of the European Parliament of 26 May 1993 (OJ C176/93, p 95); Council Common Position of 29 June 1995 (OJ C288/95, p 1) and Decision of the European Parliament of 13 December 1995 (OJ C17/96, p 51); Decision of the European Parliament of 16 January 1997 and Council Decision of 20 January 1997.

business outside their country, even if it has a subsidiary in the consumer's country of residence;

(4)   Whereas the introduction of new technologies is increasing the number of ways for consumers to obtain information about offers anywhere in the Community and to place orders; whereas some Member States have already taken different or diverging measures to protect consumers in respect of distance selling, which has had a detrimental effect on competition between businesses in the internal market; whereas it is therefore necessary to introduce at Community level a minimum set of common rules in this area;

(5)   Whereas paragraphs 18 and 19 of the Annex to the Council resolution of 14 April 1975 on a preliminary programme of the European Economic Community for a consumer protection and information policy[4] point to the need to protect the purchasers of goods or services from demands for payment for unsolicited goods and from high-pressure selling methods;

(6)   Whereas paragraph 33 of the communication from the Commission to the Council entitled 'A new impetus for consumer protection policy', which was approved by the Council resolution of 23 June 1986,[5] states that the Commission will submit proposals regarding the use of new information technologies enabling consumers to place orders with suppliers from their homes;

(7)   Whereas the Council resolution of 9 November 1989 on future priorities for relaunching consumer protection policy[6] calls upon the Commission to give priority to the areas referred to in the Annex to that resolution; whereas that Annex refers to new technologies involving teleshopping; whereas the Commission has responded to that resolution by adopting a three-year action plan for consumer protection policy in the European Economic Community (1990–1992); whereas that plan provides for the adoption of a Directive;

(8)   Whereas the languages used for distance contracts are a matter for the Member States;

(9)   Whereas contracts negotiated at a distance involve the use of one or more means of distance communication; whereas the various means of communication are used as part of an organized distance sales or service-provision scheme not involving the simultaneous presence of the supplier and the consumer; whereas the constant development of those means of communication does not allow an exhaustive list to

[4] OJ C92/75, p 1.
[5] OJ C167/86, p 1.
[6] OJ C294/89, p 1.

be compiled but does require principles to be defined which are valid even for those which are not as yet in widespread use;

(10)   Whereas the same transaction comprising successive operations or a series of separate operations over a period of time may give rise to different legal descriptions depending on the law of the Member States; whereas the provisions of this Directive cannot be applied differently according to the law of the Member States, subject to their recourse to Article 14; whereas, to that end, there is therefore reason to consider that there must at least be compliance with the provisions of this Directive at the time of the first of a series of successive operations or the first of a series of separate operations over a period of time which may be considered as forming a whole, whether that operation or series of operations are the subject of a single contract or successive, separate contracts;

(11)   Whereas the use of means of distance communication must not lead to a reduction in the information provided to the consumer; whereas the information that is required to be sent to the consumer should therefore be determined, whatever the means of communication used; whereas the information supplied must also comply with the other relevant Community rules, in particular those in Council Directive 84/450/EEC of 10 September 1984 relating to the approximation of the laws, regulations and administrative provisions of the Member States concerning misleading advertising;[7] whereas, if exceptions are made to the obligation to provide information, it is up to the consumer, on a discretionary basis, to request certain basic information such as the identity of the supplier, the main characteristics of the goods or services and their price;

(12)   Whereas in the case of communication by telephone it is appropriate that the consumer receive enough information at the beginning of the conversation to decide whether or not to continue;

(13)   Whereas information disseminated by certain electronic technologies is often ephemeral in nature insofar as it is not received on a permanent medium; whereas the consumer must therefore receive written notice in good time of the information necessary for proper performance of the contract;

(14)   Whereas the consumer is not able actually to see the product or ascertain the nature of the service provided before concluding the contract; whereas provision should be made, unless otherwise specified in this Directive, for a right of withdrawal from the contract; whereas, if this right is to be more than formal, the costs, if any, borne by the consumer when exercising the right of withdrawal must be limited to the direct costs for returning the goods; whereas this right

[7] OJ L250/84, p 17.

of withdrawal shall be without prejudice to the consumer's rights under national laws, with particular regard to the receipt of damaged products and services or of products and services not corresponding to the description given in the offer of such products or services; whereas it is for the Member States to determine the other conditions and arrangements following exercise of the right of withdrawal;

(15) Whereas it is also necessary to prescribe a time limit for performance of the contract if this is not specified at the time of ordering;

(16) Whereas the promotional technique involving the dispatch of a product or the provision of a service to the consumer in return for payment without a prior request from, or the explicit agreement of, the consumer cannot be permitted, unless a substitute product or service is involved;

(17) Whereas the principles set out in Articles 8 and 10 of the European Convention for the Protection of Human Rights and Fundamental Freedoms of 4 November 1950 apply; whereas the consumer's right to privacy, particularly as regards freedom from certain particularly intrusive means of communication, should be recognized; whereas specific limits on the use of such means should therefore be stipulated; whereas Member States should take appropriate measures to protect effectively those consumers, who do not wish to be contacted through certain means of communication, against such contacts, without prejudice to the particular safeguards available to the consumer under Community legislation concerning the protection of personal data and privacy;

(18) Whereas it is important for the minimum binding rules contained in this Directive to be supplemented where appropriate by voluntary arrangements among the traders concerned, in line with Commission recommendation 92/295/EEC of 7 April 1992 on codes of practice for the protection of consumers in respect of contracts negotiated at a distance;[8]

(19) Whereas in the interest of optimum consumer protection it is important for consumers to be satisfactorily informed of the provisions of this Directive and of codes of practice that may exist in this field;

(20) Whereas non-compliance with this Directive may harm not only consumers but also competitors; whereas provisions may therefore be laid down enabling public bodies or their representatives, or consumer organizations which, under national legislation, have a legitimate interest in consumer protection, or professional organizations which have a legitimate interest in taking action, to monitor the application thereof;

[8] OJ L156/92, p 21.

(21)   Whereas it is important, with a view to consumer protection, to address the question of cross-border complaints as soon as this is feasible; whereas the Commission published on 14 February 1996 a plan of action on consumer access to justice and the settlement of consumer disputes in the internal market; whereas that plan of action includes specific initiatives to promote out-of-court procedures; whereas objective criteria (Annex II) are suggested to ensure the reliability of those procedures and provision is made for the use of standardized claims forms (Annex III);

(22)   Whereas in the use of new technologies the consumer is not in control of the means of communication used; whereas it is therefore necessary to provide that the burden of proof may be on the supplier;

(23)   Whereas there is a risk that, in certain cases, the consumer may be deprived of protection under this Directive through the designation of the law of a non-member country as the law applicable to the contract; whereas provisions should therefore be included in this Directive to avert that risk;

(24)   Whereas a Member State may ban, in the general interest, the marketing on its territory of certain goods and services through distance contracts; whereas that ban must comply with Community rules; whereas there is already provision for such bans, notably with regard to medicinal products, under Council Directive 89/552/EEC of 3 October 1989 on the coordination of certain provisions laid down by law, regulation or administrative action in Member States concerning the pursuit of television broadcasting activities[9] and Council Directive 92/28/EEC of 31 March 1992 on the advertising of medicinal products for human use,[10]

ADOPTED THIS DIRECTIVE:

Article 1

Object

The object of this Directive is to approximate the laws, regulations and administrative provisions of the Member States concerning distance contracts between consumers and suppliers.

[9] OJ L298/89, p 23.
[10] OJ L113/92, p 13.

Article 2

Definitions

For the purposes of this Directive:

1. 'distance contract' means any contract concerning goods or services concluded between a supplier and a consumer under an organized distance sales or service-provision scheme run by the supplier, who, for the purpose of the contract, makes exclusive use of one or more means of distance communication up to and including the moment at which the contract is concluded;

2. 'consumer' means any natural person who, in contracts covered by this Directive, is acting for purposes which are outside his trade, business or profession;

3. 'supplier' means any natural or legal person who, in contracts covered by this Directive, is acting in his commercial or professional capacity;

4. 'means of distance communication' means any means which, without the simultaneous physical presence of the supplier and the consumer, may be used for the conclusion of a contract between those parties. An indicative list of the means covered by this Directive is contained in Annex I;

5. 'operator of a means of communication' means any public or private natural or legal person whose trade, business or profession involves making one or more means of distance communication available to suppliers.

Article 3

Exemptions

(1) This Directive shall not apply to contracts:
   – relating to any financial service to which directive 2002/65/EC of the European Parliament and of the Council of 23 September 2002 concerning the distance marketing of consumer financial services and amending Council Directive 90/619 and Directives 97/7/EC and 98/27/EC(13) applies,
   – concluded by means of automatic vending machines or automated commercial premises,
   – concluded with telecommunications operators through the use of public payphones,
   – concluded for the construction and sale of immovable property or relating to other immovable property rights, except for rental,
   – concluded at an auction.

(2) Articles 4, 5, 6 and 7(1) shall not apply:
- to contracts for the supply of foodstuffs, beverages or other goods intended for everyday consumption supplied to the home of the consumer, to his residence or to his workplace by regular roundsmen,
- to contracts for the provision of accommodation, transport, catering or leisure services, where the supplier undertakes, when the contract is concluded, to provide these services on a specific date or within a specific period; exceptionally, in the case of outdoor leisure events, the supplier can reserve the right not to apply Article 7 (2) in specific circumstances.

Article 4

Prior information

(1) In good time prior to the conclusion of any distance contract, the consumer shall be provided with the following information:
a) the identity of the supplier and, in the case of contracts requiring payment in advance, his address;
b) the main characteristics of the goods or services;
c) the price of the goods or services including all taxes;
d) delivery costs, where appropriate;
e) the arrangements for payment, delivery or performance;
f) the existence of a right of withdrawal, except in the cases referred to in Article 6 (3);
g) the cost of using the means of distance communication, where it is calculated other than at the basic rate;
h) the period for which the offer or the price remains valid;
i) where appropriate, the minimum duration of the contract in the case of contracts for the supply of products or services to be performed permanently or recurrently.

(2) The information referred to in paragraph 1, the commercial purpose of which must be made clear, shall be provided in a clear and comprehensible manner in any way appropriate to the means of distance communication used, with due regard, in particular, to the principles of good faith in commercial transactions, and the principles governing the protection of those who are unable, pursuant to the legislation of the Member States, to give their consent, such as minors.

(3) Moreover, in the case of telephone communications, the identity of the supplier and the commercial purpose of the call shall be made explicitly clear at the beginning of any conversation with the consumer.

Article 5

Written confirmation of information

(1) The consumer must receive written confirmation or confirmation in another durable medium available and accessible to him of the information referred to in Article 4 (1) (a) to (f), in good time during the performance of the contract, and at the latest at the time of delivery where goods not for delivery to third parties are concerned, unless the information has already been given to the consumer prior to conclusion of the contract in writing or on another durable medium available and accessible to him.

In any event the following must be provided:
- written information on the conditions and procedures for exercising the right of withdrawal, within the meaning of Article 6, including the cases referred to in the first indent of Article 6(3),
- the geographical address of the place of business of the supplier to which the consumer may address any complaints,
- information on after-sales services and guarantees which exist,
- the conclusion for cancelling the contract, where it is of unspecified duration or a duration exceeding one year.

(2) Paragraph 1 shall not apply to services which are performed through the use of a means of distance communication, where they are supplied on only one occasion and are invoiced by the operator of the means of distance communication. Nevertheless, the consumer must in all cases be able to obtain the geographical address of the place of business of the supplier to which he may address any complaints.

Article 6

Right of withdrawal

(1) For any distance contract the consumer shall have a period of at least seven working days in which to withdraw from the contract without penalty and without giving any reason. The only charge that may be made to the consumer because of the exercise of his right of withdrawal is the direct cost of returning the goods.

The period for exercise of this right shall begin:
- in the case of goods, from the day of receipt by the consumer where the obligations laid down in Article 5 have been fulfilled,
- in the case of services, from the day of conclusion of the contract or from the day on which the obligations laid down in

Article 5 were fulfilled if they are fulfilled after conclusion of the contract, provided that this period does not exceed the three-month period referred to in the following subparagraph.

If the supplier has failed to fulfil the obligations laid down in Article 5, the period shall be three months. The period shall begin:
– in the case of goods, from the day of receipt by the consumer,
– in the case of services, from the day of conclusion of the contract.

If the information referred to in Article 5 is supplied within this three-month period, the seven working day period referred to in the first subparagraph shall begin as from that moment.

(2) Where the right of withdrawal has been exercised by the consumer pursuant to this Article, the supplier shall be obliged to reimburse the sums paid by the consumer free of charge. The only charge that may be made to the consumer because of the exercise of his right of withdrawal is the direct cost of returning the goods. Such reimbursement must be carried out as soon as possible and in any case within 30 days.

(3) Unless the parties have agreed otherwise, the consumer may not exercise the right of withdrawal provided for in paragraph 1 in respect of contracts:
– for the provision of services if performance has begun, with the consumer's agreement, before the end of the seven working day period referred to in paragraph 1,
– for the supply of goods or services the price of which is dependent on fluctuations in the financial market which cannot be controlled by the supplier,
– for the supply of goods made to the consumer's specifications or clearly personalized or which, by reason of their nature, cannot be returned or are liable to deteriorate or expire rapidly,
– for the supply of audio or video recordings or computer software which were unsealed by the consumer,
– for the supply of newspapers, periodicals and magazines,
– for gaming and lottery services.

(4) The Member States shall make provision in their legislation to ensure that:
– if the Price of goods or sevices is fuly or partly covered by credit granted by the supplier or
– if that price is fully or partly covered by credit granted to the consumer by a third party on the basis of an agreement between the third party and the supplier,

the credit agreement shall be cancelled, without any penalty, if the consumer exercises his right to withdraw from the contract in accordance with paragraph 1.

Member States shall determine the detailed rules for cancellation of the credit agreement.

Article 7

Performance

(1) Unless the parties have agreed otherwise, the supplier must execute the order within a maximum of 30 days from the day following that on which the consumer forwarded his order to the supplier.

(2) Where a supplier fails to perform his side of the contract on the grounds that the goods or services ordered are unavailable, the consumer must be informed of this situation and must be able to obtain a refund of any sums he has paid as soon as possible and in any case within 30 days.

(3) Nevertheless, Member States may lay down that the supplier may provide the consumer with goods or services of equivalent quality and price provided that this possibility was provided for prior to the conclusion of the contract or in the contract. The consumer shall be informed of this possibility in a clear and comprehensible manner. The cost of returning the goods following exercise of the right of withdrawal shall, in this case, be borne by the supplier, and the consumer must be informed of this. In such cases the supply of goods or services may not be deemed to constitute inertia selling within the meaning of Article 9.

Article 8

Payment by card

Member States shall ensure that appropriate measures exist to allow a consumer:

- to request cancellation of a payment where fraudulent use has been made of his payment card in connection with distance contracts covered by this Directive,
- in the event of fraudulent use, to be recredited with the sums paid or have them returned.

Article 9

Inertia selling

Member States shall take the measures necessary to:

- prohibit the supply of goods or services to a consumer without their being ordered by the consumer beforehand, where such supply involves a demand for payment,

– exempt the consumer from the provision of any consideration in cases of unsolicited supply, the absence of a response not constituting consent.

Article 10

Restrictions on the use of certain means of distance communication

(1) Use by a supplier of the following means requires the prior consent of the consumer:
   – automated calling system without human intervention (automatic calling machine),
   – facsimile machine (fax).
(2) Member States shall ensure that means of distance communication, other than those referred to in paragraph 1, which allow individual communications may be used only where there is no clear objection from the consumer.

Article 11

Judicial or administrative redress

(1) Member States shall ensure that adequate and effective means exist to ensure compliance with this Directive in the interests of consumers.
(2) The means referred to in paragraph 1 shall include provisions whereby one or more of the following bodies, as determined by national law, may take action under national law before the courts or before the competent administrative bodies to ensure that the national provisions for the implementation of this Directive are applied:
   a) public bodies or their representatives;
   b) consumer organizations having a legitimate interest in protecting consumers;
   c) professional organizations having a legitimate interest in acting.
(3) a) Member States may stipulate that the burden of proof concerning the existence of prior information, written confirmation, compliance with time-limits or consumer consent can be placed on the supplier.
   b) Member States shall take the measures needed to ensure that suppliers and operators of means of communication, where they are able to do so, cease practices which do not comply with measures adopted pursuant to this Directive.

(4)   Member States may provide for voluntary supervision by self-regulatory bodies of compliance with the provisions of this Directive and recourse to such bodies for the settlement of disputes to be added to the means which Member States must provided to ensure compliance with the provisions of this Directive.

Article 12

Binding nature

(1)   The consumer may not waive the rights conferred on him by the transposition of this Directive into national law.
(2)   Member States shall take the measures needed to ensure that the consumer does not lose the protection granted by this Directive by virtue of the choice of the law of a non-member country as the law applicable to the contract if the latter has close connection with the territory of one or more Member States.

Article 13

Community rules

(1)   The provisions of this Directive shall apply insofar as there are no particular provisions in rules of Community law governing certain types of distance contracts in their entirety.
(2)   Where specific Community rules contain provisions governing only certain aspects of the supply of goods or provision of services, those provisions, rather than the provisions of this Directive, shall apply to these specific aspects of the distance contracts.

Article 14

Minimal clause

Member States may introduce or maintain, in the area covered by this Directive, more stringent provisions compatible with the Treaty, to ensure a higher level of consumer protection. Such provisions shall, where appropriate, include a ban, in the general interest, on the marketing of certain goods or services, particularly medicinal products, within their territory by means of distance contracts, with due regard for the Treaty.

Article 15

Implementation

(1) Member States shall bring into force the laws, regulations and administrative provisions necessary to comply with this Directive no later than three years after it enters into force. They shall forthwith inform the Commission thereof.

(2) When Member States adopt the measures referred to in paragraph 1, these shall contain a reference to this Directive or shall be accompanied by such reference on the occasion of their official publication. The procedure for such reference shall be laid down by Member States.

(3) Member States shall communicate to the Commission the text of the provisions of national law which they adopt in the field governed by this Directive.

(4) No later than four years after the entry into force of this Directive the Commission shall submit a report to the European Parliament and the Council on the implementation of this Directive, accompanied if appropriate by a proposal for the revision thereof.

Article 16

Consumer information

Member States shall take appropriate measures to inform the consumer of the national law transposing this Directive and shall encourage, where appropriate, professional organizations to inform consumers of their codes of practice.

Article 17

Complaints systems

The Commission shall study the feasibility of establishing effective means to deal with consumers' complaints in respect of distance selling. Within two years after the entry into force of this Directive the Commission shall submit a report to the European Parliament and the Council on the results of the studies, accompanied if appropriate by proposals.

Article 18

This Directive shall enter into force on the day of its publication in the Official Journal of the European Communities.

Article 19

This Directive is addressed to the Member States.

ANNEX I

Means of communication covered by Article 2(4)

- Unaddressed printed matter
- Addressed printed matter
- Standard letter
- Press advertising with order form
- Catalogue
- Telephone with human intervention
- Telephone without human intervention (automatic calling machine, audiotext)
- Radio
- Videophone (telephone with screen)
- Videotex (microcomputer and television screen) with keyboard or touch screen
- Electronic mail
- Facsimile machine (fax)
- Television (teleshopping).

Statement by the Council and the Parliament re Article 6(1)

The Council and the Parliament note that the Commission will examine the possibility and desirability of harmonizing the method of calculating the cooling-off period under existing consumer-protection legislation, notably Directive 85/577/EEC of 20 December 1985 on the protection of consumers in respect of contracts negotiated away from commercial establishments ('door-to-door sales').[11]

Sement by the Commission re Article 3(1), first indent

Commission recognizes the importance of protecting consumers in respect of distance contracts concerning financial services and has published a Green Paper entitled 'Financial services: meeting consumers' expectations'. In the light of reactions to the Green Paper the Commission will examine ways of incorporating consumer protection into the policy on financial services and the possible legislative implications and, if need be, will submit appropriate proposals.

---

[11] OJ L372/85, p 31.

Denmark	Lov om ændring af lov om visse forbrugeraftaler, markedsføringsloven og visse andre love, Lov Nr 442 af 31.5.2000
EIRE	European Communities (Protection of Consumers in Respect of Contracts made by Means of Distance Communication) Regulations 2001, S.I. No. 207/2001
Finland	1. – Laki kuluttajansuojalain muuttamisesta, 15/12/2000 ref : Suomen säädöskokoelma 2000 N 1072 (page 2809), SG(2001)A/868 du 22/01/2001
	2. – Laki sopimattomasta menettelystä elinkeinotoiminnassa annetun lain n muuttamisesta, 15/12/2000 ref : Suomen säädöskokoelma 2000 N 1073 (page 2817), SG(2001)A/868 du 22/01/2001
Sweden	Lag om konsumentskydd vid distansavtal och hemförsäljningsavtal, SFS 2000:274.
United Kingdom	Consumer Protection (Distance Selling) Regulations 2000, S.I. No. 2000/2334

DIRECTIVE 1999/44/EC OF THE EUROPEAN PARLIAMENT AND OF THE COUNCIL

of 25 May 1999

on certain aspects of the sale of consumer goods and associated guarantees

(Official Journal L171/99, p 12)

THE EUROPEAN PARLIAMENT AND THE COUNCIL OF THE EUROPEAN UNION –

Having regard to the Treaty establishing the European Community, and in particular Article 95 thereof,

Having regard to the proposal from the Commission,[1]

Having regard to the opinion of the Economic and Social Committee,[2]

Acting in accordance with the procedure laid down in Article 251 of the Treaty in the light of the joint text approved by the Conciliation Committee on 18 May 1999,[3]

(1) Whereas Article 153(1) and (3) of the Treaty provides that the Community should contribute to the achievement of a high level of consumer protection by the measures it adopts pursuant to Article 95 thereof;

(2) Whereas the internal market comprises an area without internal frontiers in which the free movement of goods, persons, services and capital is guaranteed; whereas free movement of goods concerns not only transactions by persons acting in the course of a business but also transactions by private individuals; whereas it implies that consumers resident in one Member State should be free to purchase goods in the territory of another Member State on the basis of a uniform minimum set of fair rules governing the sale of consumer goods;

(3) Whereas the laws of the Member States concerning the sale of consumer goods are somewhat disparate, with the result that national consumer

---

[1] OJ C307/96, p 8 and OJ C148/98, p 12.

[2] OJ C66/97, p 5.

[3] Opinion of the European Parliament of 10 March 1998 (OJ C104/98, p 30); Council Common Position of 24 September 1998 (OJ C333/98, p 46) and the Decision of the European Parliament of 17 December 1998 (OJ C98/99, p 226); Decision of the European Parliament of 5 May 1999; Council Decision of 17 May 1999.

goods markets differ from one another and that competition between sellers may be distorted;

(4) Whereas consumers who are keen to benefit from the large market by purchasing goods in Member States other than their State of residence play a fundamental role in the completion of the internal market; whereas the artificial reconstruction of frontiers and the compartmentalisation of markets should be prevented; whereas the opportunities available to consumers have been greatly broadened by new communication technologies which allow ready access to distribution systems in other Member States or in third countries; whereas, in the absence of minimum harmonisation of the rules governing the sale of consumer goods, the development of the sale of goods through the medium of new distance communication technologies risks being impeded;

(5) Whereas the creation of a common set of minimum rules of consumer law, valid no matter where goods are purchased within the Community, will strengthen consumer confidence and enable consumers to make the most of the internal market;

(6) Whereas the main difficulties encountered by consumers and the main source of disputes with sellers concern the non-conformity of goods with the contract; whereas it is therefore appropriate to approximate national legislation governing the sale of consumer goods in this respect, without however impinging on provisions and principles of national law relating to contractual and non-contractual liability;

(7) Whereas the goods must, above all, conform with the contractual specifications; whereas the principle of conformity with the contract may be considered as common to the different national legal traditions; whereas in certain national legal traditions it may not be possible to rely solely on this principle to ensure a minimum level of protection for the consumer; whereas under such legal traditions, in particular, additional national provisions may be useful to ensure that the consumer is protected in cases where the parties have agreed no specific contractual terms or where the parties have concluded contractual terms or agreements which directly or indirectly waive or restrict the rights of the consumer and which, to the extent that these rights result from this Directive, are not binding on the consumer;

(8) Whereas, in order to facilitate the application of the principle of conformity with the contract, it is useful to introduce a rebuttable presumption of conformity with the contract covering the most common situations; whereas that presumption does not restrict the principle of freedom of contract; whereas, furthermore, in the absence of specific contractual terms, as well as where the minimum protection clause is applied, the elements mentioned in this presumption may be used to determine the lack of conformity of the goods with the contract;

whereas the quality and performance which consumers can reasonably expect will depend inter alia on whether the goods are new or second-hand; whereas the elements mentioned in the presumption are cumulative; whereas, if the circumstances of the case render any particular element manifestly inappropriate, the remaining elements of the presumption nevertheless still apply;

(9) Whereas the seller should be directly liable to the consumer for the conformity of the goods with the contract; whereas this is the traditional solution enshrined in the legal orders of the Member States; whereas nevertheless the seller should be free, as provided for by national law, to pursue remedies against the producer, a previous seller in the same chain of contracts or any other intermediary, unless he has renounced that entitlement; whereas this Directive does not affect the principle of freedom of contract between the seller, the producer, a previous seller or any other intermediary; whereas the rules governing against whom and how the seller may pursue such remedies are to be determined by national law;

(10) Whereas, in the case of non-conformity of the goods with the contract, consumers should be entitled to have the goods restored to conformity with the contract free of charge, choosing either repair or replacement, or, failing this, to have the price reduced or the contract rescinded;

(11) Whereas the consumer in the first place may require the seller to repair the goods or to replace them unless those remedies are impossible or disproportionate; whereas whether a remedy is disproportionate should be determined objectively; whereas a remedy would be disproportionate if it imposed, in comparison with the other remedy, unreasonable costs; whereas, in order to determine whether the costs are unreasonable, the costs of one remedy should be significantly higher than the costs of the other remedy;

(12) Whereas in cases of a lack of conformity, the seller may always offer the consumer, by way of settlement, any available remedy; whereas it is for the consumer to decide whether to accept or reject this proposal;

(13) Whereas, in order to enable consumers to take advantage of the internal market and to buy consumer goods in another Member State, it should be recommended that, in the interests of consumers, the producers of consumer goods that are marketed in several Member States attach to the product a list with at least one contact address in every Member State where the product is marketed;

(14) Whereas the references to the time of delivery do not imply that Member States have to change their rules on the passing of the risk;

(15) Whereas Member States may provide that any reimbursement to the consumer may be reduced to take account of the use the consumer has had of the goods since they were delivered to him; whereas the

detailed arrangements whereby rescission of the contract is effected may be laid down in national law;

(16) Whereas the specific nature of second-hand goods makes it generally impossible to replace them; whereas therefore the consumer's right of replacement is generally not available for these goods; whereas for such goods, Member States may enable the parties to agree a shortened period of liability;

(17) Whereas it is appropriate to limit in time the period during which the seller is liable for any lack of conformity which exists at the time of delivery of the goods; whereas Member States may also provide for a limitation on the period during which consumers can exercise their rights, provided such a period does not expire within two years from the time of delivery; whereas where, under national legislation, the time when a limitation period starts is not the time of delivery of the goods, the total duration of the limitation period provided for by national law may not be shorter than two years from the time of delivery;

(18) Whereas Member States may provide for suspension or interruption of the period during which any lack of conformity must become apparent and of the limitation period, where applicable and in accordance with their national law, in the event of repair, replacement or negotiations between seller and consumer with a view to an amicable settlement;

(19) Whereas Member States should be allowed to set a period within which the consumer must inform the seller of any lack of conformity; whereas Member States may ensure a higher level of protection for the consumer by not introducing such an obligation; whereas in any case consumers throughout the Community should have at least two months in which to inform the seller that a lack of conformity exists;

(20) Whereas Member States should guard against such a period placing at a disadvantage consumers shopping across borders; whereas all Member States should inform the Commission of their use of this provision; whereas the Commission should monitor the effect of the varied application of this provision on consumers and on the internal market; whereas information on the use made of this provision by a Member State should be available to the other Member States and to consumers and consumer organisations throughout the Community; whereas a summary of the situation in all Member States should therefore be published in the Official Journal of the European Communities;

(21) Whereas, for certain categories of goods, it is current practice for sellers and producers to offer guarantees on goods against any defect which becomes apparent within a certain period; whereas this practice can stimulate competition; whereas, while such guarantees are legitimate marketing tools, they should not mislead the consumer; whereas, to ensure that consumers are not misled, guarantees should contain certain information, including a statement that the guarantee does not affect the consumer's legal rights;

(22) Whereas the parties may not, by common consent, restrict or waive the rights granted to consumers, since otherwise the legal protection afforded would be thwarted; whereas this principle should apply also to clauses which imply that the consumer was aware of any lack of conformity of the consumer goods existing at the time the contract was concluded; whereas the protection granted to consumers under this Directive should not be reduced on the grounds that the law of a non-member State has been chosen as being applicable to the contract;

(23) Whereas legislation and case-law in this area in the various Member States show that there is growing concern to ensure a high level of consumer protection; whereas, in the light of this trend and the experience acquired in implementing this Directive, it may be necessary to envisage more far-reaching harmonisation, notably by providing for the producer's direct liability for defects for which he is responsible;

(24) Whereas Member States should be allowed to adopt or maintain in force more stringent provisions in the field covered by this Directive to ensure an even higher level of consumer protection;

(25) Whereas, according to the Commission recommendation of 30 March 1998 on the principles applicable to the bodies responsible for out-of-court settlement of consumer disputes,[4] Member States can create bodies that ensure impartial and efficient handling of complaints in a national and cross-border context and which consumers can use as mediators;

(26) Whereas it is appropriate, in order to protect the collective interests of consumers, to add this Directive to the list of Directives contained in the Annex to Directive 98/27/EC of the European Parliament and of the Council of 19 May 1998 on injunctions for the protection of consumers' interests,[5]

HAVE ADOPTED THIS DIRECTIVE:

Article 1

Scope and definitions

(1) The purpose of this Directive is the approximation of the laws, regulations and administrative provisions of the Member States on certain aspects of the sale of consumer goods and associated guarantees in order to ensure a uniform minimum level of consumer protection in the context of the internal market.

---

[4] OJ L115/98, p 31.
[5] OJ L166/98, p 51.

(2) For the purposes of this Directive:

a) *consumer*: shall mean any natural person who, in the contracts covered by this Directive, is acting for purposes which are not related to his trade, business or profession;

b) *consumer goods*: shall mean any tangible movable item, with the exception of:
  - goods sold by way of execution or otherwise by authority of law,
  - water and gas where they are not put up for sale in a limited volume or set quantity,
  - electricity;

c) *seller*: shall mean any natural or legal person who, under a contract, sells consumer goods in the course of his trade, business or profession;

d) *producer*: shall mean the manufacturer of consumer goods, the importer of consumer goods into the territory of the Community or any person purporting to be a producer by placing his name, trade mark or other distinctive sign on the consumer goods;

e) *guarantee*: shall mean any undertaking by a seller or producer to the consumer, given without extra charge, to reimburse the price paid or to replace, repair or handle consumer goods in any way if they do not meet the specifications set out in the guarantee statement or in the relevant advertising;

f) *repair*: shall mean, in the event of lack of conformity, bringing consumer goods into conformity with the contract of sale.

(3) Member States may provide that the expression 'consumer goods' does not cover second-hand goods sold at public auction where consumers have the opportunity of attending the sale in person.

(4) Contracts for the supply of consumer goods to be manufactured or produced shall also be deemed contracts of sale for the purpose of this Directive.

Article 2

Conformity with the contract

(1) The seller must deliver goods to the consumer which are in conformity with the contract of sale.

(2) Consumer goods are presumed to be in conformity with the contract if they:

a) comply with the description given by the seller and possess the qualities of the goods which the seller has held out to the consumer as a sample or model;

b) are fit for any particular purpose for which the consumer requires them and which he made known to the seller at the time of conclusion of the contract and which the seller has accepted;

c) are fit for the purposes for which goods of the same type are normally used;

d) show the quality and performance which are normal in goods of the same type and which the consumer can reasonably expect, given the nature of the goods and taking into account any public statements on the specific characteristics of the goods made about them by the seller, the producer or his representative, particularly in advertising or on labelling.

(3) There shall be deemed not to be a lack of conformity for the purposes of this Article if, at the time the contract was concluded, the consumer was aware, or could not reasonably be unaware of, the lack of conformity, or if the lack of conformity has its origin in materials supplied by the consumer.

(4) The seller shall not be bound by public statements, as referred to in paragraph 2(d) if he:

– shows that he was not, and could not reasonably have been, aware of the statement in question,

– shows that by the time of conclusion of the contract the statement had been corrected, or

– shows that the decision to buy the consumer goods could not have been influenced by the statement.

(5) Any lack of conformity resulting from incorrect installation of the consumer goods shall be deemed to be equivalent to lack of conformity of the goods if installation forms part of the contract of sale of the goods and the goods were installed by the seller or under his responsibility. This shall apply equally if the product, intended to be installed by the consumer, is installed by the consumer and the incorrect installation is due to a shortcoming in the installation instructions.

Article 3

Rights of the consumer

(1) The seller shall be liable to the consumer for any lack of conformity which exists at the time the goods were delivered.

(2) In the case of a lack of conformity, the consumer shall be entitled to have the goods brought into conformity free of charge by repair or replacement, in accordance with paragraph 3, or to have an appropriate reduction made in the price or the contract rescinded with regard to those goods, in accordance with paragraphs 5 and 6.

(3) In the first place, the consumer may require the seller to repair the goods or he may require the seller to replace them, in either case free of charge, unless this is impossible or disproportionate.

A remedy shall be deemed to be disproportionate if it imposes costs on the seller which, in comparison with the alternative remedy, are unreasonable, taking into account:
- the value the goods would have if there were no lack of conformity,
- the significance of the lack of conformity, and
- whether the alternative remedy could be completed without significant inconvenience to the consumer.

Any repair or replacement shall be completed within a reasonable time and without any significant inconvenience to the consumer, taking account of the nature of the goods and the purpose for which the consumer required the goods.

(4) The terms 'free of charge' in paragraphs 2 and 3 refer to the necessary costs incurred to bring the goods into conformity, particularly the cost of postage, labour and materials.

(5) The consumer may require an appropriate reduction of the price or have the contract rescinded:
- if the consumer is entitled to neither repair nor replacement, or
- if the seller has not completed the remedy within a reasonable time, or
- if the seller has not completed the remedy without significant inconvenience to the consumer.

(6) The consumer is not entitled to have the contract rescinded if the lack of conformity is minor.

Article 4

Right of redress

Where the final seller is liable to the consumer because of a lack of conformity resulting from an act or omission by the producer, a previous seller in the same chain of contracts or any other intermediary, the final seller shall be entitled to pursue remedies against the person or persons liable in the contractual chain. The person or persons liable against whom the final seller may pursue remedies, together with the relevant actions and conditions of exercise, shall be determined by national law.

Article 5

Time limits

(1) The seller shall be held liable under Article 3 where the lack of conformity becomes apparent within two years as from delivery of the goods.

If, under national legislation, the rights laid down in Article 3(2) are subject to a limitation period, that period shall not expire within a period of two years from the time of delivery.

(2)   Member States may provide that, in order to benefit from his rights, the consumer must inform the seller of the lack of conformity within a period of two months from the date on which he detected such lack of conformity.

Member States shall inform the Commission of their use of this paragraph. The Commission shall monitor the effect of the existence of this option for the Member States on consumers and on the internal market.

Not later than 7 January 2003, the Commission shall prepare a report on the use made by Member States of this paragraph. This report shall be published in the Official Journal of the European Communities.

(3)   Unless proved otherwise, any lack of conformity which becomes apparent within six months of delivery of the goods shall be presumed to have existed at the time of delivery unless this presumption is incompatible with the nature of the goods or the nature of the lack of conformity.

Article 6

Guarantees

(1)   A guarantee shall be legally binding on the offerer under the conditions laid down in the guarantee statement and the associated advertising.

(2)   The guarantee shall:
   –   state that the consumer has legal rights under applicable national legislation governing the sale of consumer goods and make clear that those rights are not affected by the guarantee,
   –   set out in plain intelligible language the contents of the guarantee and the essential particulars necessary for making claims under the guarantee, notably the duration andterritorial scope of the guarantee as well as the name and address of the guarantor.

(3)   On request by the consumer, the guarantee shall be made available in writing or feature in another durable medium available and accessible to him.

(4)   Within its own territory, the Member State in which the consumer goods are marketed may, in accordance with the rules of the Treaty, provide that the guarantee be drafted in one or more languages which it shall determine from among the official languages of the Community.

(5)   Should a guarantee infringe the requirements of paragraphs 2, 3 or 4, the validity of this guarantee shall in no way be affected, and the consumer can still rely on the guarantee and require that it be honoured.

Article 7

Binding nature

(1) Any contractual terms or agreements concluded with the seller before the lack of conformity is brought to the seller's attention which directly or indirectly waive or restrict the rights resulting from this Directive shall, as provided for by national law, not be binding on the consumer.

Member States may provide that, in the case of second-hand goods, the seller and consumer may agree contractual terms or agreements which have a shorter time period for the liability of the seller than that set down in Article 5(1). Such period may not be less than one year.

(2) Member States shall take the necessary measures to ensure that consumers are not deprived of the protection afforded by this Directive as a result of opting for the law of a non-member State as the law applicable to the contract where the contract has a close connection with the territory of the Member States.

Article 8

National law and minimum protection

(1) The rights resulting from this Directive shall be exercised without prejudice to other rights which the consumer may invoke under the national rules governing contractual or non-contractual liability.

(2) Member States may adopt or maintain in force more stringent provisions, compatible with the Treaty in the field covered by this Directive, to ensure a higher level of consumer protection.

Article 9

Member States shall take appropriate measures to inform the consumer of the national law transposing this Directive and shall encourage, where appropriate, professional organisations to inform consumers of their rights.

Article 10

The Annex to Directive 98/27/EC shall be completed as follows:

'10. Directive 1999/44/EC of the European Parliament and of the Council of 25 May 1999 on certain aspects of the sale of consumer goods and associated guarantees (OJ L 171, 7.7.1999, p. 12).'

Article 11

Transposition

(1) Member States shall bring into force the laws, regulations and administrative provisions necessary to comply with this Directive not later than 1 January 2002. They shall forthwith inform the Commission thereof.

When Member States adopt these measures, they shall contain a reference to this Directive, or shall be accompanied by such reference at the time of their official publication. The procedure for such reference shall be adopted by Member States.

(2) Member States shall communicate to the Commission the provisions of national law which they adopt in the field covered by this Directive.

Article 12

Review

The Commission shall, not later than 7 July 2006, review the application of this Directive and submit to the European Parliament and the Council a report. The report shall examine, inter alia, the case for introducing the producer's direct liability and, if appropriate, shall be accompanied by proposals.

Article 13

Entry into force

This Directive shall enter into force on the day of its publication in *the Official Journal of the European Communities*.

Article 14

This Directive is addressed to the Member States.

Denmark	1. – Lov om aendring af lov om markedsforing ref: Lov Nr 342 af 02/06/1999.
	2. – Lov om aendring af lov omkob ref: Lov Nr 213 af 22/04/2002
EIRE	European Communities (Certain Aspects of the Sale of Consumer Goods and Associated Guarantees) Regulations 2003, S.I. No. 11/2003.
Finland	Laki kuluttajansuojalain muuttamiesta ref: Suomen Säädökokoelma n 1258/2001 du 19/12/2001, page 3509

Sweden	1. – Lag om ändring i konsumentköplagen (1990 : 932), SFS 2002/587.
	2. – Lag om ändring i konsumenttjänstlagen (1985 : 716), SFS 2002/588.
	3. – Lag om ändring i marknadsföringslagen (1995 : 450), SFS 2002/565.
United Kingdom	The Sale and Supply of Goods and Services Regulations 2002, S.I. No. 3045/2002.

COUNCIL DIRECTIVE 76/207/EEC

of 9 February 1976

on the implementation of the principle of equal treatment for men and women as regards access to employment, vocational training and promotion, and working conditions*

(Official Journal L 39/76, p 40)

THE COUNCIL OF THE EUROPEAN COMMUNITIES —

Having regard to the Treaty establishing the European Economic Community, and in particular Article 235 thereof,

Having regard to the proposal from the Commission,

Having regard to the opinion of the European Parliament,[1]

Having regard to the opinion of the Economic and Social Committee,[2]

Whereas the Council, in its resolution of 21 January 1974 concerning a social action programme,[3] included among the priorities action for the purpose of achieving equality between men and women as regards access to employment and vocational training and promotion and as regards working conditions, including pay;

Whereas, with regard to pay, the Council adopted on 10 February 1975 Directive 75/117/EEC on the approximation of the laws of the Member States relating to the application of the principle of equal pay for men and women;[4]

Whereas Community action to achieve the principle of equal treatment for men and women in respect of access to employment and vocational training and promotion and in respect of other working conditions also appears to be necessary; whereas, equal treatment for male and female workers constitutes one of the objectives of the Community, in so far as the harmonization of living and working conditions while maintaining their improvement are inter alia to be furthered; whereas the Treaty does not confer the necessary specific powers for this purpose;

Whereas the definition and progressive implementation of the principle of equal treatment in matters of social security should be ensured by means of subsequent instruments,

---

* This Directive was incorporated into the law of the United Kingdom by the Sex Discrimination Act 1975, the Sex Discrimination Order (Northern Ireland) 1976, Statutory Instruments No 1042 of 1976, and by the Operations at Unfenced Machinery (Amendment) Regulations 1976, Statutory Instruments No 955 of 1976.

[1] OJ C111/75, p 14.

[2] OJ C286/75, p 8.

[3] OJ C13/74, p 1.

[4] OJ L45/75, p 19.

HAS ADOPTED THIS DIRECTIVE:

Article 1

(1) The purpose of this Directive is to put into effect in the Member States the principle of equal treatment for men and women as regards access to employment, including promotion, and to vocational training and as regards working conditions and, on the conditions referred to in paragraph 2, social security. This principle is hereinafter referred to as 'the principle of equal treatment.'

(1a) Member States shall actively take into account the objective of equality between men and women when formulating and implementing laws, regulations, administrative provisions, policies and activities in the areas referred to in paragraph 1.

(2) With a view to ensuring the progressive implementation of the principle of equal treatment in matters of social security, the Council, acting on a proposal from the Commission, will adopt provisions defining its substance, its scope and the arrangements for its application.

Article 2

(1) For the purposes of the following provisions, the principle of equal treatment shall mean that there shall be no discrimination whatsoever on grounds of sex either directly or indirectly by reference in particular to marital or family status.

(2) For the purposes of this Directive, the following definitions shall apply:
— direct discrimination: where one person is treated less favourably on grounds of sex than another is, has been or would be treated in a comparable situation,
— indirect discrimination: where an apparently neutral provision, criterion or practice would put persons of one sex at a particular disadvantage compared with persons of the other sex, unless that provision, criterion or practice is objectively justified by a legitimate aim, and the means of achieving that aim are appropriate and necessary,
— harassment: where an unwanted conduct related to the sex of a person occurs with the purpose or effect of violating the dignity of a person, and of creating an intimidating, hostile, degrading, humiliating or offensive environment,
— sexual harassment: where any form of unwanted verbal, non-verbal or physical conduct of a sexual nature occurs, with the purpose or effect of violating the dignity of a person, in particular when creating an intimidating, hostile, degrading, humiliating or offensive environment.

(3) Harassment and sexual harassment within the meaning of this Directive shall be deemed to be discrimination on the grounds of sex and therefore prohibited.

A person's rejection of, or submission to, such conduct may not be used as a basis for a decision affecting that person.

(4) An instruction to discriminate against persons on grounds of sex shall be deemed to be discrimination within the meaning of this Directive.

(5) Member States shall encourage, in accordance with national law, collective agreements or practice, employers and those responsible for access to vocational training to take measures to prevent all forms of discrimination on grounds of sex, in particular harassment and sexual harassment at the workplace.

(6) Member States may provide, as regards access to employment including the training leading thereto, that a difference of treatment which is based on a characteristic related to sex shall not constitute discrimination where, by reason of the nature of the particular occupational activities concerned or of the context in which they are carried out, such a characteristic constitutes a genuine and determining occupational requirement, provided that the objective is legitimate and the requirement is proportionate.

(7) This Directive shall be without prejudice to provisions concerning the protection of women, particularly as regards pregnancy and maternity.

A woman on maternity leave shall be entitled, after the end of her period of maternity leave, to return to her job or to an equivalent post on terms and conditions which are no less favourable to her and to benefit from any improvement in working conditions to which she would be entitled during her absence.

Less favourable treatment of a woman related to pregnancy or maternity leave within the meaning of Directive 92/85/EEC shall constitute discrimination within the meaning of this Directive.

This Directive shall also be without prejudice to the provisions of Council Directive 96/34/EC of 3 June 1996 on the framework agreement on parental leave concluded by UNICE, CEEP and the ETUC(14) and of Council Directive 92/85/EEC of 19 October 1992 on the introduction of measures to encourage improvements in the safety and health at work of pregnant workers and workers who have recently given birth or are breastfeeding (tenth individual Directive within the meaning of Article 16(1) of Directive 89/391/EEC)(15). It is also without prejudice to the right of Member States to recognise distinct rights to paternity and/or adoption leave. Those Member States which recognise such rights shall take the necessary measures to protect working men and women against dismissal due to exercising those rights and ensure that, at the end of such leave, they shall be entitled to return to their jobs or to equivalent posts on terms and conditions which are no less favourable to them, and to benefit from any improvement in working conditions to which they would have been entitled during their absence.

(8) Member States may maintain or adopt measures within the meaning of Article 141(4) of the Treaty with a view to ensuring full equality in practice between men and women.

Article 3

(1) Application of the principle of equal treatment means that there shall be no direct or indirect discrimination on the grounds of sex in the public or private sectors, including public bodies, in relation to:

(a) conditions for access to employment, to self-employment or to occupation, including selection criteria and recruitment conditions, whatever the branch of activity and at all levels of the professional hierarchy, including promotion;

(b) access to all types and to all levels of vocational guidance, vocational training, advanced vocational training and retraining, including practical work experience;

(c) employment and working conditions, including dismissals, as well as pay as provided for in Directive 75/117/EEC;

(d) membership of, and involvement in, an organisation of workers or employers, or any organisation whose members carry on a particular profession, including the benefits provided for by such organisations.

(2) To that end, Member States shall take the necessary measures to ensure that:

(a) any laws, regulations and administrative provisions contrary to the principle of equal treatment are abolished;

(b) any provisions contrary to the principle of equal treatment which are included in contracts or collective agreements, internal rules of undertakings or rules governing the independent occupations and professions and workers' and employers' organisations shall be, or may be declared, null and void or are amended.

Article 4

Repealed

Article 5

Repealed

Article 6

(1) Member States shall ensure that judicial and/or administrative procedures, including where they deem it appropriate conciliation procedures, for the enforcement of obligations under this Directive are available to all persons who consider themselves wronged by failure to apply the principle of equal treatment to them, even after the relationship in which the discrimination is alleged to have occurred has ended.

(2) Member States shall introduce into their national legal systems such measures as are necessary to ensure real and effective compensation or reparation as the Member States so determine for the loss and damage sustained by a person injured as a result of discrimination contrary to Article 3, in a way which is dissuasive and proportionate to the damage suffered; such compensation or reparation may not be restricted by the fixing of a prior upper limit, except in cases where the employer can prove that the only damage suffered by an applicant as a result of discrimination within the meaning of this Directive is the refusal to take his/her job application into consideration.

(3) Member States shall ensure that associations, organisations or other legal entities which have, in accordance with the criteria laid down by their national law, a legitimate interest in ensuring that the provisions of this Directive are complied with, may engage, either on behalf or in support of the complainants, with his or her approval, in any judicial and/or administrative procedure provided for the enforcement of obligations under this Directive.

(4) Paragraphs 1 and 3 are without prejudice to national rules relating to time limits for bringing actions as regards the principle of equal treatment.

Article 7

Member States shall introduce into their national legal systems such measures as are necessary to protect employees, including those who are employees' representatives provided for by national laws and/or practices, against dismissal or other adverse treatment by the employer as a reaction to a complaint within the undertaking or to any legal proceedings aimed at enforcing compliance with the principle of equal treatment.

Article 8

Member States shall take care that the provisions adopted pursuant to this Directive, together with the relevant provisions already in force, are brought to the attention of employees by all appropriate means, for example at their place of employment.

Article 8a

(1) Member States shall designate and make the necessary arrangements for a body or bodies for the promotion, analysis, monitoring and support of equal treatment of all persons without discrimination on the grounds of sex. These bodies may form part of agencies charged at national level with the defence of human rights or the safeguard of individuals' rights.

(2) Member States shall ensure that the competences of these bodies include:

   (a) without prejudice to the right of victims and of associations, organisations or other legal entities referred to in Article 6(3), providing independent assistance to victims of discrimination in pursuing their complaints about discrimination;

   (b) conducting independent surveys concerning discrimination;

   (c) publishing independent reports and making recommendations on any issue relating to such discrimination.

Article 8b

(1) Member States shall, in accordance with national traditions and practice, take adequate measures to promote social dialogue between the social partners with a view to fostering equal treatment, including through the monitoring of workplace practices, collective agreements, codes of conduct, research or exchange of experiences and good practices.

(2) Where consistent with national traditions and practice, Member States shall encourage the social partners, without prejudice to their autonomy, to promote equality between women and men and to conclude, at the appropriate level, agreements laying down anti-discrimination rules in the fields referred to in Article 1 which fall within the scope of collective bargaining. These agreements shall respect the minimum requirements laid down by this Directive and the relevant national implementing measures.

(3) Member States shall, in accordance with national law, collective agreements or practice, encourage employers to promote equal treatment for men and women in the workplace in a planned and systematic way.

(4) To this end, employers should be encouraged to provide at appropriate regular intervals employees and/or their representatives with appropriate information on equal treatment for men and women in the undertaking.

Such information may include statistics on proportions of men and women at different levels of the organisation and possible measures to improve the situation in cooperation with employees' representatives.

Article 8c

Member States shall encourage dialogue with appropriate non-governmental organisations which have, in accordance with their national law and practice, a legitimate interest in contributing to the fight against discrimination on grounds of sex with a view to promoting the principle of equal treatment.

Article 8d

Member States shall lay down the rules on sanctions applicable to infringements of the national provisions adopted pursuant to this Directive, and shall take all measures necessary to ensure that they are applied.

The sanctions, which may comprise the payment of compensation to the victim, must be effective, proportionate and dissuasive. The Member States shall notify those provisions to the Commission by 5 October 2005 at the latest and shall notify it without delay of any subsequent amendment affecting them.

Article 8e

(1) Member States may introduce or maintain provisions which are more favourable to the protection of the principle of equal treatment than those laid down in this Directive.

(2) The implementation of this Directive shall under no circumstances constitute grounds for a reduction in the level of protection against discrimination already afforded by Member States in the fields covered by this Directive.

Article 9

(1) Member States shall put into force the laws, regulations and administrative provisions necessary in order to comply with this Directive within 30 months of its notification and shall immediately inform the Commission thereof.

However, as regards the first part of Article 3(2)(c) and the first part of Article 5(2)(c), Member States shall carry out a first examination and if necessary a first revision of the laws, regulations and administrative provisions referred to therein within four years of notification of this Directive.

(2) Member States shall periodically assess the occupational activities referred to in Article 2(2) in order to decide, in the light of social developments, whether there is justification for maintaining the exclusions concerned. They shall notify the Commission of the results of this assessment.

(3)   Member States shall also communicate to the Commission the texts of laws, regulations and administrative provisions which they adopt in the field covered by this Directive.

Article 10

Within two years following expiry of the 30-month period laid down in the first subparagraph of Article 9(1), Member States shall forward all necessary information to the Commission to enable it to draw up a report on the application of this Directive for submission to the Council.

Article 11

This Directive is addressed to the Member States.

Denmark	1. – Lov Nr 161 af 12/04/1978.
	2. – Lov Nr 162 af 12/04/1978.
EIRE	1. – Employment Equality Act 1998
	2. – European Communities (Employment Equality) Regulations 1982, S.I. No. 302/1982
	3. – European Communities (Employment Equality) Regulations 1985, S.I. No. 331/1985
Finland	Laki naisten ja miesten välisestä tasa-arvosta (609/86) 08/08/1986
Sweden	1. – Jämställdhetslag, SFS 1991:433.
	2. – Lag om ändring i jämställdhetslagen (1991:433), SFS 1994:292.
	3. – Förordning med instruktion för jämställdhetsombudsmannen, SFS 1991:1438.
United Kingdom	1. – The Sex Discrimination Act 1975, as amended by the Employment Act 1989.
	2. – The Operations at Unfenced Machinery (Amendment) Regulations 1976, S.I. No. 1976/955
	3. – The Sex Discrimination Order (Northern Ireland) 1976 ref: S.I. No. 1976/1042.
	4. – The Sex Discrimination (Amendment) Order 1988, S.I. No. 1988/249.
	5. – The Sex Discrimination Act 1975 (Application to Armed Forces etc) Regulations 1994, S.I. No. 1994/3276.
	6. – The Employment Protection (Part Time) Employees Regulations 1995, S.I. No. 31/1995.
	7. – The Sex Discrimination and Equal Pay (Miscellaneous Amendments) Regulations 1996, S.I. No. 1996/438
	8. – The Sex Discrimination Act 1975 (Amendment) Regulations 2003, S.I. No. 2003/1657

COUNCIL DIRECTIVE 2001/23/EC*

of 12 March 2001

on the approximation of the laws of the Member States relating to the safeguarding of employees' rights in the event of transfers of undertakings, businesses or parts of undertakings or businesses

(Official Journal L 82/16, p 16)

THE COUNCIL OF THE EUROPEAN UNION,

Having regard to the Treaty establishing the European Community, and in particular Article 94 thereof,

Having regard to the proposal from the Commission,

Having regard to the opinion of the European Parliament,[1]

Having regard to the opinion of the Economic and Social Committee,[2]

Whereas:

(1)   Council Directive 77/187/EEC of 14 February 1977 on the approximation of the laws of the Member States relating to the safeguarding of employees' rights in the event of transfers of undertakings, businesses or parts of undertakings or businesses[3] has been substantially amended.[4] In the interests of clarity and rationality, it should therefore be codified.

(2)   Economic trends are bringing in their wake, at both national and Community level, changes in the structure of undertakings, through transfers of undertakings, businesses or parts of undertakings or businesses to other employers as a result of legal transfers or mergers.

(3)   It is necessary to provide for the protection of employees in the event of a change of employer, in particular, to ensure that their rights are safeguarded.

---

* Editors' Note: Please note that this directive has consolidated the old Directive 77/187/EEC and the subsequent amendments. A table of comparison between the old and new numberings may be found in Annex II of the Directive. Domestic implementation measures only had to change in Finland as a result of this consolidation, and can be found in the appended Implementation Table.

[1] Opinion delivered on 25 October 2000 (not yet published in the Official Journal).

[2] OJ C 367, 20.12.2000, p 21.

[3] OJ L 61, 5.3.1977, p 26.

[4] See Annex I, Part A.

(4)   Differences still remain in the Member States as regards the extent of the protection of employees in this respect and these differences should be reduced.

(5)   The Community Charter of the Fundamental Social Rights of Workers adopted on 9 December 1989 ("Social Charter") states, in points 7, 17 and 18 in particular that: "The completion of the internal market must lead to an improvement in the living and working conditions of workers in the European Community. The improvement must cover, where necessary, the development of certain aspects of employment regulations such as procedures for collective redundancies and those regarding bankruptcies. Information, consultation and participation for workers must be developed along appropriate lines, taking account of the practice in force in the various Member States. Such information, consultation and participation must be implemented in due time, particularly in connection with restructuring operations in undertakings or in cases of mergers having an impact on the employment of workers".

(6)   In 1977 the Council adopted Directive 77/187/EEC to promote the harmonisation of the relevant national laws ensuring the safeguarding of the rights of employees and requiring transferors and transferees to inform and consult employees' representatives in good time.

(7)   That Directive was subsequently amended in the light of the impact of the internal market, the legislative tendencies of the Member States with regard to the rescue of undertakings in economic difficulties, the case-law of the Court of Justice of the European Communities, Council Directive 75/129/EEC of 17 February 1975 on the approximation of the laws of the Member States relating to collective redundancies[5] and the legislation already in force in most Member States.

(8)   Considerations of legal security and transparency required that the legal concept of transfer be clarified in the light of the case-law of the Court of Justice. Such clarification has not altered the scope of Directive 77/187/EEC as interpreted by the Court of Justice.

(9)   The Social Charter recognises the importance of the fight against all forms of discrimination, especially based on sex, colour, race, opinion and creed.

(10)   This Directive should be without prejudice to the time limits set out in Annex I Part B within which the Member States are to comply with Directive 77/187/EEC, and the act amending it,

---

[5] OJ L 48, 22.2.1975, p 29. Directive replaced by Directive 98/59/EC (OJ L 225, 12.8.1998, p 16).

HAS ADOPTED THIS DIRECTIVE:

CHAPTER I

Scope and definitions

Article 1

(1) a) This Directive shall apply to any transfer of an undertaking, business, or part of an undertaking or business to another employer as a result of a legal transfer or merger.

    b) Subject to subparagraph (a) and the following provisions of this Article, there is a transfer within the meaning of this Directive where there is a transfer of an economic entity which retains its identity, meaning an organised grouping of resources which has the objective of pursuing an economic activity, whether or not that activity is central or ancillary.

    c) This Directive shall apply to public and private undertakings engaged in economic activities whether or not they are operating for gain. An administrative reorganisation of public administrative authorities, or the transfer of administrative functions between public administrative authorities, is not a transfer within the meaning of this Directive.

(2) This Directive shall apply where and insofar as the undertaking, business or part of the undertaking or business to be transferred is situated within the territorial scope of the Treaty.

(3) This Directive shall not apply to sea-going vessels.

Article 2

(1) For the purposes of this Directive:

    a) 'transferor' shall mean any natural or legal person who, by reason of a transfer within the meaning of Article 1(1), ceases to be the employer in respect of the undertaking, business or part of the undertaking or business;

    b) 'transferee' shall mean any natural or legal person who, by reason of a transfer within the meaning of Article 1(1), becomes the employer in respect of the undertaking, business or part of the undertaking or business;

    c) 'representatives of employees' and related expressions shall mean the representatives of the employees provided for by the laws or practices of the Member States;

d)   'employee' shall mean any person who, in the Member State concerned, is protected as an employee under national employment law.

(2)   This Directive shall be without prejudice to national law as regards the definition of contract of employment or employment relationship.

However, Member States shall not exclude from the scope of this Directive contracts of employment or employment relationships solely because:

a)   of the number of working hours performed or to be performed,

b)   they are employment relationships governed by a fixed-duration contract of employment within the meaning of Article 1(1) of Council Directive 91/383/EEC of 25 June 1991 supplementing the measures to encourage improvements in the safety and health at work of workers with a fixed-duration employment relationship or a temporary employment relationship,[6] or

c)   they are temporary employment relationships within the meaning of Article 1(2) of Directive 91/383/EEC, and the undertaking, business or part of the undertaking or business transferred is, or is part of, the temporary employment business which is the employer.

CHAPTER II

Safeguarding of employees' rights

Article 3

(1)   The transferor's rights and obligations arising from a contract of employment or from an employment relationship existing on the date of a transfer shall, by reason of such transfer, be transferred to the transferee.

Member States may provide that, after the date of transfer, the transferor and the transferee shall be jointly and severally liable in respect of obligations which arose before the date of transfer from a contract of employment or an employment relationship existing on the date of the transfer.

(2)   Member States may adopt appropriate measures to ensure that the transferor notifies the transferee of all the rights and obligations which will be transferred to the transferee under this Article, so far as those rights and obligations are or ought to have been known to the transferor at the time of the transfer. A failure by the transferor to notify

---

[6] OJ L206/91, p 19.

the transferee of any such right or obligation shall not affect the transfer of that right or obligation and the rights of any employees against the transferee and/or transferor in respect of that right or obligation.

(3) Following the transfer, the transferee shall continue to observe the terms and conditions agreed in any collective agreement on the same terms applicable to the transferor under that agreement, until the date of termination or expiry of the collective agreement or the entry into force or application of another collective agreement.

Member States may limit the period for observing such terms and conditions with the proviso that it shall not be less than one year.

(4) a) Unless Member States provide otherwise, paragraphs 1 and 3 shall not apply in relation to employees' rights to old-age, invalidity or survivors' benefits under supplementary company or inter-company pension schemes outside the statutory social security schemes in Member States.

b) Even where they do not provide in accordance with subparagraph (a) that paragraphs 1 and 3 apply in relation to such rights, Member States shall adopt the measures necessary to protect the interests of employees and of persons no longer employed in the transferor's business at the time of the transfer in respect of rights conferring on them immediate or prospective entitlement to old age benefits, including survivors' benefits, under supplementary schemes referred to in subparagraph (a).

Article 4

(1) The transfer of the undertaking, business or part of the undertaking or business shall not in itself constitute grounds for dismissal by the transferor or the transferee. This provision shall not stand in the way of dismissals that may take place for economic, technical or organisational reasons entailing changes in the workforce.

Member States may provide that the first subparagraph shall not apply to certain specific categories of employees who are not covered by the laws or practice of the Member States in respect of protection against dismissal.

(2) If the contract of employment or the employment relationship is terminated because the transfer involves a substantial change in working conditions to the detriment of the employee, the employer shall be regarded as having been responsible for termination of the contract of employment or of the employment relationship.

Article 5

(1) Unless Member States provide otherwise, Articles 3 and 4 shall not apply to any transfer of an undertaking, business or part of an undertaking or

business where the transferor is the subject of bankruptcy proceedings or any analogous insolvency proceedings which have been instituted with a view to the liquidation of the assets of the transferor and are under the supervision of a competent public authority (which may be an insolvency practitioner authorised by a competent public authority).

(2) Where Articles 3 and 4 apply to a transfer during insolvency proceedings which have been opened in relation to a transferor (whether or not those proceedings have been instituted with a view to the liquidation of the assets of the transferor) and provided that such proceedings are under the supervision of a competent public authority (which may be an insolvency practitioner determined by national law) a Member State may provide that:

a) notwithstanding Article 3(1), the transferor's debts arising from any contracts of employment or employment relationships and payable before the transfer or before the opening of the insolvency proceedings shall not be transferred to the transferee, provided that such proceedings give rise, under the law of that Member State, to protection at least equivalent to that provided for in situations covered by Council Directive 80/987/EEC of 20 October 1980 on the approximation of the laws of the Member States relating to the protection of employees in the event of the insolvency of their employer;[7] and, or alternatively, that

b) the transferee, transferor, or person or persons exercising the transferor's functions, on the one hand, and the representatives of the employees on the other hand may agree alterations, insofar as current law or practice permits, to the employees' terms and conditions of employment designed to safeguard employment opportunities by ensuring the survival of the undertaking, business or part of the undertaking or business.

(3) A Member State may apply paragraph 2(b) to any transfers where the transferor is in a situation of serious economic crisis, as defined by national law, provided that the situation is declared by a competent public authority and open to judicial supervision, on condition that such provisions already exist in national law by 17 July 1998.

The Commission shall present a report on the effects of this provision before 17 July 2003 and shall submit any appropriate proposals to the Council.

(4) Member States shall take appropriate measures with a view to preventing misuse of insolvency proceedings in such a way as to deprive employees of the rights provided for in this Directive.

---

[7] OJ L283/80, p 23. Regulation amended by Regulation 87/164/EEC (OJ L66/87, p 11).

Article 6

(1) If the undertaking, business or part of an undertaking or business preserves its autonomy, the status and function of the representatives or of the representation of the employees affected by the transfer shall be preserved on the same terms and subject to the same conditions as existed before the date of the transfer by virtue of law, regulation, administrative provision or agreement, provided that the conditions necessary for the constitution of the employees' representation are fulfilled.

The first subparagraph shall not apply if, under the laws, regulations, administrative provisions or practice in the Member States, or by agreement with the representatives of the employees, the conditions necessary for the reappointment of the representatives of the employees or for the reconstitution of the representation of the employees are fulfilled.

Where the transferor is the subject of bankruptcy proceedings or any analogous insolvency proceedings which have been instituted with a view to the liquidation of the assets of the transferor and are under the supervision of a competent public authority (which may be an insolvency practitioner authorised by a competent public authority), Member States may take the necessary measures to ensure that the transferred employees are properly represented until the new election or designation of representatives of the employees.

If the undertaking, business or part of an undertaking or business does not preserve its autonomy, the Member States shall take the necessary measures to ensure that the employees transferred who were represented before the transfer continue to be properly represented during the period necessary for the reconstitution or reappointment of the representation of employees in accordance with national law or practice.

(2) If the term of office of the representatives of the employees affected by the transfer expires as a result of the transfer, the representatives shall continue to enjoy the protection provided by the laws, regulations, administrative provisions or practice of the Member States.

CHAPTER III

Information and consultation

Article 7

(1) The transferor and transferee shall be required to inform the representatives of their respective employees affected by the transfer of the following:
 – the date or proposed date of the transfer,
 – the reasons for the transfer,

  –   the legal, economic and social implications of the transfer for the
      employees,
  –   any measures envisaged in relation to the employees.
      The transferor must give such information to the representatives of
  his employees in good time before the transfer is carried out.
      The transferee must give such information to the representatives of
  his employees in good time, and in any event before his employees are
  directly affected by the transfer as regards their conditions of work and
  employment.

(2) Where the transferor or the transferee envisages measures in relation
     to his employees, he shall consult the representatives of his employees
     in good time on such measures with a view to reaching an agreement.

(3) Member States whose laws, regulations or administrative provisions
     provide that representatives of the employees may have recourse to an
     arbitration board to obtain a decision on the measures to be taken in
     relation to employees may limit the obligations laid down in para-
     graphs 1 and 2 to cases where the transfer carried out gives rise to a
     change in the business likely to entail serious disadvantages for a con-
     siderable number of the employees.
     The information and consultations shall cover at least the measures
     envisaged in relation to the employees.
     The information must be provided and consultations taken place in
     good time before the change in the business as referred to in the first
     subparagraph is effected.

(4) The obligations laid down in this Article shall apply irrespective of
     whether the decision resulting in the transfer is taken by the employer
     or an undertaking controlling the employer.
     In considering alleged breaches of the information and consultation
     requirements laid down by this Directive, the argument that such a
     breach occurred because the information was not provided by an under-
     taking controlling the employer shall not be accepted as an excuse.

(5) Member States may limit the obligations laid down in paragraphs 1, 2
     and 3 to undertakings or businesses which, in terms of the number of
     employees, meet the conditions for the election or nomination of a
     collegiate body representing the employees.

(6) Member States shall provide that, where there are no representatives of
     the employees in an undertaking or business through no fault of their
     own, the employees concerned must be informed in advance of:
     –   the date or proposed date of the transfer,
     –   the reason for the transfer,
     –   the legal, economic and social implications of the transfer for the
         employees,
     –   any measures envisaged in relation to the employees.

CHAPTER IV

Final provisions

Article 8

This Directive shall not affect the right of Member States to apply or introduce laws, regulations or administrative provisions which are more favourable to employees or to promote or permit collective agreements or agreements between social partners more favourable to employees.

Article 9

Member States shall introduce into their national legal systems such measures as are necessary to enable all employees and representatives of employees who consider themselves wronged by failure to comply with the obligations arising from this Directive to pursue their claims by judicial process after possible recourse to other competent authorities.

Article 10

The Commission shall submit to the Council an analysis of the effects of the provisions of this Directive before 17 July 2006. It shall propose any amendment which may seem necessary.

Article 11

Member States shall communicate to the Commission the texts of the laws, regulations and administrative provisions which they adopt in the field covered by this Directive.

Article 12

Directive 77/187/EEC, as amended by the Directive referred to in Annex I, Part A, is repealed, without prejudice to the obligations of the Member States concerning the time limits for implementation set out in Annex I, Part B.

References to the repealed Directive shall be construed as references to this Directive and shall be read in accordance with the correlation table in Annex II.

Article 13

This Directive shall enter into force on the 20th day following its publication in the Official Journal of the European Communities.

Article 14

This Directive is addressed to the Member States.

Denmark	1. – Lov om lønmodtageres retsstilling, Lov Nr 111 af 1979
	2. – Lov om ændring af lov om lønmodtageres retstilling ved virksomhedsoverdragelse, Lov Nr 441 af 2001.
EIRE	European Communities (Safeguarding of Employees' Rights on Transfer of Undertakings) Regulations 1980, S.I. No. 306/1980.
Finland	Arbetsavtalslag ref: nr 55 du 26/01/2001, page 142
Sweden	No implementation provision indicated.
England	1. – Transfer of Undertakings (Protection of Employment) Regulations 1981, S.I. No 1981/1794.
	2. – Transfer of Undertakings (Protection of Employment) (Amendment) Regulations 1987, S.I. No. 1987/442
	3. – The Collective Redundancies and Transfer of Undertakings (Protection of Employment) (Amendment) Regulations 1999, S.I. No. 1999/1925
	4. – Transfer of Undertakings (Protection of Employment) (Amendment) Regulations 1999, S.I. No. 1999/2402
	5. – Transfer of Undertakings (Protection of Employment) (Rent Officer Service) Regulations 1999, S.I. No. 1999/2511.
	6. – Transfer of Undertakings (Protection of Employment) (Greater London Authority) Order 2000, S.I. No. 2000/686.

ANNEX I

PART A

Repealed Directive and its amending Directive

(referred to in Article 12)

Council Directive 77/187/EEC (OJ L 61, 5.3.1977, p 26)
Council Directive 98/50/EC (OJ L 201, 17.7.1998, p 88)

PART B

Deadlines for transposition into national law

(referred to in Article 12)

Omitted

ANNEX II

CORRELATION TABLE

Directive 77/187/EEC	This Directive
Article 1	Article 1
Article 2	Article 2
Article 3	Article 3
Article 4	Article 4
Article 4a	Article 5
Article 5	Article 6
Article 6	Article 7
Article 7	Article 8
Article 7a	Article 9
Article 7b	Article 10
Article 8	Article 11
–	Article 12
–	Article 13
–	Article 14
–	ANNEX I
–	ANNEX II

COUNCIL DIRECTIVE 86/653/EEC

of 18 December 1986

on the coordination of the laws of the Member States relating to self-employed commercial agents

(Official Journal, L382/86, p 17)

THE COUNCIL OF THE EUROPEAN COMMUNITIES –

Having regard to the Treaty establishing the European Economic Community, and in particular Articles 57(2) and 100 thereof,

Having regard to the proposal from the Commission,[1]

Having regard to the opinion of the European Parliament,[2]

Having regard to the opinion of the Economic and Social Committee,[3]

Whereas the restrictions on the freedom of establishment and the freedom to provide services in respect of activities of intermediaries in commerce, industry and small craft industries were abolished by Directive 64/224/EEC;[4]

Whereas the differences in national laws concerning commercial representation substantially affect the conditions of competition and the carrying-on of that activity within the Community and are detrimental both to the protection available to commercial agents vis-à-vis their principals and to the security of commercial transactions; whereas moreover those differences are such as to inhibit substantially the conclusion and operation of commercial representation contracts where principal and commercial agents are established in different Member States;

Whereas trade in goods between Member States should be carried on under conditions which are similar to those of a single market, and this necessitates approximation of the legal systems of the Member States to the extent required for the proper functioning of the common market; whereas in this regard the rules concerning conflict of laws do not, in the matter of commercial representation, remove the inconsistencies referred to above, nor would they even if they were made uniform, and accordingly the proposed harmonization is necessary notwithstanding the existence of those rules;

Whereas in this regard the legal relationship between commercial agent and principal must be given priority;

Whereas it is appropriate to be guided by the principles of Article 117 of the Treaty and to maintain improvements already made, when harmonizing the laws of the Member States relating to commercial agents;

---

[1] OJ C13/77, p 2; OJ C56/79, p 5.
[2] OJ C239/78, p 17.
[3] OJ C59/78, p 31.
[4] OJ 56/64, p 869/64.

Whereas additional transitional periods should be allowed for certain Member States which have to make a particular effort to adapt their regulations, especially those concerning indemnity for termination of contract between the principal and the commercial agent, to the requirements of this Directive,

HAS ADOPTED THIS DIRECTIVE:

CHAPTER I

Scope

Article 1

(1) The harmonization measures prescribed by this Directive shall apply to the laws, regulations and administrative provisions of the Member States governing the relations between commercial agents and their principals.

(2) For the purposes of this Directive, 'commercial agent' shall mean a self-employed intermediary who has continuing authority to negotiate the sale or the purchase of goods on behalf of another person, hereinafter called the 'principal', or to negotiate and conclude such transactions on behalf of and in the name of that principal.

(3) A commercial agent shall be understood within the meaning of this Directive as not including in particular:
   – a person who, in his capacity as an officer, is empowered to enter into commitments binding on a company or association,
   – a partner who is lawfully authorized to enter into commitments binding on his partners,
   – a receiver, a receiver and manager, a liquidator or a trustee in bankruptcy.

Article 2

(1) This Directive shall not apply to:
   – commercial agents whose activities are unpaid,
   – commercial agents when they operate on commodity exchanges or in the commodity market, or
   – the body known as the Crown Agents for Overseas Governments and Administrations, as set up under the Crown Agents Act 1979 in the United Kingdom, or its subsidiaries.

(2) Each of the Member States shall have the right to provide that the Directive shall not apply to those persons whose activities as commercial agents are considered secondary by the law of that Member State.

CHAPTER II

Rights and obligations

Article 3

(1)   In performing his activities a commercial agent must look after his principal's interests and act dutifully and in good faith.

(2)   In particular, a commercial agent must:
   a)   make proper efforts to negotiate and, where appropriate, conclude the transactions he is instructed to take care of;
   b)   communicate to his principal all the necessary information available to him;
   c)   comply with reasonable instructions given by his principal.

Article 4

(1)   In his relations with his commercial agent a principal must act dutifully and in good faith.

(2)   A principal must in particular:
   a)   provide his commercial agent with the necessary documentation relating to the goods concerned;
   b)   obtain for his commercial agent the information necessary for the performance of the agency contract, and in particular notify the commercial agent within a reasonable period once he anticipates that the volume of commercial transactions will be significantly lower than that which the commercial agent could normally have expected.

(3)   A principal must, in addition, inform the commercial agent within a reasonable period of his acceptance, refusal, and of any non-execution of a commercial transaction which the commercial agent has procured for the principal.

Article 5

The parties may not derogate from the provisions of Articles 3 and 4.

CHAPTER III

Remuneration

Article 6

(1)   In the absence of any agreement on this matter between the parties, and without prejudice to the application of the compulsory provisions

of the Member States concerning the level of remuneration, a commercial agent shall be entitled to the remuneration that commercial agents appointed for the goods forming the subject of his agency contract are customarily allowed in the place where he carries on his activities. If there is no such customary practice a commercial agent shall be entitled to reasonable remuneration taking into account all the aspects of the transaction.

(2)   Any part of the remuneration which varies with the number or value of business transactions shall be deemed to be commission within the meaning of this Directive.

(3)   Articles 7 to 12 shall not apply if the commercial agent is not remunerated wholly or in part by commission.

Article 7

(1)   A commercial agent shall be entitled to commission on commercial transactions concluded during the period covered by the agency contract:

a)   where the transaction has been concluded as a result of his action; or

b)   where the transaction is concluded with a third party whom he has previously acquired as a customer for transactions of the same kind.

(2)   A commercial agent shall also be entitled to commission on transactions concluded during the period covered by the agency contract:

–   either where he is entrusted with a specific geographical area or group of customers,

–   or where he has an exclusive right to a specific geographical area or group of customers, and where the transaction has been entered into with a customer belonging to that area or group.

Member State shall include in their legislation one of the possibilities referred to in the above two indents.

Article 8

A commercial agent shall be entitled to commission on commercial transactions concluded after the agency contract has terminated:

a)   if the transaction is mainly attributable to the commercial agent's efforts during the period covered by the agency contract and if the transaction was entered into within a reasonable period after that contract terminated; or

b) if, in accordance with the conditions mentioned in Article 7, the order of the third party reached the principal or the commercial agent before the agency contract terminated.

Article 9

A commercial agent shall not be entitled to the commission referred to in Article 7, if that commission is payable, pursuant to Article 8, to the previous commercial agent, unless it is equitable because of the circumstances for the commission to be shared between the commercial agents.

Article 10

(1) The commission shall become due as soon as and to the extent that one of the following circumstances obtains:
   a) the principal has executed the transaction; or
   b) the principal should, according to his agreement with the third party, have executed the transaction; or
   c) the third party has executed the transaction.
(2) The commission shall become due at the latest when the third party has executed his part of the transaction or should have done so if the principal had executed his part of the transaction, as he should have.
(3) The commission shall be paid not later than on the last day of the month following the quarter in which it became due.
(4) Agreements to derogate from paragraphs 2 and 3 to the detriment of the commercial agent shall not be permitted.

Article 11

(1) The right to commission can be extinguished only if and to the extent that:
   – it is established that the contract between the third party and the principal will not be executed, and
   – that fact is due to a reason for which the principal is not to blame.
(2) Any commission which the commercial agent has already received shall be refunded if the right to it is extinguished.
(3) Agreements to derogate from paragraph 1 to the detriment of the commercial agent shall not be permitted.

Article 12

(1) The principal shall supply his commercial agent with a statement of the commission due, not later than the last day of the month following

the quarter in which the commission has become due. This statement shall set out the main components used in calculating the amount of commission.

(2) A commercial agent shall be entitled to demand that he be provided with all the information, and in particular an extract from the books, which is available to his principal and which he needs in order to check the amount of the commission due to him.

(3) Agreements to derogate from paragraphs 1 and 2 to the detriment of the commercial agent shall not be permitted.

(4) This Directive shall not conflict with the internal provisions of Member States which recognize the right of a commercial agent to inspect a principal's books.

CHAPTER IV

Conclusion and termination of the agency contract

Article 13

(1) Each party shall be entitled to receive from the other on request a signed written document setting out the terms of the agency contract including any terms subsequently agreed. Waiver of this right shall not be permitted.

(2) Notwithstanding paragraph 1 a Member State may provide that an agency contract shall not be valid unless evidenced in writing.

Article 14

An agency contract for a fixed period which continues to be performed by both parties after that period has expired shall be deemed to be converted into an agency contract for an indefinite period.

Article 15

(1) Where an agency contract is concluded for an indefinite period either party may terminate it by notice.

(2) The period of notice shall be one month for the first year of the contract, two months for the second year commenced, and three months for the third year commenced and subsequent years. The parties may not agree on shorter periods of notice.

(3) Member States may fix the period of notice at four months for the fourth year of the contract, five months for the fifth year and six

months for the sixth and subsequent years. They may decide that the parties may not agree to shorter periods.

(4) If the parties agree on longer periods than those laid down in paragraphs 2 and 3, the period of notice to be observed by the principal must not be shorter than that to be observed by the commercial agent.

(5) Unless otherwise agreed by the parties, the end of the period of notice must coincide with the end of a calendar month.

(6) The provision of this Article shall apply to an agency contract for a fixed period where it is converted under Article 14 into an agency contract for an indefinite period, subject to the proviso that the earlier fixed period must be taken into account in the calculation of the period of notice.

Article 16

Nothing in this Directive shall affect the application of the law of the Member States where the latter provides for the immediate termination of the agency contract:

a) because of the failure of one party to carry out all or part of his obligations;

b) where exceptional circumstances arise.

Article 17

(1) Member States shall take the measures necessary to ensure that the commercial agent is, after termination of the agency contract, indemnified in accordance with paragraph 2 or compensated for damage in accordance with paragraph 3.

(2) a) The commercial agent shall be entitled to an indemnity if and to the extent that:
   – he has brought the principal new customers or has significantly increased the volume of business with existing customers and the principal continues to derive substantial benefits from the business with such customers, and
   – the payment of this indemnity is equitable having regard to all the circumstances and, in particular, the commission lost by the commercial agent on the business transacted with such customers. Member States may provide forsuch circumstances also to include the application or otherwise of a restraint of trade clause, within the meaning of Article 20;

b)   The amount of the indemnity may not exceed a figure equivalent to an indemnity for one year calculated from the commercial agent's average annual remuneration over the preceding five years and if the contract goes back less than five years the indemnity shall be calculated on the average for the period in question;

c)   The grant of such an indemnity shall not prevent the commercial agent from seeking damages.

(3)   The commercial agent shall be entitled to compensation for the damage he suffers as a result of the termination of his relations with the principal.

Such damage shall be deemed to occur particularly when the termination takes place in circumstances:

–   depriving the commercial agent of the commission which proper performance of the agency contract would have procured him whilst providing the principal with substantial benefits linked to the commercial agent's activities,

–   and/or which have not enabled the commercial agent to amortize the costs and expenses that he had incurred for the performance of the agency contract on the principal's advice.

(4)   Entitlement to the indemnity as provided for in paragraph 2 or to compensation for damage as provided for under paragraph 3, shall also arise where the agency contract is terminated as a result of the commercial agent's death.

(5)   The commercial agent shall lose his entitlement to the indemnity in the instances provided for in paragraph 2 or to compensation for damage in the instances provided for in paragraph 3, if within one year following termination of the contract he has not notified the principal that he intends pursuing his entitlement.

(6)   The Commission shall submit to the Council, within eight years following the date of notification of this Directive, a report on the implementation of this Article, and shall if necessary submit to it proposals for amendments.

Article 18

The indemnity or compensation referred to in Article 17 shall not be payable:

a)   where the principal has terminated the agency contract because of default attributable to the commercial agent which would justify immediate termination of the agency contract under national law;

b)   where the commercial agent has terminated the agency contract, unless such termination is justified by circumstances attributable to the principal or on grounds of age, infirmity or illness of the commercial agent in consequence of which he cannot reasonably be required to continue his activities;

c) where, with the agreement of the principal, the commercial agent assigns his rights and duties under the agency contract to another person.

Article 19

The parties may not derogate from Articles 17 and 18 to the detriment of the commercial agent before the agency contract expires.

Article 20

(1) For the purposes of this Directive an agreement restricting the business activities of a commercial agent following termination of the agency contract is hereinafter referred to as a restraint of trade clause.

(2) A restraint of trade clause shall be valid only if and to the extent that:
 a) it is concluded in writing; and
 b) it relates to the geographical area or the group of customers and the geographical area entrusted to the commercial agent and to the kind of goods covered by his agency under the contract.

(3) A restraint of trade clause shall be valid for not more than two years after termination of the agency contract.

(4) This Article shall not affect provisions of national law which impose other restrictions on the validity or enforceability of restraint of trade clauses or which enable the courts to reduce the obligations on the parties resulting from such an agreement.

CHAPTER V

General and final provisions

Article 21

Nothing in this Directive shall require a Member State to provide for the disclosure of information where such disclosure would be contrary to public policy.

Article 22

(1) Member States shall bring into force the provisions necessary to comply with this Directive before 1 January 1990. They shall forthwith inform the Commission thereof. Such provisions shall apply at least to contracts concluded after their entry into force. They shall apply to contracts in operation by 1 January 1994 at the latest.

(2) As from the notification of this Directive, Member States shall communicate to the Commission the main laws, regulations and administrative provisions which they adopt in the field governed by this Directive.

(3) However, with regard to Ireland and the United Kingdom, 1 January 1990 referred to in paragraph 1 shall be replaced by 1 January 1994.

With regard to Italy, 1 January 1990 shall be replaced by 1 January 1993 in the case of the obligations deriving from Article 17.

Article 23

This Directive is addressed to the Member States.

Denmark	Lov om handelsagenter og handelsrejsender, Lov Nr 272 af 02/05/1990
EIRE	1. – European Communities (Commercial Agents) Regulations 1994, S.I. No. 33/1994
	2. – European Communities (Commercial Agents) Regulations, 1997, S.I. No. 31/1997
Finland	Laki kauppaedustajista ja myyntimiehistä (417/92) 08/05/1992
Sweden	Lag om handelsagentur, SFS 1991:351.
United Kingdom	1. – The Commercial Agents (Council Directive) Regulations 1993, S.I. No. 1993/3053
	2. – The Commercial Agents (Council Directive) Regulations 1998, S.I. No. 1998/2868

COUNCIL DIRECTIVE 90/314/EEC

of 13 June 1990

on package travel, package holidays and package tours

(Official Journal, L158/90, p 59)

THE COUNCIL OF THE EUROPEAN COMMUNITIES –

Having regard to the Treaty establishing the European Economic Community, and in particular Article 100a thereof,

Having regard to the proposal from the Commission,[1]

In cooperation with the European Parliament,[2]

Having regard to the opinion of the Economic and Social Committee,[3]

Whereas one of the main objectives of the Community is to complete the internal market, of which the tourist sector is an essential part;

Whereas the national laws of Member States concerning package travel, package holidays and package tours, hereinafter referred to as 'packages', show many disparities and national practices in this field are markedly different, which gives rise to obstacles to the freedom to provide services in respect of packages and distortions of competition amongst operators established in different Member States;

Whereas the establishment of common rules on packages will contribute to the elimination of these obstacles and thereby to the achievement of a common market in services, thus enabling operators established in one Member State to offer their services in other Member States and Community consumers to benefit from comparable conditions when buying a package in any Member State;

Whereas paragraph 36(b) of the Annex to the Council resolution of 19 May 1981 on a second programme of the European Economic Community for a consumer protection and information policy[4] invites the Commission to study, inter alia, tourism and, if appropriate, to put forward suitable proposals, with due regard for their significance for consumer protection and the effects of differences in Member States' legislation on the proper functioning of the common market;

Whereas in the resolution on a Community policy on tourism on 10 April 1984[5] the Council welcomed the Commission's initiative in drawing attention to the importance of tourism and took note of the Commission's initial guidelines for a Community policy on tourism;

[1] OJ C96/88, p 5.
[2] OJ C69/89, p 120, and OJ C149/90.
[3] OJ C102/89, p 27.
[4] OJ C165/81, p 24.
[5] OJ C115/84, p 1.

Whereas the Commission communication to the Council entitled 'A New Impetus for Consumer Protection Policy', which was approved by resolution of the Council on 6 May 1986,[6] lists in paragraph 37, among the measures proposed by the Commission, the harmonization of legislation on packages;

Whereas tourism plays an increasingly important role in the economies of the Member States; whereas the package system is a fundamental part of tourism; whereas the package travel industry in Member States would be stimulated to greater growth and productivity if at least a minimum of common rules were adopted in order to give it a Community dimension; whereas this would not only produce benefits for Community citizens buying packages organized on the basis of those rules, but would attract tourists from outside the Community seeking the advantages of guaranteed standards in packages;

Whereas disparities in the rules protecting consumers in different Member States are a disincentive to consumers in one Member State from buying packages in another Member State;

Whereas this disincentive is particularly effective in deterring consumers from buying packages outside their own Member State, and more effective than it would be in relation to the acquisition of other services, having regard to the special nature of the services supplied in a package which generally involve the expenditure of substantial amounts of money in advance and the supply of the services in a State other than that in which the consumer is resident;

Whereas the consumer should have the benefit of the protection introduced by this Directive irrespective of whether he is a direct contracting party, a transferee or a member of a group on whose behalf another person has concluded a contract in respect of a package;

Whereas the organizer of the package and/or the retailer of it should be under obligation to ensure that in descriptive matter relating to packages which they respectively organize and sell, the information which is given is not misleading and brochures made available to consumers contain information which is comprehensible and accurate;

Whereas the consumer needs to have a record of the terms of contract applicable to the package; whereas this can conveniently be achieved by requiring that all the terms of the contract be stated in writing or such other documentary form as shall be comprehensible and accessible to him, and that he be given a copy thereof;

Whereas the consumer should be at liberty in certain circumstances to transfer to a willing third person a booking made by him for a package;

Whereas the price established under the contract should not in principle be subject to revision except where the possibility of upward or downward revision is expressly provided for in the contract; whereas that possibility should nonetheless be subject to certain conditions;

Whereas the consumer should in certain circumstances be free to withdraw before departure from a package travel contract;

Whereas there should be a clear definition of the rights available to the consumer in circumstances where the organizer of the package cancels it before the agreed date of departure;

[6] OJ C118/86, p 28.

Whereas if, after the consumer has departed, there occurs a significant failure of performance of the services for which he has contracted or the organizer perceives that he will be unable to procure a significant part of the services to be provided; the organizer should have certain obligations towards the consumer;

Whereas the organizer and/or retailer party to the contract should be liable to the consumer for the proper performance of the obligations arising from the contract; whereas, moreover, the organizer and/or retailer should be liable for the damage resulting for the consumer from failure to perform or improper performance of the contract unless the defects in the performance of the contract are attributable neither to any fault of theirs nor to that of another supplier of services;

Whereas in cases where the organizer and/or retailer is liable for failure to perform or improper performance of the services involved in the package, such liability should be limited in accordance with the international conventions governing such services, in particular the Warsaw Convention of 1929 in International Carriage by Air, the Berne Convention of 1961 on Carriage by Rail, the Athens Convention of 1974 on Carriage by Sea and the Paris Convention of 1962 on the Liability of Hotel-keepers; whereas, moreover, with regard to damage other than personal injury, it should be possible for liability also to be limited under the package contract provided, however, that such limits are not unreasonable;

Whereas certain arrangements should be made for the information of consumers and the handling of complaints;

Whereas both the consumer and the package travel industry would benefit if organizers and/or retailers were placed under an obligation to provide sufficient evidence of security in the event of insolvency;

Whereas Member States should be at liberty to adopt, or retain, more stringent provisions relating to package travel for the purpose of protecting the consumer,

HAS ADOPTED THIS DIRECTIVE:

Article 1

The purpose of this Directive is to approximate the laws, regulations and administrative provisions of the Member States relating to packages sold or offered for sale in the territory of the Community.

Article 2

For the purposes of this Directive:

1. 'package' means the pre-arranged combination of not fewer than two of the following when sold or offered for sale at an inclusive price and when the service covers a period of more than twenty-four hours or includes overnight accommodation:
    a) transport;
    b) accommodation;

    c)   other tourist services not ancillary to transport or accommodation and accounting for a significant proportion of the package.

          The separate billing of various components of the same package shall not absolve the organizer or retailer from the obligations under this Directive;

2.   'organizer' means the person who, other than occasionally, organizes packages and sells or offers them for sale, whether directly or through a retailer;

3.   'retailer' means the person who sells or offers for sale the package put together by the organizer;

4.   'consumer' means the person who takes or agrees to take the package ('the principal contractor'), or any person on whose behalf the principal contractor agrees to purchase the package ('the other beneficiaries') or any person to whom the principal contractor or any of the other beneficiaries transfers the package ('the transferee');

5.   'contract' means the agreement linking the consumer to the organizer and/or the retailer.

Article 3

(1)   Any descriptive matter concerning a package and supplied by the organizer or the retailer to the consumer, the price of the package and any other conditions applying to the contract must not contain any misleading information.

(2)   When a brochure is made available to the consumer, it shall indicate in a legible, comprehensible and accurate manner both the price and adequate information concerning:

    a)   the destination and the means, characteristics and categories of transport used;

    b)   the type of accommodation, its location, category or degree of comfort and its main features, its approval and tourist classification under the rules of the host Member State concerned;

    c)   the meal plan;

    d)   the itinerary;

    e)   general information on passport and visa requirements for nationals of the Member State or States concerned and health formalities required for the journey and the stay;

    f)   either the monetary amount or the percentage of the price which is to be paid on account, and the timetable for payment of the balance;

    g)   whether a minimum number of persons is required for the package to take place and, if so, the deadline for informing the consumer in the event of cancellation.

The particulars contained in the brochure are binding on the organizer or retailer, unless:

– changes in such particulars have been clearly communicated to the consumer before conclusion of the contract, in which case the brochure shall expressly state so,
– changes are made later following an agreement between the parties to the contract.

Article 4

(1) a) The organizer and/or the retailer shall provide the consumer, in writing or any other appropriate form, before the contract is concluded, with general information on passport and visa requirements applicable to nationals of the Member State or States concerned and in particular on the periods for obtaining them, as well as with information on the health formalities required for the journey and the stay;

   b) The organizer and/or retailer shall also provide the consumer, in writing or any other appropriate form, with the following information in good time before the start of the journey:

   i) the times and places of intermediate stops and transport connections as well as details of the place to be occupied by the traveller, e.g. cabin or berth on ship, sleeper compartment on train;

   ii) the name, address and telephone number of the organizer's and/or retailer's local representative or, failing that, of local agencies on whose assistance a consumer in difficulty could call.

   Where no such representatives or agencies exist, the consumer must in any case be provided with an emergency telephone number or any other information that will enable him to contract the organizer and/or the retailer;

   iii) in the case of journeys or stays abroad by minors, information enabling direct contact to be established with the child or the person responsible at the child's place of stay;

   iv) information on the optional conclusion of an insurance policy to cover the cost of cancellation by the consumer or the cost of assistance, including repatriation, in the event of accident or illness.

(2) Member States shall ensure that in relation to the contract the following principles apply:

   a) depending on the particular package, the contract shall contain at least the elements listed in the Annex;

   b)   all the terms of the contract are set out in writing or such other
        form as is comprehensible and accessible to the consumer and must
        be communicated to him before the conclusion of the contract; the
        consumer is given a copy of these terms;
   c)   the provision under (b) shall not preclude the belated conclusion
        of last-minute reservations or contracts.
(3) Where the consumer is prevented from proceeding with the package,
    he may transfer his booking, having first given the organizer or the
    retailer reasonable notice of his intention before departure, to a person
    who satisfies all the conditions applicable to the package. The trans-
    feror of the package and the transferee shall be jointly and severally
    liable to the organizer or retailer party to the contract for payment of
    the balance due and for any additional costs arising from such transfer.
(4) a)   The prices laid down in the contract shall not be subject to revi-
         sion unless the contract expressly provides for the possibility of
         upward or downward revision and states precisely how
         the revised price is to be calculated, and solely to allow for
         variations in:
         –   transportation costs, including the cost of fuel,
         –   dues, taxes or fees chargeable for certain services, such as
              landing taxes or embarkation or disembarkation fees at ports
              and airports,
         –   the exchange rates applied to the particular package.
   b)   During the twenty days prior to the departure date stipulated, the
        price stated in the contract shall not be increased.
(5) If the organizer finds that before the departure he is constrained to
    alter significantly any of the essential terms, such as the price, he shall
    notify the consumer as quickly as possible in order to enable him to
    take appropriate decisions and in particular:
    –   either to withdraw from the contract without penalty,
    –   or to accept a rider to the contract specifying the alterations made
         and their impact on the price.
              The consumer shall inform the organizer or the retailer of his
         decision as soon as possible.
(6) If the consumer withdraws from the contract pursuant to paragraph 5,
    or if, for whatever cause, other than the fault of the consumer, the
    organizer cancels the package before the agreed date of departure, the
    consumer shall be entitled:
    a)   either to take a substitute package of equivalent or higher quality
         where the organizer and/or retailer is able to offer him such a sub-
         stitute. If the replacement package offered is of lower quality, the
         organizer shall refund the difference in price to the consumer;
    b)   or to be repaid as soon as possible all sums paid by him under the
         contract.

In such a case, he shall be entitled, if appropriate, to be compensated by either the organizer or the retailer, whichever the relevant Member State's law requires, for non-performance of the contract, except where:

i) cancellation is on the grounds that the number of persons enrolled for the package is less than the minimum number required and the consumer is informed of the cancellation, in writing, within the period indicated in the package description; or

ii) cancellation, excluding overbooking, is for reasons of force majeure, i.e. unusual and unforeseeable circumstances beyond the control of the party by whom it is pleaded, the consequences of which could not have been avoided even if all due care had been exercised.

(7) Where, after departure, a significant proportion of the services contracted for is not provided or the organizer perceives that he will be unable to procure a significant proportion of the services to be provided, the organizer shall make suitable alternative arrangements, at no extra cost to the consumer, for the continuation of the package, and where appropriate compensate the consumer for the difference between the services offered and those supplied.

If it is impossible to make such arrangements or these are not accepted by the consumer for good reasons, the organizer shall, where appropriate, provide the consumer, at no extra cost, with equivalent transport back to the place of departure, or to another return-point to which the consumer has agreed and shall, where appropriate, compensate the consumer.

Article 5

(1) Member States shall take the necessary steps to ensure that the organizer and/or retailer party to the contract is liable to the consumer for the proper performance of the obligations arising from the contract, irrespective of whether such obligations are to be performed by that organizer and/or retailer or by other suppliers of services without prejudice to the right of the organizer and/or retailer to pursue those other suppliers of services.

(2) With regard to the damage resulting for the consumer from the failure to perform or the improper performance of the contract, Member States shall take the necessary steps to ensure that the organizer and/or retailer is/are liable unless such failure to perform or improper performance is attributable neither to any fault of theirs nor to that of another supplier of services, because:

−   the failures which occur in the performance of the contract are attributable to the consumer,

- such failures are attributable to a third party unconnected with the provision of the services contracted for, and are unforeseeable or unavoidable,
- such failures are due to a case of force majeure such as that defined in Article 4 (6), second subparagraph (ii), or to an event which the organizer and/or retailer or the supplier of services, even with all due care, could not foresee or forestall.

    In the cases referred to in the second and third indents, the organizer and/or retailer party to the contract shall be required to give prompt assistance to a consumer in difficulty.

    In the matter of damages arising from the non-performance or improper performance of the services involved in the package, the Member States may allow compensation to be limited in accordance with the international conventions governing such services.

    In the matter of damage other than personal injury resulting from the non-performance or improper performance of the services involved in the package, the Member States may allow compensation to be limited under the contract. Such limitation shall not be unreasonable.

(3) Without prejudice to the fourth subparagraph of paragraph 2, there may be no exclusion by means of a contractual clause from the provisions of paragraphs 1 and 2.

(4) The consumer must communicate any failure in the performance of a contract which he perceives on the spot to the supplier of the services concerned and to the organizer and/or retailer in writing or any other appropriate form at the earliest opportunity.

This obligation must be stated clearly and explicitly in the contract.

Article 6

In cases of complaint, the organizer and/or retailer or his local representative, if there is one, must make prompt efforts to find appropriate solutions.

Article 7

The organizer and/or retailer party to the contract shall provide sufficient evidence of security for the refund of money paid over and for the repatriation of the consumer in the event of insolvency.

Article 8

Member States may adopt or return more stringent provisions in the field covered by this Directive to protect the consumer.

Article 9

(1) Member States shall bring into force the measures necessary to comply with this Directive before 31 December 1992. They shall forthwith inform the Commission thereof.

(2) Member States shall communicate to the Commission the texts of the main provisions of national law which they adopt in the field governed by this Directive. The Commission shall inform the other Member States thereof.

Article 10

This Directive is addressed to the Member States.

ANNEX

Elements to be included in the contract if relevant to the particular package:

a) the travel destination(s) and, where periods of stay are involved, the relevant periods, with dates;

b) the means, characteristics and categories of transport to be used, the dates, times and points of departure and return;

c) where the package includes accommodation, its location, its tourist category or degree of comfort, its main features, its compliance with the rules of the host Member State concerned and the meal plan;

d) whether a minimum number of persons is required for the package to take place and, if so, the deadline for informing the consumer in the event of cancellation;

e) the itinerary;

f) visits, excursions or other services which are included in the total price agreed for the package;

g) the name and address of the organizer, the retailer and, where appropriate, the insurer;

h) the price of the package, an indication of the possibility of price revisions under Article 4(4) and an indication of any dues, taxes or fees chargeable for certain services (landing, embarkation or disembarkation fees at ports and airports, tourist taxes) where such costs are not included in the package;

i) the payment schedule and method of payment;

j) special requirements which the consumer has communicated to the organizer or retailer when making the booking, and which both have accepted;

k) periods within which the consumer must make any complaint concerning failure to perform or improper performance of the contract.

Denmark	1. – Lov om ændring af lov om rejsegarantifond, Lov Nr. 454 af 30/06/1993, 2. – Lov om pakkerrejser, Lov Nr 472 af 30/06/1993, 3. – Bekendtgørelse nr. 776 af 21/09/1993, om ændring af lov em rejsegarantifond 4. – Lov om markedsføring, Lov Nr 428 af 01/06/1994 5. – Lov om en rejsegarantifond, Lov Nr 315 af 14/05/1997
EIRE	The Package Holidays and Travel Trade Act 1995
Finland	1. – Valmismatkalaki (1079/94) 28/11/1994 2. – Laki valmismatkaliikkeistä (1080/94) 28/11/1994 3. – Landskapslag om resebyrårörelse (56/75) 26/11/1975 4. – Asetus valmismatkasta annettavista tiedoista annetun asetuksen 5 ja 7 :n muuttamisesta/Förordning om ändring av 5 och 7 förordningen om de uppgifter som skall ges om paketresor (372/98) 29/05/1998
Sweden	1. – Lag om paketresor, SFS 1992:1672 2. – Lag om ändring i resegarantilagen (1972:204), SFS 1992:1673 3. – Lag om ändring i sjölagen (1891:35 s. 1), SFS 1992:1674 4. – Konsumentverkets föreskrifter och allmänna råd om paketresor, Konsumentverkets författningssamling (KOVFS) 1993:3
United Kingdom	1. – The Package Travel, Package Holidays and Package Tours Regulations 1992, S.I. No 1992/3288. 3. – The Package Travel, Package Holidays and Package Tours (Amendment) Regulations 1998, S.I. No. 1998/1208.

DIRECTIVE 97/5/EC OF THE EUROPEAN PARLIAMENT AND OF THE COUNCIL

of 27 January 1997

on cross-border credit transfers*

(Official Journal, L43/97, p 25)

THE EUROPEAN PARLIAMENT AND THE COUNCIL OF THE EUROPEAN UNION –

Having regard to the Treaty establishing the European Community, and in particular Article 100a thereof,

Having regard to the proposal from the Commission,[1]

Having regard to the opinion of the Economic and Social Committee,[2]

Having regard to the opinion of the European Monetary Institute,

Acting in accordance with the procedure laid down in Article 189b of the Treaty[3] in the light of the joint text approved on 22 November 1996 by the Conciliation Committee,

(1) Whereas the volume of cross-border payments is growing steadily as completion of the internal market and progress towards full economic and monetary union lead to greater trade and movement of people within the Community; whereas cross-border credit transfers account for a substantial part of the volume and value of cross-border payments;

(2) Whereas it is essential for individuals and businesses, especially small and medium-sized enterprises, to be able to make credit transfers rapidly, reliably and cheaply from one part of the Community to another; whereas, in conformity with the Commission Notice on the application of the EC competition rules to cross-border credit transfers,[4] greater competition in the market for cross-border credit transfers should lead to improved services and reduced prices;

---

* This Directive was implemented in the United Kingdom by the Cross-Border Credit Transfer Regulations 1999 (SI 1999/1876), which came into force on 14 August 1999.

[1] OJ C360/94, p 13, and OJ C199/95, p 16.

[2] OJ C236/95, p 1.

[3] Opinion of the European Parliament of 19 May 1995 (OJ C151/95, p 370); Council common position of 4 December 1995 (OJ C353/95, p 52) and Decision of the European Parliament of 13 March 1996 (OJ C96/96, p 74); Decision of the Council of 19 December 1996 and Decision of the European Parliament of 16 January 1997.

[4] OJ C251/95, p 3.

(3) Whereas this Directive seeks to follow up the progress made towards completion of the internal market, in particular towards liberalization of capital movements, with a view to the implementation of economic and monetary union; whereas its provisions must apply to credit transfers in the currencies of the Member States and in ecus;

(4) Whereas the European Parliament, in its resolution of 12 February 1993,[5] called for a Council Directive to lay down rules in the area of transparency and performance of cross-border payments;

(5) Whereas the issues covered by this Directive must be dealt with separately from the systemic issues which remain under consideration within the Commission; whereas it may become necessary to make a further proposal to cover these systemic issues, particularly the problem of settlement finality;

(6) Whereas the purpose of this Directive is to improve cross-border credit transfer services and thus assist the European Monetary Institute (EMI) in its task of promoting the efficiency of cross-border payments with a view to the preparation of the third stage of economic and monetary union;

(7) Whereas, in line with the objectives set out in the second recital, this Directive should apply to any credit transfer of an amount of less than ECU 50 000;

(8) Whereas, having regard to the third paragraph of Article 3b of the Treaty, and with a view to ensuring transparency, this Directive lays down the minimum requirements needed to ensure an adequate level of customer information both before and after the execution of a cross-border credit transfer; whereas these requirements include indication of the complaints and redress procedures offered to customers, together with the arrangements for access thereto; whereas this Directive lays down minimum execution requirements, in particular in terms of performance, which institutions offering cross-border credit transfer services should adhere to, including the obligation to execute a cross-border credit transfer in accordance with the customer's instructions; whereas this Directive fulfils the conditions deriving from the principles set out in Commission Recommendation 90/109/EEC of 14 February 1990 on the transparency of banking conditions relating to cross-border financial transactions;[6] whereas this Directive is without prejudice to Council Directive 91/308/EEC of 10 June 1991 on prevention of the use of the financial system for the purpose of money laundering;[7]

(9) Whereas this Directive should contribute to reducing the maximum time taken to execute a cross-border credit transfer and encourage

[5] OJ C72/93, p 158.
[6] OJ L67/90, p 39.
[7] OJ L166/91, p 77.

those institutions which already take a very short time to do so to maintain that practice;

(10) Whereas the Commission, in the report it will submit to the European Parliament and the Council within two years of implementation of this Directive, should particularly examine the time-limit to be applied in the absence of a time-limit agreed between the originator and his institution, taking into account both technical developments and the situation existing in each Member State;

(11) Whereas there should be an obligation upon institutions to refund in the event of a failure to successfully complete a credit transfer; whereas the obligation to refund imposes a contingent liability on institutions which might, in the absence of any limit, have a prejudicial effect on solvency requirements; whereas that obligation to refund should therefore be applicable up to ECU 12 500;

(12) Whereas Article 8 does not affect the general provisions of national law whereby an institution has responsibility towards the originator when a cross-border credit transfer has not been completed because of an error committed by that institution;

(13) Whereas it is necessary to distinguish, among the circumstances with which institutions involved in the execution of a cross-border credit transfer may be confronted, including circumstances relating to insolvency, those caused by force majeure; whereas for that purpose the definition of force majeure given in Article 4(6) of Directive 90/314/EEC of 13 June 1990 on package travel, package holidays and package tours[8] should be taken as a basis;

(14) Whereas there need to be adequate and effective complaints and redress procedures in the Member States for the settlement of possible disputes between customers and institutions, using existing procedures where appropriate.

HAVE ADOPTED THIS DIRECTIVE:

SECTION I

SCOPE AND DEFINITIONS

Article 1

Scope

The provisions of this Directive shall apply to cross-border credit transfers in the currencies of the Member States and the ECU up to the equivalent of ECU 50 000

---

[8] OJ L158/90, p 59.

ordered by persons other than those referred to in Article 2(a), (b) and (c) and executed by credit institutions or other institutions.

Article 2

Definitions

For the purposes of this Directive:

a) 'credit institution' means an institution as defined in Article 1 of Council Directive 77/780/EEC,[9] and includes branches, within the meaning of the third indent of that Article and located in the Community, of credit institutions which have their head offices outside the Community and which by way of business execute cross-border credit transfers;

b) 'other institution' means any natural or legal person, other than a credit institution, that by way of business executes cross-border credit transfers;

c) 'financial institution' means an institution as defined in Article 4(1) of Council Regulation (EC) No. 3604/93 of 13 December 1993 specifying definitions for the application of the prohibition of privileged access referred to in Article 104a of the Treaty;[10]

d) 'institution' means a credit institution or other institution; for the purposes of Articles 6, 7 and 8, branches of one credit institution situated in different Member States which participate in the execution of a cross-border credit transfer shall be regarded as separate institutions;

e) 'intermediary institution' means an institution which is neither that of the originator nor that of the beneficiary and which participates in the execution of a cross-border credit transfer;

f) 'cross-border credit transfer' means a transaction carried out on the initiative of an originator via an institution or its branch in one Member State, with a view to making available an amount of money to a beneficiary at an institution or its branch in another Member State; the originator and the beneficiary may be one and the same person;

g) 'cross-border credit transfer order' means an unconditional instruction in any form, given directly by an originator to an institution to execute a cross-border credit transfer;

[9] OJ L322/77, p 30. Directive as last amended by Directive 95/26/EC (OJ L168/95, p 7).
[10] OJ L332/93, p 4.

h) 'originator' means a natural or legal person that orders the making of a cross-border credit transfer to a beneficiary;

i) 'beneficiary' means the final recipient of a cross-border credit transfer for whom the corresponding funds are made available in an account to which he has access;

j) 'customer' means the originator or the beneficiary, as the context may require;

k) 'reference interest rate' means an interest rate representing compensation and established in accordance with the rules laid down by the Member State in which the establishment which must pay the compensation to the customer is situated;

l) 'date of acceptance' means the date of fulfilment of all the conditions required by the institution as to the execution of the cross-border credit transfer order and relating to the availability of adequate financial cover and the information required to execute that order.

SECTION II

TRANSPARENCY OF CONDITIONS FOR CROSS-BORDER CREDIT TRANSFERS

Article 3

Prior information on conditions for cross-border credit transfers

The institutions shall make available to their actual and prospective customers in writing, including where appropriate by electronic means, and in a readily comprehensible form, information on conditions for cross-border credit transfers. This information shall include at least:

–   indication of the time needed, when a cross-border credit transfer order given to the institution is executed, for the funds to be credited to the account of the beneficiary's institution; the start of that period must be clearly indicated,

–   indication of the time needed, upon receipt of a cross-border credit transfer, for the funds credited to the account of the institution to be credited to the beneficiary's account,

–   the manner of calculation of any commission fees and charges payable by the customer to the institution, including where appropriate the rates,

–   the value date, if any, applied by the institution,

–   details of the complaint and redress procedures available to the customer and arrangements for access to them,
–   indication of the reference exchange rates used.

Article 4

Information subsequent to a cross-border credit transfer

The institutions shall supply their customers, unless the latter expressly forgo this, subsequent to the execution or receipt of a cross-border credit transfer, with clear information in writing, including where appropriate by electronic means, and in a readily comprehensible form. This information shall include at least:

–   a reference enabling the customer to identify the cross-border credit transfer,
–   the original amount of the cross-border credit transfer,
–   the amount of all charges and commission fees payable by the customer,
–   the value date, if any, applied by the institution.

Where the originator has specified that the charges for the cross-border credit transfer are to be wholly or partly borne by the beneficiary, the latter shall be informed thereof by his own institution.

Where any amount has been converted, the institution which converted it shall inform its customer of the exchange rate used.

SECTION III

MINIMUM OBLIGATIONS OF INSTITUTIONS IN RESPECT OF CROSS-BORDER CREDIT TRANSFERS

Article 5

Specific undertakings by the institution

Unless it does not wish to do business with that customer, an institution must at a customer's request, for a cross-border credit transfer with stated specifications, give an undertaking concerning the time needed for execution of the transfer and the commission fees and charges payable, apart from those relating to the exchange rate used.

Article 6

Obligations regarding time taken

(1)   The originator's institution shall execute the cross-border credit transfer in question within the time limit agreed with the originator.

Where the agreed time limit is not complied with or, in the absence of any such time limit, where, at the end of the fifth banking business day following the date of acceptance of the cross-border credit transfer order, the funds have not been credited to the account of the beneficiary's institution, the originator's institution shall compensate the originator.

Compensation shall comprise the payment of interest calculated by applying the reference rate of interest to the amount of the cross-border credit transfer for the period from:

– the end of the agreed time limit or, in the absence of any such time limit, the end of the fifth banking business day following the date of acceptance of the cross-border credit transfer order, to

– the date on which the funds are credited to the account of the beneficiary's institution.

Similarly, where non-execution of the cross-border credit transfer within the time limit agreed or, in the absence of any such time limit, before the end of the fifth banking business day following the date of acceptance of the cross-border credit transfer is attributable to an intermediary institution, that institution shall be required to compensate the originator's institution.

(2)   The beneficiary's institution shall make the funds resulting from the cross-border credit transfer available to the beneficiary within the time limit agreed with the beneficiary.

Where the agreed time limit is not complied with or, in the absence of any such time limit, where, at the end of the banking business day following the day on which the funds were credited to the account of the beneficiary's institution, the funds have not been credited to the beneficiary's account, the beneficiary's institution shall compensate the beneficiary.

Compensation shall comprise the payment of interest calculated by applying the reference rate of interest to the amount of the cross-border credit transfer for the period from:

– the end of the agreed time limit or, in the absence of any such time limit, the end of the banking business day following the day on which the funds were credited to the account of the beneficiary's institution, to

–   the date on which the funds are credited to the beneficiary's account.

(3)   No compensation shall be payable pursuant to paragraphs 1 and 2 where the originator's institution or, as the case may be, the beneficiary's institution can establish that the delay is attributable to the originator or, as the case may be, the beneficiary.

(4)   Paragraphs 1, 2 and 3 shall be entirely without prejudice to the other rights of customers and institutions that have participated in the execution of a cross-border credit transfer order.

Article 7

Obligation to execute the cross-border transfer in accordance with instructions

(1)   The originator's institution, any intermediary institution and the beneficiary's institution, after the date of acceptance of the cross-border credit transfer order, shall each be obliged to execute that credit transfer for the full amount thereof unless the originator has specified that the costs of the cross-border credit transfer are to be borne wholly or partly by the beneficiary.

The first subparagraph shall be without prejudice to the possibility of the beneficiary's institution levying a charge on the beneficiary relating to the administration of his account, in accordance with the relevant rules and customs. However, such a charge may not be used by the institution to avoid the obligations imposed by the said subparagraph.

(2)   Without prejudice to any other claim which may be made, where the originator's institution or an intermediary institution has made a deduction from the amount of the cross-border credit transfer in breach of paragraph 1, the originator's institution shall, at the originator's request, credit, free of all deductions and at its own cost, the amount deducted to the beneficiary unless the originator requests that the amount be credited to him.

Any intermediary institution which has made a deduction in breach of paragraph 1 shall credit the amount deducted, free of all deductions and at its own cost, to the originator's institution or, if the originator's institution so requests, to the beneficiary of the cross-border credit transfer.

(3)   Where a breach of the duty to execute the cross-border credit transfer order in accordance with the originator's instructions has been caused by the beneficiary's institution, and without prejudice to any other claim which may be made, the beneficiary's institution shall be liable to credit to the beneficiary, at its own cost, any sum wrongly deducted.

Article 8

Obligation upon institutions to refund in the event of non-execution of transfers

(1)   If, after a cross-border credit transfer order has been accepted by the originator's institution, the relevant amounts are not credited to the account of the beneficiary's institution, and without prejudice to any other claim which may be made, the originator's institution shall credit the originator, up to ECU 12 500, with the amount of the cross-border credit transfer plus:

– interest calculated by applying the reference interest rate to the amount of the cross-border credit transfer for the period between the date of the cross-border credit transfer order and the date of the credit, and

– the charges relating to the cross-border credit transfer paid by the originator.

These amounts shall be made available to the originator within fourteen banking business days following the date of his request, unless the funds corresponding to the cross-border credit transfer have in the meantime been credited to the account of the beneficiary's institution.

Such a request may not be made before expiry of the time limit agreed between the originator's institution and the originator for the execution of the cross-border credit transfer order or, in the absence of any such time limit, before expiry of the time limit laid down in the second subparagraph of Article 6(1).

Similarly, each intermediary institution which has accepted the cross-border credit transfer order owes an obligation to refund at its own cost the amount of the credit transfer, including the related costs and interest, to the institution which instructed it to carry out the order. If the cross-border credit transfer was not completed because of errors or omissions in the instructions given by that institution, the intermediary institution shall endeavour as far as possible to refund the amount of the transfer.

(2)   By way of derogation from paragraph 1, if the cross-border credit transfer was not completed because of its non-execution by an intermediary institution chosen by the beneficiary's institution, the latter institution shall be obliged to make the funds available to the beneficiary up to ECU 12 500.

(3)   By way of derogation from paragraph 1, if the cross-border credit transfer was not completed because of an error or omission in the instructions given by the originator to his institution or because of non-execution of the cross-border credit transfer by an intermediary institution expressly chosen by the originator, the originator's

institution and the other institutions involved shall endeavour as far as possible to refund the amount of the transfer.

Where the amount has been recovered by the originator's institution, it shall be obliged to credit it to the originator. The institutions, including the originator's institution, are not obliged in this case to refund the charges and interest accruing, and can deduct the costs arising from the recovery if specified.

Article 9

Situation of force majeure

Without prejudice to the provisions of Directive 91/308/EEC, institutions participating in the execution of a cross-border credit transfer order shall be released from the obligations laid down in this Directive where they can adduce reasons of force majeure, namely abnormal and unforeseeable circumstances beyond the control of the person pleading force majeure, the consequences of which would have been unavoidable despite all efforts to the contrary, which are relevant to its provisions.

Article 10

Settlement of disputes

Member States shall ensure that there are adequate and effective complaints and redress procedures for the settlement of disputes between an originator and his institution or between a beneficiary and his institution, using existing procedures where appropriate.

SECTION IV

FINAL PROVISIONS

Article 11

Implementation

(1) Member States shall bring into force the laws, regulations and administrative provisions necessary to comply with this Directive by 14 August 1999 at the latest. They shall forthwith inform the Commission thereof.

When Member States adopt these provisions, they shall contain a reference to this Directive or shall be accompanied by such reference on the occasion of their official publication. The methods of making such reference shall be laid down by Member States.

(2) Member States shall communicate to the Commission the text of the main laws, regulations or administrative provisions which they adopt in the field governed by this Directive.

Article 12

Report to the European Parliament and the Council

No later than two years after the date of implementation of this Directive, the Commission shall submit a report to the European Parliament and the Council on the application of this Directive, accompanied where appropriate by proposals for its revision.

This report shall, in the light of the situation existing in each Member State and of the technical developments that have taken place, deal particularly with the question of the time limit set in Article 6(1).

Article 13

Entry into force

This Directive shall enter into force on the date of its publication in the Official Journal of the European Communities.

Article 14

Addressees

This Directive is addressed to the Member States.

Denmark	Lov om graenseoverskridende pengeoverforsler, Lov Nr 237 af 21/04/1999.
EIRE	European Communities (Cross-Border Credit Transfers) Regulations 1999, S.I. No. 231/1999.
Finland	Lag om betalningöverföringar (821/1999).
Sweden	Lag om betalningöverföringar inom Europeiska ekonomiska samarbetsomradet, SFS 1999:268.
United Kingdom	The Cross-Border Credit Transfers Regulations 1999, S.I. No. 1999/1876

DIRECTIVE 97/66/EC OF THE EUROPEAN PARLIAMENT AND OF THE COUNCIL

of 15 December 1997

concerning the processing of personal data and the protection of privacy in the telecommunications sector

(Official Journal, L24/98, p 1)

THE EUROPEAN PARLIAMENT AND THE COUNCIL OF THE EUROPEAN UNION –

Having regard to the Treaty establishing the European Community, and in particular Article 100a thereof,

Having regard to the proposal from the Commission,[1]

Having regard to the opinion of the Economic and Social Committee,[2]

Acting in accordance with the procedure laid down in Article 189b of the Treaty,[3] in the light of the joint text approved by the Conciliation Committee on 6 November 1997,

(1) Whereas Directive 95/46/EC of the European Parliament and of the Council of 24 October 1995 on the protection of individuals with regard to the processing of personal data and on the free movement of such data[4] requires Member States to ensure the rights and freedoms of natural persons with regard to the processing of personal data, and in particular their right to privacy, in order to ensure the free flow of personal data in the Community;

(2) Whereas confidentiality of communications is guaranteed in accordance with the international instruments relating to human rights (in particular the European Convention for the Protection of Human Rights and Fundamental Freedoms) and the constitutions of the Member States;

---

[1] OJ C200/94, p 4.
[2] OJ C159/91, p 38.
[3] Opinion of the European Parliament of 11 March 1992 (OJ C94/92, p 198); Council Common Position of 12 September 1996 (OJ C315/96, p 30) and Decision of the European Parliament of 16 January 1997 (OJ C33/97, p 78); Decision of the European Parliament of 20 November 1997 (OJ C371/97); Council Decision of 1 December 1997.
[4] OJ L281/95, p 31.

(3)   Whereas currently in the Community new advanced digital technologies are introduced in public telecommunications networks, which give rise to specific requirements concerning the protection of personal data and privacy of the user; whereas the development of the information society is characterised by the introduction of new telecommunications services; whereas the successful cross-border development of these services, such as video-on-demand, interactive television, is partly dependent on the confidence of the users that their privacy will not be at risk;

(4)   Whereas this is the case, in particular, with the introduction of the Integrated Services Digital Network (ISDN) and digital mobile networks;

(5)   Whereas the Council, in its Resolution of 30 June 1988 on the development of the common market for telecommunications services and equipment up to 1992,[5] called for steps to be taken to protect personal data, in order to create an appropriate environment for the future development of telecommunications in the Community; whereas the Council re-emphasised the importance of the protection of personal data and privacy in its Resolution of 18 July 1989 on the strengthening of the coordination for the introduction of the Integrated Services Digital Network (ISDN) in the European Community up to 1992;[6]

(6)   Whereas the European Parliament has underlined the importance of the protection of personal data and privacy in the telecommunications networks, in particular with regard to the introduction of the Integrated Services Digital Network (ISDN);

(7)   Whereas, in the case of public telecommunications networks, specific legal, regulatory, and technical provisions must be made in order to protect fundamental rights and freedoms of natural persons and legitimate interests of legal persons, in particular with regard to the increasing risk connected with automated storage and processing of data relating to subscribers and users;

(8)   Whereas legal, regulatory, and technical provisions adopted by the Member States concerning the protection of personal data, privacy and the legitimate interest of legal persons, in the telecommunications sector, must be harmonised in order to avoid obstacles to the internal market for telecommunications in conformity with the objective set out in Article 7a of the Treaty; whereas the harmonisation is limited to requirements that are necessary to guarantee that the promotion and development of new telecommunications services and networks between Member States will not be hindered;

[5] OJ C257/88, p 1.
[6] OJ C196/89, p 4.

(9) Whereas the Member States, providers and users concerned, together with the competent Community bodies, should cooperate in introducing and developing the relevant technologies where this is necessary to apply the guarantees provided for by the provisions of this Directive.

(10) Whereas these new services include interactive television and video on demand;

(11) Whereas, in the telecommunications sector, in particular for all matters concerning protection of fundamental rights and freedoms, which are not specifically covered by the provisions of this Directive, including the obligations on the controller and the rights of individuals, Directive 95/46/EC applies; whereas Directive 95/46/EC applies to non-publicly available telecommunications services;

(12) Whereas this Directive, similarly to what is provided for by Article 3 of Directive 95/46/EC, does not address issues of protection of fundamental rights and freedoms related to activities which are not governed by Community law; whereas it is for Member States to take such measures as they consider necessary for the protection of public security, defence, State security (including the economic well-being of the State when the activities relate to State security matters) and the enforcement of criminal law; whereas this Directive shall not affect the ability of Member States to carry out lawful interception of telecommunications, for any of these purposes;

(13) Whereas subscribers of a publicly available telecommunications service may be natural or legal persons; whereas the provisions of this Directive are aimed to protect, by supplementing Directive 95/46/EC, the fundamental rights of natural persons and particularly their right to privacy, as well as the legitimate interests of legal persons; whereas these provisions may in no case entail an obligation for Member States to extend the application of Directive 95/46/EC to the protection of the legitimate interests of legal persons; whereas this protection is ensured within the framework of the applicable Community and national legislation;

(14) Whereas the application of certain requirements relating to presentation and restriction of calling and connected line identification and to automatic call forwarding to subscriber lines connected to analogue exchanges must not be made mandatory in specific cases where such application would prove to be technically impossible or would require a disproportionate economic effort; whereas it is important for interested parties to be informed of such cases and the Member States should therefore notify them to the Commission;

(15) Whereas service providers must take appropriate measures to safeguard the security of their services, if necessary in conjunction with the provider of the network, and inform subscribers of any special

risks of a breach of the security of the network; whereas security is appraised in the light of the provision of Article 17 of Directive 95/46/EC;

(16)   Whereas measures must be taken to prevent the unauthorised access to communications in order to protect the confidentiality of communications by means of public telecommunications networks and publicly available telecommunications services; whereas national legislation in some Member States only prohibits intentional unauthorized access to communications;

(17)   Whereas the data relating to subscribers processed to establish calls contain information on the private life of natural persons and concern the right to respect for their correspondence or concern the legitimate interests of legal persons; whereas such data may only be stored to the extent that is necessary for the provision of the service for the purpose of billing and for interconnection payments, and for a limited time; whereas any further processing which the provider of the publicly available telecommunications services may want to perform for the marketing of its own telecommunications services may only be allowed if the subscriber has agreed to this on the basis of accurate and full information given by the provider of the publicly available telecommunications services about the types of further processing he intends to perform;

(18)   Whereas the introduction of itemized bills has improved the possibilities for the subscriber to verify the correctness of the fees charged by the service provider; whereas, at the same time, it may jeopardise the privacy of the users of publicly available telecommunications services; whereas therefore, in order to preserve the privacy of the user, Member States must encourage the development of telecommunications service options such as alternative payment facilities which allow anonymous or strictly private access to publicly available telecommunications services, for example calling cards and facilities for payment by credit card; whereas, alternatively, Member States may, for the same purpose, require the deletion of a certain number of digits from the called numbers mentioned in itemized bills;

(19)   Whereas it is necessary, as regards calling line identification, to protect the right of the calling party to withhold the presentation of the identification of the line from which the call is being made and the right of the called party to reject calls from unidentified lines; whereas it is justified to override the elimination of calling line identification presentation in specific cases; whereas certain subscribers, in particular helplines and similar organizations, have an interest in guaranteeing the anonymity of their callers; whereas it is necessary, as regards connected line identification, to protect the right and the legitimate interest of the called party to withhold the presentation of the identification of the line to which the calling party is actually connected, in particular in

the case of forwarded calls; whereas the providers of publicly available telecommunications services must inform their subscribers of the existence of calling and connected line identification in the network and of all services which are offered on the basis of calling and connected line identification and about the privacy options which are available; whereas this will allow the subscribers to make an informed choice about the privacy facilities they may want to use; whereas the privacy options which are offered on a per-line basis do not necessarily have to be available as an automatic network service but may be obtainable through a simple request to the provider of the publicly available telecommunications service;

(20) Whereas safeguards must be provided for subscribers against the nuisance which may be caused by automatic call forwarding by others; whereas, in such cases, it must be possible for subscribers to stop the forwarded calls being passed on to their terminals by simple request to the provider of the publicly available telecommunications service;

(21) Whereas directories are widely distributed and publicly available; whereas the right to privacy of natural persons and the legitimate interest of legal persons require that subscribers are able to determine the extent to which their personal data are published in a directory; whereas Member States may limit this possibility to subscribers who are natural persons;

(22) Whereas safeguards must be provided for subscribers against intrusion into their privacy by means of unsolicited calls and telefaxes; whereas Member States may limit such safeguards to subscribers who are natural persons;

(23) Whereas it is necessary to ensure that the introduction of technical features of telecommunications equipment for data protection purposes is harmonised in order to be compatible with the implementation of the internal market;

(24) Whereas in particular, similarly to what is provided for by Article 13 of Directive 95/46/EC, Member States can restrict the scope of subscribers' obligations and rights in certain circumstances, for example by ensuring that the provider of a publicly available telecommunications service may override the elimination of the presentation of calling line identification in conformity with national legislation for the purpose of prevention or detection of criminal offences or State security;

(25) Whereas where the rights of the users and subscribers are not respected, national legislation must provide for judicial remedy; whereas sanctions must be imposed on any person, whether governed by private or public law, who fails to comply with the national measures taken under this Directive;

(26) Whereas it is useful in the field of application of this Directive to draw on the experience of the Working Party on the protection of individuals

with regard to the processing of personal data composed of representatives of the supervisory authorities of the Member States, set up by Article 29 of Directive 95/46/EC;

(27) Whereas, given the technological developments and the attendant evolution of the services on offer, it will be necessary technically to specify the categories of data listed in the Annex to this Directive for the application of Article 6 of this Directive with the assistance of the Committee composed of representatives of the Member States set up in Article 31 of Directive 95/46/EC in order to ensure a coherent application of the requirements set out in this Directive regardless of changes in technology; whereas this procedure applies solely to specifications necessary to adapt the Annex to new technological developments, taking into consideration changes in market and consumer demand; whereas the Commission must duly inform the European Parliament of its intention to apply this procedure and whereas, otherwise, the procedure laid down in Article 100a of the Treaty shall apply;

(28) Whereas, to facilitate compliance with the provisions of this Directive, certain specific arrangements are needed for processing of data already under way on the date that national implementing legislation pursuant to this Directive enters into force,

HAVE ADOPTED THIS DIRECTIVE:

Article 1

Object and scope

(1) This Directive provides for the harmonisation of the provisions of the Member States required to ensure an equivalent level of protection of fundamental rights and freedoms, and in particular the right to privacy, with respect to the processing of personal data in the telecommunications sector and to ensure the free movement of such data and of telecommunications equipment and services in the Community.

(2) The provisions of this Directive particularise and complement Directive 95/46/EC for the purposes mentioned in paragraph 1. Moreover, they provide for protection of legitimate interests of subscribers who are legal persons.

(3) This Directive shall not apply to the activities which fall outside the scope of Community law, such as those provided for by Titles V and VI of the Treaty on European Union, and in any case to activities concerning public security, defence, State security (including the

economic well-being of the State when the activities relate to State security matters) and the activities of the State in areas of criminal law.

Article 2

Definitions

In addition to the definitions given in Directive 95/46/EC, for the purposes of this Directive:

a) 'subscriber' shall mean any natural or legal person who or which is party to a contract with the provider of publicly available telecommunications services for the supply of such services;

b) 'user' shall mean any natural person using a publicly available telecommunications service, for private or business purposes, without necessarily having subscribed to this service;

c) 'public telecommunications network' shall mean transmission systems and, where applicable, switching equipment and other resources which permit the conveyance of signals between defined termination points by wire, by radio, by optical or by other electromagnetic means, which are used, in whole or in part, for the provision of publicly available telecommunications services;

d) 'telecommunications service' shall mean services whose provision consists wholly or partly in the transmission and routing of signals on telecommunications networks, with the exception of radio- and television broadcasting.

Article 3

Services concerned

(1) This Directive shall apply to the processing of personal data in connection with the provision of publicly available telecommunications services in public telecommunications networks in the Community, in particular via the Integrated Services Digital Network (ISDN) and public digital mobile networks.

(2) Articles 8, 9 and 10 shall apply to subscriber lines connected to digital exchanges and, where technically possible and if it does not require a disproportionate economic effort, to subscriber lines connected to analogue exchanges.

(3) Cases where it would be technically impossible or require a disproportionate investment to fulfil the requirements of Articles 8, 9 and 10 shall be notified to the Commission by the Member States.

Article 4

Security

(1) The provider of a publicly available telecommunications service must take appropriate technical and organisational measures to safeguard security of its services, if necessary in conjunction with the provider of the public telecommunications network with respect to network security. Having regard to the state of the art and the cost of their implementation, these measures shall ensure a level of security appropriate to the risk presented.

(2) In case of a particular risk of a breach of the security of the network, the provider of a publicly available telecommunications service must inform the subscribers concerning such risk and any possible remedies, including the costs involved.

Article 5

Confidentiality of the communications

(1) Member States shall ensure via national regulations the confidentiality of communications by means of a public telecommunications network and publicly available telecommunications services. In particular, they shall prohibit listening, tapping, storage or other kinds of interception or surveillance of communications, by others than users, without the consent of the users concerned, except when legally authorised, in accordance with Article 14(1).

(2) Paragraph 1 shall not affect any legally authorised recording of communications in the course of lawful business practice for the purpose of providing evidence of a commercial transaction or of any other business communication.

Article 6

Traffic and billing data

(1) Traffic data relating to subscribers and users processed to establish calls and stored by the provider of a public telecommunications network and/or publicly available telecommunications service must be erased or made anonymous upon termination of the call without prejudice to the provisions of paragraphs 2, 3 and 4.

(2) For the purpose of subscriber billing and interconnection payments, data indicated in the Annex may be processed. Such processing is

permissible only up to the end of the period during which the bill may lawfully be challenged or payment may be pursued.

(3) For the purpose of marketing its own telecommunications services, the provider of a publicly available telecommunications service may process the data referred to in paragraph 2, if the subscriber has given his consent.

(4) Processing of traffic and billing data must be restricted to persons acting under the authority of providers of the public telecommunications networks and/or publicly available telecommunications services handling billing or traffic management, customer enquiries, fraud detection and marketing the provider's own telecommunications services and it must be restricted to what is necessary for the purposes of such activities.

(5) Paragraphs 1, 2, 3 and 4 shall apply without prejudice to the possibility for competent authorities to be informed of billing or traffic data in conformity with applicable legislation in view of settling disputes, in particular interconnection or billing disputes.

Article 7

Itemized billing

(1) Subscribers shall have the right to receive non-itemized bills.

(2) Member States shall apply national provisions in order to reconcile the rights of subscribers receiving itemised bills with the right to privacy of calling users and called subscribers, for example by ensuring that sufficient alternative modalities for communications or payments are available to such users and subscribers.

Article 8

Presentation and restriction of calling and connected line identification

(1) Where presentation of calling-line identification is offered, the calling user must have the possibility via a simple means, free of charge, to eliminate the presentation of the calling-line identification on a per-call basis. The calling subscriber must have this possibility on a per-line basis.

(2) Where presentation of calling-line identification is offered, the called subscriber must have the possibility via a simple means, free of charge for reasonable use of this function, to prevent the presentation of the calling line identification of incoming calls.

(3) Where presentation of calling line identification is offered and where the calling line identification is presented prior to the call being

established, the called subscriber must have the possibility via a simple means to reject incoming calls where the presentation of the calling line identification has been eliminated by the calling user or subscriber.

(4) Where presentation of connected line identification is offered, the called subscriber must have the possibility via a simple means, free of charge, to eliminate the presentation of the connected line identification to the calling user.

(5) The provisions set out in paragraph 1 shall also apply with regard to calls to third countries originating in the Community; the provisions set out in paragraphs 2, 3 and 4 shall also apply to incoming calls originating in third countries.

(6) Member States shall ensure that where presentation of calling and/or connected line identification is offered, the providers of publicly available telecommunications services inform the public thereof and of the possibilities set out in paragraphs 1, 2, 3 and 4.

Article 9

Exceptions

Member States shall ensure that there are transparent procedures governing the way in which a provider of a public telecommunications network and/or a publicly available telecommunications service may override the elimination of the presentation of calling line identification:

a) on a temporary basis, upon application of a subscriber requesting the tracing of malicious or nuisance calls; in this case, in accordance with national law, the data containing the identification of the calling subscriber will be stored and be made available by the provider of a public telecommunications network and/or publicly available telecommunications service;

b) on a per-line basis for organisations dealing with emergency calls and recognized as such by a Member State, including law enforcement agencies, ambulance services and fire brigades, for the purpose of answering such calls.

Article 10

Automatic call forwarding

Member States shall ensure that any subscriber is provided, free of charge and via a simple means, with the possibility to stop automatic call forwarding by a third party to the subscriber's terminal.

Article 11

Directories of subscribers

(1) Personal data contained in printed or electronic directories of subscribers available to the public or obtainable through directory enquiry services should be limited to what is necessary to identify a particular subscriber, unless the subscriber has given his unambiguous consent to the publication of additional personal data. The subscriber shall be entitled, free of charge, to be omitted from a printed or electronic directory at his or her request, to indicate that his or her personal data may not be used for the purpose of direct marketing, to have his or her address omitted in part and not to have a reference revealing his or her sex, where this is applicable linguistically.

(2) Notwithstanding paragraph 1, Member States may allow operators to require a payment from subscribers wishing to ensure that their particulars are not entered in a directory, provided that the sum involved does not act as a disincentive to the exercise of this right, and that, taking account of the quality requirements of the public directory in the light of the universal service, it is limited to the actual costs incurred by the operator for the adaptation and updating of the list of subscribers not to be included in the public directory.

(3) The rights conferred by paragraph 1 shall apply to subscribers who are natural persons. Member States shall also guarantee, in the framework of Community law and applicable national legislation, that the legitimate interests of subscribers other than natural persons with regard to their entry in public directories are sufficiently protected.

Article 12

Unsolicited calls

(1) The use of automated calling systems without human intervention (automatic calling machine) or facsimile machines (fax) for the purposes of direct marketing may only be allowed in respect of subscribers who have given their prior consent.

(2) Member States shall take appropriate measures to ensure that, free of charge, unsolicited calls for purposes of direct marketing, by means other than those referred to in paragraph 1, are not allowed either without the consent of the subscribers concerned or in respect of subscribers who do not wish to receive these calls, the choice between these options to be determined by national legislation.

(3) The rights conferred by paragraphs 1 and 2 shall apply to subscribers who are natural persons. Member States shall also guarantee, in the

framework of Community law and applicable national legislation, that the legitimate interests of subscribers other than natural persons with regard to unsolicited calls are sufficiently protected.

Article 13

Technical features and standardisation

(1) In implementing the provisions of this Directive, Member States shall ensure, subject to paragraphs 2 and 3, that no mandatory requirements for specific technical features are imposed on terminal or other telecommunications equipment which could impede the placing of equipment on the market and the free circulation of such equipment in and between Member States.

(2) Where provisions of this Directive can be implemented only by requiring specific technical features, Member States shall inform the Commission according to the procedures provided for by Directive 83/189/EEC[7] which lays down a procedure for the provision of information in the field of technical standards and regulations.

(3) Where required, the Commission will ensure the drawing up of common European standards for the implementation of specific technical features, in accordance with Community legislation on the approximation of the laws of the Member States concerning telecommunications terminal equipment, including the mutual recognition of their conformity, and Council Decision 87/95/EEC of 22 December 1986 on standardisation in the field of information technology and telecommunications.[8]

Article 14

Extension of the scope of application of certain provisions of Directive 95/46/EC

(1) Member States may adopt legislative measures to restrict the scope of the obligations and rights provided for in Articles 5, 6 and Article 8(1), (2), (3) and (4), when such restriction constitutes a necessary measure to safeguard national security, defence, public security, the prevention, investigation, detection and prosecution of criminal offences or of unauthorised use of the telecommunications system, as referred to in Article 13(1) of Directive 95/46/EC.

---

[7] OJ L109/83, p 8. Directive as last amended by Directive 94/10/EC (OJ L100/94, p 30).
[8] OJ L36/87, p 31. Decision as last amended by the 1994 Act of Accession.

(2) The provisions of Chapter III on judicial remedies, liability and sanctions of Directive 95/46/EC shall apply with regard to national provisions adopted pursuant to this Directive and with regard to the individual rights derived from this Directive.

(3) The Working Party on the Protection of Individuals with regard to the Processing of Personal Data established according to Article 29 of Directive 95/46/EC shall carry out the tasks laid down in Article 30 of the abovementioned Directive also with regard to the protection of fundamental rights and freedoms and of legitimate interests in the telecommunications sector, which is the subject of this Directive.

(4) The Commission, assisted by the Committee established by Article 31 of Directive 95/46/EC, shall technically specify the Annex according to the procedure mentioned in this Article. The aforesaid Committee shall be convened specifically for the subjects covered by this Directive.

Article 15

Implementation of the Directive

(1) Member States shall bring into force the laws, regulations and administrative provisions necessary for them to comply with this Directive not later than 24 October 1998.

By way of derogation from the first subparagraph, Member States shall bring into force the laws, regulations and administrative provisions necessary for them to comply with Article 5 of this Directive not later than 24 October 2000.

When Member States adopt these measures, they shall contain a reference to this Directive or shall be accompanied by such a reference at the time of their official publication. The procedure for such reference shall be adopted by Member States.

(2) By way of derogation from Article 6(3), consent is not required with respect to processing already under way on the date the national provisions adopted pursuant to this Directive enter into force. In those cases the subscribers shall be informed of this processing and if they do not express their dissent within a period to be determined by the Member State, they shall be deemed to have given their consent.

(3) Article 11 shall not apply to editions of directories which have been published before the national provisions adopted pursuant to this Directive enter into force.

(4) Member States shall communicate to the Commission the text of the provisions of national law which they adopt in the field governed by this Directive.

Article 16

Addressees

This Directive is addressed to the Member States.

ANNEX

List of data

For the purpose referred to in Article 6(2) the following data may be processed:
Data containing the:

- number or identification of the subscriber station,
- address of the subscriber and the type of station,
- total number of units to be charged for the accounting period,
- called subscriber number,
- type, starting time and duration of the calls made and/or the data volume transmitted,
- date of the call/service,
- other information concerning payments such as advance payment, payments by instalments, disconnection and reminders.

Denmark	1. – Bekendtgørelse om nummeroplysingningdatabaser
	2. – Bekendtgorelse af straffeloven
EIRE	European Communities (Data Protection and Privacy in Telecommunications) Regulations 2002, S.I. No. 192/2002.
Finland	1. – Laki venajän federaation kanssa sijoitusten edistämistä ja molemminpuolisa suojelua koskevan sopimuksen muutamisesta tehdyn pöytäkirjan eräiden määräysten hyväksymisestä.
	2. – Laki yksityisyyden suosjasta televiestinnassä ja teletoiminnan tietoturvasta
	3. – Laki telemakkinalain muutamisesta
	4. – Laki rikoslain 38 luvun muutamisesta
	5. – Lag om integritetsskydd vid telekommunikation och dataskyd inom televerksamhet. FFS nr 565 s. 1379
Sweden	Lag om ändring i telelagen (1993:597)
United Kingdom	1. – Section 98 of Postal and Telecommunications Services Act, 1983.
	2. – The Telecommunications (Open Network Provision) (Voice Telephony) Regulations 1998 S.I. No.1998/1580.
	3. – The Telecommunications (Data Protection and Privacy) (Direct Marketing) Regulations 1998, S.I. No. 1998/3170.

4. – The Telecommunications (Data Protection and Privacy) Regulations 1999, S.I. No. 1999/2093.

5. – The Telecommunications (Licence Modification) (Standard Schedules) Regulations 1999, S.I. No. 1999/2450.

6. – The Telecommunications (Data Protection and Privacy) (Amendment) Regulations 2000, S.I. No. 2000/157.

7. – The Data Protection Tribunal (National Security Appeals) (Telecommunications) Rules, S.I. No. 2000/731.

8. – Regulation of Investigatory Powers Act 2000.

9. – The Prison (Amendment) (No.2) Rules 2000, S.I. No. 2000/2641.

10. – The Young Offender Institution (Amendment) (No. 3) Rules 2000, S.I. No. 2000/2642.

11. – The Telecommunications (Lawful Business Practice) (Interception of Communications) Regulations 2000, S.I. No. 2000/2699.

12. – The Electronic Commerce (EC Directive) Regulations 2002, S.I. No 2000/2013.

13. – Regulation of Investigatory Powers Act 2000.

COUNCIL DIRECTIVE 85/374/EEC

of 25 July 1985

on the approximation of the laws, regulations and administrative provisions of the Member States concerning liability for defective products

(Official Journal L210/1985, p 29)

Amendments

Article	Nature of Amzendment	Effected by	Date	Source
2, 15	Amended	Directive 1999/34/EC	10 May 1999	

THE COUNCIL OF THE EUROPEAN COMMUNITIES –

Having regard to the Treaty establishing the European Economic Community, and in particular Article 100 thereof,

Having regard to the proposal from the Commission,[1]

Having regard to the opinion of the European Parliament,[2]

Having regard to the opinion of the Economic and Social Committee,[3]

Whereas approximation of the laws of the Member States concerning the liability of the producer for damage caused by the defectiveness of his products is necessary because the existing divergences may distort competition and affect the movement of goods within the common market and entail a differing degree of protection of the consumer against damage caused by a defective product to his health or property;

Whereas liability without fault on the part of the producer is the sole means of adequately solving the problem, peculiar to our age of increasing technicality, of a fair apportionment of the risks inherent in modern technological production;

Whereas liability without fault should apply only to movables which have been industrially produced; whereas, as a result, it is appropriate to exclude liability for agricultural products and game, except where they have undergone a processing of an industrial nature which could cause a defect in these products; whereas the

[1] OJ C241/76, p 9 and OJ C271/79, p 3.
[2] OJ C127/79, p 61.
[3] OJ C114/79, p 15.

liability provided for in this Directive should also apply to movables which are used in the construction of immovables or are installed in immovables;

Whereas protection of the consumer requires that all producers involved in the production process should be made liable, in so far as their finished product, component part or any raw material supplied by them was defective; whereas, for the same reason, liability should extend to importers of products into the Community and to persons who present themselves as producers by affixing their name, trade mark or other distinguishing feature or who supply a product the producer of which cannot be identified;

Whereas, in situations where several persons are liable for the same damage, the protection of the consumer requires that the injured person should be able to claim full compensation for the damage from any one of them;

Whereas, to protect the physical well-being and property of the consumer, the defectiveness of the product should be determined by reference not to its fitness for use but to the lack of the safety which the public at large is entitled to expect; whereas the safety is assessed by excluding any misuse of the product not reasonable under the circumstances;

Whereas a fair apportionment of risk between the injured person and the producer implies that the producer should be able to free himself from liability if he furnishes proof as to the existence of certain exonerating circumstances;

Whereas the protection of the consumer requires that the liability of the producer remains unaffected by acts or omissions of other persons having contributed to cause the damage; whereas, however, the contributory negligence of the injured person may be taken into account to reduce or disallow such liability;

Whereas the protection of the consumer requires compensation for death and personal injury as well as compensation for damage to property; whereas the latter should nevertheless be limited to goods for private use or consumption and be subject to a deduction of a lower threshold of a fixed amount in order to avoid litigation in an excessive number of cases; whereas this Directive should not prejudice compensation for pain and suffering and other non-material damages payable, where appropriate, under the law applicable to the case;

Whereas a uniform period of limitation for the bringing of action for compensation is in the interests both of the injured person and of the producer;

Whereas products age in the course of time, higher safety standards are developed and the state of science and technology progresses; whereas, therefore, it would not be reasonable to make the producer liable for an unlimited period for the defectiveness of his product; whereas, therefore, liability should expire after a reasonable length of time, without prejudice to claims pending at law;

Whereas, to achieve effective protection of consumers, no contractual derogation should be permitted as regards the liability of the producer in relation to the injured person;

Whereas under the legal systems of the Member States an injured party may have a claim for damages based on grounds of contractual liability or on grounds of non-contractual liability other than that provided for in this Directive; in so far as these provisions also serve to attain the objective of effective protection of consumers, they should remain unaffected by this Directive; whereas, in so far as effective protection of consumers in the sector of pharmaceutical products is already also attained in a Member State under a special liability system, claims based on this system should similarly remain possible;

Whereas, to the extent that liability for nuclear injury or damage is already covered in all Member States by adequate special rules, it has been possible to exclude damage of this type from the scope of this Directive;

Whereas, since the exclusion of primary agricultural products and game from the scope of this Directive may be felt, in certain Member States, in view of what is expected for the protection of consumers, to restrict unduly such protection, it should be possible for a Member State to extend liability to such products;

Whereas, for similar reasons, the possibility offered to a producer to free himself from liability if he proves that the state of scientific and technical knowledge at the time when he put the product into circulation was not such as to enable the existence of a defect to be discovered may be felt in certain Member States to restrict unduly the protection of the consumer; whereas it should therefore be possible for a Member State to maintain in its legislation or to provide by new legislation that this exonerating circumstance is not admitted; whereas, in the case of new legislation, making use of this derogation should, however, be subject to a Community stand-still procedure, in order to raise, if possible, the level of protection in a uniform manner throughout the Community;

Whereas, taking into account the legal traditions in most of the Member States, it is inappropriate to set any financial ceiling on the producer's liability without fault; whereas, in so far as there are, however, differing traditions, it seems possible to admit that a Member State may derogate from the principle of unlimited liability by providing a limit for the total liability of the producer for damage resulting from a death or personal injury and caused by identical items with the same defect, provided that this limit is established at a level sufficiently high to guarantee adequate protection of the consumer and the correct functioning of the common market;

Whereas the harmonization resulting from this cannot be total at the present stage, but opens the way towards greater harmonization; whereas it is therefore necessary that the Council receive at regular intervals, reports from the Commission on the application of this Directive, accompanied, as the case may be, by appropriate proposals;

Whereas it is particularly important in this respect that a re-examination be carried out of those parts of the Directive relating to the derogations open to the Member States, at the expiry of a period of sufficient length to gather practical experience on the effects of these derogations on the protection of consumers and on the functioning of the common market,

— *Considerations underpinning Regulation 1999/34/EC:*

THE EUROPEAN PARLIAMENT AND THE COUNCIL OF THE EUROPEAN UNION,

Having regard to the Treaty establishing the European Community, and in particular Article 95 thereof,

 Having regard to the proposal from the Commission,[4]
 Having regard to the opinion of the Economic and Social Committee,[5]
 Acting in accordance with the procedure laid down in Article 251 of the Treaty,[6]

---

[4] OJ C337/97, p 54.
[5] OJ C95/98, p 69.
[6] Opinion of the European Parliament of 5 November 1998 (OJ C359/98, p 25); Common Position of the Council of 17 December 1998 (OJ C49/99, p 1) and Decision of the European Parliament of 23 March 1999 (not yet published in the Official Journal); Decision of the Council of 29 April 1999.

(1)   *Whereas product safety and compensation for damage caused by defective products are social imperatives which must be met within the internal market; whereas the Community has responded to those requirements by means of Directive 85/374/EEC[7] and* Council Directive 92/59/EEC of 29 June 1992 on general product safety;[8]

(2)   *Whereas Directive 85/374/EEC established a fair apportionment of the risks inherent in a modern society in which there is a high degree of technicality; whereas that Directive therefore struck a reasonable balance between the interests involved, in particular the protection of consumer health, encouraging innovation and scientific and technological development, guaranteeing undistorted competition and facilitating trade under a harmonised system of civil liability; whereas that Directive has thus helped to raise awareness among traders of the issue of product safety and the importance accorded to it;*

(3)   *Whereas the degree of harmonisation of Member States' laws achieved by Directive 85/374/EEC is not complete in view of the derogations provided for, in particular with regard to its scope, from which unprocessed agricultural products are excluded;*

(4)   *Whereas the Commission monitors the implementation and effects of Directive 85/374/EEC and in particular its aspects relating to consumer protection and the functioning of the internal market, which have already been the subject of a first report; whereas, in this context, the Commission is required by Article 21 of that Directive to submit a second report on its application;*

(5)   *Whereas including primary agricultural products within the scope of Directive 85/374/EEC would help restore consumer confidence in the safety of agricultural products; whereas such a measure would meet the requirements of a high level of consumer protection;*

(6)   *Whereas circumstances call for Directive 85/374/EEC to be amended in order to facilitate, for the benefit of consumers, legitimate compensation for damage to health caused by defective agricultural products;*

(7)   *Whereas this Directive has an impact on the functioning of the internal market in so far as trade in agricultural products will no longer be affected by differences between rules on producer liability;*

(8)   *Whereas the principle of liability without fault laid down in Directive 85/374/EEC must be extended to all types of product, including agricultural products as defined by the second sentence of Article 32 of the Treaty and those listed in Annex II to the said Treaty;*

(9)   *Whereas, in accordance with the principle of proportionality, it is necessary and appropriate in order to achieve the fundamental objectives of increased protection for all consumers and the proper functioning of the*

---

[7] OJ L210/85, p 29.
[8] OJ L228/92, p 24.

internal market to include agricultural products within the scope of Directive 85/374/EEC; whereas this Directive is limited to what is necessary to achieve the objectives pursued in accordance with the third paragraph of Article 5 of the Treaty –

HAS ADOPTED THIS DIRECTIVE:

Article 1

The producer shall be liable for damage caused by a defect in his product.

Article 2

For the purpose of this Directive 'product' means all movables, with the exception of primary agricultural products and game, even though incorporated into another movable or into an immovable. 'Primary agricultural products' means the products of the soil, of stock-farming and of fisheries, excluding products which have undergone initial processing. 'Product' includes electricity.

Article 3

(1) 'Producer' means the manufacturer of a finished product, the producer of any raw material or the manufacturer of a component part and any person who, by putting his name, trade mark or other distinguishing feature on the product presents himself as its producer.

(2) Without prejudice to the liability of the producer, any person who imports into the Community a product for sale, hire, leasing or any form of distribution in the course of his business shall be deemed to be a producer within the meaning of this Directive and shall be responsible as a producer.

(3) Where the producer of the product cannot be identified, each supplier of the product shall be treated as its producer unless he informs the injured person, within a reasonable time, of the identity of the producer or of the person who supplied him with the product. The same shall apply, in the case of an imported product, if this product does not indicate the identity of the importer referred to in paragraph 2, even if the name of the producer is indicated.

Article 4

The injured person shall be required to prove the damage, the defect and the causal relationship between defect and damage.

Article 5

Where, as a result of the provisions of this Directive, two or more persons are liable for the same damage, they shall be liable jointly and severally, without prejudice to the provisions of national law concerning the rights of contribution or recourse.

Article 6

(1) A product is defective when it does not provide the safety which a person is entitled to expect, taking all circumstances into account, including:
   a) the presentation of the product;
   b) the use to which it could reasonably be expected that the product would be put;
   c) the time when the product was put into circulation.
(2) A product shall not be considered defective for the sole reason that a better product is subsequently put into circulation.

Article 7

The producer shall not be liable as a result of this Directive if he proves:

   a) that he did not put the product into circulation; or
   b) that, having regard to the circumstances, it is probable that the defect which caused the damage did not exist at the time when the product was put into circulation by him or that this defect came into being afterwards; or
   c) that the product was neither manufactured by him for sale or any form of distribution for economic purpose nor manufactured or distributed by him in the course of his business; or
   d) that the defect is due to compliance of the product with mandatory regulations issued by the public authorities; or
   e) that the state of scientific and technical knowledge at the time when he put the product into circulation was not such as to enable the existence of the defect to be discovered; or
   f) in the case of a manufacturer of a component, that the defect is attributable to the design of the product in which the component has been fitted or to the instructions given by the manufacturer of the product.

Article 8

(1) Without prejudice to the provisions of national law concerning the right of contribution or recourse, the liability of the producer shall not be reduced when the damage is caused both by a defect in product and by the act or omission of a third party.

(2) The liability of the producer may be reduced or disallowed when, having regard to all the circumstances, the damage is caused both by a defect in the product and by the fault of the injured person or any person for whom the injured person is responsible.

Article 9

For the purpose of Article 1, 'damage' means:

a) damage caused by death or by personal injuries;
b) damage to, or destruction of, any item of property other than the defective product itself, with a lower threshold of 500 ECU, provided that the item of property:
   i) is of a type ordinarily intended for private use or consumption, and
   ii) was used by the injured person mainly for his own private use or consumption.

This Article shall be without prejudice to national provisions relating to non-material damage.

Article 10

(1) Member States shall provide in their legislation that a limitation period of three years shall apply to proceedings for the recovery of damages as provided for in this Directive. The limitation period shall begin to run from the day on which the plaintiff became aware, or should reasonably have become aware, of the damage, the defect and the identity of the producer.
(2) The laws of Member States regulating suspension or interruption of the limitation period shall not be affected by this Directive.

Article 11

Member States shall provide in their legislation that the rights conferred upon the injured person pursuant to this Directive shall be extinguished upon the expiry of a period of 10 years from the date on which the producer put into circulation the actual product which caused the damage, unless the injured person has in the meantime instituted proceedings against the producer.

Article 12

The liability of the producer arising from this Directive may not, in relation to the injured person, be limited or excluded by a provision limiting his liability or exempting him from liability.

Article 13

This Directive shall not affect any rights which an injured person may have according to the rules of the law of contractual or non-contractual liability or a special liability system existing at the moment when this Directive is notified.

Article 14

This Directive shall not apply to injury or damage arising from nuclear accidents and covered by international conventions ratified by the Member States.

Article 15

(1) Each Member State may:

  a)   by way of derogation from Article 2, provide in its legislation that within the meaning of Article 1 of this Directive 'product' also means primary agricultural products and game;

  b)   by way of derogation from Article 7 (e), maintain or, subject to the procedure set out in paragraph 2 of this Article, provide in this legislation that the producer shall be liable even if he proves that the state of scientific and technical knowledge at the time when he put the product into circulation was not such as to enable the existence of a defect to be discovered.

(2) A Member State wishing to introduce the measure specified in paragraph 1 (b) shall communicate the text of the proposed measure to the Commission. The Commission shall inform the other Member States thereof.

   The Member State concerned shall hold the proposed measure in abeyance for nine months after the Commission is informed and provided that in the meantime the Commission has not submitted to the Council a proposal amending this Directive on the relevant matter. However, if within three months of receiving the said information, the Commission does not advise the Member State concerned that it intends submitting such a proposal to the Council, the Member State may take the proposed measure immediately.

   If the Commission does submit to the Council such a proposal amending this Directive within the aforementioned nine months, the Member State concerned shall hold the proposed measure in abeyance for a further period of 18 months from the date on which the proposal is submitted.

(3) Ten years after the date of notification of this Directive, the Commission shall submit to the Council a report on the effect that rulings by the courts as to the application of Article 7 (e) and of paragraph 1 (b) of this Article have on consumer protection and the functioning of the

common market. In the light of this report the Council, acting on a proposal from the Commission and pursuant to the terms of Article 100 of the Treaty, shall decide whether to repeal Article 7 (e).

Article 16

(1) Any Member State may provide that a producer's total liability for damage resulting from a death or personal injury and caused by identical items with the same defect shall be limited to an amount which may not be less than 70 million ECU.

(2) Ten years after the date of notification of this Directive, the Commission shall submit to the Council a report on the effect on consumer protection and the functioning of the common market of the implementation of the financial limit on liability by those Member States which have used the option provided for in paragraph 1. In the light of this report the Council, acting on a proposal from the Commission and pursuant to the terms of Article 100 of the Treaty, shall decide whether to repeal paragraph 1.

Article 17

This Directive shall not apply to products put into circulation before the date on which the provisions referred to in Article 19 enter into force.

Article 18

(1) For the purposes of this Directive, the ECU shall be that defined by Regulation (EEC) No 3180/78,[9] as amended by Regulation (EEC) No 2626/84.[10] The equivalent in national currency shall initially be calculated at the rate obtaining on the date of adoption of this Directive.

(2) Every five years the Council, acting on a proposal from the Commission, shall examine and, if need be, revise the amounts in this Directive, in the light of economic and monetary trends in the Community.

Article 19

(1) Member States shall bring into force, not later than three years from the date of notification of this Directive, the laws, regulations and administrative provisions necessary to comply with this Directive. They shall forthwith inform the Commission thereof.[11]

[9] OJ L379/78, p 1.
[10] OJ L247/84, p 1.
[11] This Directive was notified to Member States on 30 July 1985.

(2)   The procedure set out in Article 15(2) shall apply from the date of notification of this Directive.

Article 20

Member States shall communicate to the Commission the texts of the main provisions of national law which they subsequently adopt in the field governed by this Directive.

Article 21

Every five years the Commission shall present a report to the Council on the application of this Directive and, if necessary, shall submit appropriate proposals to it.

Article 22

This Directive is addressed to the Member States.

(1) This Directive was notified to the Member States on 30 July 1985.

Denmark	1. – Lov om produktansvar, Lov Nr 371 af 07/06/1989.
	2. – Lov om Produktsikkerhed, Lov Nr 364 af 18/05/1994.
EIRE	1. – Liability for Defective Products Act 1991
	2. – European Communities (Liability for Defective Products) Regulations, 2000, S.I. No. 401/2000.
Finland	1. – Tuotevastuulaki (694/90) 17/08/1990, muutokset (99/93) 08/01/1993 ja (879/93) 22/10/1993.
	2. – Lov om aendring af produktansvarsloven (Ophaevelse af undtagelsen for uforarbejdede produkter hidrorende fra jordbrug, husdyrbrug, fiskeri og jagt) ref : Lovtidende A, haefte 168 nr 1041–29/11/2000 (page 7623).
	3. – Forslag til Lov om aendring af produktansvarsloven (Ophaevelse af undtagelsen for uforarbejdede produkter hidrorende fra jordbrug, husdyrbrug, fiskeri og jagt) ref : Lovforslag nr 18 Folketinget 2000-01
Sweden	1. – Produktansvarslag, SFS 1992:18.
	2. – Lag om ändring i produktansvarslagen (1992:18), SFS 1992:1137.
	3. – Lag om ändring i lagen (1992:1137) om ändring i produktansvarslagen (1992:18), SFS 1993:647.
	4. – Lag om ändring i lagen (1902:71 s.1), innefattande vissa bestämmelser om elektriska anläggningar, SFS 1992:668.
England	1. – Consumer Protection Act 1987.
	2. – The Consumer Protection (Northern Ireland) Order 1987, S.I. No 1987/2049.
	3. – The Consumer Protection Act 1987 (Product Liability) (Modification) Order 2000, S.I. No. 2000/2771.
	4. – Product Liability (Amendment) Act (Northern Ireland) 2001.
	5. – The Consumer protection Act 1987 (Product liability) (Modification) (Scotland) Order 2001, S.I. No 2001/265.

DIRECTIVE 94/47/EC OF THE EUROPEAN PARLIAMENT AND THE COUNCIL

of 26 October 1994

on the protection of purchasers in respect of certain aspects of contracts relating to the purchase of the right to use immovable properties on a timeshare basis

(Official Journal L280/94, p 83)

THE EUROPEAN PARLIAMENT AND THE COUNCIL OF THE EUROPEAN UNION –

Having regard to the Treaty establishing the European Community, and in particular Article 100a thereof,

Having regard to the proposal from the Commission,[1]

Having regard to the opinion of the Economic and Social Committee,[2]

Acting in accordance with the procedure laid down in Article 189b of the Treaty (3),

1. Whereas the disparities between national legislations on contracts relating to the purchase of the right to use one or more immovable properties on a timeshare basis are likely to create barriers to the proper operation of the internal market and distortions of competition and lead to the compartmentalization of national markets;

2. Whereas the aim of this Directive is to establish a minimum basis of common rules on such matters which will make it possible to ensure that the internal market operates properly and will thereby protect purchasers; whereas it is sufficient for those rules to cover contractual transactions only with regard to those aspects that relate to information on the constituent parts of contracts, the arrangements for communicating such information and the procedures and arrangements for cancellation and withdrawal; whereas the appropriate instrument to achieve that aim is a Directive; whereas this Directive is therefore consistent with the principle of subsidiarity;

3. Whereas the legal nature of the rights which are the subject of the contracts covered by this Directive varies considerably from one

[1] OJ C299/93, p 8.
[2] OJ C108/93, p 1.

Member State to another; whereas reference should therefore be made in summary form to those variations, giving a sufficiently broad definition of such contracts, without thereby implying harmonization within the Community of the legal nature of the rights in question;

4. Whereas this Directive is not designed to regulate the extent to which contracts for the use of one or more immovable properties on a time-share basis may be concluded in Member States or the legal basis for such contracts;

5. Whereas, in practice, contracts relating to the purchase of the right to use one or more immovable properties on a timeshare basis differ from tenancy agreements; whereas that difference can be seen from, inter alia, the means of payment;

6. Whereas it may be seen from the market that hotels, residential hotels and other similar residential tourist premises are involved in contractual transactions similar to those which have made this Directive necessary;

7. Whereas it is necessary to avoid any misleading or incomplete details in information concerned specifically with the sale of the rights to use one or more immovable properties on a timeshare basis; whereas such information should be supplemented by a document which must be made available to anyone who requests it; whereas the information therein must constitute part of the contract for the purchase of the right to use one or more immovable properties on a timeshare basis;

8. Whereas, in order to give purchasers a high level of protection and in view of the specific characteristics of systems for using immovable properties on a timeshare basis, contracts for the purchase of the right to use one or more immovable properties on a timeshare basis must include certain minimal items;

9. Whereas, with a view to establishing effective protection for purchasers in this field, it is necessary to stipulate minimum obligations with which vendors must comply vis-à-vis purchasers;

10. Whereas the contract for the purchase of the right to use one or more immovable properties on a timeshare basis must be drawn up in the official language or one of the official languages of the Member State in which the purchaser is resident or in the official language or one of the official languages of the Member State of which he is a national which must be one of the official languages of the Community; whereas, however, the Member State in which the purchaser is resident may require that the contract be drawn up in its language or its languages which must be an official language or official languages of the Community; whereas provision should be made for a certified translation of each contract for the purposes of the formalities to be completed in the Member State in which the relevant property is situated;

11. Whereas to give the purchaser the chance to realize more fully what his obligations and rights under the contract are he should be

allowed a period during which he may withdraw from the contract without giving reasons since the property in question is often situated in a State and subject to legislation which are different from his own;

12. Whereas the requirement on the vendor's part that advance payments be made before the end of the period during which the purchaser may withdraw without giving reasons may reduce the purchaser's protection; whereas, therefore, advance payments before the end of that period should be prohibited;

13. Whereas in the event of cancellation of or withdrawal from a contract for the purchase of the right to use one or more immovable properties on a timeshare basis the price of which is entirely or partly covered by credit granted to the purchaser by the vendor or by a third party on the basis of an agreement concluded between that third party and the vendor, it should be provided that the credit agreement should be cancelled without penalty;

14. Whereas there is a risk, in certain cases, that the consumer may be deprived of the protection provided for in this Directive if the law of a non-Member State is specified as the law applicable to the contract; whereas this Directive should therefore include provisions intended to obviate that risk;

15. Whereas it is for the Member States to adopt measures to ensure that the vendor fulfils his obligations.

HAVE ADOPTED THIS DIRECTIVE:

Article 1

The purpose of this Directive shall be to approximate the laws, regulations and administrative provisions of the Member States on the protection of purchasers in respect of certain aspects of contracts relating directly or indirectly to the purchase of the right to use one or more immovable properties on a timeshare basis.

This Directive shall cover only those aspects of the above provisions concerning contractual transactions that relate to:

- information on the constituent parts of a contract and the arrangements for the communication of that information,
- the procedures and arrangements for cancellation and withdrawal.

With due regard to the general rules of the Treaty, the Member States shall remain competent for other matters, inter alia determination of the legal nature of the rights which are the subject of the contracts covered by this Directive.

Article 2

For the purposes of this Directive:

-   'contract relating directly or indirectly to the purchase of the right to use one or more immovable properties on a timeshare basis', hereinafter referred to as 'contract', shall mean any contract or group of contracts concluded for at least three years under which, directly or indirectly, on payment of a certain global price, a real property right or any other right relating to the use of one or more immovable properties for a specified or specifiable period of the year, which may not be less than one week, is established or is the subject of a transfer or an undertaking to transfer,
-   'immovable property' shall mean any building or part of a building for use as accommodation to which the right which is the subject of the contract relates,
-   'vendor' shall mean any natural or legal person who, acting in transactions covered by this Directive and in his professional capacity, establishes, transfers or undertakes to transfer the right which is the subject of the contract,
-   'purchaser' shall mean any natural person who, acting in transactions covered by this Directive, for purposes which may be regarded as being outwith his professional capacity, has the right which is the subject of the contract transferred to him or for whom the right which is the subject of the contract is established.

Article 3

(1) The Member States shall make provision in their legislation for measures to ensure that the vendor is required to provide any person requesting information on the immovable property or properties with a document which, in addition to a general description of the property or properties, shall provide at least brief and accurate information on the particulars referred to in points (a) to (g), (i) and (l) of the Annex and on how further information may be obtained.

(2) The Member States shall make provision in their legislation to ensure that all the information referred to in paragraph 1 which must be provided in the document referred to in paragraph 1 forms an integral part of the contract.

Unless the parties expressly agree otherwise, only changes resulting from circumstances beyond the vendor's control may be made to the information provided in the document referred to in paragraph 1.

Any changes to that information shall be communicated to the purchaser before the contract is concluded. The contract shall expressly mention any such changes.

(3) Any advertising referring to the immovable property concerned shall indicate the possibility of obtaining the document referred to in paragraph 1 and where it may be obtained.

Article 4

The Member States shall make provision in their legislation to ensure that:

– the contract, which shall be in writing, includes at least the items referred to in the Annex,
– the contract and the document referred to in Article 3(1) are drawn up in the language or one of the languages of the Member State in which the purchaser is resident or in the language or one of the languages of the Member State of which he is national which shall be an official language or official languages of the Community, at the purchaser's option. The Member State in which the purchaser is resident may, however, require that the contract be drawn up in all cases in at least its language or languages which must be an official language or official languages of the Community, and
– the vendor provides the purchaser with a certified translation of the contract in the language or one of the languages of the Member State in which the immovable property is situated which shall be an official language or official languages of the Community.

Article 5

The Member States shall make provision in their legislation to ensure that:

1. in addition to the possibilities available to the purchaser under national laws on the nullity of contracts, the purchaser shall have the right:
    – to withdraw without giving any reason within 10 calendar days of both parties' signing the contract or of both parties' signing a binding preliminary contract. If the 10th day is a public holiday, the period shall be extended to the first working day thereafter,
    – if the contract does not include the information referred to in points (a), (b), (c), (d) (1), (d) (2), (h), (i), (k), (l) and (m) of the Annex, at the time of both parties' signing the contract or of both parties' signing a binding preliminary contract, to cancel the contract within three months thereof. If the information in question is provided within those three months, the purchaser's withdrawal period provided for in the first indent, shall then start,

—   if by the end of the three-month period provided for in the second indent the purchaser has not exercised the right to cancel and the contract does not include the information referred to in points (a), (b), (c), (d) (1), (d) (2), (h), (i), (k), (l) and (m) of the Annex, to the withdrawal period provided for in the first indent from the day after the end of that three-month period;

2.   if the purchaser intends to exercise the rights provided for in paragraph 1 he shall, before the expiry of the relevant deadline, notify the person whose name and address appear in the contract for that purpose by a means which can be proved in accordance with national law in accordance with the procedures specified in the contract pursuant to point (l) of the Annex. The deadline shall be deemed to have been observed if the notification, if it is in writing, is dispatched before the deadline expires;

3.   where the purchaser exercises the right provided for in the first indent of paragraph 1, he may be required to defray, where appropriate, only those expenses which, in accordance with national law, are incurred as a result of the conclusion of and withdrawal from the contract and which correspond to legal formalities which must be completed before the end of the period referred to in the first indent of paragraph 1. Such expenses shall be expressly mentioned in the contract;

4.   where the purchaser exercises the right of cancellation provided for in the second indent of paragraph 1 he shall not be required to make any defrayal.

Article 6

The Member States shall make provision in their legislation to prohibit any advance payments by a purchaser before the end of the period during which he may exercise the right of withdrawal.

Article 7

The Member States shall make provision in their legislation to ensure that:

—   if the price is fully or partly covered by credit granted by the vendor, or
—   if the price is fully or partly covered by credit granted to the purchaser by a third party on the basis of an agreement between the third party and the vendor,

the credit agreement shall be cancelled, without any penalty, if the purchaser exercises his right to cancel or withdraw from the contract as provided for in Article 5.

The Member States shall lay down detailed arrangements to govern the cancellation of credit agreements.

Article 8

The Member States shall make provision in their legislation to ensure that any clause whereby a purchaser renounces the enjoyment of rights under this Directive or whereby a vendor is freed from the responsibilities arising from this Directive shall not be binding on the purchaser, under conditions laid down by national law.

Article 9

The Member States shall take the measures necessary to ensure that, whatever the law applicable may be, the purchaser is not deprived of the protection afforded by this Directive, if the immovable property concerned is situated within the territory of a Member State.

Article 10

The Member States shall make provision in their legislation for the consequences of non-compliance with this Directive.

Article 11

This Directive shall not prevent Member States from adopting or maintaining provisions which are more favourable as regards the protection of purchasers in the field in question, without prejudice to their obligations under the Treaty.

Article 12

(1) Member States shall bring into force the laws, regulations and administrative provisions necessary for them to comply with this Directive no later than 30 months after its publication in the Official Journal of the European Communities. They shall immediately inform the Commission thereof.

When Member States adopt those measures, they shall include references to this Directive or shall accompany them with such references on their official publication. The Member States shall lay down the manner in which such references shall be made.

(2) The Member States shall communicate to the Commission the texts of the provisions of national law which they adopt in the field governed by this Directive.

Article 13

This Directive is addressed to the Member States.

ANNEX

Minimum list of items to be included in the contract referred to in Article 4

a)   The identities and domiciles of the parties, including specific information on the vendor's legal status at the time of the conclusion of the
contract and the identity and domicile of the owner.

b)   The exact nature of the right which is the subject of the contract and a
clause setting out the conditions governing the exercise of that right
within the territory of the Member State(s) in which the property or
properties concerned relates is or are situated and if those conditions
have been fulfilled or, if they have not, what conditions remain to be
fulfilled.

c)   When the property has been determined, an accurate description of
that property and its location.

d)   Where the immovable property is under construction:
1.   the state of completion;
2.   a reasonable estimate of the deadline for completion of the
immovable property;
3.   where it concerns a specific immovable property, the number of
the building permit and the name(s) and full address(es) of the
competent authority or authorities;
4.   the state of completion of the services rendering the immovable
property fully operational (gas, electricity, water and telephone
connections);
5.   a guarantee regarding completion of the immovable property or
a guarantee regarding reimbursement of any payment made if the
property is not completed and, where appropriate, the conditions
governing the operation of those guarantees.

e)   The services (lighting, water, maintenance, refuse collection) to which
the purchaser has or will have access and on what conditions.

f)   The common facilities, such as swimming pool, sauna, etc., to which
the purchaser has or may have access, and, where appropriate, on what
conditions.

g)   The principles on the basis of which the maintenance of and repairs to
the immovable property and its administration and management will
be arranged.

h)   The exact period within which the right which is the subject of the
contract may be exercised and, if necessary, its duration; the date on
which the purchaser may start to exercise the contractual right.

i)   The price to be paid by the purchaser to exercise the contractual right;
an estimate of the amount to be paid by the purchaser for the use of
common facilities and services; the basis for the calculation of the

amount of charges relating to occupation of the property, the mandatory statutory charges (for example, taxes and fees) and the administrative overheads (for example, management, maintenance and repairs).

j)   A clause stating that acquisition will not result in costs, charges or obligations other than those specified in the contract.

k)   Whether or not it is possible to join a scheme for the exchange or resale of the contractual rights, and any costs involved should an exchange and/or resale scheme be organized by the vendor or by a third party designated by him in the contract.

l)   Information on the right to cancel or withdraw from the contract and indication of the person to whom any letter of cancellation or withdrawal should be sent, specifying also the arrangements under which such letters may be sent; precise indication of the nature and amount of the costs which the purchaser will be required to defray pursuant to Article 5(3) if he exercises his right to withdraw; where appropriate, information on the arrangements for the cancellation of the credit agreement linked to the contract in the event of cancellation of the contract or withdrawal from it.

m) The date and place of each party's signing of the contract.

Denmark	1. – Lov om forbrugeraftaler, der giver brugsret til fast ajendom på timesharebasis. 2. – Lov Nr 234 af 02/04/1997.
EIRE	1. – European Communities (Contracts for Time Sharing of Immovable Property – Protection of Purchasers) Regulations, 1997 ref: S.I. No. 204/1997. 2. – European Communities (Contracts for Time Sharing of Immovable Property – Protections of Purchasers) (Amendment) Regulations 2000, S.I. No. 144/2000.
Finland	Laki kuluttajansuojalain muuttamisesta/ Lag om ändring av konsumentskyddslagen (1162/97) 11/12/1997
Sweden	Lag om konsumentskydd vid avtal om tidsdelat boende, SFS 1997:218
England	The Timeshare Regulations 1997, S.I. No. 1997/1081.

COUNCIL DIRECTIVE 93/7/EEC

of 15 March 1993

on the return of cultural objects unlawfully removed from the territory of a Member State

(Official Journal L74/1993, p 74)

Amendments

Article	Nature of Amendment	Effected by	Date
Annex	Amended	Regulation 96/100/EC of the EP and Council	17 February 1997
Annex	Amended	Directive 2001/38/EC of the EP and Council	5 June 2001

THE COUNCIL OF THE EUROPEAN COMMUNITIES –

Having regard to the Treaty establishing the European Economic Community, and in particular Article 100a thereof,

Having regard to the proposal from the Commission,[1]

In cooperation with the European Parliament,[2]

Having regard to the opinion of the Economic and Social Committee,[3]

Whereas Article 8a of the Treaty provides for the establishment, not later than 1 January 1993, of the internal market, which is to comprise an area without internal frontiers in which the free movement of goods, persons, services and capital is ensured in accordance with the provisions of the Treaty;

Whereas, under the terms and within the limits of Article 36 of the Treaty, Member States will, after 1992, retain the right to define their national treasures and to take the necessary measures to protect them in this area without internal frontiers;

Whereas arrangements should therefore be introduced enabling Member States to secure the return to their territory of cultural objects which are classified as national treasures within the meaning of the said Article 36 and have been removed

[1] OJ C53/92, p 11, and OJ C172/92, p 7.
[2] OJ C176/92, p 129, and OJ C72/93.
[3] OJ C223/92, p 10.

from their territory in breach of the abovementioned national measures or of Council Regulation (EEC) No 3911/92 of 9 December 1992 on the export of cultural goods;[4] whereas the implementation of these arrangements should be as simple and efficient as possible; whereas, to facilitate cooperation with regard to return, the scope of the arrangements should be confined to items belonging to common categories of cultural object; whereas the Annex to this Directive is consequently not intended to define objects which rank as 'national treasures' within the meaning of the said Article 36, but merely categories of object which may be classified as such and may accordingly be covered by the return procedure introduced by this Directive;

Whereas cultural objects classified as national treasures and forming an integral part of public collections or inventories of ecclesiastical institutions but which do not fall within these common categories should also be covered by this Directive;

Whereas administrative cooperation should be established between Member States as regards their national treasures, in close liaison with their cooperation in the field of stolen works of art and involving in particular the recording, with Interpol and other qualified bodies issuing similar lists, of lost, stolen or illegally removed cultural objects forming part of their national treasures and their public collections;

Whereas the procedure introduced by this Directive is a first step in establishing cooperation between Member States in this field in the context of the internal market; whereas the aim is mutual recognition of the relevant national laws; whereas provision should therefore be made, in particular, for the Commission to be assisted by an advisory committee;

Whereas Regulation (EEC) No 3911/92 introduces, together with this Directive, a Community system to protect Member States' cultural goods; whereas the date by which Member States have to comply with this Directive has to be as close as possible to the date of entry into force of that Regulation; whereas, having regard to the nature of their legal systems and the scope of the changes to their legislation necessary to implement this Directive, some Member States will need a longer period,

HAS ADOPTED THIS DIRECTIVE:

Article 1

For the purposes of this Directive:

1. 'Cultural object' shall mean an object which:
    –   is classified, before or after its unlawful removal from the territory of a Member State, among the 'national treasures possessing artistic, historic or archaeological value' under national legislation or administrative procedures within the meaning of Article 36 of the Treaty,

---

[4] OJ L395/92, p 1.

and

- belongs to one of the categories listed in the Annex or does not belong to one of these categories but forms an integral part of:
- public collections listed in the inventories of museums, archives or libraries' conservation collection.

    For the purposes of this Directive, 'public collections' shall mean collections which are the property of a Member State, local or regional authority within a Member State or an institution situated in the territory of a Member State and defined as public in accordance with the legislation of that Member State, such institution being the property of, or significantly financed by, that Member State or a local or regional authority;
- the inventories of ecclesiastical institutions.

2. 'Unlawfully removed from the territory of a Member State' shall mean:
    - removed from the territory of a Member State in breach of its rules on the protection of national treasures or in breach of Regulation (EEC) No 3911/92, or
    - not returned at the end of a period of lawful temporary removal or any breach of another condition governing such temporary removal.

3. 'Requesting Member State' shall mean the Member State from whose territory the cultural object has been unlawfully removed.

4. 'Requested Member State' shall mean the Member State in whose territory a cultural object unlawfully removed from the territory of another Member State is located.

5. 'Return' shall mean the physical return of the cultural object to the territory of the requesting Member State.

6. 'Possessor' shall mean the person physically holding the cultural object on his own account.

7. 'Holder' shall mean the person physically holding the cultural object for third parties.

Article 2

Cultural objects which have been unlawfully removed from the territory of a Member State shall be returned in accordance with the procedure and in the circumstances provided for in this Directive.

Article 3

Each Member State shall appoint one or more central authorities to carry out the tasks provided for in this Directive.

Member States shall inform the Commission of all the central authorities they appoint pursuant to this Article.

The Commission shall publish a list of these central authorities and any changes concerning them in the C series of the Official Journal of the European Communities.

Article 4

Member States' central authorities shall cooperate and promote consultation between the Member States' competent national authorities. The latter shall in particular:

1. upon application by the requesting Member State, seek a specified cultural object which has been unlawfully removed from its territory, identifying the possessor and/or holder. The application must include all information needed to facilitate this search, with particular reference to the actual or presumed location of the object;

2. notify the Member States concerned, where a cultural object is found in their own territory and there are reasonable grounds for believing that it has been unlawfully removed from the territory of another Member State;

3. enable the competent authorities of the requesting Member State to check that the object in question is a cultural object, provided that the check is made within 2 months of the notification provided for in paragraph 2. If it is not made within the stipulated period, paragraphs 4 and 5 shall cease to apply;

4. take any necessary measures, in cooperation with the Member State concerned, for the physical preservation of the cultural object;

5. prevent, by the necessary interim measures, any action to evade the return procedure;

6. act as intermediary between the possessor and/or holder and the requesting Member State with regard to return. To this end, the competent authorities of the requested Member States may, without prejudice to Article 5, first facilitate the implementation of an arbitration procedure, in accordance with the national legislation of the requested State and provided that the requesting State and the possessor or holder give their formal approval.

Article 5

The requesting Member State may initiate, before the competent court in the requested Member State, proceedings against the possessor or, failing him, the holder, with the aim of securing the return of a cultural object which has been unlawfully removed from its territory.

Proceedings may be brought only where the document initiating them is accompanied by:

- a document describing the object covered by the request and stating that it is a cultural object,
- a declaration by the competent authorities of the requesting Member State that the cultural object has been unlawfully removed from its territory.

Article 6

The central authority of the requesting Member State shall forthwith inform the central authority of the requested Member State that proceedings have been initiated with the aim of securing the return of the object in question.

The central authority of the requested Member State shall forthwith inform the central authorities of the other Member States.

Article 7

(1) Member States shall lay down in their legislation that the return proceedings provided for in this Directive may not be brought more than one year after the requesting Member State became aware of the location of the cultural object and of the identity of its possessor or holder.

Such proceedings may, at all events, not be brought more than 30 years after the object was unlawfully removed from the territory of the requesting Member State. However, in the case of objects forming part of public collections, referred to in Article 1 (1), and ecclesiastical goods in the Member States where they are subject to special protection arrangements under national law, return proceedings shall be subject to a time-limit of 75 years, except in Member States where proceedings are not subject to a time-limit or in the case of bilateral agreements between Member States laying down a period exceeding 75 years.

(2) Return proceedings may not be brought if removal from the national territory of the requesting Member State is no longer unlawful at the time when they are to be initiated.

Article 8

Save as otherwise provided in Articles 7 and 13, the competent court shall order the return of the cultural object in question where it is found to be a cultural object within the meaning of Article 1(1) and to have been removed unlawfully from national territory.

Article 9

Where return of the object is ordered, the competent court in the requested States shall award the possessor such compensation as it deems fair according to the circumstances of the case, provided that it is satisfied that the possessor exercised due care and attention in acquiring the object.

The burden of proof shall be governed by the legislation of the requested Member State.

In the case of a donation or succession, the possessor shall not be in a more favourable position than the person from whom he acquired the object by that means.

The requesting Member State shall pay such compensation upon return of the object.

Article 10

Expenses incurred in implementing a decision ordering the return of a cultural object shall be borne by the requesting Member State. The same applies to the costs of the measures referred to in Article 4(4).

Article 11

Payment of the fair compensation and of the expenses referred to in Articles 9 and 10 respectively shall be without prejudice to the requesting Member State's right to take action with a view to recovering those amounts from the persons responsible for the unlawful removal of the cultural object from its territory.

Article 12

Ownership of the cultural object after return shall be governed by that law of the requesting Member State.

Article 13

This Directive shall apply only to cultural objects unlawfully removed from the territory of a Member State on or after 1 January 1993.

Article 14

(1)   Each Member State may extend its obligation to return cultural objects to cover categories of objects other than those listed in the Annex.

(2)   Each Member State may apply the arrangements provided for by this Directive to requests for the return of cultural objects unlawfully removed from the territory of other Member States prior to 1 January 1993.

Article 15

This Directive shall be without prejudice to any civil or criminal proceedings that may be brought, under the national laws of the Member States, by the requesting Member State and/or the owner of a cultural object that has been stolen.

Article 16

(1) Member States shall send the Commission every three years, and for the first time in February 1996, a report on the application of this Directive.
(2) The Commission shall send the European Parliament, the Council and the Economic and Social Committee, every three years, a report reviewing the application of this Directive.
(3) The Council shall review the effectiveness of this Directive after a period of application of three years and, acting on a proposal from the Commission, make any necessary adaptations.
(4) In any event, the Council acting on a proposal from the Commission, shall examine every three years and, where appropriate, update the amounts indicated in the Annex, on the basis of economic and monetary indicators in the Community.

Article 17

The Commission shall be assisted by the Committee set up by Article 8 of Regulation (EEC) No 3911/92.

The Committee shall examine any question arising from the application of the Annex to this Directive which may be tabled by the chairman either on his own initiative or at the request of the representative of a Member State.

Article 18

Member States shall bring into force the laws, regulations and administrative provisions necessary to comply with this Directive within nine months of its adoption, except as far as the Kingdom of Belgium, the Federal Republic of Germany and the Kingdom of the Netherlands are concerned, which must conform to this Directive at the latest twelve months from the date of its adoption. They shall forthwith inform the Commission thereof.

When Member States adopt these measures, they shall contain a reference to this Directive or shall be accompanied by such reference on the occasion of their official publication. The methods of making such a reference shall be laid down by the Member States.

Article 19

This Directive is addressed to the Member States.

ANNEX

Categories referred to in the second indent of Article 1(1) to which objects classified as 'national treasures' within the meaning of Article 36 of the Treaty must belong in order to qualify for return under this Directive

A. 1. Archaeological objects more than 100 years old which are the products of:
  - land or underwater excavations and finds,
  - archaeological sites,
  - archaeological collections

2. Elements forming an integral part of artistic, historical or religious monuments which have been dismembered, more than 100 years old.

3. Pictures and paintings, other than those included in categories 3A or 4, executed entirely by hand, on any medium and in any material.[1]

3A. Water-colours, gouaches and pastels executed entirely by hand on any material.[1]

4. Mosaics in any material executed by hand, other than those in categories 1 or 2 and drawings in any medium, and executed entirely by hand on any material.[1]

5. Original engravings, prints, serigraphs and lithographs with their respective plates and original posters.[1]

6. Original sculptures or statuary and copies produced by the same process as the original[1] other than those in category 1.

7. Photographs, films and negatives thereof.[1]

8. Incunabula and manuscripts, including maps and musical scores, singly or in collections.[1]

9. Books more than 100 years old, singly or in collections.

10. Printed maps more than 200 years old.

11. Archives and any elements thereof, of any kind, on any medium, comprising elements more than 50 years old.

12. (a) Collections[2] and specimens from zoological, botanical, mineralogical or anatomical collections;

---

[1] Which are more than fifty years old and do not belong to their originators.

[2] As defined by the Court of Justice in its Judgment in Case 252/84, as follows: 'Collectors' pieces within the meaning of Heading No 99.05 of the Common Customs Tariff are articles which possess the requisite characteristics for inclusion in a collection, that is to say, articles which are relatively rare, are not normally used for their original purpose, are the subject of special transactions outside the normal trade in similar utility articles and are of high value.'

(b) Collections[2] of historical, palaeontological, ethnographic or numismatic interest.

13. Means of transport more than 75 years old.

14. Any other antique item not included in categories A 1 to A 13, more than 50 years old.

The cultural objects in categories A 1 to A 14 are covered by this Directive only if their value corresponds to, or exceeds, the financial thresholds under B.

B. **Financial thresholds applicable to certain categories under A (in euro)**
    Value: 0 (Zero)
    − 1 (Archaeological objects)
    − 2 (Dismembered monuments)
    − 8 (Incunabula and manuscripts)
    − 11 (Archives)

    15 000
    − 4 (Mosaics and drawings)
    − 5 (Engravings)
    − 7 (Photographs)
    − 10 (Printed maps)

    30 000
    − 3A (Water-colours, gouaches and pastels)

    50 000
    − 6 (Statuary)
    − 9 (Books)
    − 12 (Collections)
    − 13 (Means of transport)
    − 14 (Any other item)

    150 000
    − 3 (Pictures)

The assessment of whether or not the conditions relating to financial value are fulfilled must be made when return is requested. The financial value is that of the object in the requested Member State.

For the Member States which do not have the euro as their currency, the values expressed in euro in the Annex shall be converted and expressed in national currencies at the rate of exchange on 31 December 2001 published in the Official Journal of the European Communities. This countervalue in national currencies shall be reviewed every two years with effect from 31 December 2001. Calculation of this countervalue shall be based on the average daily value of those currencies, expressed in euro, during the 24 months ending on the last day of August preceding the revision which takes effect on 31 December. The Advisory Committee on Cultural Goods shall review this method of calculation, on a proposal from the

Commission, in principle two years after the first application. For each revision, the values expressed in euro and their countervalues in national currency shall be published periodically in the Official Journal of the European Communities in the first days of the month of November preceding the date on which the revision takes effect.

Denmark	1. – Lov om tilbagelevering af kulturgoder, som unlovigt er fjernet fra et EU- medlemslands område, Lov Nr 1104 af 22/12/1993
	2. – Kulturministeriets bekendtgørelse nr. 1064 af 18/12/1997 om ændring af bilag til lov om tilbagelevering af kulturgoder, som ulovligt er fjernet fra et EU-medlemslands område. Kulturmin., 2.kt., j.nr. 1997.200-3.
EIRE	1. – European Communities (Return of Cultural Objects) Regulations 1994, S.I. No. 182/1994.
	2. – European Communities (Return of Cultural Objects) (Amendment) Regulations, 1998, S.I. No. 24/1998
Finland	Laki Euroopan talousalueen valtion alueelta laittomasti — vietyjen kulttuuriesineiden palauttamisesta (1276/94) 16/12/1994
Sweden	1. – Lag om ändring i lagen (1988:950) om kulturminnen m.m., – SFS 1994:1523 — —
	2. – Förordning om ändring i förordningen (1988:1188) om kulturminnen m.m., SFS 1994:1524
	3. – Lag om ändring i lagen (1988:950) om kulturminnen m.m., SFS 2001:1047
	4. – Lag om ändring i lagen (1988:950) om kulturminnen m.m., SFS 1998:30
	5. – Lag om ändring i lagen (1998:950) om kulturminnen m.m., SFS 2001:1047
United Kingdom	1. – The Return of Cultural Objects Regulations 1994, S.I. No 1994/501.
	2. – The European Communities (Return of Cultural Objects) Regulations 1997, S.I. No 1997/1719.
	3. – The Return of Cultural Objects (Amendment) Regulations 2001, S.I. No. 2001/3972.

PART 2

UNITARY LAW

EUROPEAN CONVENTION

for the Protection of Human Rights and Fundamental Freedoms
of 4 November 1950*

– Extract –

(UKTS 71 (1953), Cmd 8969, 213 UNTS 221, ETS 5)

Amendments

Article	Nature of Amendment	Effected by	Date	Source in UK law
29, 30, 34	Amended	Protocol 3	6 May 1963	The Human Rights Act
22, 40	Amended	Protocol 5	20 January 1966	1998 incorporates the
20, 21, 23, 28–31, 34, 40, 41, 43	Amended	Protocol 8	19 March 1985	substantive rights of the Convention, and of continued...

* The Convention came into force on 3 September 1953. The United Kingdom was one of the first signatories, on 4 November 1950. Before being ratified, it was, in accordance with the 'Ponsoby' rule, ordered 'to lie upon the Table' of the House of Commons, on 23 January 1951. The instrument of ratification was deposited with the Secretary-General of the Council of Europe on 8 March 1951. In accordance with the pivotal precept of British constitutional law, to wit parliamentary sovereignty, the terms of any international treaty ratified by the UK does not become part of its domestic law unless expressly so enacted. This did not happen, as UK law was deemed already to be in full accord with the substance of the Convention rights: therefore, although UK courts could take note of the rights, they could not enforce them as such directly. This was the situation until the passage of the Human Rights Act 1998, which came into force on 2 October 2000. This Act incorporated the substantive rights of the Convention, as well as of Protocols 1 and 6 into domestic law.

The Convention came into force in the following states, on the dates indicated in brackets, and indeed often subject to reservations or declarations: Albania (2 October 1996), Andorra (22 January 1996), Austria (3 September 1958), Belgium (14 June 1955), Bulgaria (7 September 1992), Croatia (5 November 1997), Cyprus (6 October 1962), the Czech Republic (1 January 1993), Denmark (3 September 1953), Estonia (16 April 1996), the Federal Republic of Germany (3 September 1953), Finland (10 May 1990), France (3 May 1974), Greece (28 November 1974), Hungary (5 November 1992), Ireland (3 September 1953), Iceland (3 September 1953), Italy (26 November 1955), Latvia (27 June 1997), Lithuania (20 June 1995), Liechtenstein (8 September 1982), Luxembourg (3 September 1953), Moldavia (12 September 1997), Malta (23 January 1967), Macedonia, the former Yugoslavia (10 April 1997), The Netherlands (31 August 1954), Norway (3 September 1953), Poland (19 January 1993), Portugal (9 November 1978), Romania (20 June 1994), the Russian

Article	Nature of Amendment	Effected by	Date	Source in UK law
31, 44, 45	Amended	Protocol 9	19 April 1994	Protocols 2 and 6
32	Amended	Protocol 10[1]	19 April 1994	into UK law
19-51 56	Amended	Protocol 11	24 July 1995	
Articles 58 & 59 Article 57 becomes 52 Articles 60–66 become 53	Repealed			

The governments signatory hereto, being members of the Council of Europe –

Considering the Universal Declaration of Human Rights proclaimed by the General Assembly of the United Nations on 10th December 1948;

Considering that this Declaration aims at securing the universal and effective recognition and observance of the Rights therein declared;

Considering that the aim of the Council of Europe is the achievement of greater unity between its members and that one of the methods by which that aim is to be pursued is the maintenance and further realisation of human rights and fundamental freedoms;

Reaffirming their profound belief in those fundamental freedoms which are the foundation of justice and peace in the world and are best maintained on the one hand by an effective political democracy and on the other by a common understanding and observance of the human rights upon which they depend;

Being resolved, as the governments of European countries which are like-minded and have a common heritage of political traditions, ideals, freedom and the rule of law, to take the first steps for the collective enforcement of certain of the rights stated in the Universal Declaration,

Have agreed as follows:

Article 1

Obligation to respect human rights

The High Contracting Parties shall secure to everyone within their jurisdiction the rights and freedoms defined in Section I of this Convention.

Federation (5 May 1998), San Marino (22 March 1989), Sweden (3 September 1953), Switzerland (28 November 1974), Slovakia (1 January 1993), Slovenia (28 June 1994), Spain (4 October 1979), Turkey (18 May 1954) and the Ukraine (11 September 1997).
[1] Protocol 10 was rendered obsolete by Protocol 11.

Section I

Rights and freedoms

Article 2

Right to life

(1) Everyone's right to life shall be protected by law. No one shall be deprived of his life intentionally save in the execution of a sentence of a court following his conviction of a crime for which this penalty is provided by law.

(2) Deprivation of life shall not be regarded as inflicted in contravention of this article when it results from the use of force which is no more than absolutely necessary:

a) in defence of any person from unlawful violence;

b) in order to effect a lawful arrest or to prevent the escape of a person lawfully detained;

c) in action lawfully taken for the purpose of quelling a riot or insurrection.

Article 3

Prohibition of torture

No one shall be subjected to torture or to inhuman or degrading treatment or punishment.

Article 4

Prohibition of slavery and forced labour

(1) No one shall be held in slavery or servitude.

(2) No one shall be required to perform forced or compulsory labour.

(3) For the purpose of this article the term 'forced or compulsory labour' shall not include:

a) any work required to be done in the ordinary course of detention imposed according to the provisions of Article 5 of this Convention or during conditional release from such detention;

b) any service of a military character or, in case of conscientious objectors in countries where they are recognised, service exacted instead of compulsory military service;

c)   any service exacted in case of an emergency or calamity threatening the life or well-being of the community;

d)   any work or service which forms part of normal civic obligations.

Article 5

Right to liberty and security

(1) Everyone has the right to liberty and security of person. No one shall be deprived of his liberty save in the following cases and in accordance with a procedure prescribed by law:

a)   the lawful detention of a person after conviction by a competent court;

b)   the lawful arrest or detention of a person for non-compliance with the lawful order of a court or in order to secure the fulfilment of any obligation prescribed by law;

c)   the lawful arrest or detention of a person effected for the purpose of bringing him before the competent legal authority on reasonable suspicion of having committed an offence or when it is reasonably considered necessary to prevent his committing an offence or fleeing after having done so;

d)   the detention of a minor by lawful order for the purpose of educational supervision or his lawful detention for the purpose of bringing him before the competent legal authority;

e)   the lawful detention of persons for the prevention of the spreading of infectious diseases, of persons of unsound mind, alcoholics or drug addicts or vagrants;

f)   the lawful arrest or detention of a person to prevent his effecting an unauthorised entry into the country or of a person against whom action is being taken with a view to defsportation orextradition.

(2) Everyone who is arrested shall be informed promptly, in a language which he understands, of the reasons for his arrest and of any charge against him.

(3) Everyone arrested or detained in accordance with the provisions of paragraph 1.c of this article shall be brought promptly before a judge or other officer authorised by law to exercise judicial power and shall be entitled to trial within a reasonable time or to release pending trial. Release may be conditioned by guarantees to appear for trial.

(4) Everyone who is deprived of his liberty by arrest or detention shall be entitled to take proceedings by which the lawfulness of his detention shall be decided speedily by a court and his release ordered if the detention is not lawful.

(5) Everyone who has been the victim of arrest or detention in contravention of the provisions of this article shall have an enforceable right to compensation.

Article 6

Right to a fair trial

(1) In the determination of his civil rights and obligations or of any criminal charge against him, everyone is entitled to a fair and public hearing within a reasonable time by an independent and impartial tribunal established by law. Judgment shall be pronounced publicly but the press and public may be excluded from all or part of the trial in the interests of morals, public order or national security in a democratic society, where the interests of juveniles or the protection of the private life of the parties so require, or to the extent strictly necessary in the opinion of the court in special circumstances where publicity would prejudice the interests of justice.

(2) Everyone charged with a criminal offence shall be presumed innocent until proved guilty according to law.

(3) Everyone charged with a criminal offence has the following minimum rights:

a) to be informed promptly, in a language which he understands and in detail, of the nature and cause of the accusation against him;

b) to have adequate time and facilities for the preparation of his defence;

c) to defend himself in person or through legal assistance of his own choosing or, if he has not sufficient means to pay for legal assistance, to be given it free when the interests of justice so require;

d) to examine or have examined witnesses against him and to obtain the attendance and examination of witnesses on his behalf under the same conditions as witnesses against him;

e) to have the free assistance of an interpreter if he cannot understand or speak the language used in court.

Article 7

No punishment without law

(1) No one shall be held guilty of any criminal offence on account of any act or omission which did not constitute a criminal offence under national or international law at the time when it was committed. Nor shall a heavier penalty be imposed than the one that was applicable at the time the criminal offence was committed.

(2) This article shall not prejudice the trial and punishment of any person for any act or omission which, at the time when it was committed, was criminal according to the general principles of law recognised by civilised nations.

Article 8

Right to respect for private and family life

(1) Everyone has the right to respect for his private and family life, his home and his correspondence.
(2) There shall be no interference by a public authority with the exercise of this right except such as is in accordance with the law and is necessary in a democratic society in the interests of national security, public safety or the economic well-being of the country, for the prevention of disorder or crime, for the protection of health or morals, or for the protection of the rights and freedoms of others.

Article 9

Freedom of thought, conscience and religion

(1) Everyone has the right to freedom of thought, conscience and religion; this right includes freedom to change his religion or belief and freedom, either alone or in community with others and in public or private, to manifest his religion or belief, in worship, teaching, practice and observance.
(2) Freedom to manifest one's religion or beliefs shall be subject only to such limitations as are prescribed by law and are necessary in a democratic society in the interests of public safety, for the protection of public order, health or morals, or for the protection of the rights and freedoms of others.

Article 10

Freedom of expression

(1) Everyone has the right to freedom of expression. This right shall include freedom to hold opinions and to receive and impart information and ideas without interference by public authority and regardless of frontiers. This article shall not prevent States from requiring the licensing of broadcasting, television or cinema enterprises.
(2) The exercise of these freedoms, since it carries with it duties and responsibilities, may be subject to such formalities, conditions, restrictions or penalties as are prescribed by law and are necessary in a democratic society, in the interests of national security, territorial integrity or public safety, for the prevention of disorder or crime, for the protection of health or morals, for the protection of the reputation or rights of others, for preventing the disclosure of information received in confidence, or for maintaining the authority and impartiality of the judiciary.

Article 11

Freedom of assembly and association

(1) Everyone has the right to freedom of peaceful assembly and to freedom of association with others, including the right to form and to join trade unions for the protection of his interests.

(2) No restrictions shall be placed on the exercise of these rights other than such as are prescribed by law and are necessary in a democratic society in the interests of national security or public safety, for the prevention of disorder or crime, for the protection of health or morals or for the protection of the rights and freedoms of others. This article shall not prevent the imposition of lawful restrictions on the exercise of these rights by members of the armed forces, of the police or of the administration of the State.

Article 12

Right to marry

Men and women of marriageable age have the right to marry and to found a family, according to the national laws governing the exercise of this right.

Article 13

Right to an effective remedy

Everyone whose rights and freedoms as set forth in this Convention are violated shall have an effective remedy before a national authority notwithstanding that the violation has been committed by persons acting in an official capacity.

Article 14

Prohibition of discrimination

The enjoyment of the rights and freedoms set forth in this Convention shall be secured without discrimination on any ground such as sex, race, colour, language, religion, political or other opinion, national or social origin, association with a national minority, property, birth or other status.

Article 15

Derogation in time of emergency

(1) In time of war or other public emergency threatening the life of the nation any High Contracting Party may take measures derogating from

its obligations under this Convention to the extent strictly required by the exigencies of the situation, provided that such measures are not inconsistent with its other obligations under international law.

(2) No derogation from Article 2, except in respect of deaths resulting from lawful acts of war, or from Articles 3, 4 (paragraph 1) and 7 shall be made under this provision.

(3) Any High Contracting Party availing itself of this right of derogation shall keep the Secretary General of the Council of Europe fully informed of the measures which it has taken and the reasons therefor. It shall also inform the Secretary General of the Council of Europe when such measures have ceased to operate and the provisions of the Convention are again being fully executed.

Article 16

Restrictions on political activity of aliens

Nothing in Articles 10, 11 and 14 shall be regarded as preventing the High Contracting Parties from imposing restrictions on the political activity of aliens.

Article 17

Prohibition of abuse of rights

Nothing in this Convention may be interpreted as implying for any State, group or person any right to engage in any activity or perform any act aimed at the destruction of any of the rights and freedoms set forth herein or at their limitation to a greater extent than is provided for in the Convention.

Article 18

Limitation on use of restrictions on rights

The restrictions permitted under this Convention to the said rights and freedoms shall not be applied for any purpose other than those for which they have been prescribed.

Section II

European Court of Human Rights

Article 19 to 51

(not reproduced)

Section III

Miscellaneous provisions

Article 52 to 59

(not reproduced)

PROTOCOL 1

to the European Convention for the Protection of Human Rights and Fundamental Freedoms[1]

(UKTS 46 (1954), Cmd 9221, 213 UNTS 262, ETS 9)

Amendments

Article	Nature of Amendment	Effected by	Date	Source in UK law
4	Amended	Protocol 11	24 July 1995	Human Rights Act 1998

The Governments signatory hereto, being Members of the Council of Europe,

Being resolved to take steps to ensure the collective enforcement of certain rights and freedoms other than those already included in Section I of the Convention for the Protection of Human Rights and Fundamental Freedoms signed at Rome on 4 November 1950 (hereinafter referred to as 'the Convention'),

Have agreed as follows:

Article 1

Every natural or legal person is entitled to the peaceful enjoyment of his possessions. No one shall be deprived of his possessions except in the public interest and subject to the conditions provided for by law and by the general principles of international law.

The preceding provisions shall not, however, in any way impair the right of a State to enforce such laws as it deems necessary to control the use of property in accordance with the general interest or to secure the payment of taxes or other contributions or penalties.

---

[1] The United Kingdom was one of the original signatories of Protocol 1, on 8 March 1952. The instrument of ratification was deposited with the Secretary-General of the Council of Europe on 3 November 1952. The UK made a reservation in respect of Article 2 thereof: the duty of the state to provide educational facilities in accordance with parental convictions was 'accepted by the UK only in so far as it is compatible with the provisions of efficient instruction and training, and the avoidance of unreasonable expenditure'. Protocol 1 was not made part of domestic law, until the Human Rights Act 1998 explicitly incorporated it on 2 October 2000.

Subject to certain reservations and declarations, the Protocol applies in all states in which the Convention is in force, as well as in Andorra, the Republic of Moldavia and Switzerland.

Article 2

No person shall be denied the right to education. In the exercise of any functions which it assumes in relation to education and to teaching, the State shall respect the right of parents to ensure such education and teaching in conformity with their own religions and philosophical convictions.

Article 3

The High Contracting Parties undertake to hold free elections at reasonable intervals by secret ballot, under conditions which will ensure the free expression of the opinion of the people in the choice of the legislature.

Article 4

Any High Contracting Party may at the time of signature or ratification or at any time thereafter communicate to the Secretary-General of the Council of Europe a Declaration stating the extent to which it undertakes that the provisions of the present Protocol shall apply to such of the territories for the international relations of which it is responsible as are named therein.

Any High Contracting Party which has communicated a Declaration in virtue of the preceding paragraph may from time to time communicate a further Declaration modifying the terms of any former Declaration or terminating the application of the provisions of this Protocol in respect of any territory.

A Declaration made in accordance with this article shall be deemed to have been made in accordance with paragraph 1 of Article 63 of the Convention.

Article 5

As between the High Contracting Parties the provisions of Articles 1, 2, 3 and 4 of this Protocol shall be regarded as additional articles to the Convention and all the provisions of the Convention shall apply accordingly.

Article 6

This Protocol shall be open for signature by the members of the Council of Europe, who are the signatories of the Convention; it shall be ratified at the same time as or after the ratification of the Convention. It shall enter into force after the deposit of ten instruments of ratification. As regards any signatory ratifying subsequently, the Protocol shall enter into force at the date of the deposit of its instrument of ratification.

The instruments of ratification shall be deposited with the Secretary-General of the Council of Europe, who will notify all the Members of the names of those who have ratified.

Done at Paris on the 20th day of March 1952, In English and French, both texts being equally authentic, in a single copy which shall remain deposited in the archives of the Council of Europe. The Secretary-General shall transmit certified copies to each of the signatory Governments.

(Undersigned)

PROTOCOL 4

to the Convention for the Protection of Human Rights and Fundamental Freedoms[1]

– Extract –

(Misc 6 (1964), Cmnd 2309, ETS 46)

Amendments

Article	Nature of Amendment	Effected by	Date	Source in UK law
5	Amended	Protocol 11	24 July 1995	Protocol 11 has not been ratified by the UK
6		Protocol 11	24 July 1995	

The Governments signatory hereto, being Members of the Council of Europe,

Being resolved to take steps to ensure the collective enforcement of certain rights and freedoms other than those already included in Section 1 of the Convention for the Protection of Human Rights and Fundamental Freedoms signed at Rome on 4 November 1950 (hereinafter referred to as 'the Convention') and in Articles 1 to 3 of the First Protocol to the Convention, signed at Paris on 20 March 1952,

Have agreed as follows:

Article 1

No one shall be deprived of his liberty merely on the ground of inability to fulfil a contractual obligation.

[1] The United Kingdom has not ratified Protocol 4. It has, however, come into force in the following states, on the dates indicated in brackets: Albania (2 October 1996), Austria (18 September 1969), Belgium (21 September 1970), Croatia (5 November 1997), Cyprus (3 October 1989), Czech Republic (1 January 1993), the former Czechoslovakia (18 March 1992), Denmark (2 May 1968), Estonia (16 April 1996), the Federal Republic of Germany (1 June 1968), Finland (10 May 1990), France (3 May 1974), Hungary (5 November 1992), Iceland (2 May 1968), Ireland (29 October 1968), Italy (27 May 1982), Latvia (27 June 1997), Lithuania (20 June 1995), Luxembourg (2 May 1968), Macedonia, the former Yugoslavia (10 April 1997), The Netherlands (23 June 1982), Norway (2 May 1968), Poland (10 October 1994), Portugal (9 November 1978), Romania (20 June 1994), the Russian Federation (5 May 1998), San Marino (22 March 1989), Sweden (2 May 1968), Slovakia (1 January 1993), Slovenia (28 June 1994), and the Ukraine (11 September 1997).

Article 2

(1) Everyone lawfully within the territory of a State shall, within that territory, have the right to liberty of movement and freedom to choose his residence.

(2) Everyone shall be free to leave any country, including his own.

(3) No restrictions shall be placed on the exercise of these rights other than such as are in accordance with law and are necessary in a democratic society in the interests of national security or public safety for the maintenance of 'ordre public', for the prevention of crime, for the protection of rights and freedoms of others.

(4) The rights set forth in paragraph 1 may also be subject, in particular areas, to restrictions imposes in accordance with law and justified by the public interest in a democratic society.

Article 3 to 7

(not reproduced)

PROTOCOL 7

to the Convention for the Protection of Human Rights and Fundamental Freedoms of 22 November 1984[1]

– Extract –

(ETS 117, 7 EHRR 1, 24 ILM 435)

Amendments

Article	Nature of Amendment	Effected by	Date	Source in UK law
6	Amended	Protocol 11	24 July 1995	Protocol 11 has not been ratified by the UK
7	Repealed	Protocol 11	24 July 1995	

The Member States of the Council of Europe signatory hereto,

Being resolved to take further steps to ensure the collective enforcement of certain rights and freedoms by means of the Convention for the Protection of Human Rights and Fundamental Freedoms signed at Rome on 4 November 1950 (hereinafter referred to as 'The Convention');

Have agreed as follows:

Article 1

(1) An alien lawfully resident in the territory of a State shall not be expelled therefrom except in pursuance of a decision reached in accordance with law and shall be allowed:
   a) to submit reasons against his expulsion,
   b) to have his case reviewed, and
   c) to be represented for these purposes before the competent authority or a person or persons designated by that authority.
(2) An alien may be expelled before the exercise of his rights under paragraph 1(a), (b) and (c) of this Article, when such expulsion is necessary in the interests of public order or is grounded on reasons of national security.

[1] Protocol 4 came into force on 1 November 1988, in terms of Article 9. The United Kingdom has not ratified it.

Article 2 to 4

(not reproduced)

Article 5

Spouses shall enjoy equality of rights and responsibilities of a private law character between them, and in their relations with their children, as to marriage, during marriage and in the event of its dissolution. This Article shall not prevent States from taking such measures as are necessary in the interests of the children.

Article 6

(1) Any State may at the time of signature or when depositing its instrument of ratification, acceptance or approval, specify the territory or territories to which this Protocol shall apply and state the extent to which it undertakes that the provisions of this Protocol shall apply to this or these territories.

(2) Any State may at any later date, by a declaration addressed to the Secretary-General of the Council of Europe, extend the application of this Protocol to any other territory specified in the declaration. In respect of such territory the Protocol shall enter into force on the first day of the month following the expiration of a period of two months after the date of receipt by the Secretary-General of such declaration.

(3) Any declaration made under the two preceding paragraphs may, in respect of any territory specified in such declaration, be withdrawn or modified by a notification addressed to the Secretary-General. The withdrawal or modification shall become effective on the first day of the month following the expiration of a period of two months after the date of receipt of such notification by the Secretary General.

(4) A declaration made in accordance with this Article shall be deemed to have been made in accordance with paragraph 1 of Article 63 of the Convention.

(5) The territory of any State to which this Protocol applies by virtue of ratification, acceptance or approval by that State, and each territory to which this Protocol is applied by virtue of a declaration by that State under this Article, may be treated as separate territories for the purpose of the reference in Article 1 to the territory of a State.

Article 7

As between the State Parties, the provisions of Articles 1 to 6 of this Protocol shall be regarded as additional Articles to the Convention, and all the provisions of the Convention shall apply accordingly.

Article 8 to 10

(not reproduced)

UNITED NATIONS CONVENTION

on Contracts for the International Sale of Goods
of 11 April 1980[1]

(Misc 24 (1980), Cmnd 8074, UN Doc A/Conf 97/18, 19 ILM 671)

The States Parties to this Convention,

Bearing in mind the broad objectives in the resolutions adopted by the sixth special session of the General Assembly of the United Nations on the establishment of a New International Economic Order,

Considering that the development of international trade on the basis of equality and mutual benefit is an important element in promoting friendly relations among States,

Being of the opinion that the adoption of uniform rules which govern contracts for the international sale of goods and take into account the different social, economic and legal systems would contribute to the removal of legal barriers in international trade and promote the development of international trade,

Have agreed as follows:

PART I

SPHERE OF APPLICATION AND GENERAL PROVISIONS

CHAPTER I

SPHERE OF APPLICATION

Article 1

(1) This Convention applies to contracts of sale of goods between parties whose places of business are in different States:
  a)   When the States are Contracting States; or
  b)   When the rules of private international law lead to the application of the law of a Contracting State.

---

[1] The Convention has not come into force in the United Kingdom. It has indeed come into force in the following states, on the dates indicated in brackets: Argentina (1 January 1988), Australia (1 April 1989), Austria (1 January 1989), Belgium (1 November 1997), Bosnia-Herzegovina (6 March 1992), Bulgaria (1 August 1991), Burundi (1 October 1999), Canada (1 May 1992), Chile (1 March 1991), China (1 January 1988), Croatia (8 October 1991), Cuba (1 December 1995), the Czech Republic (1 January 1993), Denmark (1 March 1990), Ecuador (1 February 1993), the former East Germany (1 March 1990), Egypt (1 January 1988), Estonia (1 October 1994), the Federal Republic of Germany (1 January 1991), Finland (1 January 1989), France (1 January 1998), Georgia (1 September 1995), Greece (1 February 1999), Guinea (1 February 1992), Hungary (1 January 1988), Iraq (1 April 1991),

(2) The fact that the parties have their places of business in different States is to be disregarded whenever this fact does not appear either from the contract or from any dealings between, or from information disclosed by, the parties at any time before or at the conclusion of the contract.

(3) Neither the nationality of the parties nor the civil or commercial character of the parties or of the contract is to be taken into consideration in determining the application of this Convention.

Article 2

This Convention does not apply to sales:

a) Of goods bought for personal, family or household use, unless the seller, at any time before or at the conclusion of the contract, neither knew nor ought to have known that the goods were bought for any such use;

b) By auction;

c) On execution or otherwise by authority of law;

d) Of stocks, shares, investment securities, negotiable instruments or money;

e) Of ships, vessels, hovercraft or aircraft;

f) Of electricity.

Article 3

(1) Contracts for the supply of goods to be manufactured or produced are to be considered sales unless the party who orders the goods undertakes to supply a substantial part of the materials necessary for such manufacture or production.

(2) This Convention does not apply to contracts in which the preponderant part of the obligations of the party who furnishes the goods consists in the supply of labour or other services.

Article 4

This Convention governs only the formation of the contract of sale and the rights and obligations of the seller and the buyer arising from such a contract. In particular,

Italy (1 January 1988), Latvia (1 August 1998), Lesotho (1 January 1988), Lithuania (1 February 1996), Luxembourg (1 January 1998), Mexico (1 January 1989), Moldavia (1 November 1995), Mongolia (1 November 1995), The Netherlands (1 January 1992), New Zealand (1 October 1995), Norway (1 August 1989), Poland (1 June 1996), Romania (1 June 1992), Russia (1 September 1991), Singapore (1 March 1996), Slovakia (1 January 1993), Slovenia (25 June 1991), Spain (1 August 1991), Sweden (1 January 1989), Switzerland (1March 1991), Syria (1 January 1988), Uganda (1 March 1993), the Ukraine (11 September 1997), the United States of America (1 January 1988), Uzbekistan (1 December 1997), White Russia (1 November 1990), the former Yugoslavia (1 January 1988), and Zambia (1 January 1988).

except as otherwise expressly provided in this Convention, it is not concerned with:

a) The validity of the contract or of any of its provisions or of any usage;
b) The effect which the contract may have on the property in the goods sold.

Article 5

This Convention does not apply to the liability of the seller for death or personal injury caused by the goods to any person.

Article 6

The parties may exclude the application of this Convention or, subject to article 12, derogate from or vary the effect of any of its provisions.

CHAPTER II

GENERAL PROVISIONS

Article 7

(1) In the interpretation of this Convention, regard is to be had to its international character and to the need to promote uniformity in its application and the observance of good faith in international trade.
(2) Questions concerning matters governed by this Convention which are not expressly settled in it are to be settled in conformity with the general principles on which it is based or, in the absence of such principles, in conformity with the law applicable by virtue of the rules of private international law.

Article 8

(1) For the purposes of this Convention statements made by and other conduct of a party are to be interpreted according to his intent where the other party knew or could not have been unaware what that intent was.
(2) If the preceding paragraph is not applicable, statements made by and other conduct of a party are to be interpreted according to the understanding that a reasonable person of the same kind as the other party would have had in the same circumstances.

(3) In determining the intent of a party or the understanding a reasonable person would have had, due consideration is to be given to all relevant circumstances of the case including the negotiations, any practices which the parties have established between themselves, usages and any subsequent conduct of the parties.

Article 9

(1) The parties are bound by any usage to which they have agreed and by any practices which they have established between themselves.
(2) The parties are considered, unless otherwise agreed, to have impliedly made applicable to their contract or its formation a usage of which the parties knew or ought to have known and which in international trade is widely known to, and regularly observed by, parties to contracts of the type involved in the particular trade concerned.

Article 10

For the purposes of this Convention:

a) If a party has more than one place of business, the place of business is that which has the closest relationship to the contract and its performance, having regard to the circumstances known to or contemplated by the parties at any time before or at the conclusion of the contract;
b) If a party does not have a place of business, reference is to be made to his habitual residence.

Article 11

A contract of sale need not be concluded in or evidenced by writing and is not subject to any other requirement as to form. It may be proved by any means, including witnesses.

Article 12

Any provision of article 11, article 29 or Part II of this Convention that allows a contract of sale or its modification or termination by agreement or any offer, acceptance or other indication of intention to be made in any form other than in writing does not apply where any party has his place of business in a Contracting State which has made a declaration under article 96 of this Convention. The parties may not derogate from or vary the effect of this article.

Article 13

For the purposes of this Convention 'writing' includes telegram and telex.

PART II

FORMATION OF THE CONTRACT

Article 14

(1) A proposal for concluding a contract addressed to one or more specific persons constitutes an offer if it is sufficiently definite and indicates the intention of the offeror to be bound in case of acceptance. A proposal is sufficiently definite if it indicates the goods and expressly or implicitly fixes or makes provision for determining the quantity and the price.

(2) A proposal other than one addressed to one or more specific persons is to be considered merely as an invitation to make offers, unless the contrary is clearly indicated by the person making the proposal.

Article 15

(1) An offer becomes effective when it reaches the offeree.

(2) An offer, even if it is irrevocable, may be withdrawn if the withdrawal reaches the offeree before or at the same time as the offer.

Article 16

(1) Until a contract is concluded an offer may be revoked if the revocation reaches the offeree before he has dispatched an acceptance.

(2) However, an offer cannot be revoked:

   a)   If it indicates, whether by stating a fixed time for acceptance or otherwise, that it is irrevocable; or

   b)   If it was reasonable for the offeree to rely on the offer as being irrevocable and the offeree has acted in reliance on the offer.

Article 17

An offer, even if it is irrevocable, is terminated when a rejection reaches the offeror.

Article 18

(1) A statement made by or other conduct of the offeree indicating assent to an offer is an acceptance. Silence or inactivity does not in itself amount to acceptance.

(2) An acceptance of an offer becomes effective at the moment the indication of assent reaches the offeror. An acceptance is not effective if the

indication of assent does not reach the offeror within the time he has fixed or, if no time is fixed, within a reasonable time, due account being taken of the circumstances of the transaction, including the rapidity of the means of communication employed by the offeror. An oral offer must be accepted immediately unless the circumstances indicate otherwise.

(3)   However, if, by virtue of the offer or as a result of practices which the parties have established between themselves or of usage, the offeree may indicate assent by performing an act, such as one relating to the dispatch of the goods or payment of the price, without notice to the offeror, the acceptance is effective at the moment the act is performed, provided that the act is performed within the period of time laid down in the preceding paragraph.

Article 19

(1)   A reply to an offer which purports to be an acceptance but contains additions, limitations or other modifications is a rejection of the offer and constitutes a counter-offer.

(2)   However, a reply to an offer which purports to be an acceptance but contains additional or different terms which do not materially alter the terms of the offer constitutes an acceptance, unless the offeror, without undue delay, objects orally to the discrepancy or dispatches a notice to that effect. If he does not so object, the terms of the contract are the terms of the offer with the modifications contained in the acceptance.

(3)   Additional or different terms relating, among other things, to the price, payment, quality and quantity of the goods, place and time of delivery, extent of one party's liability to the other or the settlement of disputes are considered to alter the terms of the offer materially.

Article 20

(1)   A period of time for acceptance fixed by the offeror in a telegram or a letter begins to run from the moment the telegram is handed in for dispatch or from the date shown on the letter or, if no such date is shown, from the date shown on the envelope. A period of time for acceptance fixed by the offeror by telephone, telex or other means of instantaneous communication, begins to run from the moment that the offer reaches the offeree.

(2)   Official holidays or non-business days occurring during the period for acceptance are included in calculating the period. However, if a notice of acceptance cannot be delivered at the address of the offeror on the last day of the period because that day falls on an official holiday or a non-business day at the place of business of the offeror, the period is extended until the first business day which follows.

Article 21

(1)   A late acceptance is nevertheless effective as an acceptance if without delay the offeror orally so informs the offeree or dispatches a notice to that effect.

(2)   If a letter or other writing containing a late acceptance shows that it has been sent in such circumstances that if its transmission had been normal it would have reached the offeror in due time, the late acceptance is effective as an acceptance unless, without delay, the offeror orally informs the offeree that he considers his offer as having lapsed or dispatches a notice to that effect.

Article 22

An acceptance may be withdrawn if the withdrawal reaches the offeror before or at the same time as the acceptance would have become effective.

Article 23

A contract is concluded at the moment when an acceptance of an offer becomes effective in accordance with the provisions of this Convention.

Article 24

For the purposes of this Part of the Convention, an offer, declaration of acceptance or any other indication of intention 'reaches' the addressee when it is made orally to him or delivered by any other means to him personally, to his place of business or mailing address or, if he does not have a place of business or mailing address, to his habitual residence.

PART III

SALE OF GOODS

CHAPTER I

GENERAL PROVISIONS

Article 25

A breach of contract committed by one of the parties is fundamental if it results in such detriment to the other party as substantially to deprive him of what he is entitled to expect under the contract, unless the party in breach did not foresee and a reasonable person of the same kind in the same circumstances would not have foreseen such a result.

Article 26

A declaration of avoidance of the contract is effective only if made by notice to the other party.

Article 27

Unless otherwise expressly provided in this Part of the Convention, if any notice, request or other communication is given or made by a party in accordance with this Part and by means appropriate in the circumstances, a delay or error in the transmission of the communication or its failure to arrive does not deprive that party of the right to rely on the communication.

Article 28

If, in accordance with the provisions of this Convention, one party is entitled to require performance of any obligation by the other party, a court is not bound to enter a judgement for specific performance unless the court would do so under its own law in respect of similar contracts of sale not governed by this Convention.

Article 29

(1) A contract may be modified or terminated by the mere agreement of the parties.

(2) A contract in writing which contains a provision requiring any modification or termination by agreement to be in writing may not be otherwise modified or terminated by agreement. However, a party may be precluded by his conduct from asserting such a provision to the extent that the other party has relied on that conduct.

CHAPTER II

OBLIGATIONS OF THE SELLER

Article 30

The seller must deliver the goods, hand over any documents relating to them and transfer the property in the goods, as required by the contract and this Convention.

SECTION I

Delivery of the goods and handing over of documents

Article 31

If the seller is not bound to deliver the goods at any other particular place, his obligation to deliver consists:

a) If the contract of sale involves carriage of the goods – in handing the goods over to the first carrier for transmission to the buyer;

b) If, in cases not within the preceding subparagraph, the contract relates to specific goods, or unidentified goods to be drawn from a specific stock or to be manufactured or produced, and at the time of the conclusion of the contract the parties knew that the goods were at, or were to be manufactured or produced at, a particular place – in placing the goods at the buyer's disposal at that place;

c) In other cases – in placing the goods at the buyer's disposal at the place where the seller had his place of business at the time of the conclusion of the contract.

Article 32

(1) If the seller, in accordance with the contract or this Convention, hands the goods over to a carrier and if the goods are not clearly identified to the contract by markings on the goods, by shipping documents or otherwise, the seller must give the buyer notice of the consignment specifying the goods.

(2) If the seller is bound to arrange for carriage of the goods, he must make such contracts as are necessary for carriage to the place fixed by means of transportation appropriate in the circumstances and according to the usual terms for such transportation.

(3) If the seller is not bound to effect insurance in respect of the carriage of the goods, he must, at the buyer's request, provide him with all available information necessary to enable him to effect such insurance.

Article 33

The seller must deliver the goods:

a) If a date is fixed by or determinable from the contract, on that date;

b) If a period of time is fixed by or determinable from the contract, at any time within that period unless circumstances indicate that the buyer is to choose a date; or

c)   In any other case, within a reasonable time after the conclusion of the contract.

Article 34

If the seller is bound to hand over documents relating to the goods, he must hand them over at the time and place and in the form required by the contract. If the seller has handed over documents before that time, he may, up to that time, cure any lack of conformity in the documents, if the exercise of this right does not cause the buyer unreasonable inconvenience or unreasonable expense. However, the buyer retains any right to claim damages as provided for in this Convention.

SECTION II

Conformity of the goods and third party claims

Article 35

(1)   The seller must deliver goods which are of the quantity, quality and description required by the contract and which are contained or packaged in the manner required by the contract.

(2)   Except where the parties have agreed otherwise, the goods do not conform with the contract unless they:

a)   Are fit for the purposes for which goods of the same description would ordinarily be used;

b)   Are fit for any particular purpose expressly or impliedly made known to the seller at the time of the conclusion of the contract, except where the circumstances show that the buyer did not rely, or that it was unreasonable for him to rely, on the seller's skill and judgement;

c)   Possess the qualities of goods which the seller had held out to the buyer as a sample or model;

d)   Are contained or packaged in the manner usual for such goods or, where there is no such manner, in a manner adequate to preserve and protect the goods.

(3)   The seller is not liable under subparagraphs (a) to (d) of the preceding paragraph for any lack of conformity of the goods if at the time of the conclusion of the contract the buyer knew or could not have been unaware of such lack of conformity.

Article 36

(1)   The seller is liable in accordance with the contract and this Convention for any lack of conformity which exists at the time when the risk passes

to the buyer, even though the lack of conformity becomes apparent only after that time.

(2) The seller is also liable for any lack of conformity which occurs after the time indicated in the preceding paragraph and which is due to a breach of any of his obligations, including a breach of any guarantee that for a period of time the goods will remain fit for their ordinary purpose or for some particular purpose or will retain specified qualities or characteristics.

Article 37

If the seller has delivered goods before the date for delivery, he may, up to that date, deliver any missing part or make up any deficiency in the quantity of the goods delivered, or deliver goods in replacement of any non-conforming goods delivered or remedy any lack of conformity in the goods delivered, provided that the exercise of this right does not cause the buyer unreasonable inconvenience or unreasonable expense. However, the buyer retains any right to claim damages as provided for in this Convention.

Article 38

(1) The buyer must examine the goods, or cause them to be examined, within as short a period as is practicable in the circumstances.

(2) If the contract involves carriage of the goods, examination may be deferred until after the goods have arrived at their destination.

(3) If the goods are redirected in transit or redispatched by the buyer without a reasonable opportunity for examination by him and at the time of the conclusion of the contract the seller knew or ought to have known of the possibility of such redirection or redispatch, examination may be deferred until after the goods have arrived at the new destination.

Article 39

(1) The buyer loses the right to rely on a lack of conformity of the goods if he does not give notice to the seller specifying the nature of the lack of conformity within a reasonable time after he has discovered it or ought to have discovered it.

(2) In any event, the buyer loses the right to rely on a lack of conformity of the goods if he does not give the seller notice thereof at the latest within a period of two years from the date on which the goods were actually handed over to the buyer, unless this time-limit is inconsistent with a contractual period of guarantee.

Article 40

The seller is not entitled to rely on the provisions of articles 38 and 39 if the lack of conformity relates to facts of which he knew or could not have been unaware and which he did not disclose to the buyer.

Article 41

The seller must deliver goods which are free from any right or claim of a third party, unless the buyer agreed to take the goods subject to that right or claim. However, if such right or claim is based on industrial property or other intellectual property, the seller's obligation is governed by article 42.

Article 42

(1) The seller must deliver goods which are free from any right or claim of a third party based on industrial property or other intellectual property, of which at the time of the conclusion of the contract the seller knew or could not have been unaware, provided that the right or claim is based on industrial property or other intellectual property:
   a) Under the law of the State where the goods will be resold or otherwise used, if it was contemplated by the parties at the time of the conclusion of the contract that the goods would be resold or otherwise used in that State; or
   b) in any other case, under the law of the State where the buyer has his place of business.
(2) The obligation of the seller under the preceding paragraph does not extend to cases where:
   a) At the time of the conclusion of the contract the buyer knew or could not have been unaware of the right or claim; or
   b) The right or claim results from the seller's compliance with technical drawings, designs, formulae or other such specifications furnished by the buyer.

Article 43

(1) The buyer loses the right to rely on the provisions of article 41 or article 42 if he does not give notice to the seller specifying the nature of the right or claim of the third party within a reasonable time after he has become aware or ought to have become aware of the right or claim.
(2) The seller is not entitled to rely on the provisions of the preceding paragraph if he knew of the right or claim of the third party and the nature of it.

Article 44

Notwithstanding the provisions of paragraph (1) of article 39 and paragraph (1) of article 43, the buyer may reduce the price in accordance with article 50 or claim damages, except for loss of profit, if he has a reasonable excuse for his failure to give the required notice.

SECTION III

Remedies for breach of contract by the seller

Article 45

(1) If the seller fails to perform any of his obligations under the contract or this Convention, the buyer may:
    a)   Exercise the rights provided in articles 46 to 52;
    b)   Claim damages as provided in articles 74 to 77.
(2) The buyer is not deprived of any right he may have to claim damages by exercising his right to other remedies.
(3) No period of grace may be granted to the seller by a court or arbitral tribunal when the buyer resorts to a remedy for breach of contract.

Article 46

(1) The buyer may require performance by the seller of his obligations unless the buyer has resorted to a remedy which is inconsistent with this requirement.
(2) If the goods do not conform with the contract, the buyer may require delivery of substitute goods only if the lack of conformity constitutes a fundamental breach of contract and a request for substitute goods is made either in conjunction with notice given under article 39 or within a reasonable time thereafter.
(3) If the goods do not conform with the contract, the buyer may require the seller to remedy the lack of conformity by repair, unless this is unreasonable having regard to all the circumstances. A request for repair must be made either in conjunction with notice given under article 39 or within a reasonable time thereafter.

Article 47

(1) The buyer may fix an additional period of time of reasonable length for performance by the seller of his obligations.
(2) Unless the buyer has received notice from the seller that he will not perform within the period so fixed, the buyer may not, during that

period, resort to any remedy for breach of contract. However, the buyer is not deprived thereby of any right he may have to claim damages for delay in performance.

Article 48

(1) Subject to article 49, the seller may, even after the date for delivery, remedy at his own expense any failure to perform his obligations, if he can do so without unreasonable delay and without causing the buyer unreasonable inconvenience or uncertainty of reimbursement by the seller of expenses advanced by the buyer. However, the buyer retains any right to claim damages as provided for in this Convention.

(2) If the seller requests the buyer to make known whether he will accept performance and the buyer does not comply with the request within a reasonable time, the seller may perform within the time indicated in his request. The buyer may not, during that period of time, resort to any remedy which is inconsistent with performance by the seller.

(3) A notice by the seller that he will perform within a specified period of time is assumed to include a request, under the preceding paragraph, that the buyer make known his decision.

(4) A request or notice by the seller under paragraph (2) or (3) of this article is not effective unless received by the buyer.

Article 49

(1) The buyer may declare the contract avoided:

   a) If the failure by the seller to perform any of his obligations under the contract or this Convention amounts to a fundamental breach of contract; or

   b) In case of non-delivery, if the seller does not deliver the goods within the additional period of time fixed by the buyer in accordance with paragraph (1) of article 47 or declares that he will not deliver within the period so fixed.

(2) However, in cases where the seller has delivered the goods, the buyer loses the right to declare the contract avoided unless he does so:

   a) In respect of late delivery, within a reasonable time after he has become aware that delivery has been made;

   b) In respect of any breach other than late delivery, within a reasonable time:

      i) After he knew or ought to have known of the breach;

      ii) After the expiration of any additional period of time fixed by the buyer in accordance with paragraph (1) of artcle 47, or after the seller has declared that he will not perform his obligations within such an additional period; or

iii) After the expiration of any additional period of time indicated by the seller in accordance with paragraph (2) of article 48, or after the buyer has declared that he will not accept performance.

Article 50

If the goods do not conform with the contract and whether or not the price has already been paid, the buyer may reduce the price in the same proportion as the value that the goods actually delivered had at the time of the delivery bears to the value that conforming goods would have had at that time. However, if the seller remedies any failure to perform his obligations in accordance with article 37 or article 48 or if the buyer refuses to accept performance by the seller in accordance with those articles, the buyer may not reduce the price.

Article 51

(1) If the seller delivers only a part of the goods or if only a part of the goods delivered is in conformity with the contract, articles 46 to 50 apply in respect of the part which is missing or which does not conform.

(2) The buyer may declare the contract avoided in its entirety only if the failure to make delivery completely or in conformity with the contract amounts to a fundamental breach of the contract.

Article 52

(1) If the seller delivers the goods before the date fixed, the buyer may take delivery or refuse to take delivery.

(2) If the seller delivers a quantity of goods greater than that provided for in the contract, the buyer may take delivery or refuse to take delivery of the excess quantity. If the buyer takes delivery of all or part of the excess quantity, he must pay for it at the contract rate.

CHAPTER III

OBLIGATIONS OF THE BUYER

Article 53

The buyer must pay the price for the goods and take delivery of them as required by the contract and this Convention.

SECTION I

Payment of the price

Article 54

The buyer's obligation to pay the price includes taking such steps and complying with such formalities as may be required under the contract or any laws and regulations to enable payment to be made.

Article 55

Where a contract has been validly concluded but does not expressly or implicitly fix or make provision for determining the price, the parties are considered, in the absence of any indication to the contrary, to have impliedly made reference to the price generally charged at the time of the conclusion of the contract for such goods sold under comparable circumstances in the trade concerned.

Article 56

If the price is fixed according to the weight of the goods, in case of doubt it is to be determined by the net weight.

Article 57

(1) If the buyer is not bound to pay the price at any other particular place, he must pay it to the seller:
   a) At the seller's place of business; or
   b) If the payment is to be made against the handing over of the goods or of documents, at the place where the handing over takes place.
(2) The seller must bear any increase in the expenses incidental to payment which is caused by a change in his place of business subsequent to the conclusion of the contract.

Article 58

(1) If the buyer is not bound to pay the price at any other specific time, he must pay it when the seller places either the goods or documents controlling their disposition at the buyer's disposal in accordance with the contract and this Convention. The seller may make such payment a condition for handing over the goods or documents.
(2) If the contract involves carriage of the goods, the seller may dispatch the goods on terms whereby the goods, or documents controlling their disposition, will not be handed over to the buyer except against payment of the price.
(3) The buyer is not bound to pay the price until he has had an opportunity to examine the goods, unless the procedures for delivery or

payment agreed upon by the parties are inconsistent with his having such an opportunity.

Article 59

The buyer must pay the price on the date fixed by or determinable from the contract and this Convention without the need for any request or compliance with any formality on the part of the seller.

SECTION II

Taking delivery

Article 60

The buyer's obligation to take delivery consists:

a)   In doing all the acts which could reasonably be expected of him in order to enable the seller to make delivery; and
b)   In taking over the goods.

SECTION II

Remedies for breach of contract by the buyer

Article 61

(1) If the buyer fails to perform any of his obligations under the contract or this Convention, the seller may:
　　 a)   Exercise the rights provided in articles 62 to 65;
　　 b)   Claim damages as provided in articles 74 to 77.
(2) The seller is not deprived of any right he may have to claim damages by exercising his right to other remedies.
(3) No period of grace may be granted to the buyer by a court or arbitral tribunal when the seller resorts to a remedy for breach of contract.

Article 62

The seller may require the buyer to pay the price, take delivery or perform his other obligations, unless the seller has resorted to a remedy which is inconsistent with this requirement.

Article 63

(1) The seller may fix an additional period of time of reasonable length for performance by the buyer of his obligations.

(2) Unless the seller has received notice from the buyer that he will not perform within the period so fixed, the seller may not, during that period, resort to any remedy for breach of contract. However, the seller is not deprived thereby of any right he may have to claim damages for delay in performance.

Article 64

(1) The seller may declare the contract avoided:
    a) If the failure by the buyer to perform any of his obligations under the contract or this Convention amounts to a fundamental breach of contract; or
    b) If the buyer does not, within the additional period of time fixed by the seller in accordance with paragraph (1) of article 63, perform his obligation to pay the price or take delivery of the goods, or if he declares that he will not do so within the period so fixed.

(2) However, in cases where the buyer has paid the price, the seller loses the right to declare the contract avoided unless he does so:
    a) In respect of late performance by the buyer, before the seller has become aware that performance has been rendered; or
    b) In respect of any breach other than late performance by the buyer, within a reasonable time:
        (i) After the seller knew or ought to have known of the breach; or
        (ii) After the expiration of any additional period of time fixed by the seller in accordance with paragraph (1) of article 63, or after the buyer has declared that he will not perform his obligations within such an additional period.

Article 65

(1) If under the contract the buyer is to specify the form, measurement or other features of the goods and he fails to make such specification either on the date agreed upon or within a reasonable time after receipt of a request from the seller, the seller may, without prejudice to any other rights he may have, make the specification himself in accordance with the requirements of the buyer that may be known to him.

(2) If the seller makes the specification himself, he must inform the buyer of the details thereof and must fix a reasonable time within which the buyer may make a different specification. If, after receipt of such a

communication, the buyer fails to do so within the time so fixed, the specification made by the seller is binding.

CHAPTER IV

PASSING OF RISK

Article 66

Loss of or damage to the goods after the risk has passed to the buyer does not discharge him from his obligation to pay the price, unless the loss or damage is due to an act or omission of the seller.

Article 67

(1) If the contract of sale involves carriage of the goods and the seller is not bound to hand them over at a particular place, the risk passes to the buyer when the goods are handed over to the first carrier for transmission to the buyer in accordance with the contract of sale. If the seller is bound to hand the goods over to a carrier at a particular place, the risk does not pass to the buyer until the goods are handed over to the carrier at that place. The fact that the seller is authorized to retain documents controlling the disposition of the goods does not affect the passage of the risk.

(2) Nevertheless, the risk does not pass to the buyer until the goods are clearly identified to the contract, whether by markings on the goods, by shipping documents, by notice given to the buyer or otherwise.

Article 68

The risk in respect of goods sold in transit passes to the buyer from the time of the conclusion of the contract. However, if the circumstances so indicate, the risk is assumed by the buyer from the time the goods were handed over to the carrier who issued the documents embodying the contract of carriage. Nevertheless, if at the time of the conclusion of the contract of sale the seller knew or ought to have known that the goods had been lost or damaged and did not disclose this to the buyer, the loss or damage is at the risk of the seller.

Article 69

(1) In cases not within articles 67 and 68, the risk passes to the buyer when he takes over the goods or, if he does not do so in due time, from the time when the goods are placed at his disposal and he commits a breach of contract by failing to take delivery.

(2) However, if the buyer is bound to take over the goods at a place other than a place of business of the seller, the risk passes when delivery is due and the buyer is aware of the fact that the goods are placed at his disposal at that place.

(3) If the contract relates to goods not then identified, the goods are considered not to be placed at the disposal of the buyer until they are clearly identified to the contract.

Article 70

If the seller has committed a fundamental breach of contract, articles 67, 68 and 69 do not impair the remedies available to the buyer on account of the breach.

CHAPTER V

PROVISIONS COMMON TO THE OBLIGATIONS OF THE SELLER AND OF THE BUYER

SECTION I

Anticipatory breach and instalment contracts

Article 71

(1) A party may suspend the performance of his obligations if, after the conclusion of the contract, it becomes apparent that the other party will not perform a substantial part of his obligations as a result of:
  a) A serious deficiency in his ability to perform or in his creditworthiness; or
  b) His conduct in preparing to perform or in performing the contract.

(2) If the seller has already dispatched the goods before the grounds described in the preceding paragraph become evident, he may prevent the handing over of the goods to the buyer even though the buyer holds a document which entitles him to obtain them. The present paragraph relates only to the rights in the goods as between the buyer and the seller.

(3) A party suspending performance, whether before or after dispatch of the goods, must immediately give notice of the suspension to the other party and must continue with performance if the other party provides adequate assurance of his performance.

Article 72

(1) If prior to the date for performance of the contract it is clear that one of the parties will commit a fundamental breach of contract, the other party may declare the contract avoided.

(2) If time allows, the party intending to declare the contract avoided must give reasonable notice to the other party in order to permit him to provide adequate assurance of his performance.

(3) The requirements of the preceding paragraph do not apply if the other party has declared that he will not perform his obligations.

Article 73

(1) In the case of a contract for delivery of goods by instalments, if the failure of one party to perform any of his obligations in respect of any instalment constitutes a fundamental breach of contract with respect to that instalment, the other party may declare the contract avoided with respect to that instalment.

(2) If one party's failure to perform any of his obligations in respect of any instalment gives the other party good grounds to conclude that a fundamental breach of contract will occur with respect to future instalments, he may declare the contract avoided for the future, provided that he does so within a reasonable time.

(3) A buyer who declares the contract avoided in respect of any delivery may, at the same time, declare it avoided in respect of deliveries already made or of future deliveries if, by reason of their interdependence, those deliveries could not be used for the purpose contemplated by the parties at the time of the conclusion of the contract.

SECTION II

Damages

Article 74

Damages for breach of contract by one party consist of a sum equal to the loss, including loss of profit, suffered by the other party as a consequence of the breach. Such damages may not exceed the loss which the party in breach foresaw or ought to have foreseen at the time of the conclusion of the contract, in the light of the facts and matters of which he then knew or ought to have known, as a possible consequence of the breach of contract.

Article 75

If the contract is avoided and if, in a reasonable manner and within a reasonable time after avoidance, the buyer has bought goods in replacement or the seller has resold the goods, the party claiming damages may recover the difference between the contract price and the price in the substitute transaction as well as any further damages recoverable under article 74.

Article 76

(1) If the contract is avoided and there is a current price for the goods, the party claiming damages may, if he has not made a purchase or resale under article 75, recover the difference between the price fixed by the contract and the current price at the time of avoidance as well as any further damages recoverable under article 74. If, however, the party claiming damages has avoided the contract after taking over the goods, the current price at the time of such taking over shall be applied instead of the current price at the time of avoidance.

(2) For the purposes of the preceding paragraph, the current price is the price prevailing at the place where delivery of the goods should have been made or, if there is no current price at that place, the price at such other place as serves as a reasonable substitute, making due allowance for differences in the cost of transporting the goods.

Article 77

A party who relies on a breach of contract must take such measures as are reasonable in the circumstances to mitigate the loss, including loss of profit, resulting from the breach. If he fails to take such measures, the party in breach may claim a reduction in the damages in the amount by which the loss should have been mitigated.

SECTION III

Interest

Article 78

If a party fails to pay the price or any other sum that is in arrears, the other party is entitled to interest on it, without prejudice to any claim for damages recoverable under article 74.

SECTION IV

Exemptions

Article 79

(1) A party is not liable for a failure to perform any of his obligations if he proves that the failure was due to an impediment beyond his control and that he could not reasonably be expected to have taken the impediment into account at the time of the conclusion of the contract or to have avoided or overcome it or its consequences.

(2) If the party's failure is due to the failure by a third person whom he has engaged to perform the whole or a part of the contract, that party is exempt from liability only if:
   a) He is exempt under the preceding paragraph; and
   b) The person whom he has so engaged would be so exempt if the provisions of that paragraph were applied to him.

(3) The exemption provided by this article has effect for the period during which the impediment exists.

(4) The party who fails to perform must give notice to the other party of the impediment and its effect on his ability to perform. If the notice is not received by the other party within a reasonable time after the party who fails to perform knew or ought to have known of the impediment, he is liable for damages resulting from such non-receipt.

(5) Nothing in this article prevents either party from exercising any right other than to claim damages under this Convention.

Article 80

A party may not rely on a failure of the other party to perform, to the extent that such failure was caused by the first party's act or omission.

Article 81

(1) Avoidance of the contract releases both parties from their obligations under it, subject to any damages which may be due. Avoidance does not affect any provision of the contract for the settlement of disputes or any other provision of the contract governing the rights and obligations of the parties consequent upon the avoidance of the contract.

(2) A party who has performed the contract either wholly or in part may claim restitution from the other party of whatever the first party has supplied or paid under the contract. If both parties are bound to make restitution, they must do so concurrently.

Article 82

(1) The buyer loses the right to declare the contract avoided or to require the seller to deliver substitute goods if it is impossible for him to make restitution of the goods substantially in the condition in which he received them.

(2) The preceding paragraph does not apply:

   a)   if the impossibility of making restitution of the goods or of making restitution of the goods substantially in the condition in which the buyer received them is not due to his act oromission;

   b)   if the goods or part of the goods have perished or deteriorated as a result of the examination provided for in article 38; or

   c)   if the goods or part of the goods have been sold in the normal course of business or have been consumed or transformed by the buyer in the course of normal use before he discovered or ought to have discovered the lack of conformity.

Article 83

A buyer who has lost the right to declare the contract avoided or to require the seller to deliver substitute goods in accordance with article 82 retains all other remedies under the contract and this Convention.

Article 84

(1) If the seller is bound to refund the price, he must also pay interest on it, from the date on which the price was paid.

(2) The buyer must account to the seller for all benefits which he has derived from the goods or part of them:

   a)   if he must make restitution of the goods or part of them; or

   b)   if it is impossible for him to make restitution of all or part of the goods or to make restitution of all or part of the goods substantially in the condition in which he received them, but he has nevertheless declared the contract avoided or required the seller to deliver substitute goods.

SECTION VI

Preservation of the goods

Article 85

If the buyer is in delay in taking delivery of the goods or, where payment of the price and delivery of the goods are to be made concurrently, if he fails to pay the price, and the seller is either in possession of the goods or otherwise able to control their disposition, the seller must take such steps as are reasonable in the circumstances to preserve them. He is entitled to retain them until he has been reimbursed his reasonable expenses by the buyer.

Article 86

(1) If the buyer has received the goods and intends to exercise any right under the contract or this Convention to reject them, he must take such steps to preserve them as are reasonable in the circumstances. He is entitled to retain them until he has been reimbursed his reasonable expenses by the seller.

(2) If goods dispatched to the buyer have been placed at his disposal at their destination and he exercises the right to reject them, he must take possession of them on behalf of the seller, provided that this can be done without payment of the price and without unreasonable inconvenience or unreasonable expense. This provision does not apply if the seller or a person authorized to take charge of the goods on his behalf is present at the destination. If the buyer takes possession of the goods under this paragraph, his rights and obligations are governed by the preceding paragraph.

Article 87

A party who is bound to take steps to preserve the goods may deposit them in a warehouse of a third person at the expense of the other party provided that the expense incurred is not unreasonable.

Article 88

(1) A party who is bound to preserve the goods in accordance with article 85 or 86 may sell them by any appropriate means if there has been an unreasonable delay by the other party in taking possession of the goods or in taking them back or in paying the price or the cost of preservation, provided that reasonable notice of the intention to sell has been given to the other party.

(2) If the goods are subject to rapid deterioration or their preservation would involve unreasonable expense, a party who is bound to preserve the goods in accordance with article 85 or 86 must take reasonable measures to sell them. To the extent possible he must give notice to the other party of his intention to sell.

(3) A party selling the goods has the right to retain out of the proceeds of sale an amount equal to the reasonable expenses of preserving the

goods and of selling them. He must account to the other party for the balance.

PART IV

FINAL PROVISIONS

Article 89

The Secretary-General of the United Nations is hereby designated as the depositary for this Convention.

Article 90

This Convention does not prevail over any international agreement which has already been or may be entered into and which contains provisions concerning the matters governed by this Convention, provided that the parties have their places of business in States parties to such agreement.

Article 91

(1) This Convention is open for signature at the concluding meeting of the United Nations Conference on Contracts for the International Sale of Goods and will remain open for signature by all States at the Headquarters of the United Nations, New York until 30 September 1981.

(2) This Convention is subject to ratification, acceptance or approval by the signatory States.

(3) This Convention is open for accession by all States which are not signatory States as from the date it is open for signature.

(4) Instruments of ratification, acceptance, approval and accession are to be deposited with the Secretary-General of the United Nations.

Article 92

(1) A Contracting State may declare at the time of signature, ratification, acceptance, approval or accession that it will not be bound by Part II of this Convention or that it will not be bound by Part III of this Convention.

(2) A Contracting State which makes a declaration in accordance with the preceding paragraph in respect of Part II or Part III of this Convention is not to be considered a Contracting State within paragraph (1) of article 1 of this Convention in respect of matters governed by the Part to which the declaration applies.

Article 93

(1) If a Contracting State has two or more territorial units in which, according to its constitution, different systems of law are applicable in relation to the matters dealt with in this Convention, it may, at the time of signature, ratification, acceptance, approval or accession, declare that this Convention is to extend to all its territorial units or only to one or more of them, and may amend its declaration by submitting another declaration at any time.

(2) These declarations are to be notified to the depositary and are to state expressly the territorial units to which the Convention extends.

(3) If, by virtue of a declaration under this article, this Convention extends to one or more but not all of the territorial units of a Contracting State, and if the place of business of a party is located in that State, this place of business, for the purposes of this Convention, is considered not to be in a Contracting State, unless it is in a territorial unit to which the Convention extends.

(4) If a Contracting State makes no declaration under paragraph (1) of this article, the Convention is to extend to all territorial units of that State.

Article 94

(1) Two or more Contracting States which have the same or closely related legal rules on matters governed by this Convention may at any time declare that the Convention is not to apply to contracts of sale or to their formation where the parties have their places of business in those States. Such declarations may be made jointly or by reciprocal unilateral declarations.

(2) A Contracting State which has the same or closely related legal rules on matters governed by this Convention as one or more non-Contracting States may at any time declare that the Convention is not to apply to contracts of sale or to their formation where the parties have their places of business in those States.

(3) If a State which is the object of a declaration under the preceding paragraph subsequently becomes a Contracting State, the declaration made will, as from the date on which the Convention enters into force in respect of the new Contracting State, have the effect of a declaration made under paragraph (1), provided that the new Contracting State joins in such declaration or makes a reciprocal unilateral declaration.

Article 95

Any State may declare at the time of the deposit of its instrument of ratification, acceptance, approval or accession that it will not be bound by subparagraph (1)(b) of article 1 of this Convention.

Article 96

A Contracting State whose legislation requires contracts of sale to be concluded in or evidenced by writing may at any time make a declaration in accordance with article 12 that any provision of article 11, article 29, or Part II of this Convention, that allows a contract of sale or its modification or termination by agreement or any offer, acceptance, or other indication of intention to be made in any form other than in writing, does not apply where any party has his place of business in that State.

Article 97

(1) Declarations made under this Convention at the time of signature are subject to confirmation upon ratification, acceptance or approval.

(2) Declarations and confirmations of declarations are to be in writing and be formally notified to the depositary.

(3) A declaration takes effect simultaneously with the entry into force of this Convention in respect of the State concerned. However, a declaration of which the depositary receives formal notification after such entry into force takes effect on the first day of the month following the expiration of six months after the date of its receipt by the depositary. Reciprocal unilateral declarations under article 94 take effect on the first day of the month following the expiration of six months after the receipt of the latest declaration by the depositary.

(4) Any State which makes a declaration under this Convention may withdraw it at any time by a formal notification in writing addressed to the depositary. Such withdrawal is to take effect on the first day of the month following the expiration of six months after the date of the receipt of the notification by the depositary.

(5) A withdrawal of a declaration made under article 94 renders inoperative, as from the date on which the withdrawal takes effect, any reciprocal declaration made by another State under that article.

Article 98

No reservations are permitted except those expressly authorized in this Convention.

Article 99

(1) This Convention enters into force, subject to the provisions of paragraph (6) of this article, on the first day of the month following the expiration of twelve months after the date of deposit of the tenth instrument of ratification, acceptance, approval or accession, including an instrument which contains a declaration made under article 92.

(2) When a State ratifies, accepts, approves or accedes to this Convention after the deposit of the tenth instrument of ratification, acceptance,

approval or accession, this Convention, with the exception of the Part excluded, enters into force in respect of that State, subject to the provisions of paragraph (6) of this article, on the first day of the month following the expiration of twelve months after the date of the deposit of its instrument of ratification, acceptance, approval or accession.

(3)   A State which ratifies, accepts, approves or accedes to this Convention and is a party to either or both the Convention relating to a Uniform Law on the Formation of Contracts for the International Sale of Goods done at The Hague on 1 July 1964 (1964 Hague Formation Convention) and the Convention relating to a Uniform Law on the International Sale of Goods done at The Hague on 1 July 1964 (1964 Hague Sales Convention) shall at the same time denounce, as the case may be, either or both the 1964 Hague Sales Convention and the 1964 Hague Formation Convention by notifying the Government of the Netherlands to that effect.

(4)   A State party to the 1964 Hague Sales Convention which ratifies, accepts, approves or accedes to the present Convention and declares or has declared under article 52 that it will not be bound by Part II of this Convention shall at the time of ratification, acceptance, approval or accession denounce the 1964 Hague Sales Convention by notifying the Government of the Netherlands to that effect.

(5)   A State party to the 1964 Hague Formation Convention which ratifies, accepts, approves or accedes to the present Convention and declares or has declared under article 92 that it will not be bound by Part III of this Convention shall at the time of ratification, acceptance, approval or accession denounce the 1964 Hague Formation Convention by notifying the Government of the Netherlands to that effect.

(6)   For the purpose of this article, ratifications, acceptances, approvals and accessions in respect of this Convention by States parties to the 1964 Hague Formation Convention or to the 1964 Hague Sales Convention shall not be effective until such denunciations as may be required on the part of those States in respect of the latter two Conventions have themselves become effective. The depositary of this Convention shall consult with the Government of the Netherlands, as the depositary of the 1964 Conventions, so as to ensure necessary co-ordination in this respect.

Article 100

(1)   This Convention applies to the formation of a contract only when the proposal for concluding the contract is made on or after the date when the Convention enters into force in respect of the Contracting States referred to in subparagraph (1)(a) or the Contracting State referred to in subparagraph (1)(b) of article 1.

(2) This Convention applies only to contracts concluded on or after the date when the Convention enters into force in respect of the Contracting States referred to in subparagraph (1)(a) or the Contracting State referred to in subparagraph (1)(b) of article 1.

Article 101

(1) A Contracting State may denounce this Convention, or Part II or Part III of the Convention, by a formal notification in writing addressed to the depositary.

(2) The denunciation takes effect on the first day of the month following the expiration of twelve months after the notification is received by the depositary. Where a longer period for the denunciation to take effect is specified in the notification, the denunciation takes effect upon the expiration of such longer period after the notification is received by the depositary.

Done at Vienna, this day of eleventh day of April, one thousand nine hundred and eighty, in a single original, of which the Arabic, Chinese, English, French, Russian and Spanish texts are equally authentic.

In witness whereof the undersigned plenipotentiaries, being duly authorized by their respective Governments, have signed this Convention.

UNITED NATIONS CONVENTION

on the Limitation Period in the International Sale of Goods of 14 June 1974 (New York)[1]

(Misc 24 (1980), Cmnd 8074, UN Doc A/Conf. 63/15)

Amendments

Article	Nature of	Effected by	Source
3, 4, 31, 34, 37, 40	Amended	Protocol of 11 April 1980 (Vienna)	UN Document A/CONF. 97/18 Annex II
36 *bis*, 43 *bis*, 43 *ter*, 44 *bis*, 45 *bis*	Inserted	Protocol of 11 April 1980 (Vienna)	UN Document A/CONF. 97/18 Annex II

Preamble

The States Parties to the present Convention,

Consid ering that international trade is an important factor in the promotion of friendly relations amongst States,

Believing that the adoption of uniform rules governing the limitation period in the international sale of goods would facilitate the development of world trade,

Have agreed as follows:

---

[1] The text of the Convention is published in Yearbook of the United Nations Commission on International Trade Law 1974 210. The 1980 Protocol is published in Yearbook of the United Nations Commission on International Trade Law 1980 162.

The 1974 Convention is in force in the following states, in the version as amended by the Protocol of 1980: Argentina (1 August 1988), Cuba (1 June 1995), the Czech Republic (1 January 1993), Egypt (1 August 1988), Guinea (1 January 1991), Hungary (1 August 1988), Mexico (1 August 1988), Moldavia (1 March 1998), Poland (1 December 1995), Romania (1 November 1992), Slovakia (1 January 1993), Slovenia (1 March 1996), Uganda (1 September 1992), the United States of America (1 December 1994), Uruguay (1 November 1997), White Russia (1 August 1997), and Zambia (1 January 1988). The Convention is in force in its original form in the following states: Bosnia-Herzegovina (6 March 1992), Burundi (1 April 1999), the Dominican Republic (1 August 1988), Ghana (1 August 1988), Norway (1 August 1988), the Ukraine (1 April 1994), and the former Yugoslavia (1 August 1988).

PART I: SUBSTANTIVE PROVISIONS

Sphere of application

Article 1

(1) This Convention shall determine when claims of a buyer and a seller against each other arising from a contract of international sale of goods or relating to its breach, termination or invalidity can no longer be exercised by reason of the expiration of a period of time. Such a period of time is hereinafter referred to as 'the limitation period'.

(2) This Convention shall not affect a particular time-limit within which one party is required, as a condition for the acquisition or exercise of his claim, to give notice to the other party or perform any act other than the institution of legal proceedings.

(3) In this Convention:
   a) 'Buyer', 'seller' and 'party' mean persons who buy or sell, or agree to buy or sell, goods, and the successors to and assigns of their rights or obligations under the contract of sale;
   b) 'Creditor' means a party who asserts a claim, whether or not such a claim is for a sum of money;
   c) 'Debtor' means a party against whom a creditor asserts a claim;
   d) 'Breach of contract' means the failure of a party to perform the contract or any performance not in conformity with the contract;
   e) 'Legal proceedings' includes judicial, arbitral and administrative proceedings;
   f) 'Person' includes corporation, company, partnership, association or entity, whether private or public, which can sue or be sued;
   g) 'Writing' includes telegram and telex;
   h) 'Year' means a year according to the Gregorian calendar.

Article 2

For the purposes of this Convention:

   a) A contract of sale of goods shall be considered international if, at the time of the conclusion of the contract, the buyer and the seller have their places of business in different States;
   b) The fact that the parties have their places of business in different States shall be disregarded whenever this fact does not appear either from the contract or from any dealings between, or from information disclosed by, the parties at any time before or at the conclusion of the contract;

c) Where a party to a contract of sale of goods has places of business in more than one State, the place of business shall be that which has the closest relationship to the contract and its performance, having regard to the circumstances known to or contemplated by the parties at the time of the conclusion of the contract;

d) Where a party does not have a place of business, reference shall be made to his habitual residence;

e) Neither the nationality of the parties nor the civil or commercial character of the parties or of the contract shall be taken into consideration.

Article 3

(1) This Convention shall apply only
   a) If, at the time of the conclusion of the contract, the places of business of the parties to a contract of international sale of goods are in Contracting States; or
   b) If the rules of private international law make the law of a Contracting State applicable to the contract of sale.

(2) This Convention shall not apply when the parties have expressly excluded its application.

Article 4

This Convention shall not apply to sales:

a) Of goods bought for personal, family or household use, unless the seller, at any time before or at the conclusion of the contract, neither knew nor ought to have known that the goods were bought for any such use;

b) By auction;

c) On execution or otherwise by authority of law;

d) Of stocks, shares, investment securities, negotiable instruments or money;

e) Of ships, vessels, hovercraft or aircraft;

f) Of electricity.

Article 5

This Convention shall not apply to claims based upon:

a) Death of, or personal injury to, any person;

b) Nuclear damage caused by the goods sold;

c) A lien, mortgage or other security interest in property;

d) A judgement or award made in legal proceedings;

e) A document on which direct enforcement or execution can be obtained in accordance with the law of the place where such enforcement or execution is sought;

f) A bill of exchange, cheque or promissory note.

Article 6

(1) This Convention shall not apply to contracts in which the preponderant part of the obligations of the seller consists in the supply of labour or other services.

(2) Contracts for the supply of goods to be manufactured or produced shall be considered to be sales, unless the party who orders the goods undertakes to supply a substantial part of the materials necessary for such manufacture or production.

Article 7

In the interpretation and application of the provisions of this Convention, regard shall be had to its international character and to the need to promote uniformity.

The duration and commencement of the limitation period

Article 8

The limitation period shall be four years.

Article 9

(1) Subject to the provisions of articles 10, 11 and 12 the limitation period shall commence on the date [on] which the claim accrues.

(2) The commencement of the limitation period shall not be postponed by:
   a) A requirement that the party be given a notice as described in paragraph 2 of article 1, or
   b) A provision in an arbitration agreement that no right shall arise until an arbitration award has been made.

Article 10

(1) A claim arising from a breach of contract shall accrue on the date on which such breach occurs.

(2) A claim arising from a defect or other lack of conformity shall accrue on the date on which the goods are actually handed over to, or their tender is refused by, the buyer.

(3) A claim based on fraud committed before or at the time of the conclusion of the contract or during its performance shall accrue on the date on which the fraud was or reasonably could have been discovered.

Article 11

If the seller has given an express undertaking relating to the goods which is stated to have effect for a certain period of time, whether expressed in terms of a specific period of time or otherwise, the limitation period in respect of any claim arising from the undertaking shall commence on the date on which the buyer notifies the seller of the fact on which the claim is based, but not later than on the date of the expiration of the period of the undertaking.

Article 12

(1) If, in circumstances provided for by the law applicable to the contract, one party is entitled to declare the contract terminated before the time for performance is due, and exercises this right, the limitation period in respect of a claim based on any such circumstances shall commence on the date on which the declaration is made to the other party. If the contract is not declared to be terminated before performance becomes due, the limitation period shall commence on the date on which performance is due.

(2) The limitation period in respect of a claim arising out of a breach by one party of a contract for the delivery of or payment for goods by instalments shall, in relation to each separate instalment, commence on the date on which the particular breach occurs. If, under the law applicable to the contract, one party is entitled to declare the contract terminated by reason of such breach, and exercises this right, the limitation period in respect of all relevant instalments shall commence on the date on which the declaration is made to the other party.

Cessation and extension of the limitation period

Article 13

The limitation period shall cease to run when the creditor performs any act which, under the law of the court where the proceedings are instituted, is recognized as commencing judicial proceedings against the debtor or as asserting his claim in such proceedings already instituted against the debtor, for the purpose of obtaining satisfaction or recognition of his claim.

Article 14

(1) Where the parties have agreed to submit to arbitration, the limitation period shall cease to run when either party commences arbitral proceedings in the manner provided for in the arbitration agreement or by the law applicable to such proceedings.

(2) In the absence of any such provision, arbitral proceedings shall be
     deemed to commence on the date on which a request that the claim in
     dispute be referred to arbitration is delivered at the habitual residence
     or place of business of the other party or, if he has no such residence or
     place of business, then at his last known residence or place of business.

Article 15

In any legal proceedings other than those mentioned in articles 13 and 14,
including legal proceedings commenced upon the occurrence of:

a) The death or incapacity of the debtor,
b) The bankruptcy or any state of insolvency affecting the whole of the
    property of the debtor, or
c) The dissolution or liquidation of a corporation, company,
    partnership, association or entity when it is the debtor,
        the limitation period shall cease to run when the creditor asserts his
    claim in such proceedings for the purpose of obtaining satisfaction or
    recognition of the claim, subject to the law governing the proceedings.

Article 16

For the purposes of articles 13, 14 and 15, any act performed by way of counterclaim shall be deemed to have been performed on the same date as the act performed in relation to the claim against which the counterclaim is raised, provided
that both the claim and the counterclaim relate to the same contract or to several
contracts concluded in the course of the same transaction.

Article 17

(1) Where a claim has been asserted in legal proceedings within the limita-
     tion period in accordance with article 13, 14, 15 or 16, but such legal
     proceedings have ended without a decision binding on the merits
     of the claim, the limitation period shall be deemed to have continued to
     run.
(2) If, at the time such legal proceedings ended, the limitation period has
     expired or has less than one year to run, the creditor shall be entitled to a
     period of one year from the date on which the legal proceedings ended.

Article 18

(1) Where legal proceedings have been commenced against one debtor,
     the limitation period prescribed in this Convention shall cease to run
     against any other party jointly and severally liable with the debtor,

provided that the creditor informs such party in writing within that period that the proceedings have been commenced.

(2) Where legal proceedings have been commenced by a subpurchaser against the buyer, the limitation period prescribed in this Convention shall cease to run in relation to the buyer's claim over against the seller, if the buyer informs the seller in writing within that period that the proceedings have been commenced.

(3) Where the legal proceedings referred to in paragraphs 1 and 2 of this article have ended, the limitation period in respect of the claim of the creditor or the buyer against the party jointly and severally liable or against the seller shall be deemed not to have ceased running by virtue of paragraphs 1 and 2 of this article, but the creditor or the buyer shall be entitled to an additional year from the date on which the legal proceedings ended, if at that time the limitation period had expired or had less than one year to run.

Article 19

Where the creditor performs, in the State in which the debtor has his place of business and before the expiration of the limitation period, any act, other than the acts described in articles 13, 14, 15 and 16, which under the law of that State has the effect of recommencing a limitation period, a new limitation period of four years shall commence on the date prescribed by that law.

Article 20

(1) Where the debtor, before the expiration of the limitation period, acknowledges in writing his obligation to the creditor, a new limitation period of four years shall commence to run from the date of such acknowledgement.

(2) Payment of interest or partial performance of an obligation by the debtor shall have the same effect as an acknowledgement under paragraph (1) of this article if it can reasonably be inferred from such payment or performance that the debtor acknowledges that obligation.

Article 21

Where, as a result of a circumstance which is beyond the control of the creditor and which he could neither avoid nor overcome, the creditor has been prevented from causing the limitation period to cease to run, the limitation period shall be extended so as not to expire before the expiration of one year from the date on which the relevant circumstance ceased to exist.

Modification of the limitation period by the parties

Article 22

(1) The limitation period cannot be modified or affected by any declaration or agreement between the parties, except in the cases provided for in paragraph (2) of this article.

(2) The debtor may at any time during the running of the limitation period extend the period by a declaration in writing to the creditor. This declaration may be renewed.

(3) The provisions of this article shall not affect the validity of a clause in the contract of sale which stipulates that arbitral proceedings shall be commenced within a shorter period of limitation than that prescribed by this Convention, provided that such clause is valid under the law applicable to the contract of sale.

General limit of the limitation period

Article 23

Notwithstanding the provisions of this Convention, a limitation period shall in any event expire not later than 10 years from the date on which it commenced to run under articles 9, 10, 11 and 12 of this Convention.

Consequences of the expiration of the limitation period

Article 24

Expiration of the limitation period shall be taken into consideration in any legal proceedings only if invoked by a party to such proceedings.

Article 25

(1) Subject to the provisions of paragraph (2) of this article and of article 24, no claim shall be recognized or enforced in any legal proceedings commenced after the expiration of the limitation period.

(2) Notwithstanding the expiration of the limitation period, one party may rely on his claim as a defence or for the purpose of set-off against a claim asserted by the other party, provided that in the latter case this may only be done:

   a) If both claims relate to the same contract or to several contracts concluded in the course of the same transaction; or

   b) If the claims could have been set-off at any time before the expiration of the limitation period.

Article 26

Where the debtor performs his obligation after the expiration of the limitation period, he shall not on that ground be entitled in any way to claim restitution even if he did not know at the time when he performed his obligation that the limitation period had expired.

Article 27

The expiration of the limitation period with respect to a principal debt shall have the same effect with respect to an obligation to pay interest on that debt.

Calculation of the period

Article 28

(1) The limitation period shall be calculated in such a way that it shall expire at the end of the day which corresponds to the date on which the period commenced to run. If there is no such corresponding date, the period shall expire at the end of the last day of the last month of the limitation period.

(2) The limitation period shall be calculated by reference to the date of the place where the legal proceedings are instituted.

Article 29

Where the last day of the limitation period falls on an official holiday or other *dies non juridicus* precluding the appropriate legal action in the jurisdiction where the creditor institutes legal proceedings or asserts a claim as envisaged in article 13, 14 or 15, the limitation period shall be extended so as not to expire until the end of the first day following that official holiday or *dies non juridicus* on which such proceedings could be instituted or on which such a claim could be asserted in that jurisdiction.

International effect

Article 30

The acts and circumstances referred to in articles 13 through 19 which have taken place in one Contracting State shall have effect for the purposes of this Convention in another Contracting State, provided that the creditor has taken all reasonable steps to ensure that the debtor is informed of the relevant act or circumstances as soon as possible.

PART II: IMPLEMENTATION

Article 31

(1) If a Contracting State has two or more territorial units in which, according to its constitution, different systems of law are applicable in relation to the matters dealt with in this Convention, it may, at the time of signature, ratification or accession, declare that this Convention shall extend to all its territorial units or only to one or more of them, and may amend its declaration by submitting another declaration at any time.

(2) These declarations shall be notified to the Secretary-General of the United Nations and shall state expressly the territorial units to which the Convention applies.

(3) If a Contracting State described in paragraph (1) of this article makes no declaration at the time of signature, ratification or accession, the Convention shall have effect within all territorial units of that State.

(4) If, by virtue of a declaration under this article, this Convention extends to one or more but not all of the territorial units of a Contracting State, and if the place of business of a party to a contract is located in that State, this place of business shall, for the purposes of this Convention, be considered not to be in a Contracting State, unless it is in a territorial unit to which the Convention extends.

Article 32

Where in this Convention reference is made to the law of a State in which different systems of law apply, such reference shall be construed to mean the law of the particular legal system concerned.

Article 33

Each Contracting State shall apply the provisions of this Convention to contracts concluded on or after the date of the entry into force of this Convention.

PART III: DECLARATIONS AND RESERVATIONS

Article 34

(1) Two or more Contracting States which have the same or closely related legal rules on matters governed by this Convention may at any time declare that the Convention shall not apply to contracts of international sale of goods where the parties have their places of business in those States. Such declarations may be made jointly or by reciprocal unilateral declarations.

(2) A Contracting State which has the same or closely related legal rules on matters governed by this Convention as one or more non-Contracting States may at any time declare that the Convention shall not apply to contracts of international sale of goods where the parties have their places of business in those States.

(3) If a State which is the object of a declaration under paragraph (2) of this article subsequently becomes a Contracting State, the declaration made shall, as from the date on which this Convention enters into force in respect of the new Contracting State, have the effect of a declaration made under paragraph (1), provided that the new Contracting State joins in such declaration or makes a reciprocal unilateral declaration.

Article 35

A Contracting State may declare, at the time of the deposit of its instrument of ratification or accession, that it will not apply the provisions of this Convention to actions for annulment of the contract.

Article 36

Any State may declare, at the time of the deposit of its instrument of ratification or accession, that it shall not be compelled to apply the provisions of article 24 of this Convention.

Article 36 bis

Any State may declare at the time of the deposit of its instrument of accession or its notification under article 43 *bis* that it will not be bound by the amendments to article 3 made by article I of the 1980 Protocol. A declaration made under this article shall be in writing and be formally notified to the depositary.

Article 37

This Convention shall not prevail over any international agreement which has already been or may be entered into and which contains provisions concerning the matters governed by this Convention, provided that the seller and buyer have their places of business in States parties to such agreement.

Article 38

(1) A Contracting State which is a party to an existing convention relating to the international sale of goods may declare, at the time of the

deposit of its instrument of ratification or accession, that it will apply this Convention exclusively to contracts of international sale of goods as defined in such existing convention.

(2)　Such declaration shall cease to be effective on the first day of the month following the expiration of 12 months after a new convention on the international sale of goods, concluded under the auspices of the United Nations, shall have entered into force.

Article 39

No reservation other than those made in accordance with articles 34, 35, 36, 36 *bis* and 38 shall be permitted.

Article 40

(1)　Declarations made under this Convention shall be addressed to the Secretary-General of the United Nations and shall take effect simultaneously with the entry of this Convention into force in respect of the State concerned, except declarations made thereafter. The latterdeclarations shall take effect on the first day of the month following the expiration of six months after the date of their receipt by the Secretary-General of the United Nations. Reciprocal unilateral declarations under article 34 shall take effect on the first day of the month following the expiration of six months after the receipt of the latest declaration by the Secretary-General of the United Nations.

(2)　Any State which has made a declaration under this Convention may withdraw it at any time by a notification addressed to the Secretary-General of the United Nations. Such withdrawal shall take effect on the first day of the month following the expiration of six months after the date of the receipt of the notification by the Secretary-General of the United Nations. In the case of a declaration made under article 34 of this Convention, such withdrawal shall also render inoperative, as from the date on which the withdrawal takes effect, any reciprocal declaration made by another State under that article.

PART IV: FINAL CLAUSES

Article 41

This Convention shall be open until 31 December 1975 for signature by all States at the Headquarters of the United Nations.

Article 42

This Convention is subject to ratification. The instruments of ratification shall be deposited with the Secretary-General of the United Nations.

Article 43

This Convention shall remain open for accession by any State. The instruments of accession shall be deposited with the Secretary-General of the United Nations.

Article 43 bis

If a State ratifies or accedes to the 1974 Limitation Convention after the entry into force of the 1980 Protocol, the ratification or accession shall also constitute a ratification or an accession to the Convention as amended by the 1980 Protocol if the State notifies the depositary accordingly.

Article 43 ter

Accession to the 1980 Protocol by any State which is not a Contracting Party to the 1974 Limitation Convention shall have the effect of accession to that Convention as amended by the Protocol, subject to the provisions of article 44 *bis*.

Article 44

(1) This Convention shall enter into force on the first day of the month following the expiration of six months after the date of the deposit of the tenth instrument of ratification or accession.
(2) For each State ratifying or acceding to this Convention after the deposit of the tenth instrument of ratification or accession, this Convention shall enter into force on the first day of the month following the expiration of six months after the date of the deposit of its instrument of ratification of accession.

Article 44 bis

Any State which becomes a Contracting Party to the 1974 Limitation Convention, as amended by the 1980 Protocol, shall, unless it notifies the depositary to the contrary, be considered to be also a Contracting Party to the Convention, unamended, in relation to any Contracting Party to the Convention not yet a Contracting Party to the 1980 Protocol.

Article 45

(1) Any Contracting State may denounce this Convention by notifying the
     Secretary-General of the United Nations to that effect.
(2) The denunciation shall take effect on the first day of the month follow-
     ing the expiration of 12 months after receipt of the notification by the
     Secretary-General of the United Nations.

Article 45 bis

Any Contracting State in respect of which the 1980 Protocol ceases to have effect
by the application of paragraphs (1) and (2) of article XIII of the 1980 Protocol
shall remain a Contracting Party to the 1974 Limitation Convention, unamended,
unless it denounces the unamended Convention in accordance with article 45 of
that Convention.

Article 46

The original of this Convention, of which the Chinese, English, French,
Russian and Spanish texts are equally authentic, shall be deposited with the
Secretary-General of the United Nations.

CONVENTION

on Agency in the International Sale of Goods of 17 February 1983 (Geneva)[1]

(22 ILM 249)

The States Parties to this Convention,

Desiring to establish common provisions concerning agency in the international sale of goods,

Bearing in mind the objectives of the United Nations Convention on Contracts for the International Sale of Goods,

Considering that the development of international trade on the basis of equality and mutual benefit is an important element in promoting friendly relations among States, bearing in mind the New International Economic Order,

Being of the opinion that the adoption of uniform rules which govern agency in the international sale of goods and take into account the different social, economic and legal systems would contribute to the removal of legal barriers in international trade and promote the development of international trade,

Have agreed as follows:

CHAPTER I SPHERE OF APPLICATION AND GENERAL PROVISIONS

Article 1

(1) This Convention applies where one person, the agent, has authority or purports to have authority on behalf of another person, the principal, to conclude a contract of sale of goods with a third party.

(2) It governs not only the conclusion of such a contract by the agent but also any act undertaken by him for the purpose of concluding that contract or in relation to its performance.

(3) It is concerned only with relations between the principal or the agent on the one hand, and the third party on the other.

(4) It applies irrespective of whether the agent acts in his own name or in that of the principal.

Article 2

(1) This Convention applies only where the principal and the third party have their places of business in different States and:

    a) the agent has his place of business in a Contracting State, or

---

[1] The Convention is published in the American Journal of Comparative Law 32 (1984) 751ff.

Hitherto France and Italy have ratified the Convention. Mexico, the Netherlands, and South Africa have acceded to it. In terms of Article 33(1) of the Convention, it comes into force when seven states have ratified it.

b) the rules of private international law lead to the application of the law of a Contracting State.

(2) Where, at the time of contracting, the third party neither knew nor ought to have known that the agent was acting as an agent, the Convention only applies if the agent and the third party had their places of business in different States and if the requirements of paragraph 1 are satisfied.

(3) Neither the nationality of the parties nor the civil or commercial character of the parties or of the contract of sale is to be taken into consideration in determining the application of this Convention.

Article 3

(1) This Convention does not apply to:
  a) the agency of a dealer on a stock, commodity or other exchange;
  b) the agency of an auctioneer;
  c) agency by operation of law in family law, in the law of matrimonial property, or in the law of succession;
  d) agency arising from statutory or judicial authorization to act for a person without capacity to act;
  e) agency by virtue of a decision of a judicial or quasi-judicial authority or subject to the direct control of such an authority.

(2) Nothing in this Convention affects any rule of law for the protection of consumers.

Article 4

For the purposes of this Convention:

a) an organ, officer or partner of a corporation, association, partnership or other entity, whether or not possessing legal personality, shall not be regarded as the agent of that entity in so far as, in the exercise of his functions as such, he acts by virtue of an authority conferred by law or by the constitutive documents of that entity;

b) a trustee shall not be regarded as an agent of the trust, of the person who has created the trust, or of the beneficiaries.

Article 5

The principal, or an agent acting in accordance with the express or implied instructions of the principal, may agree with the third party to exclude the application of this Convention or, subject to Article 11, to derogate from or vary the effect of any of its provisions.

Article 6

(1) In the interpretation of this Convention, regard is to be had to its international character and to the need to promote uniformity in its application and the observance of good faith in international trade.

(2) Questions concerning matters governed by this Convention which are not expressly settled in it are to be settled in conformity with the general principles on which it is based or, in the absence of such principles, in conformity with the law applicable by virtue of the rules of private international law.

Article 7

(1) The principal or the agent on the one hand and the third party on the other are bound by any usage to which they have agreed and by any practices which they have established between themselves.

(2) They are considered, unless otherwise agreed, to have impliedly made applicable to their relations any usage of which they knew or ought to have known and which in international trade is widely known to, and regularly observed by, parties to agency relations of the type involved in the particular trade concerned.

Article 8

For the purposes of this Convention:

a) if a party has more than one place of business, the place of business is that which has the closest relationship to the contract of sale, having regard to the circumstances known to or contemplated by the parties at the time of contracting;

b) if a party does not have a place of business, reference is to be made to his habitual residence.

CHAPTER II ESTABLISHMENT AND SCOPE OF THE AUTHORITY OF THE AGENT

Article 9

(1) The authorization of the agent by the principal may be express or implied.

(2) The agent has authority to perform all acts necessary in the circumstances to achieve the purposes for which the authorization was given.

Article 10

The authorization need not be given in or evidenced by writing and is not subject to any other requirement as to form. It may be proved by any means, including witnesses.

Article 11

Any provision of Article 10, Article 15 or Chapter IV which allows an authorization, a ratification or a termination of authority to be made in any form other than in writing does not apply where the principal or the agent has his place of business in a Contracting State which has made a declaration under Article 27. The parties may not derogate from or vary the effect of this paragraph.

CHAPTER III LEGAL EFFECTS OF ACTS CARRIED OUT BY THE AGENT

Article 12

Where an agent acts on behalf of a principal within the scope of his authority and the third party knew or ought to have known that the agent was acting as an agent, the acts of the agent shall directly bind the principal and the third party to each other, unless it follows from the circumstances of the case, for example by a reference to a contract of commission, that the agent undertakes to bind himself only.

Article 13

(1) Where the agent acts on behalf of a principal within the scope of his authority, his acts shall bind only the agent and the third party if:
   a) the third party neither knew nor ought to have known that the agent was acting as an agent, or
   b) it follows from the circumstances of the case, for example by a reference to a contract of commission, that the agent undertakes to bind himself only.
(2) Nevertheless:
   a) where the agent, whether by reason of the third party's failure of performance or for any other reason, fails to fulfil or is not in a position to fulfil his obligations to the principal, the principal may exercise against the third party the rights acquired on the principal's behalf by the agent, subject to any defences which the third party may set up against the agent;
   b) where the agent fails to fulfil or is not in a position to fulfil his obligations to the third party, the third party may exercise against the principal the rights which the third party has against the agent,

subject to any defences which the agent may set up against the third party and which the principal may set up against the agent.

(3) The rights under paragraph 2 may be exercised only if notice of intention to exercise them is given to the agent and the third party or principal, as the case may be. As soon as the third party or principal has received such notice, he may no longer free himself from his obligations by dealing with the agent.

(4) Where the agent fails to fulfil or is not in a position to fulfil his obligations to the third party because of the principal's failure of performance, the agent shall communicate the name of the principal to the third party.

(5) Where the third party fails to fulfil his obligations under the contract to the agent, the agent shall communicate the name of the third party to the principal.

(6) The principal may not exercise against the third party the rights acquired on his behalf by the agent if it appears from the circumstances of the case that the third party, had he known the principal's identity, would not have entered into the contract.

(7) An agent may, in accordance with the express or implied instructions of the principal, agree with the third party to derogate from or vary the effect of paragraph 2.

Article 14

(1) Where an agent acts without authority or acts outside the scope of his authority, his acts do not bind the principal and the third party to each other.

(2) Nevertheless, where the conduct of the principal causes the third party reasonably and in good faith to believe that the agent has authority to act on behalf of the principal and that the agent is acting within the scope of that authority, the principal may not invoke against the third party the lack of authority of the agent.

Article 15

(1) An act by an agent who acts without authority or who acts outside the scope of his authority may be ratified by the principal. On ratification the act produces the same effects as if it had initially been carried out with authority.

(2) Where, at the time of the agent's act, the third party neither knew nor ought to have known of the lack of authority, he shall not be liable to the principal if, at any time before ratification, he gives notice of his refusal to become bound by a ratification. Where the principal ratifies but does not do so within a reasonable time, the third party may refuse to be bound by the ratification if he promptly notifies the principal.

(3) Where, however, the third party knew or ought to have known of the lack of authority of the agent, the third party may not refuse to become bound by a ratification before the expiration of any time agreed for ratification or, failing agreement, such reasonable time as the third party may specify.

(4) The third party may refuse to accept a partial ratification.

(5) Ratification shall take effect when notice of it reaches the third party or the ratification otherwise comes to his attention. Once effective, it may not be revoked.

(6) Ratification is effective notwithstanding that the act itself could not have been effectively carried out at the time of ratification.

(7) Where the act has been carried out on behalf of a corporation or other legal person before its creation, ratification is effective only if allowed by the law of the State governing its creation.

(8) Ratification is subject to no requirement as to form. It may be express or may be inferred from the conduct of the principal.

Article 16

(1) An agent who acts without authority or who acts outside the scope of his authority shall, failing ratification, be liable to pay the third party such compensation as will place the third party in the same position as he would have been in if the agent had acted with authority and within the scope of his authority.

(2) The agent shall not be liable, however, if the third party knew or ought to have known that the agent had no authority or was acting outside the scope of his authority.

CHAPTER IV TERMINATION OF THE AUTHORITY OF THE AGENT

Article 17

The authority of the agent is terminated:

a) when this follows from any agreement between the principal and the agent;

b) on completion of the transaction or transactions for which the authority was created;

c) on revocation by the principal or renunciation by the agent, whether or not this is consistent with the terms of their agreement.

Article 18

The authority of the agent is also terminated when the applicable law so provides.

Article 19

The termination of the authority shall not affect the third party unless he knew or ought to have known of the termination or the facts which caused it.

Article 20

Notwithstanding the termination of his authority, the agent remains authorised to perform on behalf of the principal or his successors the acts which are necessary to prevent damage to their interests.

CHAPTER V FINAL PROVISIONS

Article 21

The Government of Switzerland is hereby designated as the depositary for this Convention.

Article 22

(1) This Convention is open for signature at the concluding meeting of the Diplomatic Conference on Agency in the International Sale of Goods and will remain open for signature by all States at Berne until 31 December 1984.
(2) This Convention is subject to ratification, acceptance or approval by the signatory States.
(3) This Convention is open for accession by all States which are not signatory States as from the date it is open for signature.
(4) Instruments of ratification, acceptance, approval and accession are to be deposited with the Government of Switzerland.

Article 23

This Convention does not prevail over any international agreement which has already been or may be entered into and which contains provisions of substantive law concerning the matters governed by this Convention, provided that the principal and the third party or, in the case referred to in Article 2, paragraph 2, the agent and the third party have their places of business in States parties to such agreement.

Article 24

(1) If a Contracting State has two or more territorial units in which different systems of law are applicable in relation to the matters dealt with in this Convention, it may, at the time of signature, ratification,

acceptance, approval or accession, declare that this Convention is to extend to all its territorial units or only to one or more of them, and may amend its declaration by submitting another declaration at any time.

(2) These declarations are to be notified to the depositary and are to state expressly the territorial units to which the Convention extends.

(3) If, by virtue of a declaration under this Article, this Convention extends to one or more but not all of the territorial units of a Contracting State, and if the place of business of a party is located in that State, this place of business, for the purposes of thisConvention, is considered not to be in a Contracting State, unless it is in a territorial unit to which the Convention extends.

(4) If a Contracting State makes no declaration under paragraph 1 of this Article, the Convention is to extend to all territorial units of that State.

Article 25

Where a Contracting State has a system of government under which executive, judicial and legislative powers are distributed between central and other authorities within that State, its signature or ratification, acceptance or approval of, or accession to this Convention, or its making of any declaration in terms of Article 24 shall carry no implication as to the internal distribution of powers within that State.

Article 26

(1) Two or more Contracting States which have the same or closely related legal rules on matters governed by this Convention may at any time declare that the Convention is not to apply where the principal and the third party or, in the case referred to in Article 2, paragraph 2, the agent and the third party have their places of business in those States. Such declarations may be made jointly or by reciprocal unilateral declarations.

(2) A Contracting State which has the same or closely related legal rules on matters governed by this Convention as one or more non-Contracting States may at any time declare that the Convention is not to apply where the principal and the third party or, in the case referred to in Article 2, paragraph 2, the agent and the third party have their places of business in those States.

(3) If a State which is the object of a declaration under the preceding paragraph subsequently becomes a Contracting State, the declaration made will, as from the date on which the Convention enters into force in respect of the new Contracting State, have the effect of a declaration made under paragraph 1, provided that the new Contracting State joins in such declaration or makes a reciprocal unilateral declaration.

Article 27

A Contracting State whose legislation requires an authorization, ratification or termination of authority to be made in or evidenced by writing in all cases governed by this Convention may at any time make a declaration in accordance with Article 11 that any provision of Article 10, Article 15 or Chapter IV which allows an authorization, ratification or termination of authority to be other than in writing, does not apply where the principal or the agent has his place of business in that State.

Article 28

A Contracting State may declare at the time of signature, ratification, acceptance, approval or accession that it will not be bound by Article 2, paragraph 1(b).

Article 29

A Contracting State, the whole or specific parts of the foreign trade of which are carried on exclusively by specially authorized organizations, may at any time declare that, in cases where such organizations act either as buyers or sellers in foreign trade, all these organizations or the organizations specified in the declaration shall not be considered, for the purposes of Article 13, paragraphs 2(b) and 4, as agents in their relations with other organizations having their place of business in the same State.

Article 30

(1) A Contracting State may at any time declare that it will apply the provisions of this Convention to specified cases falling outside its sphere of application.
(2) Such declaration may, for example, provide that the Convention shall apply to:
　　a) contracts other than contracts of sale of goods;
　　b) cases where the places of business mentioned in Article 2, paragraph 1, are not situated in Contracting States.

Article 31

(1) Declarations made under this Convention at the time of signature are subject to confirmation upon ratification, acceptance or approval.
(2) Declarations and confirmations of declarations are to be in writing and to be formally notified to the depositary.
(3) A declaration takes effect simultaneously with the entry into force of this Convention in respect of the State concerned. However, a declaration of which the depositary receives formal notification after such

entry into force takes effect on the first day of the month following the expiration of six months after the date of its receipt by the depositary. Reciprocal unilateral declar:•tions under Article 26 take effect on the first day of the month following the expiration of six months after the receipt of the latest declaration by the depositary.

(4) Any State which makes a declaration under this Convention may withdraw it at any time by a formal notification in writing addressed to the depositary. Such withdrawal is to take effect on the first day of the month following the expiration of six months after the date of the receipt of the notification by the depositary.

(5) A withdrawal of a declaration made under Article 26 renders inoperative, as from the date on which the withdrawal takes effect, any reciprocal declaration made by another State under that Article.

Article 32

No reservations are permitted except those expressly authorized in this Convention.

Article 33

(1) This Convention enters into force on the first day of the month following the expiration of twelve months after the date of deposit of the tenth instrument of ratification, acceptance, approval or accession.

(2) When a State ratifies, accepts, approves or accedes to this Convention after the deposit of the tenth instrument of ratification, acceptance, approval or accession, this Convention enters into force in respect of that State on the first day of the month following the expiration of twelve months after the date of the deposit of its instrument of ratification, acceptance, approval or accession.

Article 34

This Convention applies when the agent offers to sell or purchase or accepts an offer of sale or purchase on or after the date when the Convention enters into force in respect of the Contracting State referred to in Article 2, paragraph 1.

Article 35

(1) A Contracting State may denounce this Convention by a formal notification in writing to the depositary.

(2) The denunciation takes effect on the first day of the month following the expiration of twelve months after the notification is received by the depositary. Where a longer period for the denunciation to take effect is specified in the notification, the denunciation takes effect upon the

expiration of such longer period after the notification is received by the depositary.

In witness whereof the undersigned plenipotentiaries, being duly authorized by their respective Governments, have signed this Convention.

Done at Geneva this seventeenth day of February, one thousand nine hundred and eighty-three, in a single original, of which the English and French texts are equally authentic.

UNIDROIT CONVENTION

on International Factoring of 28 May 1988 (Ottawa)*

(Misc 5 (1991), Cm 1487, 27 ILM 943)

The States Parties to this Convention,

Conscious of the fact that international factoring has a significant role to play in the development of international trade,

Recognising therefore the importance of adopting uniform rules to provide a legal framework that will facilitate international factoring, while maintaining a fair balance of interests between the different parties involved in factoring transactions,

Have agreed as follows:

CHAPTER 1–SPHERE OF APPLICATION AND GENERAL PROVISIONS

Article 1

(1) This Convention governs factoring contracts and assignments of receivables as described in this Chapter.

(2) For the purposes of this Convention, 'factoring contract' means a contract concluded between one party (the supplier) and another party (the factor) pursuant to which:

    a) the supplier may or will assign to the factor receivables arising from contracts of sale of goods made between the supplier and its customers (debtors) other than those for the sale of goods bought primarily for their personal, family or household use;

    b) the factor is to perform at least two of the following functions: finance for the supplier, including loans and advance payments; maintenance of accounts (ledgering) relating to the receivables; collection of receivables; protection against default in payment by debtors;

    c) notice of the assignment of the receivables is to be given to debtors.

(3) In this Convention references to 'goods' and 'sale of goods' shall include services and the supply of services.

(4) For the purposes of this Convention:

---

* This Convention applies, subject to various reservations and declarations, in the following states, since the dates indicated in brackets: the Federal Republic of Germany (1 December 1998), France (1 May 1995), Hungary (1 December 1996), Italy (1 May 1995), Latvia (1 March 1998), and Nigeria (1 May 1995). It does not apply in the United Kingdom.

a)   a notice in writing need not be signed but must identify the person by whom or in whose name it is given;

b)   'notice in writing' includes, but is not limited to, telegrams, telex and any other telecommunication capable of being reproduced in tangible form;

c)   a notice in writing is given when it is received by the addressee.

Article 2

(1)   This Convention applies whenever the receivables assigned pursuant to a factoring contract arise from a contract of sale of goods between a supplier and a debtor whose places of business are in different States and:

     a)   those States and the State in which the factor has its place of business are Contracting States; or

     b)   both the contract of sale of goods and the factoring contract are governed by the law of a Contracting State.

(2)   A reference in this Convention to a party's place of business shall, if it has more than one place of business, mean the place of business which has the closest relationship to the relevant contract and its performance, having regard to the circumstances known to or contemplated by the parties at any time before or at the conclusion of that contract.

Article 3

(1)   The application of this Convention may be excluded:

     a)   by the parties to the factoring contract; or

     b)   by the parties to the contract of sale of goods, as regards receivables arising at or after the time when the factor has been given notice in writing of such exclusion.

(2)   Where the application of this Convention is excluded in accordance with the previous paragraph, such exclusion may be made only as regards the Convention as a whole.

Article 4

(1)   In the interpretation of this Convention, regard is to be had to its object and purpose as set forth in the preamble, to its international character and to the need to promote uniformity in its application and the observance of good faith in international trade.

(2)   Questions concerning matters governed by this Convention which are not expressly settled in it are to be settled in conformity with the general principles on which it is based or, in the absence of such principles, in conformity with the law applicable by virtue of the rules of private international law.

CHAPTER II – RIGHTS AND DUTIES OF THE PARTIES

Article 5

As between the parties to the factoring contract:

(a) a provision in the factoring contract for the assignment of existing or future receivables shall not be rendered invalid by the fact that the contract does not specify them individually, if at the time of conclusion of the contract or when they come into existence they can be identified to the contract;

(b) a provision in the factoring contract by which future receivables are assigned operates to transfer the receivables to the factor when they come into existence without the need for any new act of transfer.

Article 6

(1) The assignment of a receivable by the supplier to the factor shall be effective notwithstanding any agreement between the supplier and the debtor prohibiting such assignment.

(2) However, such assignment shall not be effective against the debtor when, at the time of conclusion of the contract of sale of goods, it has its place of business in a Contracting State which has made a declaration under Article 18 of this Convention.

(3) Nothing in paragraph 1 shall affect any obligation of good faith owed by the supplier to the debtor or any liability of the supplier to the debtor in respect of an assignment made in breach of the terms of the contract of sale of goods.

Article 7

A factoring contract may validly provide as between the parties thereto for the transfer, with or without a new act of transfer, of all or any of the supplier's rights deriving from the contract of sale of goods, including the benefit of any provision in the contract of sale of goods reserving to the supplier title to the goods or creating any security interest.

Article 8

(1) The debtor is under a duty to pay the factor if, and only if, the debtor does not have knowledge of any other person's superior right to payment and notice in writing of the assignment:
   a) is given to the debtor by the supplier or by the factor with the supplier's authority;

b)   reasonably identifies the receivables which have been assigned and the factor to whom or for whose account the debtor is required to make payment; and

c)   relates to receivables arising under a contract of sale of goods made at or before the time the notice is given.

(2) Irrespective of any other ground on which payment by the debtor to the factor discharges the debtor from liability, payment shall be effective for this purpose if made in accordance with the previous paragraph.

Article 9

(1) In a claim by the factor against the debtor for payment of a receivable arising under a contract of sale of goods the debtor may set up against the factor all defences arising under that contract of which the debtor could have availed itself if such claim had been made by the supplier.

(2) The debtor may also assert against the factor any right of set-off in respect of claims existing against the supplier in whose favour the receivable arose and available to the debtor at the time a notice in writing of assignment conforming to Article 8(1) was given to the debtor.

Article 10

(1) Without prejudice to the debtor's rights under Article 9, non-performance or defective or late performance of the contract of sale of goods shall not by itself entitle the debtor to recover a sum paid by the debtor to the factor if the debtor has a right to recover that sum from the supplier.

(2) The debtor who has such a right to recover from the supplier a sum paid to the factor in respect of a receivable shall nevertheless be entitled to recover that sum from the factor to the extent that:

a)   the factor has not discharged an obligation to make payment to the supplier in respect of that receivable; or

b)   the factor made such payment at a time when it knew of the supplier's non-performance or defective or late performance as regards the goods to which the debtor's payment relates.

CHAPTER III – SUBSEQUENT ASSIGNMENTS

Article 11

(1) Where a receivable is assigned by a supplier to a factor pursuant to a factoring contract governed by this Convention:

a)   the rules set out in Articles 5 to 10 shall, subject to sub-paragraph (b)of this paragraph, apply to any subsequent assignment of the receivable by the factor or by a subsequent assignee;

b)   the provisions of Articles 8 to 10 shall apply as if the subsequent assignee were the factor.

(2) For the purposes of this Convention, notice to the debtor of the subsequent assignment also constitutes notice of the assignment to the factor.

Article 12

This Convention shall not apply to a subsequent assignment which is prohibited by the terms of the factoring contract.

Article 13 to 23

(not reproduced)

UNIDROIT CONVENTION

on International Financial Leasing
of 20 May 1988 (Ottawa)*

(27 ILM 931)

The States Parties to this Convention,

Recognising the importance of removing certain legal impediments to the international financial leasing of equipment, while maintaining a fair balance of interests between the different parties to the transaction,

Aware of the need to make international financial leasing more available,

Conscious of the fact that the rules of law governing the traditional contract of hire need to be adapted to the distinctive triangular relationship created by the financial leasing transaction,

Recognising therefore the desirability of formulating certain uniform rules relating primarily to the civil and commercial law aspects of international financial leasing,

Have agreed as follows:

CHAPTER I – SPHERE OF APPLICATION
AND GENERAL PROVISIONS

Article 1

(1) This Convention governs a financial leasing transaction as described in paragraph 2 in which one party (the lessor),

    a)   on the specifications of another party (the lessee), enters into an agreement (the supply agreement) with a third party (the supplier) under which the lessor acquires plant, capital goods or other equipment (the equipment) on terms approved by the lessee so far as they concern its interests, and

    b)   enters into an agreement (the leasing agreement) with the lessee, granting to the lessee the right to use the equipment in return for the payment of rentals.

(2) The financial leasing transaction referred to in the previous paragraph is a transaction which includes the following characteristics:

---

* This Convention applies, subject to various reservations and declarations, in the following states, since the dates indicated in brackets: France (1 May 1995), Italy (1 May 1995), Latvia (1 March 1998), Nigeria (1 May 1995), Panama (1 October 1997), the Russian Federation (1 January 1999), Hungary (1 December 1996), and White Russia (1 March 1999).

a) the lessee specifies the equipment and selects the supplier without relying primarily on the skill and judgment of the lessor;

b) the equipment is acquired by the lessor in connection with a leasing agreement which, to the knowledge of the supplier, either has been made or is to be made between the lessor and the lessee; and

c) the rentals payable under the leasing agreement are calculated so as to take into account in particular the amortisation of the whole or a substantial part of the cost of the equipment.

(3) This Convention applies whether or not the lessee has or subsequently acquires the option to buy the equipment or to hold it on lease FSfor a further period, and whether or not for a nominal price or rental.

(4) This Convention applies to financial leasing transactions in relation to all equipment save that which is to be used primarily for the lessee's personal, family or household purposes.

Article 2

In the case of one or more sub-leasing transactions involving the same equipment, this Convention applies to each transaction which is a financial leasing transaction and is otherwise subject to this Convention as if the person from whom the first lessor (as defined in paragraph 1 of the previous article) acquired the equipment were the supplier and as if the agreement under which the equipment was so acquired were the supply agreement.

Article 3

(1) This Convention applies when the lessor and the lessee have their places of business in different States and:

a) those States and the State in which the supplier has its place of business are Contracting States; or

b) both the supply agreement and the leasing agreement are governed by the law of a Contracting State.

(2) A reference in this Convention to a party's place of business shall, if it has more than one place of business, mean the place of business which has the closest relationship to the relevant agreement and its performance, having regard to the circumstances known to or contemplated by the parties at any time before or at the conclusion of that agreement.

Article 4

(1) The provisions of this Convention shall not cease to apply merely because the equipment has become a fixture to or incorporated in land.

(2) Any question whether or not the equipment has become a fixture to or incorporated in land, and if so the effect on the rights *inter se* of the

lessor and a person having real rights in the land, shall be determined by the law of the State where the land is situated.

Article 5

(1) The application of this Convention may be excluded only if each of the parties to the supply agreement and each of the parties to the leasing agreement agree to exclude it.

(2) Where the application of this Convention has not been excluded in accordance with the previous paragraph, the parties may, in their relations with each other, derogate from or vary the effect of any of its provisions except as stated in Articles 8(3) and 13(3)(b) and (4).

Article 6

(1) In the interpretation of this Convention, regard is to be had to its object and purpose as set forth in the preamble, to its international character and to the need to promote uniformity in its application and the observance of good faith in international trade.

(2) Questions concerning matters governed by this Convention which are not expressly settled in it are to be settled in conformity with the general principles on which it is based or, in the absence of such principles, in conformity with the law applicable by virtue of the rules of private international law.

CHAPTER II – RIGHTS AND DUTIES OF THE PARTIES

Article 7

(1) a) The lessor's real rights in the equipment shall be valid against the lessee's trustee in bankruptcy and creditors, including creditors who have obtained an attachment or execution.

   b) For the purposes of this paragraph 'trustee in bankruptcy' includes a liquidator, administrator or other person appointed to administer the lessee's estate for the benefit of the general body of creditors.

(2) Where by the applicable law the lessor's real rights in the equipment are valid against a person referred to in the previous paragraph only on compliance with rules as to public notice, those rights shall be valid against that person only if there has been compliance with such rules.

(3) For the purposes of the previous paragraph the applicable law is the law of the State which, at the time when a person referred to in paragraph 1 becomes entitled to invoke the rules referred to in the previous paragraph, is:

a) in the case of a registered ship, the State in which it is registered in the name of the owner (for the purposes of this sub-paragraph a bareboat charterer is deemed not to be the owner);

b) in the case of an aircraft which is registered pursuant to the Convention on International Civil Aviation done at Chicago on 7 December 1944, the State in which it is so registered;

c) in the case of other equipment of a kind normally moved from one State to another, including an aircraft engine, the State in which the lessee has its principal place of business;

d) in the case of all other equipment, the State in which the equipment is situated.

(4) Paragraph 2 shall not affect the provisions of any other treaty under which the lessor's real rights in the equipment are required to be recognised.

(5) This article shall not affect the priority of any creditor having:

a) a consensual or non-consensual lien or security interest in the equipment arising otherwise than by virtue of an attachment or execution, or

b) any right of arrest, detention or disposition conferred specifically in relation to ships or aircraft under the law applicable by virtue of the rules of private international law.

Article 8

(1) a) Except as otherwise provided by this Convention or stated in the leasing agreement, the lessor shall not incur any liability to the lessee in respect of the equipment save to the extent that the lessee has suffered loss as the result of its reliance on the lessor's skill and judgment and of the lessor's intervention in the selection of the supplier or the specifications of the equipment.

b) The lessor shall not, in its capacity of lessor, be liable to third parties for death, personal injury or damage to property caused by the equipment.

c) The above provisions of this paragraph shall not govern any liability of the lessor in any other capacity, for example as owner.

(2) The lessor warrants that the lessee's quiet possession will not be disturbed by a person who has a superior title or right, or who claims a superior title or right and acts under the authority of a court, where such title, right or claim is not derived from an act or omission of the lessee.

(3) The parties may not derogate from or vary the effect of the provisions of the previous paragraph in so far as the superior title, right or claim is derived from an intentional or grossly negligent act or omission of the lessor.

(4) The provisions of paragraphs 2 and 3 shall not affect any broader warranty of quiet possession by the lessor which is mandatory under the law applicable by virtue of the rules of private international law.

Article 9

(1) The lessee shall take proper care of the equipment, use it in a reasonable manner and keep it in the condition in which it was delivered, subject to fair wear and tear and to any modification of the equipment agreed by the parties.

(2) When the leasing agreement comes to an end the lessee, unless exercising a right to buy the equipment or to hold the equipment on lease for a further period, shall return the equipment to the lessor in the condition specified in the previous paragraph.

Article 10

(1) The duties of the supplier under the supply agreement shall also be owed to the lessee as if it were a party to that agreement and as if the equipment were to be supplied directly to the lessee. However, the supplier shall not be liable to both the lessor and the lessee in respect of the same damage.

(2) Nothing in this article shall entitle the lessee to terminate or rescind the supply agreement without the consent of the lessor.

Article 11

The lessee's rights derived from the supply agreement under this Convention shall not be affected by a variation of any term of the supply agreement previously approved by the lessee unless it consented to that variation.

Article 12

(1) Where the equipment is not delivered or is delivered late or fails to conform to the supply agreement:
   a) the lessee has the right as against the lessor to reject the equipment or to terminate the leasing agreement; and
   b) the lessor has the right to remedy its failure to tender equipment in conformity with the supply agreement,
      as if the lessee had agreed to buy the equipment from the lessor under the same terms as those of the supply agreement.

(2) A right conferred by the previous paragraph shall be exercisable in the same manner and shall be lost in the same circumstances as if the lessee had agreed to buy the equipment from the lessor under the same terms as those of the supply agreement.

(3) The lessee shall be entitled to withhold rentals payable under the leasing agreement until the lessor has remedied its failure to tender equipment in conformity with the supply agreement or the lessee has lost the right to reject the equipment.

(4) Where the lessee has exercised a right to terminate the leasing agreement, the lessee shall be entitled to recover any rentals and other sums paid in advance, less a reasonable sum for any benefit the lessee has derived from the equipment.

(5) The lessee shall have no other claim against the lessor for non-delivery, delay in delivery or delivery of non-conforming equipment except to the extent to which this results from the act or omission of the lessor.

(6) Nothing in this article shall affect the lessee's rights against the supplier under Article 10.

Article 13

(1) In the event of default by the lessee, the lessor may recover accrued unpaid rentals, together with interest and damages.

(2) Where the lessee's default is substantial, then subject to paragraph 5 the lessor may also require accelerated payment of the value of the future rentals, where the leasing agreement so provides, or may terminate the leasing agreement and after such termination:

    a) recover possession of the equipment; and

    b) recover such damages as will place the lessor in the position in which it would have been had the lessee performed the leasing agreement in accordance with its terms.

(3) a) The leasing agreement may provide for the manner in which the damages recoverable under paragraph 2(b) are to be computed.

    b) Such provision shall be enforceable between the parties unless it would result in damages substantially in excess of those provided for under paragraph 2(b). The parties may not derogate from or vary the effect of the provisions of the present sub-paragraph.

(4) Where the lessor has terminated the leasing agreement, it shall not be entitled to enforce a term of that agreement providing for acceleration of payment of future rentals, but the value of such rentals may be taken into account in computing damages under paragraphs 2(b) and 3. The parties may not derogate from or vary the effect of the provisions of the present paragraph.

(5) The lessor shall not be entitled to exercise its right of acceleration or its right of termination under paragraph 2 unless it has by notice given the lessee a reasonable opportunity of remedying the default so far as the same may be remedied.

(6) The lessor shall not be entitled to recover damages to the extent that it has failed to take all reasonable steps to mitigate its loss.

Article 14

(1) The lessor may transfer or otherwise deal with all or any of its rights in the equipment or under the leasing agreement. Such a transfer shall not relieve the lessor of any of its duties under the leasing agreement or alter either the nature of the leasing agreement or its legal treatment as provided in this Convention.

(2) The lessee may transfer the right to the use of the equipment or any other rights under the leasing agreement only with the consent of the lessor and subject to the rights of third parties.

CHAPTER III – FINAL PROVISIONS

Article 15

(1) This Convention is open for signature at the concluding meeting of the Diplomatic Conference for the Adoption of the Draft Unidroit Conventions on International Factoring and International Financial Leasing and will remain open for signature by all States at Ottawa until 31 December 1990.

(2) This Convention is subject to ratification, acceptance or approval by States which have signed it.

(3) This Convention is open for accession by all States which are not signatory States as from the date it is open for signature.

(4) Ratification, acceptance, approval or accession is effected by the deposit of a formal instrument to that effect with the depositary.

Article 16

(1) This convention enters into force on the first day of the month following the expiration of six months after the date of deposit of the third instrument of ratification, acceptance, approval or accession.

(2) For each State that ratifies, accepts, approves, or accedes to this Convention after the deposit of the third instrument of ratification, acceptance, approval or accession, this Convention enters into force in respect of that State on the first day of the month following the expiration of six months after the date of the deposit of its instrument of ratification, acceptance, approval or accession.

Article 17

This Convention does not prevail over any treaty which has already been or may be entered into; in particular it shall not affect any liability imposed on any person by existing or future treaties.

Article 18

(1) If a Contracting State has two or more territorial units in which different systems of law are applicable in relation to the matters dealt with in this Convention, it may, at the time of signature, ratification, acceptance, approval or accession, declare that this Convention is to extend to all its territorial units or only to one or more of them, and may substitute its declaration by another declaration at any time.

(2) These declarations are to be notified to the depositary and are to state expressly the territorial units to which the Convention extends.

(3) If, by virtue of a declaration under this article, this Convention extends to one or more but not all of the territorial units of a Contracting State, and if the place of business of a party is located in that State, this place of business, for the purposes of this Convention, is considered not to be in a Contracting State, unless it is in a territorial unit to which the Convention extends.

(4) If a Contracting State makes no declaration under paragraph 1, the Convention is to extend to all territorial units of that State.

Article 19

(1) Two or more Contracting States which have the same or closely related legal rules on matters governed by this Convention may at any time declare that the Convention is not to apply where the supplier, the lessor and the lessee have their places of business in those States. Such declarations may be made jointly or by reciprocal unilateral declarations.

(2) A Contracting State which has the same or closely related legal rules on matters governed by this Convention as one or more non-Contracting States may at any time declare that the Convention is not to apply where the supplier, the lessor and the lessee have their places of business in those States.

(3) If a State which is the object of a declaration under the previous paragraph subsequently becomes a Contracting State, the declaration made will, as from the date on which the Convention enters into force in respect of the new Contracting State, have the affect of a declaration made under paragraph 1, provided that the new Contracting State joins in such declaration or makes a reciprocal unilateral declaration.

Article 20

A Contracting State may declare at the time of signature, ratification, acceptance, approval or accession that it will substitute its domestic law for Article 8(3) if its domestic law does not permit the lessor to exclude its liability for its default or negligence.

Article 21

(1) Declarations made under this Convention at the time of signature are subject to confirmation upon ratification, acceptance or approval.

(2) Declarations and confirmations of declarations are to be in writing and to be formally notified to the depositary.

(3) A declaration takes effect simultaneously with the entry into force of this Convention in respect of the State concerned. However, a declaration of which the depositary receives formal notification after such entry into force takes effect on the first day of the month following the expiration of six months after the date of its receipt by the depositary. Reciprocal unilateral declarations under Article 19 take effect on the first day of the month following the expiration of six months after the receipt of the latest declaration by the depositary.

(4) Any State which makes a declaration under this Convention may withdraw it at any time by a formal notification in writing addressed to the depositary. Such withdrawal is to take effect on the first day of the month following the expiration of six months after the date of the receipt of the notification by the depositary.

(5) A withdrawal of a declaration made under Article 19 renders inoperative in relation to the withdrawing State, as from the date on which the withdrawal takes effect, any joint or reciprocal unilateral declaration made by another State under that article.

Article 22

No reservations are permitted except those expressly authorised in this Convention.

Article 23

This Convention applies to a financial leasing transaction when the leasing agreement and the supply agreement are both concluded on or after the date on which the Convention enters into force in respect of the Contracting States referred to in Article 3(1)(a), or of the Contracting State or States referred to in paragraph 1(b) of that article.

Article 24

(1) This Convention may be denounced by any Contracting State at any time after the date on which it enters into force for that State.

(2) Denunciation is effected by the deposit of an instrument to that effect with the depositary.

(3) A denunciation takes effect on the first day of the month following the expiration of six months after the deposit of the instrument of denunciation with the depositary. Where a longer period for the denunciation to take effect is specified in the instrument of denunciation it takes effect upon the expiration of such longer period after its deposit with the depositary.

Article 25

(1) This Convention shall be deposited with the Government of Canada.
(2) The Government of Canada shall:
    a) inform all States which have signed or acceded to this Convention and the President of the International Institute for the Unification of Private Law (Unidroit) of:
        i) each new signature or deposit of an instrument of ratification, acceptance, approval or accession, together with the date thereof;
        ii) each declaration made under Articles 18, 19 and 20;
        iii) the withdrawal of any declaration made under Article 21(4);
        iv) the date of entry into force of this Convention;
        v) the deposit of an instrument of denunciation of this Convention together with the date of its deposit and the date on which it takes effect;
    b) transmit certified true copies of this Convention to all signatory States, to all States acceding to the Convention and to the President of the International Institute for the Unification of Private Law (Unidroit).

In witness whereof the undersigned plenipotentiaries, being duly authorised by their respective Governments, have signed this Convention.

Done at Ottawa, this twenty-eighth day of May, one thousand nine hundred and eighty-eight, in a single original, of which the English and French texts are equally authentic.

CONVENTION

on the law applicable to Contractual Obligations opened for signature in Rome on 19 June 1980*

(Misc 5(1982), Cmnd 8489, 19 ILM 1492, Official Journal, C27/98, p 36)

PREAMBLE

The High Contracting Parties to the Treaty establishing the European Economic Community,

Anxious to continue in the field of private international law the work of unification of law which has already been done within the Community, in particular in the field of jurisdiction and enforcement of judgments,

Wishing to establish uniform rules concerning the law applicable to contractual obligations,

Have agreed as follows:

TITLE I – SCOPE OF THE CONVENTION

Article 1

Scope of the Convention

(1) The rules of this Convention shall apply to contractual obligations in any situation involving a choice between the laws of different countries.

(2) They shall not apply to:
  a) questions involving the status or legal capacity of natural persons, without prejudice to Article 11;
  b) contractual obligations relating to:
  wills and succession,
  – rights in property arising out of a matrimonial relationship,

---

* This is the version of the Convention of 10 April 1984, at the time of the accession of the Republic of Greece (hereinafter referred to as 'Accession Convention of 1984'), of the Convention of 18 May 1992 at the time of the accession of the Kingdom of Spain and of the Republic of Portugal (hereinafter referred to as the 'Accession Convention of 1992'), and of the Convention at the time of the accession of the Republic of Austria, the Republic of Finland and of the Kingdom of Sweden (hereinafter referred to as the 'Convention of 1996').

The Convention of 19 June 1980 came into force in the United Kingdom, as well as in Belgium, Denmark, the Federal Republic of Germany, France, Italy, and Luxembourg on 1 April 1991. It is also in force in the Netherlands (1 September 1991) and Ireland (1 January 1992).

- rights and duties arising out of a family relationship, parentage, marriage or affinity, including maintenance obligations in respect of children who are not legitimate;

c) obligations arising under bills of exchange, cheques and promissory notes and other negotiable instruments to the extent that the obligations under such other negotiable instruments arise out of their negotiable character;

d) arbitration agreements and agreements on the choice of court;

e) questions governed by the law of companies and other bodies corporate or unincorporate such as the creation, by registration or otherwise, legal capacity, internal organization or winding up of companies and other bodies corporate or unincorporate and the personal liability of officers and members as such for the obligations of the company or body;

f) the question whether an agent is able to bind a principal, or an organ to bind a company or body corporate or unincorporate, to a third party;

g) the constitution of trusts and the relationship between settlors, trustees and beneficiaries;

h) evidence and procedure, without prejudice to Article 14.

(3) The rules of this Convention do not apply to contracts of insurance which cover risks situated in the territories of the Member States of the European Economic Community. In order to determine whether a risk is situated in those territories the court shall apply its internal law.

(4) The preceding paragraph does not apply to contracts of re-insurance.

Article 2

Application of law of non-contracting States

Any law specified by this Convention shall be applied whether or not it is the law of a Contracting State.

The Accession Convention of 1984 cameinto force in the Federal Republic of Germany on 1 April 1991 (BGBl 1988 II p. 563). In regard to the abovementioned states, except for the Netherlands and Ireland, the date on which the Convention of 19 June 1980 came into force is identical with that of the Convention of 10 April 1984. It became applicable in Ireland on 1 January 1992. The Accession Convention of 1992 came into force in the United Kingdom on 1 December 1997, in Belgium on 1 June 1998, in the Federal Republic of Germany on 1 September 1995, in France on 1 December 1995, in Italy on 1 March 1994, in Luxembourg on 1 April 1997, in the Netherlands on 1 September 1993, in Portugal on 1 September 1994, and in Spain on 1 September 1993.

The Accession Convention of 1996 (BGBl. 1998 II p. 1421) envisages the accession of the Republic of Austria, the Republic of Finland and the Kingdom of Sweden to the Convention of 19 June 1980.

The European Union contemplates the enactment of a regulation??? which should take the place of the Convention.

TITLE II – UNIFORM RULES

Article 3

Freedom of choice

(1) A contract shall be governed by the law chosen by the parties. The choice must be expressed or demonstrated with reasonable certainty by the terms of the contract or the circumstances of the case. By their choice the parties can select the law applicable to the whole or a part only of the contract.

(2) The parties may at any time agree to subject the contract to a law other than that which previously governed it, whether as a result of an earlier choice under this Article or of other provisions of this Convention. Any variation by the parties of the law to be applied made after the conclusion of the contract shall not prejudice its formal validity under Article 9 or adversely affect the rights of third parties.

(3) The fact that the parties have chosen a foreign law, whether or not accompanied by the choice of a foreign tribunal, shall not, where all the other elements relevant to the situation at the time of the choice are connected with one country only, prejudice the application of rules of the law at the country which cannot be derogated from by contract, hereinafter called 'mandatory rules'.

(4) The existence and validity of the consent of the parties as to the choice of the applicable law shall be determined in accordance with the provisions of Articles 8, 9 and 11.

Article 4

Applicable law in the absence of choice

(1) To the extent that the law applicable to the contract has not been chosen in accordance with Article 3, the contract shall be governed by the law of the country with which it is most closely connected. Nevertheless, a separable part of the contract which has a closer connection with another country may by way of exception be governed by the law of that other country.

(2) Subject to the provisions of paragraph 5 of this Article, it shall be presumed that the contract is most closely connected with the country where the party who is to effect the performance which is characteristic of the contract has, at the time of conclusion of the contract, his habitual residence, or, in the case of a body corporate or unincorporate, its central administration. However, if the contract is entered into in the course of that party's trade or profession, that country shall be

the country in which the principal place of business is situated or, where under the terms of the contract the performance is to be effected through a place of business other than the principal place of business, the country in which that other place of business is situated.

(3) Notwithstanding the provisions of paragraph 2 of this Article, to the extent that the subject matter of the contract is a right in immovable property or a right to use immovable property it shall be presumed that the contract is most closely connected with the country where the immovable property is situated.

(4) A contract for the carriage of goods shall not be subject to the presumption in paragraph 2. In such a contract if the country in which, at the time the contract is concluded, the carrier has his principal place of business is also the country in which the place of loading or the place of discharge or the principal place of business of the consignor is situated, it shall be presumed that the contract is most closely connected with that country. In applying this paragraph single voyage charter-parties and other contracts the main purpose of which is the carriage of goods shall be treated as contracts for the carriage of goods.

(5) Paragraph 2 shall not apply if the characteristic performance cannot be determined, and the presumptions in paragraphs 2, 3 and 4 shall be disregarded if it appears from the circumstances as a whole that the contract is more closely connected with another country.

Article 5

Certain consumer contracts

(1) This Article applies to a contract the object of which is the supply of goods or services to a person ('the consumer') for a purpose which can be regarded as being outside his trade or profession, or a contract for the provision of credit for that object.

(2) Notwithstanding the provisions of Article 3, a choice of law made by the parties shall not have the result of depriving the consumer of the protection afforded to him by the mandatory rules of the law of the country in which he has his habitual residence:

if in that country the conclusion of the contract was preceded by a specific invitation addressed to him or by advertising, and he had taken in that country all the steps necessary on his part for the conclusion of the contract, or

if the other party or his agent received the consumer's order in that country, or

if the contract is for the sale of goods and the consumer travelled from that country to another country and there gave his order, provided that the consumer's journey was arranged by the seller for the purpose of inducing the consumer to buy.

(3) Notwithstanding the provisions of Article 4, a contract to which this Article applies shall, in the absence of choice in accordance with Article 3, be governed by the law of the country in which the consumer has his habitual residence if it is entered into in the circumstances described in paragraph 2 of this Article.

(4) This Article shall not apply to:

a)   a contract of carriage;

b)   a contract for the supply of services where the services are to be supplied to the consumer exclusively in a country other than that in which he has his habitual residence.

(5) Notwithstanding the provisions of paragraph 4, this Article shall apply to a contract which, for an inclusive price, provides for a combination of travel and accommodation.

Article 6

Individual employment contracts

(1) Notwithstanding the provisions of Article 3, in a contract of employment a choice of law made by the parties shall not have the result of depriving the employee of the protection afforded to him by the mandatory rules of the law which would be applicable under paragraph 2 in the absence of choice.

(2) Notwithstanding the provisions of Article 4, a contract of employment shall, in the absence of choice in accordance with Article 3, be governed:

a)   by the law of the country in which the employee habitually carries out his work in performance of the contract, even if he is temporarily employed in another country; or

b)   if the employee does not habitually carry out his work in any one country, by the law of the country in which the place of business through which he was engaged is situated;

unless it appears from the circumstances as a whole that the contract is more closely connected with another country, in which case the contract shall be governed by the law of that country.

Article 7

Mandatory rules

(1) When applying under this Convention the law of a country, effect may be given to the mandatory rules of the law of another country with which the situation has a close connection, if and in so far as, under

the law of the latter country, those rules must be applied whatever the law applicable to the contract. In considering whether to give effect to these mandatory rules, regard shall be had to their nature and purpose and to the consequences of their application or non-application.

(2) Nothing in this Convention shall restrict the application of the rules of the law of the forum in a situation where they are mandatory irrespective of the law otherwise applicable to the contract.

Article 8

Material validity

(1) The existence and validity of a contract, or of any term of a contract, shall be determined by the law which would govern it under this Convention if the contract or term were valid.

(2) Nevertheless a party may rely upon the law of the country in which he has his habitual residence to establish that he did not consent if it appears from the circumstances that it would not be reasonable to determine the effect of his conduct in accordance with the law specified in the preceding paragraph.

Article 9

Formal validity

(1) A contract concluded between persons who are in the same country is formally valid if it satisfies the formal requirements of the law which governs it under this Convention or of the law of the country where it is concluded.

(2) A contract concluded between persons who are in different countries is formally valid if it satisfies the formal requirements of the law which governs it under this Convention or of the law of one of those countries.

(3) Where a contract is concluded by an agent, the country in which the agent acts is the relevant country for the purposes of paragraphs 1 and 2.

(4) An act intended to have legal effect relating to an existing or contemplated contract is formally valid if it satisfies the formal requirements of the law which under this Convention governs or would govern the contract or of the law of the country where the act was done.

(5) The provisions of the preceding paragraphs shall not apply to a contract to which Article 5 applies, concluded in the circumstances described in paragraph 2 of Article 5. The formal validity of such a contract is governed by the law of the country in which the consumer has his habitual residence.

(6) Notwithstanding paragraphs 1 to 4 of this Article, a contract the subject matter of which is a right in immovable property or a right to use immovable property shall be subject to the mandatory requirements of form of the law of the country where the property is situated if by that law those requirements are imposed irrespective of the country where the contract is concluded and irrespective of the law governing the contract.

Article 10

Scope of applicable law

(1) The law applicable to a contract by virtue of Articles 3 to 6 and 12 of this Convention shall govern in particular:
   a) interpretation;
   b) performance;
   c) within the limits of the powers conferred on the court by its procedural law, the consequences of breach, including the assessment of damages in so far as it is governed by rules of law;
   d) the various ways of extinguishing obligations, and prescription and limitation of actions;
   e) the consequences of nullity of the contract.
(2) In relation to the manner of performance and the steps to be taken in the event of defective performance regard shall be had to the law of the country in which performance takes place.

Article 11

Incapacity

In a contract concluded between persons who are in the same country, a natural person who would have capacity under the law of that country may invoke his incapacity resulting from another law only if the other party to the contract was aware of this incapacity at the time of the conclusion of the contract or was not aware thereof as a result of negligence.

Article 12

Voluntary assignment

(1) The mutual obligations of assignor and assignee under a voluntary assignment of a right against another person ('the debtor') shall be governed by the law which under this Convention applies to the contract between the assignor and assignee.

(2) The law governing the right to which the assignment relates shall determine its assignability, the relationship between the assignee and the debtor, the conditions under which the assignment can be invoked against the debtor and any question whether the debtor's obligations have been discharged.

Article 13

Subrogation

(1) Where a person ('the creditor') has a contractual claim upon another ('the debtor'), and a third person has a duty to satisfy the creditor, or has in fact satisfied the creditor in discharge of that duty, the law which governs the third person's duty to satisfy the creditor shall determine whether the third person is entitled to exercise against the debtor the rights which the creditor had against the debtor under the law governing their relationship and, if so, whether he may do so in full or only to a limited extent.

(2) The same rule applies where several persons are subject to the same contractual claim and one of them has satisfied the creditor.

Article 14

Burden of proof

(1) The law governing the contract under this Convention applies to the extent that it contains, in the law of contract, rules which raise presumptions of law or determine the burden of proof.

(2) A contract or an act intended to have legal effect may be proved by any mode of proof recognized by the law of the forum or by any of the laws referred to in Article 9 under which that contract or act is formally valid, provided that such mode of proof can be administered by the forum.

Article 15

Exclusion of convoi

The application of the law of any country specified by this Convention means the application of the rules of law in force in that country other than its rules of private international law.

Article 16

'Ordre public'

The application of a rule of the law of any country specified by this Convention may be refused only if such application is manifestly incompatible with the public policy ('ordre public') of the forum.

Article 17

No retrospective effect

This Convention shall apply in a Contracting State to contracts made after the date on which this Convention has entered into force with respect to that State.

Article 18

Uniform interpretation

In the interpretation and application of the preceding uniform rules, regard shall be had to their international character and to the desirability of achieving uniformity in their interpretation and application.

Article 19

States with more than one legal system

(1) Where a State comprises several territorial units each of which has its own rules of law in respect of contractual obligations, each territorial unit shall be considered as a country for the purposes of identifying the law applicable under this Convention.
(2) A State within which different territorial units have their own rules of law in respect of contractual obligations shall not be bound to apply this Convention to conflicts solely between the laws of such units.

Article 20

Precedence of Community law

This Convention shall not affect the application of provisions which, in relation to particular matters, lay down choice of law rules relating to contractual obligations and which are or will be contained in acts of the institutions of the European Communities or in national laws harmonized in implementation of such acts.

Article 21

Relationship with other conventions

This Convention shall not prejudice the application of international conventions to which a Contracting State is, or becomes, a party.

Article 22

Reservations

(1) Any Contracting State may, at the time of signature, ratification, acceptance or approval, reserve the right not to apply:
   a)   the provisions of Article 7(1);
   b)   the provisions of Article 10(1)(e).
(2) ...
(3) Any Contracting State may at any time withdraw a reservation which it has made; the reservation shall cease to have effect on the first day of the third calendar month after notification of the withdrawal.

TITLE III – FINAL PROVISIONS

Article 23

(1) If, after the date on which this Convention has entered into force for a Contracting State, that State wishes to adopt any new choice of law rule in regard to any particular category of contract within the scope of this Convention, it shall communicate its intention to the other signatory States through the Secretary-General of the Council of the European Communities.
(2) Any signatory State may, within six months from the date of the communication made to the Secretary-General, request him to arrange consultations between signatory States in order to reach agreement.
(3) If no signatory State has requested consultations within this period or if within two years following the communication made to the Secretary-General no agreement is reached in the course of consultations, the Contracting State concerned may amend its law in the manner indicated. The measures taken by that State shall be brought to the knowledge of the other signatory States through the Secretary-General of the Council of the European Communities.

Article 24

(1) If, after the date on which this Convention has entered into force with respect to a Contracting State, that State wishes to become a party to a multilateral convention whose principal aim or one of whose principal aims is to lay down rules of private international law concerning any of the matters governed by this Convention, the procedure set out in Article 23 shall apply. However, the period of two years, referred to in paragraph 3 of that Article, shall be reduced to one year.

(2) The procedure referred to in the preceding paragraph need not be followed if a Contracting State or one of the European Communities is already a party to the multilateral convention, or if its object is to revise a convention to which the State concerned is already a party, or if it is a convention concluded within the framework of the Treaties establishing the European Communities.

Article 25

If a Contracting State considers that the unification achieved by this Convention is prejudiced by the conclusion of agreements not covered by Article 24(1), that State may request the Secretary-General of the Council of the European Communities to arrange consultations between the signatory States of this Convention.

Article 26

Any Contracting State may request the revision of this Convention. In this event a revision conference shall be convened by the President of the Council of the European Communities.

Article 27

Article 28

(1) This Convention shall be open from 19 June 1980 for signature by the States party to the Treaty establishing the European Economic Community.

(2) This Convention shall be subject to ratification, acceptance or approval by the signatory States. The instruments of ratification, acceptance or approval shall be deposited with the Secretary-General of the Council of the European Communities (4).

Article 29

(1) This Convention shall enter into force on the first day of the third month following the deposit of the seventh instrument of ratification, acceptance or approval.

(2)   This Convention shall enter into force for each signatory State ratifying, accepting or approving at a later date on the first day of the third month following the deposit of its instrument of ratification, acceptance or approval.

Article 30

(1)   This Convention shall remain in force for 10 years from the date of its entry into force in accordance with Article 29(1), even for States for which it enters into force at a later date.

(2)   If there has been no denunciation it shall be renewed tacitly every five years.

(3)   A Contracting State which wishes to denounce shall, not less than six months before the expiration of the period of 10 or five years, as the case may be, give notice to the Secretary-General of the Council of the European Communities. Denunciation may be limited to any territory to which the Convention has been extended by a declaration under Article 27(2).

(4)   The denunciation shall have effect only in relation to the State which has notified it. The Convention will remain in force as between all other Contracting States.

Article 31

The Secretary-General of the Council of the European Communities shall notify the States party to the Treaty establishing the European Economic Community of:

a)   the signatures;
b)   deposit of each instrument of ratification, acceptance or approval;
c)   the date of entry into force of this Convention;
d)   communications made in pursuance of Articles 23, 24, 25, 26 and 30;
e)   the reservations and withdrawals of reservations referred to in Article 22.

Article 32

The Protocol annexed to this Convention shall form an integral part thereof.

Article 33

This Convention, drawn up in a single original in the Danish, Dutch, English, French, German, Irish and Italian languages, these texts being equally authentic, shall be deposited in the archives of the Secretariat of the Council of the European Communities. The Secretary-General shall transmit a certified copy thereof to the Government of each signatory State.

In witness whereof the undersigned, being duly authorized thereto, having signed this Convention.

Done at Rome on the nineteenth day of June in the year one thousand nine hundred and eighty.

(Signatures of the plenipotentiaries)

PROTOCOL

The High Contracting Parties have agreed upon the following provision which shall be annexed to the Convention:

'Notwithstanding the provisions of the Convention, Denmark, Sweden and Finland may retain national provisions concerning the law applicable to questions relating to the carriage of goods by sea and may amend such provisions without following the procedure provided for in Article 23 of the Convention of Rome. The national provisions applicable in this respect are the following:

in Denmark, paragraphs 252 and 321(3) and (4) of the 'Solov' (maritime law),

in Sweden, Chapter 13, Article 2(1) and (2), and Chapter 14, Article 1(3), of 'sjölagen' (maritime law),

in Finland, Chapter 13, Article 2(1) and (2), and Chapter 14, Article 1(3), of 'merilaki'/'sjölagen' (maritime law).'

In witness whereof the undersigned, being duly authorized thereto, have signed this Protocol.

Done at Rome on the nineteenth day of June in the year one thousand nine hundred and eighty.

(Signatures of the Plenipotentiaries)

JOINT DECLARATION

At the time of the signature of the Convention on the law applicable to contractual obligations, the Governments of the Kingdom of Belgium, the Kingdom of Denmark, the Federal Republic of Germany, the French Republic, Ireland, the Italian Republic, the Grand Duchy of Luxembourg, the Kingdom of the Netherlands and the United Kingdom of Great Britain and Northern Ireland

I.   anxious to avoid, as far as possible, dispersion of choice of law rules among several instruments and differences between these rules, express the wish that the institutions of the European Communities, in the exercise of their powers under the Treaties by which they were established, will, where the need arises, endeavour to adopt choice of law rules which are as far as possible consistent with those of this Convention;

II. declare their intention as from the date of signature of this Convention until becoming bound by Article 24, to consult with each other if any one of the signatory States wishes to become a party to any convention to which the procedure referred to in Article 24 would apply;

III.   having regard to the contribution of the Convention on the law applicable to contractual obligations to the unification of choice of law rules within the European Communities, express the view that any State which becomes a member of the European Communities should accede to this Convention.

In witness whereof the undersigned, being duly authorized thereto, have signed this Joint Declaration.

Done at Rome on the nineteenth day of June in the year one thousand nine hundred and eighty.

(Signatures of the Plenipotentiaries)

JOINT DECLARATION

The Governments of the Kingdom of Belgium, the Kingdom of Denmark, the Federal Republic of Germany, the French Republic, Ireland, the Italian Republic, the Grand Duchy of Luxembourg, the Kingdom of the Netherlands and the United Kingdom of Great Britain and Northern Ireland,

On signing the Convention on the law applicable to contractual obligations;

Desiring to ensure that the Convention is applied as effectively as possible;

Anxious to prevent differences of interpretation of the Convention from impairing its unifying effect;

Declare themselves ready:

1. to examine the possibility of conferring jurisdiction in certain matters on the Court of Justice of the European Communities and, if necessary, to negotiate an agreement to this effect;

2. to arrange meetings at regular intervals between their representatives.

In witness whereof the undersigned, being duly authorized thereto, have signed this Joint Declaration.

Done at Rome on the nineteenth day of June in the year one thousand nine hundred and eighty.

(Signatures of the Plenipotentiaries)

CONVENTION

on the law applicable to Trusts and their Recognition
of 1 July 1985 (The Hague)

UKTS 14 (1992), Cm 1823)

The States signatory to the present Convention

Considering that the trust, as developed in courts of equity in common law jurisdictions and adopted with some modifications in other jurisdictions, is a unique legal institution,

Desiring to establish common provisions on the law applicable to trusts and to deal with the most important issues concerning the recognition of trusts,

Have resolved to conclude a Convention to this effect, and have agreed upon the following provisions:

CHAPTER I – SCOPE

Article 1

This Convention specifies the law applicable to trusts and governs their recognition.

Article 2

For the purposes of this Convention, the term 'trust' refers to the legal relationships created—*inter vivos* or on death—by a person, the settlor, when assets have been placed under the control of a trustee for the benefit of a beneficiary or for a specified purpose.

A trust has the following characteristics—

a) the assets constitute a separate fund and are not a part of the trustee's own estate;

b) title to the trust assets stands in the name of the trustee or in the name of another person on behalf of the trustee;

c) the trustee has the power and the duty, in respect of which he is accountable, to manage, employ or dispose of the assets in accordance with the terms of the trust and the special duties imposed upon him by law.

The reservation by the settlor of certain rights and powers, and the fact that the trustee may himself have rights as a beneficiary, are not necessarily inconsistent with the existence of a trust.

Article 3

The Convention applies only to trusts created voluntarily and evidenced in writing.

Article 4

The Convention does not apply to preliminary issues relating to the validity of wills or of other acts by virtue of which assets are transferred to the trustee.

Article 5

The Convention does not apply to the extent that the law specified by Chapter II does not provide for trusts or the category of trusts involved.

CHAPTER II – APPLICABLE LAW

Article 6

A trust shall be governed by the law chosen by the settlor. The choice must be express or be implied in the terms of the instrument creating or the writing evidencing the trust, interpreted, if necessary, in the light of the circumstances of the case.

Where the law chosen under the previous paragraph does not provide for trusts or the category of trust involved, the choice shall not be effective and the law specified in Article 7 shall apply.

Article 7

Where no applicable law has been chosen, a trust shall be governed by the law with which it is most closely connected.

In ascertaining the law with which a trust is most closely connected reference shall be made in particular to—

a)   the place of administration of the trust designated by the settlor;
b)   the situs of the assets of the trust;
c)   the place of residence or business of the trustee;
d)   the objects of the trust and the places where they are to be fulfilled.

Article 8

The law specified by Article 6 or 7 shall govern the validity of the trust, its construction, its effects, and the administration of the trust.

In particular that law shall govern—

a)   the appointment, resignation and removal of trustees, the capacity to act as a trustee, and the devolution of the office of trustee;
b)   the rights and duties of trustees among themselves;
c)   the right of trustees to delegate in whole or in part the discharge of their duties or the exercise of their powers;

d) the power of trustees to administer or to dispose of trust assets, to create security interests in the trust assets, or to acquire new assets;
e) the powers of investment of trustees;
f) restrictions upon the duration of the trust, and upon the power to accumulate the income of the trust;
g) the relationships between the trustees and the beneficiaries including the personal liability of the trustees to the beneficiaries;
h) the variation or termination of the trust;
i) the distribution of the trust assets;
j) the duty of trustees to account for their administration.

Article 9

In applying this Chapter a severable aspect of the trust, particularly matters of administration, may be governed by a different law.

Article 10

The law applicable to the validity of the trust shall determine whether that law or the law governing a severable aspect of the trust may be replaced by another law.

CHAPTER III – RECOGNITION

Article 11

A trust created in accordance with the law specified by the preceding Chapter shall be recognized as a trust. Such recognition shall imply, as a minimum, that the trust property constitutes a separate fund, that the trustee may sue and be sued in his capacity as trustee, and that he may appear or act in this capacity before a notary or any person acting in an official capacity.

In so far as the law applicable to the trust requires or provides, such recognition shall imply, in particular—

a) that personal creditors of the trustee shall have no recourse against the trust assets;
b) that the trust assets shall not form part of the trustee's estate upon his insolvency or bankruptcy;
c) that the trust assets shall not form part of the matrimonial property of the trustee or his spouse nor part of the trustee's estate upon his death;
d) that the trust assets may be recovered when the trustee, in breach of trust, has mingled trust assets with his own property or has alienated trust assets. However, the rights and obligations of any third party holder of the assets shall remain subject to the law determined by the choice of law rules of the forum.

Article 12

Where the trustee desires to register assets, movable or immovable, or documents of title to them, he shall be entitled, in so far as this is not prohibited by or inconsistent with the law of the State where registration is sought, to do so in his capacity as trustee or in such other way that the existence of the trust is disclosed.

Article 13

No State shall be bound to recognize a trust the significant elements of which, except for the choice of the applicable law, the place of administration and the habitual residence of the trustee, are more closely connected with States which do not have the institution of the trust or the category of trust involved.

Article 14

The Convention shall not prevent the application of rules of law more favourable to the recognition of trusts.

CHAPTER IV – GENERAL CLAUSES

Article 15

The Convention does not prevent the application of provisions of the law designated by the conflicts rules of the forum, in so far as those provisions cannot be derogated from by voluntary act, relating in particular to the following matters -

a)   the protection of minors and incapable parties;
b)   the personal and proprietary effects of marriage;
c)   succession rights, testate and intestate, especially the indefeasible shares of spouses and relatives;
d)   the transfer of title to property and security interests in property;
e)   the protection of creditors in matters of insolvency;
f)   the protection, in other respects, of third parties acting in good faith.

Article 16

The Convention does not prevent the application of those provisions of the law of the forum which must be applied even to international situations, irrespective of rules of conflict of laws.

If another State has a sufficiently close connection with a case then, in exceptional circumstances, effect may also be given to rules of that State which have the same character as mentioned in the preceding paragraph.

Any Contracting State may, by way of reservation, declare that it will not apply the second paragraph of this Article.

Article 17

In the Convention the word 'law' means the rules of law in force in a State other than its rules of conflict of laws.

Article 18

The provisions of the Convention may be disregarded when their application would be manifestly incompatible with public policy (*ordre public*).

Article 19

Nothing in the Convention shall prejudice the powers of States in fiscal matters.

Article 20

Any Contracting State may, at any time, declare that the provisions of the Convention will be extended to trusts declared by judicial decisions.

This declaration shall be notified to the Ministry of Foreign Affairs of the Kingdom of the Netherlands and will come into effect on the day when this notification is received.

Article 31 is applicable to the withdrawal of the declaration in the same way as it applies to a denunciation of the Convention.

Article 21

Any Contracting State may reserve the right to apply the provisions of Chapter III only to trusts the validity of which is governed by the law of a Contracting State.

Article 22

The Convention applies to trusts regardless of the date on which they were created.

However, a Contracting State may reserve the right not to apply the Convention to trusts created before the date on which, in relation to that State, the Convention enters into force.

Article 23

For the purpose of identifying the law applicable under the Convention, where a State comprises several territorial units each of which has its own rules of law in respect of trusts, any reference to the law of the State is to be construed as referring to the law in force in the territorial unit in question.

Article 24

A State within which different territorial units have their own rules of law in respect of trusts is not bound to apply the Convention to conflicts solely between the laws of such units.

Article 25

The Convention shall not affect any other international instrument containing provisions on matters governed by this Convention to which a Contracting State is, or becomes, a party.

CHAPTER V – FINAL CLAUSES

Article 26

Any State may, at the time of signature, ratification, acceptance, approval or accession, or at the time of making a declaration in terms of Article 29, make the reservations provided for in Articles 16, 21 and 22.

No other reservation shall be permitted.

Any Contracting State may at any time withdraw a reservation which it has made; the reservation shall cease to have effect on the first day of the third calendar month after notification of the withdrawal.

Article 27

The Convention shall be open for signature by the States which were Members of the Hague Conference on Private International Law at the time of its Fifteenth Session.

It shall be ratified, accepted or approved and the instruments of ratification, acceptance or approval shall be deposited with the Ministry of Foreign Affairs of the Kingdom of the Netherlands.

Article 28

Any other State may accede to the Convention after it has entered into force in accordance with Article 30, paragraph 1.

The instrument of accession shall be deposited with the Ministry of Foreign Affairs of the Kingdom of the Netherlands.

The accession shall have effect only as regards the relations between the acceding State and those Contracting States which have not raised an objection to its accession in the twelve months after the receipt of the notification referred to in Article 32. Such an objection may also be raised by Member States at the time when they ratify, accept or approve the Convention after an accession. Any such objection shall be notified to the Ministry of Foreign Affairs of the Kingdom of the Netherlands.

Article 29

If a State has two or more territorial units in which different systems of law are applicable, it may at the time of signature, ratification, acceptance, approval or accession declare that this Convention shall extend to all of its territorial units or only to one or more of them and may modify this declaration by submitting another declaration at any time.

Any such declaration shall be notified to the Ministry of Foreign Affairs of the Kingdom of the Netherlands and shall state expressly the territorial units to which the Convention applies.

If a State makes no declaration under this Article, the Convention is to extend to all territorial units of that State.

Article 30

The Convention shall enter into force on the first day of the third calendar month after the deposit of the third instrument of ratification, acceptance or approval referred to in Article 27.

Thereafter the Convention shall enter into force—

a) for each State ratifying, accepting or approving it subsequently, on the first day of the third calendar month after the deposit of its instrument of ratification, acceptance or approval;

b) for each acceding State, on the first day of the third calendar month after the expiry of the period referred to in Article 28;

c) for a territorial unit to which the Convention has been extended in conformity with Article 29, on the first day of the third calendar month after the notification referred to in that Article.

Article 31

Any Contracting State may denounce this Convention by a formal notification in writing addressed to the Ministry of Foreign Affairs of the Kingdom of the Netherlands, depositary of the Convention.

The denunciation takes effect on the first day of the month following the expiration of six months after the notification is received by the depositary or on such later date as is specified in the notification.

Article 32

The Ministry of Foreign Affairs of the Kingdom of the Netherlands shall notify the States Members of the Conference, and the States which have acceded in accordance with Article 28, of the following—

a) the signatures and ratifications, acceptances or approvals referred to in Article 27;

b) the date on which the Convention enters into force in accordance with Article 30;

  c)   the accessions and the objections raised to accessions referred to in
       Article 28;
  d)   the extensions referred to in Article 29;
  e)   the declarations referred to in Article 20;
  f)   the reservation or withdrawals referred to in Article 26;
  g)   the denunciations referred to in Article 31.

In witness whereof the undersigned, being duly authorized thereto, have signed
this Convention.

Done at The Hague, on the first day of July, 1985, in English and French, both
texts being equally authentic, in a single copy which shall be deposited in the
archives of the Government of the Kingdom of the Netherlands, and of which a
certified copy shall be sent, through diplomatic channels, to each of the States
Members of the Hague Conference on Private International Law at the date of its
Fifteenth Session.

UNITED NATIONS CONVENTION ON THE ASSIGNMENT OF RECEIVABLES IN INTERNATIONAL TRADE

PREAMBLE

The Contracting States,

Reaffirming their conviction that international trade on the basis of equality and mutual benefit is an important element in the promotion of friendly relations among States,

Considering that problems created by uncertainties as to the content and the choice of legal regime applicable to the assignment of receivables constitute an obstacle to international trade,

Desiring to establish principles and to adopt rules relating to the assignment of receivables that would create certainty and transparency and promote the modernization of the law relating to assignments of receivables, while protecting existing assignment practices and facilitating the development of new practices,

Desiring also to ensure adequate protection of the interests of debtors in assignments of receivables,

Being of the opinion that the adoption of uniform rules governing the assignment of receivables would promote the availability of capital and credit at more affordable rates and thus facilitate the development of international trade,

Have agreed as follows:

CHAPTER I

Scope of application

Article 1

Scope of application

1. This Convention applies to:
    (a) Assignments of international receivables and to international assignments of receivables as defined in this chapter, if, at the time of conclusion of the contract of assignment, the assignor is located in a Contracting State; and
    (b) Subsequent assignments, provided that any prior assignment is governed by this Convention.
2. This Convention applies to subsequent assignments that satisfy the criteria set forth in paragraph 1(a) of this article, even if it did not apply to any prior assignment of the same receivable.

3. This Convention does not affect the rights and obligations of the debtor unless, at the time of conclusion of the original contract, the debtor is located in a Contracting State or the law governing the original contract is the law of a Contracting State.

4. The provisions of chapter V apply to assignments of international receivables and to international assignments of receivables as defined in this chapter independently of paragraphs 1 to 3 of this article. However, those provisions do not apply if a State makes a declaration under article 39.

5. The provisions of the annex to this Convention apply as provided in article 42.

Article 2

Assignment of receivables

For the purposes of this Convention:

(a) 'Assignment' means the transfer by agreement from one person ('assignor') to another person ('assignee') of all or part of or an undivided interest in the assignor's contractual right to payment of a monetary sum ('receivable') from a third person ('the debtor'). The creation of rights in receivables as security for indebtedness or other obligation is deemed to be a transfer;

(b) In the case of an assignment by the initial or any other assignee ('subsequent assignment'), the person who makes that assignment is the assignor and the person to whom that assignment is made is the assignee.

Article 3

Internationality

A receivable is international if, at the time of conclusion of the original contract, the assignor and the debtor are located in different States. An assignment is international if, at the time of conclusion of the contract of assignment, the assignor and the assignee are located in different States.

Article 4

Exclusions and other limitations

1. This Convention does not apply to assignments made:
    (a) To an individual for his or her personal, family or household purposes;

    (b)   As part of the sale or change in the ownership or legal status of the business out of which the assigned receivables arose.

2.   This Convention does not apply to assignments of receivables arising under or from:

    (a)   Transactions on a regulated exchange;

    (b)   Financial contracts governed by netting agreements, except a receivable owed on the termination of all outstanding transactions;

    (c)   Foreign exchange transactions;

    (d)   Inter-bank payment systems, inter-bank payment agreements or clearance and settlement systems relating to securities or other financial assets or instruments;

    (e)   The transfer of security rights in, sale, loan or holding of or agreement to repurchase securities or other financial assets or instruments held with an intermediary;

    (f)   Bank deposits;

    (g)   A letter of credit or independent guarantee.

3.   Nothing in this Convention affects the rights and obligations of any person under the law governing negotiable instruments.

4.   Nothing in this Convention affects the rights and obligations of the assignor and the debtor under special laws governing the protection of parties to transactions made for personal, family or household purposes.

5.   Nothing in this Convention:

    (a)   Affects the application of the law of a State in which real property is situated to either:

        (i)   An interest in that real property to the extent that under that law the assignment of a receivable confers such an interest; or

       (ii)   The priority of a right in a receivable to the extent that under that law an interest in the real property confers such a right; or

    (b)   Makes lawful the acquisition of an interest in real property not permitted under the law of the State in which the real property is situated.

CHAPTER II

General provisions

Article 5

Definitions and rules of interpretation

For the purposes of this Convention:

    (a)   'Original contract' means the contract between the assignor and the debtor from which the assigned receivable arises;

(b) 'Existing receivable' means a receivable that arises upon or before conclusion of the contract of assignment and 'future receivable' means a receivable that arises after conclusion of the contract of assignment;

(c) 'Writing' means any form of information that is accessible so as to be usable for subsequent reference. Where this Convention requires a writing to be signed, that requirement is met if, by generally accepted means or a procedure agreed to by the person whose signature is required, the writing identifies that person and indicates that person's approval of the information contained in the writing;

(d) 'Notification of the assignment' means a communication in writing that reasonably identifies the assigned receivables and the assignee;

(e) 'Insolvency administrator' means a person or body, including one appointed on an interim basis, authorized in an insolvency proceeding to administer the reorganization or liquidation of the assignor's assets or affairs;

(f) 'Insolvency proceeding' means a collective judicial or administrative proceeding, including an interim proceeding, in which the assets and affairs of the assignor are subject to control or supervision by a court or other competent authority for the purpose of reorganization or liquidation;

(g) 'Priority' means the right of a person in preference to the right of another person and, to the extent relevant for such purpose, includes the determination whether the right is a personal or a property right, whether or not it is a security right for indebtedness or other obligation and whether any requirements necessary to render the right effective against a competing claimant have been satisfied;

(h) A person is located in the State in which it has its place of business. If the assignor or the assignee has a place of business in more than one State, the place of business is that place where the central administration of the assignor or the assignee is exercised. If the debtor has a place of business in more than one State, the place of business is that which has the closest relationship to the original contract. If a person does not have a place of business, reference is to be made to the habitual residence of that person;

(i) 'Law' means the law in force in a State other than its rules of private international law;

(j) 'Proceeds' means whatever is received in respect of an assigned receivable, whether in total or partial payment or other satisfaction of the receivable. The term includes whatever is received in respect of proceeds. The term does not include returned goods;

(k) 'Financial contract' means any spot, forward, future, option or swap transaction involving interest rates, commodities, currencies, equities, bonds, indices or any other financial instrument, any repurchase or securities lending transaction, and any other transaction similar to any transaction referred to above entered into in financial markets and any combination of the transactions mentioned above;

(l) 'Netting agreement' means an agreement between two or more parties that provides for one or more of the following:

(i) The net settlement of payments due in the same currency on the same date whether by novation or otherwise;

(ii) Upon the insolvency or other default by a party, the termination of all outstanding transactions at their replacement or fair market values, conversion of such sums into a single currency and netting into a single payment by one party to the other; or

(iii) The set-off of amounts calculated as set forth in subparagraph (l) (ii) of this article under two or more netting agreements;

(m) 'Competing claimant' means:

(i) Another assignee of the same receivable from the same assignor, including a person who, by operation of law, claims a right in the assigned receivable as a result of its right in other property of the assignor, even if that receivable is not an international receivable and the assignment to that assignee is not an international assignment;

(ii) A creditor of the assignor; or

(iii) The insolvency administrator.

Article 6

Party autonomy

Subject to article 19, the assignor, the assignee and the debtor may derogate from or vary by agreement provisions of this Convention relating to their respective rights and obligations. Such an agreement does not affect the rights of any person who is not a party to the agreement.

Article 7

Principles of interpretation

1. In the interpretation of this Convention, regard is to be had to its object and purpose as set forth in the preamble, to its international character and to the need to promote uniformity in its application and the observance of good faith in international trade.

2. Questions concerning matters governed by this Convention that are not expressly settled in it are to be settled in conformity with the general principles on which it is based or, in the absence of such principles, in conformity with the law applicable by virtue of the rules of private international law.

CHAPTER III

Effects of assignment

Article 8

Effectiveness of assignments

1. An assignment is not ineffective as between the assignor and the assignee or as against the debtor or as against a competing claimant, and the right of an assignee may not be denied priority, on the ground that it is an assignment of more than one receivable, future receivables or parts of or undivided interests in receivables, provided that the receivables are described:
    (a) Individually as receivables to which the assignment relates; or
    (b) In any other manner, provided that they can, at the time of the assignment or, in the case of future receivables, at the time of conclusion of the original contract, be identified as receivables to which the assignment relates.
2. Unless otherwise agreed, an assignment of one or more future receivables is effective without a new act of transfer being required to assign each receivable.
3. Except as provided in paragraph 1 of this article, article 9 and article 10, paragraphs 2 and 3, this Convention does not affect any limitations on assignments arising from law.

Article 9

Contractual limitations on assignments

1. An assignment of a receivable is effective notwithstanding any agreement between the initial or any subsequent assignor and the debtor or any subsequent assignee limiting in any way the assignor's right to assign its receivables.
2. Nothing in this article affects any obligation or liability of the assignor for breach of such an agreement, but the other party to such agreement may not avoid the original contract or the assignment contract on the sole ground of that breach. A person who is not party to such an agreement is not liable on the sole ground that it had knowledge of the agreement.
3. This article applies only to assignments of receivables:
    (a) Arising from an original contract that is a contract for the supply or lease of goods or services other than financial services, a construction contract or a contract for the sale or lease of real property;

(b) Arising from an original contract for the sale, lease or licence of industrial or other intellectual property or of proprietary information;

(c) Representing the payment obligation for a credit card transaction; or

(d) Owed to the assignor upon net settlement of payments due pursuant to a netting agreement involving more than two parties.

Article 10

Transfer of security rights

1. A personal or property right securing payment of the assigned receivable is transferred to the assignee without a new act of transfer. If such a right, under the law governing it, is transferable only with a new act of transfer, the assignor is obliged to transfer such right and any proceeds to the assignee.

2. A right securing payment of the assigned receivable is transferred under paragraph 1 of this article notwithstanding any agreement between the assignor and the debtor or other person granting that right, limiting in any way the assignor's right to assign the receivable or the right securing payment of the assigned receivable.

3. Nothing in this article affects any obligation or liability of the assignor for breach of any agreement under paragraph 2 of this article, but the other party to that agreement may not avoid the original contract or the assignment contract on the sole ground of that breach. A person who is not a party to such an agreement is not liable on the sole ground that it had knowledge of the agreement.

4. Paragraphs 2 and 3 of this article apply only to assignments of receivables:

(a) Arising from an original contract that is a contract for the supply or lease of goods or services other than financial services, a construction contract or a contract for the sale or lease of real property;

(b) Arising from an original contract for the sale, lease or licence of industrial or other intellectual property or of proprietary information;

(c) Representing the payment obligation for a credit card transaction; or

(d) Owed to the assignor upon net settlement of payments due pursuant to a netting agreement involving more than two parties.

5. The transfer of a possessory property right under paragraph 1 of this article does not affect any obligations of the assignor to the debtor or the person granting the property right with respect to the property transferred existing under the law governing that property right.

6.   Paragraph 1 of this article does not affect any requirement under rules
     of law other than this Convention relating to the form or registration of
     the transfer of any rights securing payment of the assigned receivable.

CHAPTER IV

Rights, obligations and defences

SECTION I

Assignor and assignee

Article 11

Rights and obligations of the assignor and the assignee

1.   The mutual rights and obligations of the assignor and the assignee aris-
     ing from their agreement are determined by the terms and conditions
     set forth in that agreement, including any rules or general conditions
     referred to therein.
2.   The assignor and the assignee are bound by any usage to which they
     have agreed and, unless otherwise agreed, by any practices they have
     established between themselves.
3.   In an international assignment, the assignor and the assignee
     are considered, unless otherwise agreed, implicitly to have made appli-
     cable to the assignment a usage that in international trade is widely
     known to, and regularly observed by, parties to the particular type
     of assignment or to the assignment of the particular category of
     receivables.

Article 12

Representations of the assignor

1.   Unless otherwise agreed between the assignor and the assignee, the
     assignor represents at the time of conclusion of the contract of assign-
     ment that:
     (a)   The assignor has the right to assign the receivable;
     (b)   The assignor has not previously assigned the receivable to another
           assignee; and
     (c)   The debtor does not and will not have any defences or rights of
           set-off.

2. Unless otherwise agreed between the assignor and the assignee, the assignor does not represent that the debtor has, or will have, the ability to pay.

Article 13

Right to notify the debtor

1. Unless otherwise agreed between the assignor and the assignee, the assignor or the assignee or both may send the debtor notification of the assignment and a payment instruction, but after notification has been sent only the assignee may send such an instruction.

2. Notification of the assignment or a payment instruction sent in breach of any agreement referred to in paragraph 1 of this article is not ineffective for the purposes of article 17 by reason of such breach. However, nothing in this article affects any obligation or liability of the party in breach of such an agreement for any damages arising as a result of the breach.

Article 14

Right to payment

1. As between the assignor and the assignee, unless otherwise agreed and whether or not notification of the assignment has been sent:

    (a) If payment in respect of the assigned receivable is made to the assignee, the assignee is entitled to retain the proceeds and goods returned in respect of the assigned receivable;

    (b) If payment in respect of the assigned receivable is made to the assignor, the assignee is entitled to payment of the proceeds and also to goods returned to the assignor in respect of the assigned receivable; and

    (c) If payment in respect of the assigned receivable is made to another person over whom the assignee has priority, the assignee is entitled to payment of the proceeds and also to goods returned to such person in respect of the assigned receivable.

2. The assignee may not retain more than the value of its right in the receivable.

SECTION II

Debtor

Article 15

Principle of debtor protection

1. Except as otherwise provided in this Convention, an assignment does
    not, without the consent of the debtor, affect the rights and obligations
    of the debtor, including the payment terms contained in the original
    contract.
2. A payment instruction may change the person, address or account to
    which the debtor is required to make payment, but may not change:
    (a) The currency of payment specified in the original contract; or
    (b) The State specified in the original contract in which payment is to
         be made to a State other than that in which the debtor is located.

Article 16

Notification of the debtor

1. Notification of the assignment or a payment instruction is effective
    when received by the debtor if it is in a language that is reasonably
    expected to inform the debtor about its contents. It is sufficient if noti-
    fication of the assignment or a payment instruction is in the language
    of the original contract.
2. Notification of the assignment or a payment instruction may relate to
    receivables arising after notification.
3. Notification of a subsequent assignment constitutes notification of all
    prior assignments.

Article 17

Debtor's discharge by payment

1. Until the debtor receives notification of the assignment, the debtor is
    entitled to be discharged by paying in accordance with the original
    contract.
2. After the debtor receives notification of the assignment, subject to para-
    graphs 3 to 8 of this article, the debtor is discharged only by
    paying the assignee or, if otherwise instructed in the notification of the
    assignment or subsequently by the assignee in a writing received by the
    debtor, in accordance with such payment instruction.

3. If the debtor receives more than one payment instruction relating to a single assignment of the same receivable by the same assignor, the debtor is discharged by paying in accordance with the last payment instruction received from the assignee before payment.

4. If the debtor receives notification of more than one assignment of the same receivable made by the same assignor, the debtor is discharged by paying in accordance with the first notification received.

5. If the debtor receives notification of one or more subsequent assignments, the debtor is discharged by paying in accordance with the notification of the last of such subsequent assignments.

6. If the debtor receives notification of the assignment of a part of or an undivided interest in one or more receivables, the debtor is discharged by paying in accordance with the notification or in accordance with this article as if the debtor had not received the notification. If the debtor pays in accordance with the notification, the debtor is discharged only to the extent of the part or undivided interest paid.

7. If the debtor receives notification of the assignment from the assignee, the debtor is entitled to request the assignee to provide within a reasonable period of time adequate proof that the assignment from the initial assignor to the initial assignee and any intermediate assignment have been made and, unless the assignee does so, the debtor is discharged by paying in accordance with this article as if the notification from the assignee had not been received. Adequate proof of an assignment includes but is not limited to any writing emanating from the assignor and indicating that the assignment has taken place.

8. This article does not affect any other ground on which payment by the debtor to the person entitled to payment, to a competent judicial or other authority, or to a public deposit fund discharges the debtor.

Article 18

Defences and rights of set-off of the debtor

1. In a claim by the assignee against the debtor for payment of the assigned receivable, the debtor may raise against the assignee all defences and rights of set-off arising from the original contract, or any other contract that was part of the same transaction, of which the debtor could avail itself as if the assignment had not been made and such claim were made by the assignor.

2. The debtor may raise against the assignee any other right of set-off, provided that it was available to the debtor at the time notification of the assignment was received by the debtor.

3. Notwithstanding paragraphs 1 and 2 of this article, defences and rights of set-off that the debtor may raise pursuant to article 9 or 10 against the assignor for breach of an agreement limiting in any way the assignor's right to make the assignment are not available to the debtor against the assignee.

Article 19

Agreement not to raise defences or rights of set-off

1. The debtor may agree with the assignor in a writing signed by the debtor not to raise against the assignee the defences and rights of set-off that it could raise pursuant to article 18. Such an agreement precludes the debtor from raising against the assignee those defences and rights of set-off.
2. The debtor may not waive defences:
   (a) Arising from fraudulent acts on the part of the assignee; or
   (b) Based on the debtor's incapacity.
3. Such an agreement may be modified only by an agreement in a writing signed by the debtor. The effect of such a modification as against the assignee is determined by article 20, paragraph 2.

Article 20

Modification of the original contract

1. An agreement concluded before notification of the assignment between the assignor and the debtor that affects the assignee's rights is effective as against the assignee, and the assignee acquires corresponding rights.
2. An agreement concluded after notification of the assignment between the assignor and the debtor that affects the assignee's rights is ineffective as against the assignee unless:
   (a) The assignee consents to it; or
   (b) The receivable is not fully earned by performance and either the modification is provided for in the original contract or, in the context of the original contract, a reasonable assignee would consent to the modification.
3. Paragraphs 1 and 2 of this article do not affect any right of the assignor or the assignee arising from breach of an agreement between them.

Article 21

Recovery of payments

Failure of the assignor to perform the original contract does not entitle the debtor to recover from the assignee a sum paid by the debtor to the assignor or the assignee.

SECTION III

Third parties

Article 22

Law applicable to competing rights

With the exception of matters that are settled elsewhere in this Convention and subject to articles 23 and 24, the law of the State in which the assignor is located governs the priority of the right of an assignee in the assigned receivable over the right of a competing claimant.

Article 23

Public policy and mandatory rules

1. The application of a provision of the law of the State in which the assignor is located may be refused only if the application of that provision is manifestly contrary to the public policy of the forum State.
2. The rules of the law of either the forum State or any other State that are mandatory irrespective of the law otherwise applicable may not prevent the application of a provision of the law of the State in which the assignor is located.
3. Notwithstanding paragraph 2 of this article, in an insolvency proceeding commenced in a State other than the State in which the assignor is located, any preferential right that arises, by operation of law, under the law of the forum State and is given priority over the rights of an assignee in insolvency proceedings under the law of that State may be given priority notwithstanding article 22. A State may deposit at any time a declaration identifying any such preferential right.

Article 24

Special rules on proceeds

1. If proceeds are received by the assignee, the assignee is entitled to retain those proceeds to the extent that the assignee's right in the assigned receivable had priority over the right of a competing claimant in the assigned receivable.
2. If proceeds are received by the assignor, the right of the assignee in those proceeds has priority over the right of a competing claimant in

those proceeds to the same extent as the assignee's right had priority over the right in the assigned receivable of that claimant if:

(a) The assignor has received the proceeds under instructions from the assignee to hold the proceeds for the benefit of the assignee; and

(b) The proceeds are held by the assignor for the benefit of the assignee separately and are reasonably identifiable from the assets of the assignor, such as in the case of a separate deposit or securities account containing only proceeds consisting of cash or securities.

3. Nothing in paragraph 2 of this article affects the priority of a person having against the proceeds a right of set-off or a right created by agreement and not derived from a right in the receivable.

Article 25

Subordination

An assignee entitled to priority may at any time subordinate its priority unilaterally or by agreement in favour of any existing or future assignees.

CHAPTER V

Autonomous conflict-of-laws rules

Article 26

Application of chapter V

The provisions of this chapter apply to matters that are:

(a) Within the scope of this Convention as provided in article 1, paragraph 4; and

(b) Otherwise within the scope of this Convention but not settled elsewhere in it.

Article 27

Form of a contract of assignment

1. A contract of assignment concluded between persons who are located in the same State is formally valid as between them if it satisfies the

requirements of either the law which governs it or the law of the State in which it is concluded.

2. A contract of assignment concluded between persons who are located in different States is formally valid as between them if it satisfies the requirements of either the law which governs it or the law of one of those States.

Article 28

Law applicable to the mutual rights and obligations of the assignor and the assignee

1. The mutual rights and obligations of the assignor and the assignee arising from their agreement are governed by the law chosen by them.
2. In the absence of a choice of law by the assignor and the assignee, their mutual rights and obligations arising from their agreement are governed by the law of the State with which the contract of assignment is most closely connected.

Article 29

Law applicable to the rights and obligations of the assignee and the debtor

The law governing the original contract determines the effectiveness of contractual limitations on assignment as between the assignee and the debtor, the relationship between the assignee and the debtor, the conditions under which the assignment can be invoked against the debtor and whether the debtor's obligations have been discharged.

Article 30

Law applicable to priority

1. The law of the State in which the assignor is located governs the priority of the right of an assignee in the assigned receivable over the right of a competing claimant.
2. The rules of the law of either the forum State or any other State that are mandatory irrespective of the law otherwise applicable may not prevent the application of a provision of the law of the State in which the assignor is located.
3. Notwithstanding paragraph 2 of this article, in an insolvency proceeding commenced in a State other than the State in which the assignor is located, any preferential right that arises, by operation of law, under the law of the forum State and is given priority over the rights of an assignee in insolvency proceedings under the law of that State may be given priority notwithstanding paragraph 1 of this article.

Article 31

Mandatory rules

1. Nothing in articles 27 to 29 restricts the application of the rules of the law of the forum State in a situation where they are mandatory irrespective of the law otherwise applicable.
2. Nothing in articles 27 to 29 restricts the application of the mandatory rules of the law of another State with which the matters settled in those articles have a close connection if and insofar as, under the law of that other State, those rules must be applied irrespective of the law otherwise applicable.

Article 32

Public policy

With regard to matters settled in this chapter, the application of a provision of the law specified in this chapter may be refused only if the application of that provision is manifestly contrary to the public policy of the forum State.

CHAPTER VI

Final provisions

Article 33

Depositary

The Secretary-General of the United Nations is the depositary of this Convention.

Article 34

Signature, ratification, acceptance, approval, accession

1. This Convention is open for signature by all States at the Headquarters of the United Nations in New York until 31 December 2003.
2. This Convention is subject to ratification, acceptance or approval by the signatory States.
3. This Convention is open to accession by all States that are not signatory States as from the date it is open for signature.
4. Instruments of ratification, acceptance, approval and accession are to be deposited with the Secretary-General of the United Nations.

Article 35

Application to territorial units

1. If a State has two or more territorial units in which different systems of law are applicable in relation to the matters dealt with in this Convention, it may at any time declare that this Convention is to extend to all its territorial units or only one or more of them, and may at any time substitute another declaration for its earlier declaration.
2. Such declarations are to state expressly the territorial units to which this Convention extends.
3. If, by virtue of a declaration under this article, this Convention does not extend to all territorial units of a State and the assignor or the debtor is located in a territorial unit to which this Convention does not extend, this location is considered not to be in a Contracting State.
4. If, by virtue of a declaration under this article, this Convention does not extend to all territorial units of a State and the law governing the original contract is the law in force in a territorial unit to which this Convention does not extend, the law governing the original contract is considered not to be the law of a Contracting State.
5. If a State makes no declaration under paragraph 1 of this article, the Convention is to extend to all territorial units of that State.

Article 36

Location in a territorial unit

If a person is located in a State which has two or more territorial units, that person is located in the territorial unit in which it has its place of business. If the assignor or the assignee has a place of business in more than one territorial unit, the place of business is that place where the central administration of the assignor or the assignee is exercised. If the debtor has a place of business in more than one territorial unit, the place of business is that which has the closest relationship to the original contract. If a person does not have a place of business, reference is to be made to the habitual residence of that person. A State with two or more territorial units may specify by declaration at any time other rules for determining the location of a person within that State.

Article 37

Applicable law in territorial units

Any reference in this Convention to the law of a State means, in the case of a State which has two or more territorial units, the law in force in the territorial unit. Such a State may specify by declaration at any time other rules for determining the applicable law, including rules that render applicable the law of another territorial unit of that State.

Article 38

Conflicts with other international agreements

1. This Convention does not prevail over any international agreement that has already been or may be entered into and that specifically governs a transaction otherwise governed by this Convention.
2. Notwithstanding paragraph 1 of this article, this Convention prevails over the Unidroit Convention on International Factoring ('the Ottawa Convention'). To the extent that this Convention does not apply to the rights and obligations of a debtor, it does not preclude the application of the Ottawa Convention with respect to the rights and obligations of that debtor.

Article 39

Declaration on application of chapter V

A State may declare at any time that it will not be bound by chapter V.

Article 40

Limitations relating to Governments and other public entities

A State may declare at any time that it will not be bound or the extent to which it will not be bound by articles 9 and 10 if the debtor or any person granting a personal or property right securing payment of the assigned receivable is located in that State at the time of conclusion of the original contract and is a Government, central or local, any subdivision thereof, or an entity constituted for a public purpose. If a State has made such a declaration, articles 9 and 10 do not affect the rights and obligations of that debtor or person. A State may list in a declaration the types of entity that are the subject of a declaration.

Article 41

Other exclusions

1. A State may declare at any time that it will not apply this Convention to specific types of assignment or to the assignment of specific categories of receivables clearly described in a declaration.
2. After a declaration under paragraph 1 of this article takes effect:
   (a) This Convention does not apply to such types of assignment or to the assignment of such categories of receivables if the assignor is

located at the time of conclusion of the contract of assignment in such a State; and

(b) The provisions of this Convention that affect the rights and obligations of the debtor do not apply if, at the time of conclusion of the original contract, the debtor is located in such a State or the law governing the original contract is the law of such a State.

3. This article does not apply to assignments of receivables listed in article 9, paragraph 3.

Article 42

Application of the annex

1. A State may at any time declare that it will be bound by:
   (a) The priority rules set forth in section I of the annex and will participate in the international registration system established pursuant to section II of the annex;
   (b) The priority rules set forth in section I of the annex and will effectuate such rules by use of a registration system that fulfils the purposes of such rules, in which case, for the purposes of section I of the annex, registration pursuant to such a system has the same effect as registration pursuant to section II of the annex;
   (c) The priority rules set forth in section III of the annex;
   (d) The priority rules set forth in section IV of the annex; or
   (e) The priority rules set forth in articles 7 and 9 of the annex.

2. For the purposes of article 22:
   (a) The law of a State that has made a declaration pursuant to paragraph 1(a) or (b) of this article is the set of rules set forth in section I of the annex, as affected by any declaration made pursuant to paragraph 5 of this article;
   (b) The law of a State that has made a declaration pursuant to paragraph 1(c) of this article is the set of rules set forth in section III of the annex, as affected by any declaration made pursuant to paragraph 5 of this article;
   (c) The law of a State that has made a declaration pursuant to paragraph 1(d) of this article is the set of rules set forth in section IV of the annex, as affected by any declaration made pursuant to paragraph 5 of this article; and
   (d) The law of a State that has made a declaration pursuant to paragraph 1(e) of this article is the set of rules set forth in articles 7 and 9 of the annex, as affected by any declaration made pursuant to paragraph 5 of this article.

3. A State that has made a declaration pursuant to paragraph 1 of this article may establish rules pursuant to which contracts of assignment concluded before the declaration takes effect become subject to those rules within a reasonable time.

4. A State that has not made a declaration pursuant to paragraph 1 of this article may, in accordance with priority rules in force in that State, utilize the registration system established pursuant to section II of the annex.

5. At the time a State makes a declaration pursuant to paragraph 1 of this article or thereafter, it may declare that:

   (a) It will not apply the priority rules chosen under paragraph 1 of this article to certain types of assignment or to the assignment of certain categories of receivables; or

   (b) It will apply those priority rules with modifications specified in that declaration.

6. At the request of Contracting or Signatory States to this Convention comprising not less than one third of the Contracting and Signatory States, the depositary shall convene a conference of the Contracting and Signatory States to designate the supervising authority and the first registrar and to prepare or revise the regulations referred to in section II of the annex.

Article 43

Effect of declaration

1. Declarations made under articles 35, paragraph 1, 36, 37 or 39 to 42 at the time of signature are subject to confirmation upon ratification, acceptance or approval.

2. Declarations and confirmations of declarations are to be in writing and to be formally notified to the depositary.

3. A declaration takes effect simultaneously with the entry into force of this Convention in respect of the State concerned. However, a declaration of which the depositary receives formal notification after such entry into force takes effect on the first day of the month following the expiration of six months after the date of its receipt by the depositary.

4. A State that makes a declaration under articles 35, paragraph 1, 36, 37 or 39 to 42 may withdraw it at any time by a formal notification in writing addressed to the depositary. Such withdrawal takes effect on the first day of the month following the expiration of six months after the date of the receipt of the notification by the depositary.

5. In the case of a declaration under articles 35, paragraph 1, 36, 37 or 39 to 42 that takes effect after the entry into force of this Convention in

respect of the State concerned or in the case of a withdrawal of any such declaration, the effect of which in either case is to cause a rule in this Convention, including any annex, to become applicable:

(a) Except as provided in paragraph 5(b) of this article, that rule is applicable only to assignments for which the contract of assignment is concluded on or after the date when the declaration or withdrawal takes effect in respect of the Contracting State referred to in article 1, paragraph 1(a);

(b) A rule that deals with the rights and obligations of the debtor applies only in respect of original contracts concluded on or after the date when the declaration or withdrawal takes effect in respect of the Contracting State referred to in article 1, paragraph 3.

6. In the case of a declaration under articles 35, paragraph 1, 36, 37 or 39 to 42 that takes effect after the entry into force of this Convention in respect of the State concerned or in the case of a withdrawal of any such declaration, the effect of which in either case is to cause a rule in this Convention, including any annex, to become inapplicable:

(a) Except as provided in paragraph 6(b) of this article, that rule is inapplicable to assignments for which the contract of assignment is concluded on or after the date when the declaration or withdrawal takes effect in respect of the Contracting State referred to in article 1, paragraph 1(a);

(b) A rule that deals with the rights and obligations of the debtor is inapplicable in respect of original contracts concluded on or after the date when the declaration or withdrawal takes effect in respect of the Contracting State referred to in article 1, paragraph 3.

7. If a rule rendered applicable or inapplicable as a result of a declaration or withdrawal referred to in paragraph 5 or 6 of this article is relevant to the determination of priority with respect to a receivable for which the contract of assignment is concluded before such declaration or withdrawal takes effect or with respect to its proceeds, the right of the assignee has priority over the right of a competing claimant to the extent that, under the law that would determine priority before such declaration or withdrawal takes effect, the right of the assignee would have priority.

Article 44

Reservations

No reservations are permitted except those expressly authorized in this Convention.

Article 45

Entry into force

1. This Convention enters into force on the first day of the month following the expiration of six months from the date of deposit of the fifth instrument of ratification, acceptance, approval or accession with the depositary.
2. For each State that becomes a Contracting State to this Convention after the date of deposit of the fifth instrument of ratification, acceptance, approval or accession, this Convention enters into force on the first day of the month following the expiration of six months after the date of deposit of the appropriate instrument on behalf of that State.
3. This Convention applies only to assignments if the contract of assignment is concluded on or after the date when this Convention enters into force in respect of the Contracting State referred to in article 1, paragraph 1(a), provided that the provisions of this Convention that deal with the rights and obligations of the debtor apply only to assignments of receivables arising from original contracts concluded on or after the date when this Convention enters into force in respect of the Contracting State referred to in article 1, paragraph 3.
4. If a receivable is assigned pursuant to a contract of assignment concluded before the date when this Convention enters into force in respect of the Contracting State referred to in article 1, paragraph 1(a), the right of the assignee has priority over the right of a competing claimant with respect to the receivable to the extent that, under the law that would determine priority in the absence of this Convention, the right of the assignee would have priority.

Article 46

Denunciation

1. A Contracting State may denounce this Convention at any time by written notification addressed to the depositary.
2. The denunciation takes effect on the first day of the month following the expiration of one year after the notification is received by the depositary. Where a longer period is specified in the notification, the denunciation takes effect upon the expiration of such longer period after the notification is received by the depositary.
3. This Convention remains applicable to assignments if the contract of assignment is concluded before the date when the denunciation takes effect in respect of the Contracting State referred to in article 1, paragraph 1(a), provided that the provisions of this Convention that deal with the rights and obligations of the debtor remain applicable only to

assignments of receivables arising from original contracts concluded before the date when the denunciation takes effect in respect of the Contracting State referred to in article 1, paragraph 3.

4. If a receivable is assigned pursuant to a contract of assignment concluded before the date when the denunciation takes effect in respect of the Contracting State referred to in article 1, paragraph 1(a), the right of the assignee has priority over the right of a competing claimant with respect to the receivable to the extent that, under the law that would determine priority under this Convention, the right of the assignee would have priority.

Article 47

Revision and amendment

1. At the request of not less than one third of the Contracting States to this Convention, the depositary shall convene a conference of the Contracting States to revise or amend it.
2. Any instrument of ratification, acceptance, approval or accession deposited after the entry into force of an amendment to this Convention is deemed to apply to the Convention as amended.

Annex to the Convention

SECTION I

Priority rules based on registration

Article 1

Priority among several assignees

As between assignees of the same receivable from the same assignor, the priority of the right of an assignee in the assigned receivable is determined by the order in which data about the assignment are registered under section II of this annex, regardless of the time of transfer of the receivable. If no such data are registered, priority is determined by the order of conclusion of the respective contracts of assignment.

Article 2

Priority between the assignee and the insolvency administrator or creditors of the assignor

The right of an assignee in an assigned receivable has priority over the right of an insolvency administrator and creditors who obtain a right in the assigned receivable by attachment, judicial act or similar act of a competent authority that gives rise to such right, if the receivable was assigned, and data about the assignment were registered under section II of this annex, before the commencement of such insolvency proceeding, attachment, judicial act or similar act.

SECTION II

Registration

Article 3

Establishment of a registration system

A registration system will be established for the registration of data about assignments, even if the relevant assignment or receivable is not international, pursuant to the regulations to be promulgated by the registrar and the supervising authority. Regulations promulgated by the registrar and the supervising authority under this annex shall be consistent with this annex. The regulations will prescribe in detail the manner in which the registration system will operate, as well as the procedure for resolving disputes relating to that operation.

Article 4

Registration

1. Any person may register data with regard to an assignment at the registry in accordance with this annex and the regulations. As provided in the regulations, the data registered shall be the identification of the assignor and the assignee and a brief description of the assigned receivables.

2. A single registration may cover one or more assignments by the assignor to the assignee of one or more existing or future receivables, irrespective of whether the receivables exist at the time of registration.

3. A registration may be made in advance of the assignment to which it relates. The regulations will establish the procedure for the cancellation of a registration in the event that the assignment is not made.

4. Registration or its amendment is effective from the time when the data set forth in paragraph 1 of this article are available to searchers. The registering party may specify, from options set forth in the regulations, a period of effectiveness for the registration. In the absence of such a specification, a registration is effective for a period of five years.

5. Regulations will specify the manner in which registration may be renewed, amended or cancelled and regulate such other matters as are necessary for the operation of the registration system.

6. Any defect, irregularity, omission or error with regard to the identification of the assignor that would result in data registered not being found upon a search based on a proper identification of the assignor renders the registration ineffective.

Article 5

Registry searches

1. Any person may search the records of the registry according to identification of the assignor, as set forth in the regulations, and obtain a search result in writing.

2. A search result in writing that purports to be issued by the registry is admissible as evidence and is, in the absence of evidence to the contrary, proof of the registration of the data to which the search relates, including the date and hour of registration.

SECTION III

Priority rules based on the time of the contract of assignment

Article 6

Priority among several assignees

As between assignees of the same receivable from the same assignor, the priority of the right of an assignee in the assigned receivable is determined by the order of conclusion of the respective contracts of assignment.

Article 7

Priority between the assignee and the insolvency administrator or creditors of the assignor

The right of an assignee in an assigned receivable has priority over the right of an insolvency administrator and creditors who obtain a right in the assigned receivable by attachment, judicial act or similar act of a competent authority that gives rise to such right, if the receivable was assigned before the commencement of such insolvency proceeding, attachment, judicial act or similar act.

Article 8

Proof of time of contract of assignment

The time of conclusion of a contract of assignment in respect of articles 6 and 7 of this annex may be proved by any means, including witnesses.

SECTION IV

Priority rules based on the time of notification of assignment

Article 9

Priority among several assignees

As between assignees of the same receivable from the same assignor, the priority of the right of an assignee in the assigned receivable is determined by the order in which notification of the respective assignments is received by the debtor. However, an assignee may not obtain priority over a prior assignment of which the assignee had knowledge at the time of conclusion of the contract of assignment to that assignee by notifying the debtor.

Article 10

Priority between the assignee and the insolvency administrator or creditors of the assignor

The right of an assignee in an assigned receivable has priority over the right of an insolvency administrator and creditors who obtain a right in the assigned receivable by attachment, judicial act or similar act of a competent authority that gives rise to such right, if the receivable was assigned and notification was received by the debtor before the commencement of such insolvency proceeding, attachment, judicial act or similar act.

DONE at New York, this 12th day of December two thousand one, in a single original, of which the Arabic, Chinese, English, French, Russian and Spanish texts are equally authentic.

IN WITNESS WHEREOF the undersigned plenipotentiaries, being duly authorized by their respective Governments, have signed the present Convention.

PART 3

COMMON PRINCIPLES

PRINCIPLES OF EUROPEAN CONTRACT LAW
THE COMMISSION FOR EUROPEAN CONTRACT LAW*

CHAPTER 1: GENERAL PROVISIONS

Section 1: Scope of the Principles

Article 1:101: Application of the Principles

(1) These Principles are intended to be applied as general rules of contract law in the European Union.

(2) These Principles will apply when the parties have agreed to incorporate them into their contract or that their contract is to be governed by them.

(3) These Principles may be applied when the parties:
   (a) have agreed that their contract is to be governed by 'general principles of law', the 'lex mercatoria' or the like; or
   (b) have not chosen any system or rules of law to govern their contract.

(4) These Principles may provide a solution to the issue raised where the system or rules of law applicable do not do so.

Article 1:102: Freedom of Contract

(1) Parties are free to enter into a contract and to determine its contents, subject to the requirements of good faith and fair dealing, and the mandatory rules established by these Principles.

(2) The parties may exclude the application of any of the Principles or derogate from or vary their effects, except as otherwise provided by these Principles.

Article 1:103: Mandatory Law

(1) Where the law otherwise applicable so allows, the parties may choose to have their contract governed by the Principles, with the effect that national mandatory rules are not applicable.

(2) Effect should nevertheless be given to those mandatory rules of national, supranational and international law which, according to the relevant rules of private international law, are applicable irrespective of the law governing the contract.

*The text of The Principles is published in O Lando & H Beale (eds) *Principles of European Contract Law Parts I & II*. In addition to the text reprinted here this volume contains a commentary as well as comparative observations.

Article 1:104: Application to Questions of Consent

(1) The existence and validity of the agreement of the parties to adopt or incorporate these Principles shall be determined by these Principles.

(2) Nevertheless, a party may rely upon the law of the country in which it has its habitual residence to establish that it did not consent if it appears from the circumstances that it would not be reasonable to determine the effect of the party's conduct in accordance with these Principles.

Article 1:105: Usages and Practices

(1) The parties are bound by any usage to which they have agreed and by any practice they have established between themselves.

(2) The parties are bound by a usage which would be considered generally applicable by persons in the same situation as the parties, except where the application of such usage would be unreasonable.

Article 1:106: Interpretation and Supplementation

(1) These Principles should be interpreted and developed in accordance with their purposes. In particular, regard should be had to the need to promote good faith and fair dealing, certainty in contractual relationships and uniformity of application.

(2) Issues within the scope of these Principles but not expressly settled by them are so far as possible to be settled in accordance with the ideas underlying the Principles. Failing this, the legal system applicable by virtue of the rules of private international law is to be applied.

Article 1:107: Application of the Principles by Way of Analogy

These Principles apply with appropriate modifications to agreements to modify or end a contract, to unilateral promises and to other statements and conduct indicating intention.

Section 2: General Duties

Article 1:201: Good Faith and Fair Dealing

(1) Each party must act in accordance with good faith and fair dealing.

(2) The parties may not exclude or limit this duty.

Article 1:202: Duty to Co-operate

Each party owes to the other a duty to co-operate in order to give full effect to the contract.

Section 3: Terminology and Other Provisions

Article 1:301: Meaning of Terms

In these Principles, except where the context otherwise requires:

(1) 'act' includes omission;

(2) 'court' includes arbitral tribunal;

(3) an 'intentional' act includes an act done recklessly;

(4) 'non-performance' denotes any failure to perform an obligation under the contract, whether or not excused, and includes delayed performance, defective performance and failure to co-operate in order to give full effect to the contract;

(5) a matter is 'material' if it is one which a reasonable person in the same situation as one party ought to have known would influence the other party in its decision whether to contract on the proposed terms or to contract at all;

(6) 'written' statements include communications made by telegram, telex, telefax and electronic mail and other means of communication capable of providing a readable record of the statement on both sides.

Article 1:302: Reasonableness

Under these Principles reasonableness is to be judged by what persons acting in good faith and in the same situation as the parties would consider to be reasonable. In particular, in assessing what is reasonable the nature and purpose of the contract, the circumstances of the case and the usages and practices of the trades or professions involved should be taken into account.

Article 1:303: Notice

(1) Any notice may be given by any means, whether in writing or otherwise, appropriate to the circumstances.

(2) Subject to paragraphs (4) and (5), any notice becomes effective when it reaches the addressee.

(3) A notice reaches the addressee when it is delivered to it or to its place of business or mailing address, or, if it does not have a place of business or mailing address, to its habitual residence.

(4) If one party gives notice to the other because of the other's non-performance or because such non-performance is reasonably anticipated by the first party, and the notice is properly dispatched or given, a delay or inaccuracy in the transmission of the notice or its failure to arrive does not prevent it from having effect. The notice shall have effect from the time at which it would have arrived in normal circumstances.

(5) A notice has no effect if a withdrawal of it reaches the addressee before or at the same time as the notice.

(6) In this Article, 'notice' includes the communication of a promise, statement, offer, acceptance, demand, request or other declaration.

Article 1:304: Computation of Time

(1) A period of time set by a party in a written document for the addressee to reply or take other action begins to run from the date stated as the date of the document. If no date is shown, the period begins to run from the moment the document reaches the addressee.

(2) Official holidays and official non-working days occurring during the period are included in calculating the period. However, if the last day of the period is an official holiday or official non-working day at the address of the addressee, or at the place where a prescribed act is to be performed, the period is extended until the first following working day in that place.

(3) Periods of time expressed in days, weeks, months or years shall begin at 00.00 on the next day and shall end at 24.00 on the last day of the period; but any reply that has to reach the party which set the period must arrive, or any other act which is to be done must be completed, by the normal close of business in the relevant place on the last day of the period.

Article 1:305: Imputed Knowledge and Intention

If any person who with a party's assent was involved in making a contract, or who was entrusted with performance by a party or performed with its assent:

(a) knew or foresaw a fact, or ought to have known or foreseen it; or

(b) acted intentionally or with gross negligence, or not in accordance with good faith and fair dealing,

this knowledge, foresight or behaviour is imputed to the party itself.

CHAPTER 2: FORMATION

Section 1: General Provisions

Article 2:101: Conditions for the Conclusion of a Contract

(1) A contract is concluded if:
   (a) the parties intend to be legally bound, and
   (b) they reach a sufficient agreement
       without any further requirement.

(2)   A contract need not be concluded or evidenced in writing nor is it subject to any other requirement as to form. The contract may be proved by any means, including witnesses.

Article 2:102: Intention

The intention of a party to be legally bound by contract is to be determined from the party's statements or conduct as they were reasonably understood by the other party.

Article 2:103: Sufficient Agreement

(1)   There is sufficient agreement if the terms:
   (a)   have been sufficiently defined by the parties so that the contract can be enforced, or
   (b)   can be determined under these Principles.
(2)   However, if one of the parties refuses to conclude a contract unless the parties have agreed on some specific matter, there is no contract unless agreement on that matter has been reached.

Article 2:104: Terms Not Individually Negotiated

(1)   Contract terms which have not been individually negotiated may be invoked against a party which did not know of them only if the party invoking them took reasonable steps to bring them to the other party's attention before or when the contract was concluded.
(2)   Terms are not brought appropriately to a party's attention by a mere reference to them in a contract document, even if that party signs the document.

Article 2:105: Merger Clause

(1)   If a written contract contains an individually negotiated clause stating that the writing embodies all the terms of the contract (a merger clause), any prior statements, undertakings or agreements which are not embodied in the writing do not form part of the contract.
(2)   If the merger clause is not individually negotiated it will only establish a presumption that the parties intended that their prior statements, undertakings or agreements were not to form part of the contract. This rule may not be excluded or restricted.

(3) The parties' prior statements may be used to interpret the contract. This rule may not be excluded or restricted except by an individually negotiated clause.

(4) A party may by its statements or conduct be precluded from asserting a merger clause to the extent that the other party has reasonably relied on them.

Article 2:106: Written Modification Only

(1) A clause in a written contract requiring any modification or ending by agreement to be made in writing establishes only a presumption that an agreement to modify or end the contract is not intended to be legally binding unless it is in writing.

(2) A party may by its statements or conduct be precluded from asserting such a clause to the extent that the other party has reasonably relied on them.

Article 2:107: Promises Binding without Acceptance

A promise which is intended to be legally binding without acceptance is binding.

Section 2: Offer and Acceptance

Article 2:201: Offer

(1) A proposal amounts to an offer if:
   (a) it is intended to result in a contract if the other party accepts it, and
   (b) it contains sufficiently definite terms to form a contract.

(2) An offer may be made to one or more specific persons or to the public.

(3) A proposal to supply goods or services at stated prices made by a professional supplier in a public advertisement or a catalogue, or by a display of goods, is presumed to be an offer to sell or supply at that price until the stock of goods, or the supplier's capacity to supply the service, is exhausted.

Article 2:202: Revocation of an Offer

(1) An offer may be revoked if the revocation reaches the offeree before it has dispatched its acceptance or, in cases of acceptance by conduct, before the contract has been concluded under Article 2:205(2) or (3).

(2) An offer made to the public can be revoked by the same means as were used to make the offer.

(3)   However, a revocation of an offer is ineffective if:
    (a)   the offer indicates that it is irrevocable; or
    (b)   it states a fixed time for its acceptance; or
    (c)   it was reasonable for the offeree to rely on the offer as being irrev-
        ocable and the offeree has acted in reliance on the offer.

Article 2:203: Rejection

When a rejection of an offer reaches the offeror, the offer lapses.

Article 2:204: Acceptance

(1)   Any form of statement or conduct by the offeree is an acceptance if it
    indicates assent to the offer.
(2)   Silence or inactivity does not in itself amount to acceptance.

Article 2:205: Time of Conclusion of the Contract

(1)   If an acceptance has been dispatched by the offeree the contract is con-
    cluded when the acceptance reaches the offeror.
(2)   In the case of acceptance by conduct, the contract is concluded when
    notice of the conduct reaches the offeror.
(3)   If by virtue of the offer, of practices which the parties have established
    between themselves, or of a usage, the offeree may accept the offer by
    performing an act without notice to the offeror, the contract is con-
    cluded when the performance of the act begins.

Article 2:206: Time Limit for Acceptance

(1)   In order to be effective, acceptance of an offer must reach the offeror
    within the time fixed by it.
(2)   If no time has been fixed by the offeror acceptance must reach it
    within a reasonable time.
(3)   In the case of an acceptance by an act of performance under
    Article 2:205(3), that act must be performed within the time for
    acceptance fixed by the offeror or, if no such time is fixed, within a rea-
    sonable time.

Article 2:207: Late Acceptance

(1)   A late acceptance is nonetheless effective as an acceptance if without
    delay the offeror informs the offeree that he treats it as such.
(2)   If a letter or other writing containing a late acceptance shows that it
    has been sent in such circumstances that if its transmission had
    been normal it would have reached the offeror in due time, the late

acceptance is effective as an acceptance unless, without delay, the offeror informs the offeree that it considers its offer as having lapsed.

Article 2:208: Modified Acceptance

(1) A reply by the offeree which states or implies additional or different terms which would materially alter the terms of the offer is a rejection and a new offer.

(2) A reply which gives a definite assent to an offer operates as an acceptance even if it states or implies additional or different terms, provided these do not materially alter the terms of the offer. The additional or different terms then become part of the contract.

(3) However, such a reply will be treated as a rejection of the offer if:
  (a) the offer expressly limits acceptance to the terms of the offer; or
  (b) the offeror objects to the additional or different terms without delay; or
  (c) the offeree makes its acceptance conditional upon the offeror's assent to the additional or different terms, and the assent does not reach the offeree within a reasonable time.

Article 2:209: Conflicting General Conditions

(1) If the parties have reached agreement except that the offer and acceptance refer to conflicting general conditions of contract, a contract is nonetheless formed. The general conditions form part of the contract to the extent that they are common in substance.

(2) However, no contract is formed if one party:
  (a) has indicated in advance, explicitly, and not by way of general conditions, that it does not intend to be bound by a contract on the basis of paragraph (1); or
  (b) without delay, informs the other party that it does not intend to be bound by such contract.

(3) General conditions of contract are terms which have been formulated in advance for an indefinite number of contracts of a certain nature, and which have not been individually negotiated between the parties.

Article 2:210: Professional's Written Confirmation

If professionals have concluded a contract but have not embodied it in a final document, and one without delay sends the other a writing which purports to be a confirmation of the contract but which contains additional or different terms, such terms will become part of the contract unless:

(a) the terms materially alter the terms of the contract, or
(b) the addressee objects to them without delay.

Article 2:211: Contracts not Concluded through Offer and Acceptance

The rules in this section apply with appropriate adaptations even though the process of conclusion of a contract cannot be analysed into offer and acceptance.

Section 3: Liability for Negotiations

Article 2:301: Negotiations Contrary to Good Faith

(1) A party is free to negotiate and is not liable for failure to reach an agreement.
(2) However, a party which has negotiated or broken off negotiations contrary to good faith and fair dealing is liable for the losses caused to the other party.
(3) It is contrary to good faith and fair dealing, in particular, for a party to enter into or continue negotiations with no real intention of reaching an agreement with the other party.

Article 2:302: Breach of Confidentiality

If confidential information is given by one party in the course of negotiations, the other party is under a duty not to disclose that information or use it for its own purposes whether or not a contract is subsequently concluded. The remedy for breach of this duty may include compensation for loss suffered and restitution of the benefit received by the other party.

CHAPTER 3: AUTHORITY OF AGENTS

Section 1: General Provisions

Article 3:101: Scope of the Chapter

(1) This Chapter governs the authority of an agent or other intermediary to bind its principal in relation to a contract with a third party.
(2) This Chapter does not govern an agent's authority bestowed by law or the authority of an agent appointed by a public or judicial authority.
(3) This Chapter does not govern the internal relationship between the agent or intermediary and its principal.

Article 3:102: Categories of Representation

(1) Where an agent acts in the name of a principal, the rules on direct representation apply (Section 2). It is irrelevant whether the principal's identity is revealed at the time the agent acts or is to be revealed later.

(2) Where an intermediary acts on instructions and on behalf of, but not in the name of, a principal, or where the third party neither knows nor has reason to know that the intermediary acts as an agent, the rules on indirect representation apply (Section 3).

Section 2: Direct Representation

Article 3:201: Express, Implied and Apparent Authority

(1) The principal's grant of authority to an agent to act in its name may be express or may be implied from the circumstances.

(2) The agent has authority to perform all acts necessary in the circumstances to achieve the purposes for which the authority was granted.

(3) A person is to be treated as having granted authority to an apparent agent if the person's statements or conduct induce the third party reasonably and in good faith to believe that the apparent agent has been granted authority for the act performed by it.

Article 3:202: Agent acting in Exercise of its Authority

Where an agent is acting within its authority as defined by Article 3:201, its acts bind the principal and the third party directly to each other. The agent itself is not bound to the third party.

Article 3:203: Unidentified Principal

If an agent enters into a contract in the name of a principal whose identity is to be revealed later, but fails to reveal that identity within a reasonable time after a request by the third party, the agent itself is bound by the contract.

Article 3:204: Agent acting without or outside its Authority

(1) Where a person acting as an agent acts without authority or outside the scope of its authority, its acts are not binding upon the principal and the third party.

(2) Failing ratification by the principal according to Article 3:207, the agent is liable to pay the third party such damages as will place the third party in the same position as if the agent had acted with authority.

This does not apply if the third party knew or could not have been unaware of the agent's lack of authority.

Article 3:205: Conflict of Interest

(1) If a contract concluded by an agent involves the agent in a conflict of interest of which the third party knew or could not have been unaware, the principal may avoid the contract according to the provisions of Articles 4:112 to 4:116.

(2) There is presumed to be a conflict of interest where:
    (a) the agent also acted as agent for the third party; or
    (b) the contract was with itself in its personal capacity.

(3) However, the principal may not avoid the contract:
    (a) if it had consented to, or could not have been unaware of, the agent's so acting; or
    (b) if the agent had disclosed the conflict of interest to it and it had not objected within a reasonable time.

Article 3:206: Subagency

An agent has implied authority to appoint a subagent to carry out tasks which are not of a personal character and which it is not reasonable to expect the agent to carry out itself. The rules of this Section apply to the subagency; acts of the sub-agent which are within its and the agent's authority bind the principal and the third party directly to each other.

Article 3:207: Ratification by Principal

(1) Where a person acting as an agent acts without authority or outside its authority, the principal may ratify the agent's acts.

(2) Upon ratification, the agent's acts are considered as having been authorised, without prejudice to the rights of other persons.

Article 3:208: Third Party's Right with Respect to Confirmation of Authority

Where the statements or conduct of the principal gave the third party reason to believe that an act performed by the agent was authorised, but the third party is in doubt about the authorisation, it may send a written confirmation to the principal or request ratification from it. If the principal does not object or answer the request without delay, the agent's act is treated as having been authorised.

Article 3:209: Duration of Authority

(1) An agent's authority continues until the third party knows or ought to know that:
- (a) the agent's authority has been brought to an end by the principal, the agent, or both; or
- (b) the acts for which the authority had been granted have been completed, or the time for which it had been granted has expired; or
- (c) the agent has become insolvent or, where a natural person, has died or become incapacitated; or
- (d) the principal has become insolvent.

(2) The third party is considered to know that the agent's authority has been brought to an end under paragraph (1)(a) above if this has been communicated or publicised in the same manner in which the authority was originally communicated or publicised.

(3) However, the agent remains authorised for a reasonable time to perform those acts which are necessary to protect the interests of the principal or its successors.

Section 3: Indirect Representation

Article 3:301: Intermediaries not acting in the name of a Principal

(1) Where an intermediary acts:
- (a) on instructions and on behalf, but not in the name, of a principal, or
- (b) on instructions from a principal but the third party does not know and has no reason to know this,

the intermediary and the third party are bound to each other.

(2) The principal and the third party are bound to each other only under the conditions set out in Articles 3:302 to 3:304.

Article 3:302: Intermediary's Insolvency or Fundamental Non-performance to Principal

If the intermediary becomes insolvent, or if it commits a fundamental non-performance towards the principal, or if prior to the time for performance it is clear that there will be a fundamental non-performance:

- (a) on the principal's demand, the intermediary shall communicate the name and address of the third party to the principal; and
- (b) the principal may exercise against the third party the rights acquired on the principal's behalf by the intermediary, subject to any defences which the third party may set up against the intermediary.

Article 3:303: Intermediary's Insolvency or Fundamental
Non-performance to Third Party

If the intermediary becomes insolvent, or if it commits a fundamental non-performance towards the third party, or if prior to the time for performance it is clear that there will be a fundamental non-performance:

(a) on the third party's demand, the intermediary shall communicate the name and address of the principal to the third party; and

(b) the third party may exercise against the principal the rights which the third party has against the intermediary, subject to any defences which the intermediary may set up against the third party and those which the principal may set up against the intermediary.

CHAPTER 4: VALIDITY

Article 4:101: Matters not Covered

This chapter does not deal with invalidity arising from illegality, immorality or lack of capacity.

Article 4:102: Initial Impossibility

A contract is not invalid merely because at the time it was concluded performance of the obligation assumed was impossible, or because a party was not entitled to dispose of the assets to which the contract relates.

Article 4:103: Fundamental Mistake as to Facts or Law

(1) A party may avoid a contract for mistake of fact or law existing when the contract was concluded if:

(a)   (i)   the mistake was caused by information given by the other party; or

(ii) the other party knew or ought to have known of the mistake and it was contrary to good faith and fair dealing to leave the mistaken party in error; or

(iii) the other party made the same mistake,

and

(b) the other party knew or ought to have known that the mistaken party, had it known the truth, would not have entered the contract or would have done so only on fundamentally different terms.

(2) However a party may not avoid the contract if:

(a) in the circumstances its mistake was inexcusable, or

   (b)   the risk of the mistake was assumed, or in the circumstances
         should be borne, by it.

Article 4:104: Inaccuracy in Communication

An inaccuracy in the expression or transmission of a statement is to be treated as a
mistake of the person which made or sent the statement and Article 4:103 applies.

Article 4:105: Adaptation of Contract

   (1)   If a party is entitled to avoid the contract for mistake but the other
         party indicates that it is willing to perform, or actually does perform,
         the contract as it was understood by the party entitled to avoid it, the
         contract is to be treated as if it had been concluded as that party
         understood it. The other party must indicate its willingness to per-
         form, or render such performance, promptly after being informed of
         the manner in which the party entitled to avoid it understood the con-
         tract and before that party acts in reliance on any notice of avoidance.
   (2)   After such indication or performance the right to avoid is lost and any
         earlier notice of avoidance is ineffective.
   (3)   Where both parties have made the same mistake, the court may at the
         request of either party bring the contract into accordance with what
         might reasonably have been agreed had the mistake not occurred.

Article 4:106: Incorrect Information

A party which has concluded a contract relying on incorrect information given it
by the other party may recover damages in accordance with Article 4:117(2) and
(3) even if the information does not give rise to a fundamental mistake under
Article 4:103, unless the party which gave the information had reason to believe
that the information was correct.

Article 4:107: Fraud

   (1)   A party may avoid a contract when it has been led to conclude it by
         the other party's fraudulent representation, whether by words or con-
         duct, or fraudulent non-disclosure of any information which in accor-
         dance with good faith and fair dealing it should have disclosed.
   (2)   A party's representation or non-disclosure is fraudulent if it was
         intended to deceive.
   (3)   In determining whether good faith and fair dealing required that a
         party disclose particular information, regard should be had to all the
         circumstances, including:
         (a)   whether the party had special expertise;

(b)   the cost to it of acquiring the relevant information;

(c)   whether the other party could reasonably acquire the information for itself; and

(d)   the apparent importance of the information to the other party.

Article 4:108: Threats

A party may avoid a contract when it has been led to conclude it by the other party's imminent and serious threat of an act:

(a)   which is wrongful in itself, or

(b)   which it is wrongful to use as a means to obtain the conclusion of the contract, unless in the circumstances the first party had a reasonable alternative.

Article 4:109: Excessive Benefit or Unfair Advantage

(1)   A party may avoid a contract if, at the time of the conclusion of the contract:

(a)   it was dependent on or had a relationship of trust with the other party, was in economic distress or had urgent needs, was improvident, ignorant, inexperienced or lacking in bargaining skill, and

(b)   the other party knew or ought to have known of this and, given the circumstances and purpose of the contract, took advantage of the first party's situation in a way which was grossly unfair or took an excessive benefit.

(2)   Upon the request of the party entitled to avoidance, a court may if it is appropriate adapt the contract in order to bring it into accordance with what might have been agreed had the requirements of good faith and fair dealing been followed.

(3)   A court may similarly adapt the contract upon the request of a party receiving notice of avoidance for excessive benefit or unfair advantage, provided that this party informs the party which gave the notice promptly after receiving it and before that party has acted in reliance on it.

Article 4:110: Unfair Terms not Individually Negotiated

(1)   A party may avoid a term which has not been individually negotiated if, contrary to the requirements of good faith and fair dealing, it causes a significant imbalance in the parties' rights and obligations arising under the contract to the detriment of that party, taking into account the nature of the performance to be rendered under the contract,

all the other terms of the contract and the circumstances at the time the contract was concluded.

(2) This Article does not apply to:

   (a) a term which defines the main subject matter of the contract, provided the term is in plain and intelligible language; or to

   (b) the adequacy in value of one party's obligations compared to the value of the obligations of the other party.

Article 4:111: Third Persons

(1) Where a third person for whose acts a party is responsible, or who with a party's assent is involved in the making of a contract:

   (a) causes a mistake by giving information, or knows of or ought to have known of a mistake,

   (b) gives incorrect information,

   (c) commits fraud,

   (d) makes a threat, or

   (e) takes excessive benefit or unfair advantage,

   remedies under this Chapter will be available under the same conditions as if the behaviour or knowledge had been that of the party itself.

(2) Where any other third person:

   (a) gives incorrect information,

   (b) commits fraud,

   (c) makes a threat, or

   (d) takes excessive benefit or unfair advantage,

   remedies under this Chapter will be available if the party knew or ought to have known of the relevant facts, or at the time of avoidance it has not acted in reliance on the contract.

Article 4:112: Notice of Avoidance

Avoidance must be by notice to the other party.

Article 4:113: Time Limits

(1) Notice of avoidance must be given within a reasonable time, with due regard to the circumstances, after the avoiding party knew or ought to have known of the relevant facts or became capable of acting freely.

(2) However, a party may avoid an individual term under Article 4:110 if it gives notice of avoidance within a reasonable time after the other party has invoked the term.

Article 4:114: Confirmation

If the party who is entitled to avoid a contract confirms it, expressly or impliedly, after it knows of the ground for avoidance, or becomes capable of acting freely, avoidance of the contract is excluded.

Article 4:115: Effect of Avoidance

On avoidance either party may claim restitution of whatever it has supplied under the contract, provided it makes concurrent restitution of whatever it has received. If restitution cannot be made in kind for any reason, a reasonable sum must be paid for what has been received.

Article 4:116: Partial Avoidance

If a ground of avoidance affects only particular terms of a contract, the effect of an avoidance is limited to those terms unless, giving due consideration to all the circumstances of the case, it is unreasonable to uphold the remaining contract.

Article 4:117: Damages

(1) A party who avoids a contract under this Chapter may recover from the other party damages so as to put the avoiding party as nearly as possible into the same position as if it had not concluded the contract, provided that the other party knew or ought to have known of the mistake, fraud, threat or taking of excessive benefit or unfair advantage.

(2) If a party has the right to avoid a contract under this Chapter, but does not exercise its right or has lost its right under the provisions of Articles 4:113 or 4:114, it may recover, subject to paragraph (1), damages limited to the loss caused to it by the mistake, fraud, threat or taking of excessive benefit or unfair advantage. The same measure of damages shall apply when the party was misled by incorrect information in the sense of Article 4:106.

(3) In other respects, the damages shall be in accordance with the relevant provisions of Chapter 9, Section 5, with appropriate adaptations.

Article 4:118: Exclusion or Restriction of Remedies

(1) Remedies for fraud, threats and excessive benefit or unfair advantage-taking, and the right to avoid an unfair term which has not been individually negotiated, cannot be excluded or restricted.

(2) Remedies for mistake and incorrect information may be excluded or restricted unless the exclusion or restriction is contrary to good faith and fair dealing.

Article 4:119: Remedies for Non-performance

A party which is entitled to a remedy under this Chapter in circumstances which afford that party a remedy for non-performance may pursue either remedy.

CHAPTER 5: INTERPRETATION

Article 5:101: General Rules of Interpretation

(1) A contract is to be interpreted according to the common intention of the parties even if this differs from the literal meaning of the words.

(2) If it is established that one party intended the contract to have a particular meaning, and at the time of the conclusion of the contract the other party could not have been unaware of the first party's intention, the contract is to be interpreted in the way intended by the first party.

(3) If an intention cannot be established according to (1) or (2), the contract is to be interpreted according to the meaning that reasonable persons of the same kind as the parties would give to it in the same circumstances.

Article 5:102: Relevant Circumstances

In interpreting the contract, regard shall be had, in particular, to:

(a) the circumstances in which it was concluded, including the preliminary negotiations;

(b) the conduct of the parties, even subsequent to the conclusion of the contract;

(c) the nature and purpose of the contract;

(d) the interpretation which has already been given to similar clauses by the parties and the practices they have established between themselves;

(e) the meaning commonly given to terms and expressions in the branch of activity concerned and the interpretation similar clauses may already have received ;

(f) usages; and

(g) good faith and fair dealing.

Article 5:103: Contra Proferentem Rule

Where there is doubt about the meaning of a contract term not individually negotiated, an interpretation of the term against the party which supplied it is to be preferred.

Article 5:104: Preference to Negotiated Terms

Terms which have been individually negotiated take preference over those which have not.

Article 5:105: Reference to Contract as a Whole

Terms are to be interpreted in the light of the whole contract in which they appear.

Article 5:106: Terms to Be Given Effect

An interpretation which renders the terms of the contract lawful, or effective, is to be preferred to one which would not.

Article 5:107: Linguistic Discrepancies

Where a contract is drawn up in two or more language versions none of which is stated to be authoritative, there is, in case of discrepancy between the versions, a preference for the interpretation according to the version in which the contract was originally drawn up.

CHAPTER 6: CONTENTS AND EFFECTS

Article 6:101: Statements giving rise to Contractual Obligations

(1) A statement made by one party before or when the contract is concluded is to be treated as giving rise to a contractual obligation if that is how the other party reasonably understood it in the circumstances, taking into account:
   (a) the apparent importance of the statement to the other party;
   (b) whether the party was making the statement in the course of business; and
   (c) the relative expertise of the parties.

(2) If one of the parties is a professional supplier which gives information about the quality or use of services or goods or other property when marketing or advertising them or otherwise before the contract for them is concluded, the statement is to be treated as giving rise to a contractual obligation unless it is shown that the other party knew or could not have been unaware that the statement was incorrect.

(3) Such information and other undertakings given by a person advertising or marketing services, goods or other property for the professional supplier, or by a person in earlier links of the business chain, are to be

treated as giving rise to a contractual obligation on the part of the professional supplier unless it did not know and had no reason to know of the information or undertaking.

Article 6:102: Implied Terms

In addition to the express terms, a contract may contain implied terms which stem from

(a)   the intention of the parties,
(b)   the nature and purpose of the contract, and
(c)   good faith and fair dealing.

Article 6:103: Simulation

When the parties have concluded an apparent contract which was not intended to reflect their true agreement, as between the parties the true agreement prevails.

Article 6:104: Determination of Price

Where the contract does not fix the price or the method of determining it, the parties are to be treated as having agreed on a reasonable price.

Article 6:105: Unilateral Determination by a Party

Where the price or any other contractual term is to be determined by one party and that party's determination is grossly unreasonable, then notwithstanding any provision to the contrary, a reasonable price or other term shall be substituted.

Article 6:106: Determination by a Third Person

(1)   Where the price or any other contractual term is to be determined by a third person, and it cannot or will not do so, the parties are presumed to have empowered the court to appoint another person to determine it.
(2)   If a price or other term fixed by a third person is grossly unreasonable, a reasonable price or term shall be substituted.

Article 6:107: Reference to a Non-Existent Factor

Where the price or any other contractual term is to be determined by reference to a factor which does not exist or has ceased to exist or to be accessible, the nearest equivalent factor shall be substituted.

Article 6:108: Quality of Performance

If the contract does not specify the quality, a party must tender performance of at least average quality.

Article 6:109: Contract for an Indefinite Period

A contract for an indefinite period may be ended by either party by giving notice of reasonable length.

Article 6:110: Stipulation in Favour of a Third Party

(1) A third party may require performance of a contractual obligation when its right to do so has been expressly agreed upon between the promisor and the promisee, or when such agreement is to be inferred from the purpose of the contract or the circumstances of the case. The third party need not be identified at the time the agreement is concluded.

(2) If the third party renounces the right to performance the right is treated as never having accrued to it.

(3) The promisee may by notice to the promisor deprive the third party of the right to performance unless:

(a) the third party has received notice from the promisee that the right has been made irrevocable, or

(b) the promisor or the promisee has received notice from the third party that the latter accepts the right.

Article 6:111: Change of Circumstances

(1) A party is bound to fulfil its obligations even if performance has become more onerous, whether because the cost of performance has increased or because the value of the performance it receives has diminished.

(2) If, however, performance of the contract becomes excessively onerous because of a change of circumstances, the parties are bound to enter into negotiations with a view to adapting the contract or ending it, provided that:

(a) the change of circumstances occurred after the time of conclusion of the contract,

(b) the possibility of a change of circumstances was not one which could reasonably have been taken into account at the time of conclusion of the contract, and

(c) the risk of the change of circumstances is not one which, according to the contract, the party affected should be required to bear.

(3) If the parties fail to reach agreement within a reasonable period, the court may:

(a) end the contract at a date and on terms to be determined by the court; or

(b) adapt the contract in order to distribute between the parties in a just and equitable manner the losses and gains resulting from the change of circumstances.

In either case, the court may award damages for the loss suffered through a party refusing to negotiate or breaking off negotiations contrary to good faith and fair dealing.

CHAPTER 7: PERFORMANCE

Article 7:101: Place of Performance

(1) If the place of performance of a contractual obligation is not fixed by or determinable from the contract it shall be:
 (a) in the case of an obligation to pay money, the creditor's place of business at the time of the conclusion of the contract;
 (b) in the case of an obligation other than to pay money, the debtor's place of business at the time of conclusion of the contract.
(2) If a party has more than one place of business, the place of business for the purpose of the preceding paragraph is that which has the closest relationship to the contract, having regard to the circumstances known to or contemplated by the parties at the time of conclusion of the contract.
(3) If a party does not have a place of business its habitual residence is to be treated as its place of business.

Article 7:102: Time of Performance

A party has to effect its performance:

(a) if a time is fixed by or determinable from the contract, at that time;
(b) if a period of time is fixed by or determinable from the contract, at any time within that period unless the circumstances of the case indicate that the other party is to choose the time;
(c) in any other case, within a reasonable time after the conclusion of the contract.

Article 7:103: Early Performance

(1) A party may decline a tender of performance made before it is due except where acceptance of the tender would not unreasonably prejudice its interests.
(2) A party's acceptance of early performance does not affect the time fixed for the performance of its own obligation.

Article 7:104: Order of Performance

To the extent that the performances of the parties can be rendered simultaneously, the parties are bound to render them simultaneously unless the circumstances indicate otherwise.

Article 7:105: Alternative Performance

(1) Where an obligation may be discharged by one of alternative performances, the choice belongs to the party which is to perform, unless the circumstances indicate otherwise.

(2) If the party which is to make the choice fails to do so by the time required by the contract, then:
  (a) if the delay in choosing is fundamental, the right to choose passes to the other party;
  (b) if the delay is not fundamental, the other party may give a notice fixing an additional period of reasonable length in which the party to choose must do so. If the latter fails to do so, the right to choose passes to the other party.

Article 7:106: Performance by a Third Person

(1) Except where the contract requires personal performance the creditor cannot refuse performance by a third person if:
  (a) the third person acts with the assent of the debtor; or
  (b) the third person has a legitimate interest in performance and the debtor has failed to perform or it is clear that it will not perform at the time performance is due.

(2) Performance by the third person in accordance with paragraph (1) discharges the debtor.

Article 7:107: Form of Payment

(1) Payment of money due may be made in any form used in the ordinary course of business.

(2) A creditor which, pursuant to the contract or voluntarily, accepts a cheque or other order to pay or a promise to pay is presumed to do so only on condition that it will be honoured. The creditor may not enforce the original obligation to pay unless the order or promise is not honoured.

Article 7:108: Currency of Payment

(1) The parties may agree that payment shall be made only in a specified currency.

(2) In the absence of such agreement, a sum of money expressed in a currency other than that of the place where payment is due may be paid in the currency of that place according to the rate of exchange prevailing there at the time when payment is due.

(3) If, in a case falling within the preceding paragraph, the debtor has not paid at the time when payment is due, the creditor may require payment in the currency of the place where payment is due according to the rate of exchange prevailing there either at the time when payment is due or at the time of actual payment.

Article 7:109: Appropriation of Performance

(1) Where a party has to perform several obligations of the same nature and the performance tendered does not suffice to discharge all of the obligations, then subject to paragraph (4) the party may at the time of its performance declare to which obligation the performance is to be appropriated.

(2) If the performing party does not make such a declaration, the other party may within a reasonable time appropriate the performance to such obligation as it chooses. It shall inform the performing party of the choice. However, any such appropriation to an obligation which:

(a) is not yet due, or

(b) is illegal, or

(c) is disputed,

is invalid.

(3) In the absence of an appropriation by either party, and subject to paragraph (4), the performance is appropriated to that obligation which satisfies one of the following criteria in the sequence indicated:

(a) the obligation which is due or is the first to fall due;

(b) the obligation for which the creditor has the least security;

(c) the obligation which is the most burdensome for the debtor;

(d) the obligation which has arisen first.

If none of the preceding criteria applies, the performance is appropriated proportionately to all obligations.

(4) In the case of a monetary obligation, a payment by the debtor is to be appropriated, first, to expenses, secondly, to interest, and thirdly, to principal, unless the creditor makes a different appropriation.

Article 7:110: Property Not Accepted

(1) A party which is left in possession of tangible property other than money because of the other party's failure to accept or retake the property must take reasonable steps to protect and preserve the property.

(2) The party left in possession may discharge its duty to deliver or return:
   (a) by depositing the property on reasonable terms with a third person to be held to the order of the other party, and notifying the other party of this; or
   (b) by selling the property on reasonable terms after notice to the other party, and paying the net proceeds to that party.
(3) Where, however, the property is liable to rapid deterioration or its preservation is unreasonably expensive, the party must take reasonable steps to dispose of it. It may discharge its duty to deliver or return by paying the net proceeds to the other party.
(4) The party left in possession is entitled to be reimbursed or to retain out of the proceeds of sale any expenses reasonably incurred.

Article 7:111: Money not Accepted

Where a party fails to accept money properly tendered by the other party, that party may after notice to the first party discharge its obligation to pay by depositing the money to the order of the first party in accordance with the law of the place where payment is due.

Article 7:112: Costs of Performance

Each party shall bear the costs of performance of its obligations.

CHAPTER 8: NON-PERFORMANCE AND REMEDIES IN GENERAL

Article 8:101: Remedies Available

(1) Whenever a party does not perform an obligation under the contract and the non-performance is not excused under Article 8:108, the aggrieved party may resort to any of the remedies set out in Chapter 9.
(2) Where a party's non-performance is excused under Article 8:108, the aggrieved party may resort to any of the remedies set out in Chapter 9 except claiming performance and damages.
(3) A party may not resort to any of the remedies set out in Chapter 9 to the extent that its own act caused the other party's non-performance.

Article 8:102: Cumulation of Remedies

Remedies which are not incompatible may be cumulated. In particular, a party is not deprived of its right to damages by exercising its right to any other remedy.

Article 8:103: Fundamental Non-Performance

A non-performance of an obligation is fundamental to the contract if:

(a)   strict compliance with the obligation is of the essence of the contract; or
(b)   the non-performance substantially deprives the aggrieved party of what it was entitled to expect under the contract, unless the other party did not foresee and could not reasonably have foreseen that result; or
(c)   the non-performance is intentional and gives the aggrieved party reason to believe that it cannot rely on the other party's future performance.

Article 8:104: Cure by Non-Performing Party

A party whose tender of performance is not accepted by the other party because it does not conform to the contract may make a new and conforming tender where the time for performance has not yet arrived or the delay would not be such as to constitute a fundamental non-performance.

Article 8:105: Assurance of Performance

(1)   A party which reasonably believes that there will be a fundamental non-performance by the other party may demand adequate assurance of due performance and meanwhile may withhold performance of its own obligations so long as such reasonable belief continues.
(2)   Where this assurance is not provided within a reasonable time, the party demanding it may terminate the contract if it still reasonably believes that there will be a fundamental non-performance by the other party and gives notice of termination without delay.

Article 8:106: Notice Fixing Additional Period for Performance

(1)   In any case of non-performance the aggrieved party may by notice to the other party allow an additional period of time for performance.
(2)   During the additional period the aggrieved party may withhold performance of its own reciprocal obligations and may claim damages, but it may not resort to any other remedy. If it receives notice from the other party that the latter will not perform within that period, or if upon expiry of that period due performance has not been made, the aggrieved party may resort to any of the remedies that may be available under chapter 9.
(3)   If in a case of delay in performance which is not fundamental the aggrieved party has given a notice fixing an additional period of time of reasonable length, it may terminate the contract at the end of the period of notice. The aggrieved party may in its notice provide that if

the other party does not perform within the period fixed by the notice the contract shall terminate automatically. If the period stated is too short, the aggrieved party may terminate, or, as the case may be, the contract shall terminate automatically, only after a reasonable period from the time of the notice.

Article 8:107 Performance Entrusted to Another

A party which entrusts performance of the contract to another person remains responsible for performance.

Article 8:108: Excuse Due to an Impediment

(1)   A party's non-performance is excused if it proves that it is due to an impediment beyond its control and that it could not reasonably have been expected to take the impediment into account at the time of the conclusion of the contract, or to have avoided or overcome the impediment or its consequences.

(2)   Where the impediment is only temporary the excuse provided by this Article has effect for the period during which the impediment exists. However, if the delay amounts to a fundamental non-performance, the creditor may treat it as such.

(3)   The non-performing party must ensure that notice of the impediment and of its effect on its ability to perform is received by the other party within a reasonable time after the non-performing party knew or ought to have known of these circumstances. The other party is entitled to damages for any loss resulting from the non-receipt of such notice.

Article 8:109: Clause Excluding or Restricting Remedies

Remedies for non-performance may be excluded or restricted unless it would be contrary to good faith and fair dealing to invoke the exclusion or restriction.

CHAPTER 9: PARTICULAR REMEDIES FOR NON-PERFORMANCE

Section 1: Right to Performance

Article 9:101: Monetary Obligations

(1)   The creditor is entitled to recover money which is due.

(2)   Where the creditor has not yet performed its obligation and it is clear that the debtor will be unwilling to receive performance, the creditor

may nonetheless proceed with its performance and may recover any sum due under the contract unless:

(a)   it could have made a reasonable substitute transaction without significant effort or expense; or

(b)   performance would be unreasonable in the circumstances.

Article 9:102: Non-monetary Obligations

(1)   The aggrieved party is entitled to specific performance of an obligation other than one to pay money, including the remedying of a defective performance.

(2)   Specific performance cannot, however, be obtained where:

(a)   performance would be unlawful or impossible; or

(b)   performance would cause the debtor unreasonable effort or expense; or

(c)   the performance consists in the provision of services or work of a personal character or depends upon a personal relationship, or

(d)   the aggrieved party may reasonably obtain performance from another source.

(3)   The aggrieved party will lose the right to specific performance if it fails to seek it within a reasonable time after it has or ought to have become aware of the non-performance.

Article 9:103: Damages Not Precluded

The fact that a right to performance is excluded under this Section does not preclude a claim for damages.

Section 2: Withholding Performance

Article 9:201: Right to Withhold Performance

(1)   A party which is to perform simultaneously with or after the other party may withhold performance until the other has tendered performance or has performed. The first party may withhold the whole of its performance or a part of it as may be reasonable in the circumstances.

(2)   A party may similarly withhold performance for as long as it is clear that there will be a non-performance by the other party when the other party's performance becomes due.

Section 3: Termination of the Contract

Article 9:301: Right to Terminate the Contract

(1)   A party may terminate the contract if the other party's non-performance is fundamental.

(2) In the case of delay the aggrieved party may also terminate the contract under Article 8:106(3).

Article 9:302: Contract to be Performed in Parts

If the contract is to be performed in separate parts and in relation to a part to which a counter-performance can be apportioned, there is a fundamental non-performance, the aggrieved party may exercise its right to terminate under this Section in relation to the part concerned. It may terminate the contract as a whole only if the non-performance is fundamental to the contract as a whole.

Article 9:303: Notice of Termination

(1) A party's right to terminate the contract is to be exercised by notice to the other party.

(2) The aggrieved party loses its right to terminate the contract unless it gives notice within a reasonable time after it has or ought to have become aware of the non-performance.

(3) (a) When performance has not been tendered by the time it was due, the aggrieved party need not give notice of termination before a tender has been made. If a tender is later after it has or ought to have become aware of the tender.

    (b) If, however, the aggrieved party knows or has reason to know that the other party still intends to tender within a reasonable time, and the aggrieved party unreasonably fails to notify the other party that it will not accept performance, it loses its right to terminate if the other party in fact tenders within a reasonable time.

(4) If a party is excused under Article 8:108 through an impediment which is total and permanent, the contract is terminated automatically and without notice at the time the impediment arises.

Article 9:304: Anticipatory Non-Performance

Where prior to the time for performance by a party it is clear that there will be a fundamental non-performance by it, the other party may terminate the contract.

Article 9:305: Effects of Termination in General

(1) Termination of the contract releases both parties from their obligation to effect and to receive future performance, but, subject to Articles 9:306 to 9:308, does not affect the rights and liabilities that have accrued up to the time of termination.

(2) Termination does not affect any provision of the contract for the settlement of disputes or any other provision which is to operate even after termination.

Article 9:306: Property Reduced in Value

A party which terminates the contract may reject property previously received from the other party if its value to the first party has been fundamentally reduced as a result of the other party's non-performance.

Article 9:307: Recovery of Money Paid

On termination of the contract a party may recover money paid for a performance which it did not receive or which it properly rejected.

Article 9:308: Recovery of Property

On termination of the contract a party which has supplied property which can be returned and for which it has not received payment or other counter-performance may recover the property.

Article 9:309: Recovery for Performance that Cannot be Returned

On termination of the contract a party which has rendered a performance which cannot be returned and for which it has not received payment or other counter-performance may recover a reasonable amount for the value of the performance to the other party.

Section 4: Price Reduction

Article 9:401: Right to Reduce Price

(1) A party which accepts a tender of performance not conforming to the contract may reduce the price. This reduction shall be proportionate to the decrease in the value of the performance at the time this was tendered compared to the value which a conforming tender would have had at that time.

(2) A party which is entitled to reduce the price under the preceding paragraph and which has already paid a sum exceeding the reduced price may recover the excess from the other party.

(3) A party which reduces the price cannot also recover damages for reduction in the value of the performance but remains entitled to damages for any further loss it has suffered so far as these are recoverable under Section 5 of this Chapter.

Section 5: Damages and Interest

Article 9:501: Right to Damages

(1) The aggrieved party is entitled to damages for loss caused by the other party's non-performance which is not excused under Article 8:108.
(2) The loss for which damages are recoverable includes:
   (a) non-pecuniary loss; and
   (b) future loss which is reasonably likely to occur.

Article 9:502: General Measure of Damages

The general measure of damages is such sum as will put the aggrieved party as nearly as possible into the position in which it would have been if the contract had been duly performed. Such damages cover the loss which the aggrieved party has suffered and the gain of which it has been deprived.

Article 9:503: Foreseeability

The non-performing party is liable only for loss which it foresaw or could reasonably have foreseen at the time of conclusion of the contract as a likely result of its non-performance, unless the non-performance was intentional or grossly negligent.

Article 9:504: Loss Attributable to Aggrieved Party

The non-performing party is not liable for loss suffered by the aggrieved party to the extent that the aggrieved party contributed to the non-performance or its effects.

Article 9:505: Reduction of Loss

(1) The non-performing party is not liable for loss suffered by the aggrieved party to the extent that the aggrieved party could have reduced the loss by taking reasonable steps.
(2) The aggrieved party is entitled to recover any expenses reasonably incurred in attempting to reduce the loss.

Article 9:506: Substitute Transaction

Where the aggrieved party has terminated the contract and has made a substitute transaction within a reasonable time and in a reasonable manner, it may recover the difference between the contract price and the price of the substitute transaction as well as damages for any further loss so far as these are recoverable under this Section.

Article 9:507: Current Price

Where the aggrieved party has terminated the contract and has not made a substitute transaction but there is a current price for the performance contracted for, it may recover the difference between the contract price and the price current at the time the contract is terminated as well as damages for any further loss so far as these are recoverable under this Section.

Article 9:508: Delay in Payment of Money

(1)   If payment of a sum of money is delayed, the aggrieved party is entitled to interest on that sum from the time when payment is due to the time of payment at the average commercial bank short-term lending rate to prime borrowers prevailing for the contractual currency of payment at the place where payment is due.

(2)   The aggrieved party may in addition recover damages for any further loss so far as these are recoverable under this Section.

Article 9:509: Agreed Payment for Non-performance

(1)   Where the contract provides that a party which fails to perform is to pay a specified sum to the aggrieved party for such non-performance, the aggrieved party shall be awarded that sum irrespective of its actual loss.

(2)   However, despite any agreement to the contrary the specified sum may be reduced to a reasonable amount where it is grossly excessive in relation to the loss resulting from the non-performance and the other circumstances.

Article 9:510: Currency by which Damages to be Measured

Damages are to be measured by the currency which most appropriately reflects the aggrieved party's loss.

CHAPTER 10: PLURALITY OF PARTIES

Section 1: Plurality of Debtors

Article 10:101: Solidary, Separate and Communal Obligations

(1)   Obligations are solidary when all the debtors are bound to render one and the same performance and the creditor may require it from any one of them until full performance has been received.

(2)   Obligations are separate when each debtor is bound to render only part of the performance and the creditor may require from each debtor only that debtor's part.

(3)   An obligation is communal when all the debtors are bound to render the performance together and the creditor may require it only from all of them.

Article 10:102: When Solidary Obligations Arise

(1)   If several debtors are bound to render one and the same performance to a creditor under the same contract, they are solidarily liable, unless the contract or the law provides otherwise.

(2)   Solidary obligations also arise where several persons are liable for the same damage.

(3)   The fact that the debtors are not liable on the same terms does not prevent their obligations from being solidary.

Article 10:103: Liability Under Separate Obligations

Debtors bound by separate obligations are liable in equal shares unless the contract or the law provides otherwise.

Article 10:104: Communal Obligations: Special Rule when Money Claimed for Non-performance

Notwithstanding Article 10:101(3), when money is claimed for non-performance of a communal obligation, the debtors are solidarily liable for payment to the creditor.

Article 10:105: Apportionment between Dolidary Debtors

(1)   As between themselves, solidary debtors are liable in equal shares unless the contract or the law provides otherwise.

(2)   If two or more debtors are liable for the same damage under Article 10:102(2), their share of liability as between themselves is determined according to the law governing the event which gave rise to the liability.

Article 10:106: Recourse between Solidary Debtors

(1)   A solidary debtor who has performed more than that debtor's share may claim the excess from any of the other debtors to the extent of each debtor's unperformed share, together with a share of any costs reasonably incurred.

(2) A solidary debtor to whom paragraph (1) applies may also, subject to any prior right and interest of the creditor, exercise the rights and actions of the creditor, including accessory securities, to recover the excess from any of the other debtors to the extent of each debtor's unperformed share.

(3) If a solidary debtor who has performed more than that debtor's share is unable, despite all reasonable efforts, to recover contribution from another solidary debtor, the share of the others, including the one who has performed, is increased proportionally.

Article 10:107: Performance, Set-Off and Merger in Solidary Obligations

(1) Performance or set-off by a solidary debtor or set-off by the creditor against one solidary debtor discharges the other debtors in relation to the creditor to the extent of the performance or set-off.

(2) Merger of debts between a solidary debtor and the creditor discharges the other debtors only for the share of the debtor concerned.

Article 10:108: Release or Settlement in Solidary Obligations

(1) When the creditor releases, or reaches a settlement with, one solidary debtor, the other debtors are discharged of liability for the share of that debtor.

(2) The debtors are totally discharged by the release or settlement if it so provides.

(3) As between solidary debtors, the debtor who is discharged from that debtor's share is discharged only to the extent of the share at the time of the discharge and not from any supplementary share for which that debtor may subsequently become liable under Article 10:106(3).

Article 10:109: Effect of Judgment in Solidary Obligations

A decision by a court as to the liability to the creditor of one solidary debtor does not affect:

(a) the liability to the creditor of the other solidary debtors; or
(b) the rights of recourse between the solidary debtors under Article 10:106.

Article 10:110: Prescription in Solidary Obligations

Prescription of the creditor's right to performance ('claim') against one solidary debtor does not affect:

(a) the liability to the creditor of the other solidary debtors; or
(b) the rights of recourse between the solidary debtors under Article 10:106.

Article 10:111: Opposability of other Defences in Solidary Obligations

(1) A solidary debtor may invoke against the creditor any defence which another solidary debtor can invoke, other than a defence personal to that other debtor. Invoking the defence has no effect with regard to the other solidary debtors.

(2) A debtor from whom contribution is claimed may invoke against the claimant any personal defence that debtor could have invoked against the creditor.

Section 2: Plurality of Creditors

Article 10:201: Solidary, Separate and Communal Claims

(1) Claims are solidary when any of the creditors may require full performance from the debtor and when the debtor may render performance to any of the creditors.

(2) Claims are separate when the debtor owes each creditor only that creditor's share of the claim and each creditor may require performance only of that creditor's share.

(3) A claim is communal when the debtor must perform to all the creditors and any creditor may require performance only for the benefit of all.

Article 10:202: Apportionment of Separate Claims

Separate creditors are entitled to equal shares unless the contract or the law provides otherwise.

Article 10:203: Difficulties of Executing a Communal Claim

If one of the creditors in a communal claim refuses, or is unable to receive, the performance, the debtor may discharge the obligation to perform by depositing the property or money with a third party according to Articles 7:110 or 7:111 of the Principles.

Article 10:204: Apportionment of Solidary Claims

(1) Solidary creditors are entitled to equal shares unless the contract or the law provides otherwise.

(2) A creditor who has received more than that creditor's share must transfer the excess to the other creditors to the extent of their respective shares.

Article 10:205: Regime of Solidary Claims

(1) A release granted to the debtor by one of the solidary creditors has no effect on the other solidary creditors.

(2)   The rules of Articles 10:107, 10:109, 10:110 and 10:111(1) apply, with appropriate adaptations, to solidary claims.

CHAPTER 11: ASSIGNMENT OF CLAIMS

Section 1: General Principles

Article 11:101: Scope of Chapter

(1)   This Chapter applies to the assignment by agreement of a right to performance ('claim') under an existing or future contract.
(2)   Except where otherwise stated or the context otherwise requires, this Chapter also applies to the assignment by agreement of other transferable claims.
(3)   This Chapter does not apply:
    (a)   to the transfer of a financial instrument or investment security where, under the law otherwise applicable, such transfer must be by entry in a register maintained by or for the issuer; or
    (b)   to the transfer of a bill of exchange or other negotiable instrument or of a negotiable security or a document of title to goods where, under the law otherwise applicable, such transfer must be by delivery (with any necessary indorsement).
(4)   In this Chapter 'assignment' includes an assignment by way of security.
(5)   This Chapter also applies, with appropriate adaptations, to the granting by agreement of a right in security over a claim otherwise than by assignment.

Article 11:102: Contractual Claims Generally Assignable

(1)   Subject to Articles 11:301 and 11:302, a party to a contract may assign a claim under it.
(2)   A future claim arising under an existing or future contract may be assigned if at the time when it comes into existence, or at such other time as the parties agree, it can be identified as the claim to which the assignment relates.

Article 11:103: Partial Assignment

A claim which is divisible may be assigned in part, but the assignor is liable to the debtor for any increased costs which the debtor thereby incurs.

Article 11:104: Form of Assignment

An assignment need not be in writing and is not subject to any other requirement as to form. It may be proved by any means, including witnesses.

Section 2: Effects of Assignment As Between Assignor and Assignee

Article 11:201: Rights Transferred to Assignee

(1)   The assignment of a claim transfers to the assignee:
    (a)   all the assignor's rights to performance in respect of the claim assigned; and
    (b)   all accessory rights securing such performance.
(2)   Where the assignment of a claim under a contract is associated with the substitution of the assignee as debtor in respect of any obligation owed by the assignor under the same contract, this Article takes effect subject to Article 12:201.

Article 11:202: When Assignment Takes Effect

(1)   An assignment of an existing claim takes effect at the time of the agreement to assign or such later time as the assignor and assignee agree.
(2)   An assignment of a future claim is dependent upon the assigned claim coming into existence but thereupon takes effect from the time of the agreement to assign or such later time as the assignor and assignee agree.

Article 11:203: Preservation of Assignee's Rights Against Assignor

An assignment is effective as between the assignor and assignee, and entitles the assignee to whatever the assignor receives from the debtor, even if it is ineffective against the debtor under Article 11:301 or 11:302.

Article 11:204: Undertakings by Assignor

By assigning or purporting to assign a claim the assignor undertakes to the assignee that:

(a)   at the time when the assignment is to take effect the following conditions will be satisfied except as otherwise disclosed to the assignee:
    (i)   the assignor has the right to assign the claim;
    (ii) the claim exists and the assignee's rights are not affected by any defences or rights (including any right of set-off) which the debtor might have against the assignor; and

(iii)   the claim is not subject to any prior assignment or right in security in favour of any other party or to any other incumbrance;

(b)   the claim and any contract under which it arises will not be modified without the consent of the assignee unless the modification is provided for in the assignment agreement or is one which is made in good faith and is of a nature to which the assignee could not reasonably object; and

(c)   the assignor will transfer to the assignee all transferable rights intended to secure performance which are not accessory rights.

Section 3: Effects of Assignment As Between Assignee and Debtor

Article 11:301: Contractual Prohibition of Assignment

(1)   An assignment which is prohibited by or is otherwise not in conformity with the contract under which the assigned claim arises is not effective against the debtor unless:
(a)   the debtor has consented to it; or
(b)   the assignee neither knew nor ought to have known of the non-conformity; or
(c)   the assignment is made under a contract for the assignment of future rights to payment of money.

(2)   Nothing in the preceding paragraph affects the assignor's liability for the non-conformity.

Article 11:302: Other Ineffective Assignments

An assignment to which the debtor has not consented is ineffective against the debtor so far as it relates to a performance which the debtor, by reason of the nature of the performance or the relationship of the debtor and the assignor, could not reasonably be required to render to anyone except the assignor.

Article 11:303: Effect on Debtor's Obligation

(1)   Subject to Articles 11:301, 11:302, 11:307 and 11:308, the debtor is bound to perform in favour of the assignee if and only if the debtor has received a notice in writing from the assignor or the assignee which reasonably identifies the claim which has been assigned and requires the debtor to give performance to the assignee.

(2)   However, if such notice is given by the assignee, the debtor may within a reasonable time request the assignee to provide reliable evidence of the assignment, pending which the debtor may withhold performance.

(3)   Where the debtor has acquired knowledge of the assignment otherwise than by a notice conforming to paragraph (1), the debtor may either withhold performance from or give performance to the assignee.

(4) Where the debtor gives performance to the assignor, the debtor is discharged if and only if the performance is given without knowledge of the assignment.

Article 11:304: Protection of Debtor

A debtor who performs in favour of a person identified as assignee in a notice of assignment under Article 11:303 is discharged unless the debtor could not have been unaware that such person was not the person entitled to performance.

Article 11:305: Competing Demands

A debtor who has received notice of two or more competing demands for performance may discharge liability by conforming to the law of the due place of performance, or, if the performances are due in different places, the law applicable to the claim.

Article 11:306: Place of Performance

(1) Where the assigned claim relates to an obligation to pay money at a particular place, the assignee may require payment at any place within the same country or, if that country is a Member State of the European Union, at any place within the European Union, but the assignor is liable to the debtor for any increased costs which the debtor incurs by reason of any change in the place of performance.
(2) Where the assigned claim relates to a non-monetary obligation to be performed at a particular place, the assignee may not require performance at any other place.

Article 11:307: Defences and Rights of Set-Off

(1) The debtor may set up against the assignee all substantive and procedural defences to the assigned claim which the debtor could have used against the assignor.
(2) The debtor may also assert against the assignee all rights of set-off which would have been available against the assignor under Chapter 13 in respect of any claim against the assignor:
   (a) existing at the time when a notice of assignment, whether or not conforming to Article 11:303(1), reaches the debtor; or
   (b) closely connected with the assigned claim.

Article 11:308: Unauthorised Modification not Binding on Assignee

A modification of the claim made by agreement between the assignor and the debtor, without the consent of the assignee, after a notice of assignment, whether or not conforming to Article 11:303(1), reaches the debtor does not affect the rights of the assignee against the debtor unless the modification is provided for in the assignment agreement or is one which is made in good faith and is of a nature to which the assignee could not reasonably object.

Section 4: Order of Priority between Assignee and Competing Claimants

Article 11:401: Priorities

(1) Where there are successive assignments of the same claim, the assignee whose assignment is first notified to the debtor has priority over any earlier assignee if at the time of the later assignment the assignee under that assignment neither knew nor ought to have known of the earlier assignment.

(2) Subject to paragraph (1), the priority of successive assignments, whether of existing or future claims, is determined by the order in which they are made.

(3) The assignee's interest in the assigned claim has priority over the interest of a creditor of the assignor who attaches that claim, whether by judicial process or otherwise, after the time the assignment has taken effect under Article 11:202.

(4) In the event of the assignor's bankruptcy, the assignee's interest in the assigned claim has priority over the interest of the assignor's insolvency administrator and creditors, subject to any rules of the law applicable to the bankruptcy relating to:
   (a) publicity required as a condition of such priority;
   (b) the ranking of claims; or
   (c) the avoidance or ineffectiveness of transactions in the bankruptcy proceedings.

CHAPTER 12: SUBSTITUTION OF NEW DEBTOR: TRANSFER OF CONTRACT

Section 1: Substitution of New Debtor

Article 12:101: Substitution: General Rules

(1) A third person may undertake with the agreement of the debtor and the creditor to be substituted as debtor, with the effect that the original debtor is discharged.

(2) A creditor may agree in advance to a future substitution. In such a case the substitution takes effect only when the creditor is given notice by

the new debtor of the agreement between the new and the original debtor.

Article 12:102: Effects of Substitution on Defences and Securities

(1) The new debtor cannot invoke against the creditor any rights or defences arising from the relationship between the new debtor and the original debtor.

(2) The discharge of the original debtor also extends to any security of the original debtor given to the creditor for the performance of the obligation, unless the security is over an asset which is transferred to the new debtor as part of a transaction between the original and the new debtor.

(3) Upon discharge of the original debtor, a security granted by any person other than the new debtor for the performance of the obligation is released, unless that other person agrees that it should continue to be available to the creditor.

(4) The new debtor may invoke against the creditor all defences which the original debtor could have invoked against the creditor.

Section 2: Transfer of Contract

Article 12:201: Transfer of Contract

(1) A party to a contract may agree with a third person that person is to be substituted as the contracting party. In such a case the substitution takes effect only where, as a result of the other party's assent, the first party is discharged.

(2) To the extent that the substitution of the third person as a contracting party involves a transfer of rights to performance ('claims'), the provisions of Chapter 11 apply; to the extent that obligations are transferred, the provisions of Section 1 of this Chapter apply.

CHAPTER 13: SET-OFF

Article 13:101: Requirements for Set-Off

If two parties owe each other obligations of the same kind, either party may set off that party's right to performance ('claim') against the other party's claim, if and to the extent that, at the time of set-off, the first party:

(a) is entitled to effect performance; and
(b) may demand the other party's performance.

Article 13:102: Unascertained Claims

(1) A debtor may not set off a claim which is unascertained as to its existence or value unless the set-off will not prejudice the interests of the other party.

(2) Where the claims of both parties arise from the same legal relationship it is presumed that the other party's interests will not be prejudiced.

Article 13:103: Foreign Currency Set-Off

Where parties owe each other money in different currencies, each party may set off that party's claim against the other party's claim, unless the parties have agreed that the party declaring set-off is to pay exclusively in a specified currency.

Article 13:104: Notice of Set-Off

The right of set-off is exercised by notice to the other party.

Article 13:105: Plurality of Claims and Obligations

(1) Where the party giving notice of set-off has two or more claims against the other party, the notice is effective only if it identifies the claim to which it relates.

(2) Where the party giving notice of set-off has to perform two or more obligations towards the other party, the rules in Article 7:109 apply with appropriate adaptations.

Article 13:106: Effect of Set-Off

Set-off discharges the obligations, as far as they are coextensive, as from the time of notice.

Article 13:107: Exclusion of Right of Set-Off

Set-off cannot be effected:

(a) where it is excluded by agreement;

(b) against a claim to the extent that claim is not capable of attachment; and

(c) against a claim arising from a deliberate wrongful act.

CHAPTER 14: PRESCRIPTION

Section 1: General Provision

Article 14:101: Claims subject to Prescription

A right to performance of an obligation ('claim') is subject to prescription by the expiry of a period of time in accordance with these Principles.

Section 2: Periods of Prescription and their Commencement

Article 14:201: General Period

The general period of prescription is three years.

Article 14:202: Period for a Claim Established by Legal Proceedings

(1) The period of prescription for a claim established by judgment is ten years.
(2) The same applies to a claim established by an arbitral award or other instrument which is enforceable as if it were a judgment.

Article 14:203: Commencement

(1) The general period of prescription begins to run from the time when the debtor has to effect performance or, in the case of a right to damages, from the time of the act which gives rise to the claim.
(2) Where the debtor is under a continuing obligation to do or refrain from doing something, the general period of prescription begins to run with each breach of the obligation.
(3) The period of prescription set out in Article 14:202 begins to run from the time when the judgment or arbitral award obtains the effect of res judicata, or the other instrument becomes enforceable, though not before the debtor has to effect performance.

Section 3: Extension of Period

Article 14:301: Suspension in Case of Ignorance

The running of the period of prescription is suspended as long as the creditor does not know of, and could not reasonably know of:

(a) the identity of the debtor; or

(b)   the facts giving rise to the claim including, in the case of a right to damages, the type of damage.

Article 14:302: Suspension in Case of Judicial and Other Proceedings

(1)   The running of the period of prescription is suspended from the time when judicial proceedings on the claim are begun.

(2)   Suspension lasts until a decision has been made which has the effect of res judicata, or until the case has been otherwise disposed of.

(3)   These provisions apply, with appropriate adaptations, to arbitration proceedings and to all other proceedings initiated with the aim of obtaining an instrument which is enforceable as if it were a judgment.

Article 14:303: Suspension in Case of Impediment beyond Creditor's Control

(1)   The running of the period of prescription is suspended as long as the creditor is prevented from pursuing the claim by an impediment which is beyond the creditor's control and which the creditor could not reasonably have been expected to avoid or overcome.

(2)   Paragraph (1) applies only if the impediment arises, or subsists, within the last six months of the prescription period.

Article 14:304: Postponement of Expiry in Case of Negotiations

If the parties negotiate about the claim, or about circumstances from which a claim might arise, the period of prescription does not expire before one year has passed since the last communication made in the negotiations.

Article 14:305: Postponement of Expiry in Case of Incapacity

(1)   If a person subject to an incapacity is without a representative, the period of prescription of a claim held by or against that person does not expire before one year has passed after either the incapacity has ended or a representative has been appointed.

(2)   The period of prescription of claims between a person subject to an incapacity and that person's representative does not expire before one year has passed after either the incapacity has ended or a new representative has been appointed.

Article 14:306: Postponement of Expiry: Deceased's Estate

Where the creditor or debtor has died, the period of prescription of a claim held by or against the deceased's estate does not expire before one year has passed after the claim can be enforced by or against an heir, or by or against a representative of the estate.

Article 14:307: Maximum Length of Period

The period of prescription cannot be extended, by suspension of its running or postponement of its expiry under these Principles, to more than ten years or, in case of claims for personal injuries, to more than thirty years. This does not apply to suspension under Article 14:302.

Section 4: Renewal of Periods

Article 14:401: Renewal by Acknowledgement

(1) If the debtor acknowledges the claim, vis-à-vis the creditor, by part payment, payment of interest, giving of security, or in any other manner, a new period of prescription begins to run.

(2) The new period is the general period of prescription, regardless of whether the claim was originally subject to the general period of prescription or the ten year period under Article 14:202. In the latter case, however, this Article does not operate so as to shorten the ten year period.

Article 14:402: Renewal by Attempted Execution

The ten year period of prescription laid down in Article 14:202 begins to run again with each reasonable attempt at execution undertaken by the creditor.

Section 5: Effects of Prescription

Article 14:501: General Effect

(1) After expiry of the period of prescription the debtor is entitled to refuse performance.

(2) Whatever has been performed in order to discharge a claim may not be reclaimed merely because the period of prescription had expired.

Article 14:502: Effect on Ancillary Claims

The period of prescription for a right to payment of interest, and other claims of an ancillary nature, expires not later than the period for the principal claim.

Article 14:503: Effect on Set-Off

A claim in relation to which the period of prescription has expired may nonetheless be set off, unless the debtor has invoked prescription previously or does so within two months of notification of set-off.

Section 6: Modification by Agreement

Article 14:601: Agreements Concerning Prescription

(1) The requirements for prescription may be modified by agreement
     between the parties, in particular by either shortening or lengthening
     the periods of prescription.
(2) The period of prescription may not, however, be reduced to less than
     one year or extended to more than thirty years after the time of com-
     mencement set out in Article 14:203.

CHAPTER 15: ILLEGALITY

Article 15:101: Contracts Contrary to Fundamental Principles

A contract is of no effect to the extent that it is contrary to principles recognised
as fundamental in the laws of the Member States of the European Union.

Article 15:102: Contracts Infringing Mandatory Rules

(1) Where a contract infringes a mandatory rule of law applicable under
     Article 1:103 of these Principles, the effects of that infringement upon
     the contract are the effects, if any, expressly prescribed by that manda-
     tory rule.
(2) Where the mandatory rule does not expressly prescribe the effects of
     an infringement upon a contract, the contract may be declared to have
     full effect, to have some effect, to have no effect, or to be subject to
     modification.
(3) A decision reached under paragraph (2) must be an appropriate and
     proportional response to the infringement, having regard to all rele-
     vant circumstances, including:
     (a) the purpose of the rule which has been infringed;
     (b) the category of persons for whose protection the rule exists;
     (c) any sanction that may be imposed under the rule infringed;
     (d) the seriousness of the infringement;
     (e) whether the infringement was intentional; and
     (f) the closeness of the relationship between the infringement and
          the contract.

Article 15:103: Partial Ineffectiveness

(1) If only part of a contract is rendered ineffective under Articles 15:101
     or 15:102, the remaining part continues in effect unless, giving due

consideration to all the circumstances of the case, it is unreasonable to uphold it.

(2) Articles 15:104 and 15:105 apply, with appropriate adaptations, to a case of partial ineffectiveness.

Article 15:104: Restitution

(1) When a contract is rendered ineffective under Articles 15:101 or 15:102, either party may claim restitution of whatever that party has supplied under the contract, provided that, where appropriate, concurrent restitution is made of whatever has been received.

(2) When considering whether to grant restitution under paragraph (1), and what concurrent restitution, if any, would be appropriate, regard must be had to the factors referred to in Article 15:102(3).

(3) An award of restitution may be refused to a party who knew or ought to have known of the reason for the ineffectiveness.

(4) If restitution cannot be made in kind for any reason, a reasonable sum must be paid for what has been received.

Article 15:105: Damages

(1) A party to a contract which is rendered ineffective under Articles 15:101 or 15:102 may recover from the other party damages putting the first party as nearly as possible into the same position as if the contract had not been concluded, provided that the other party knew or ought to have known of the reason for the ineffectiveness.

(2) When considering whether to award damages under paragraph (1), regard must be had to the factors referred to in Article 15:102(3).

(3) An award of damages may be refused where the first party knew or ought to have known of the reason for the ineffectiveness.

CHAPTER 16: CONDITIONS

Article 16:101: Types of Condition

A contractual obligation may be made conditional upon the occurrence of an uncertain future event, so that the obligation takes effect only if the event occurs (suspensive condition) or comes to an end if the event occurs (resolutive condition).

Article 16:102: Interference with Conditions

(1)   If fulfilment of a condition is prevented by a party, contrary to duties of good faith and fair dealing or co-operation, and if fulfilment would have operated to that party's disadvantage, the condition is deemed to be fulfilled.

(2)   If fulfilment of a condition is brought about by a party, contrary to duties of good faith and fair dealing or co-operation, and if fulfilment operates to that party's advantage, the condition is deemed not to be fulfilled.

Article 16:103: Effect of Conditions

(1)   Upon fulfilment of a suspensive condition, the relevant obligation takes effect unless the parties otherwise agree.

(2)   Upon fulfilment of a resolutive condition, the relevant obligation comes to an end unless the parties otherwise agree.

CHAPTER 17: CAPITALISATION OF INTEREST

Article 17:101: When Interest to be Added to Capital

(1)   Interest payable according to Article 9:508(1) is added to the outstanding capital every 12 months.

(2)   Paragraph (1) of this Article does not apply if the parties have provided for interest upon delay in payment.

THE PRINCIPLES OF INTERNATIONAL COMMERCIAL CONTRACTS
(The UNIDROIT Principles)*

Preamble
(Purpose of the Principles)

These Principles set forth general rules for international commercial contracts.

They shall be applied when the parties have agreed that their contract be governed by them.

They may be applied when the parties have agreed that their contract be governed by general principles of law, the *lex mercatoria*, or the like.

They may provide a solution to an issue raised when it proves impossible to establish the relevant rule of the applicable law.

They may be used to interpret or supplement international uniform law instruments.

They may serve as a model for national and international legislators.

Chapter 1 – General Provisions

Article 1.1

(Freedom of contract)

The parties are free to enter into a contract and to determine its content.

Article 1.2

(No form required)

Nothing in these Principles requires a contract to be concluded in or evidenced by writing. It may be proved by any means, including witnesses.

Article 1.3

(Binding character of contract)

A contract validly entered into is binding upon the parties. It can only be modified or terminated in accordance with its terms or by agreement or as otherwise provided in these Principles.

---

* This text is published in UNIDROIT, *Principles of International Commercial Contracts*, Rome 1994.

Article 1.4

(Mandatory rules)

Nothing in these Principles shall restrict the application of mandatory rules, whether of national, international, or supranational origin, which are applicable in accordance with the relevant rules of private international law.

Article 1.5

(Exclusion or modification by the parties)

The parties may exclude the application of these Principles or derogate from or vary the effect of any of their provisions, except as otherwise provided in the Principles.

Article 1.6

(Interpretation and supplementation of the principles)

(1)   In the interpretation of these Principles, regard is to be had to their international character and to their purposes including the need to promote uniformity in their application.
(2)   Issues within the scope of these Principles but not expressly settled by them are as far as possible to be settled in accordance with their underlying general principles.

Article 1.7

(Good faith and fair dealing)

(1)   Each party must act in accordance with good faith and fair dealing in international trade.
(2)   The parties may not exclude or limit this duty.

Article 1.8

(Usages and Practices)

(1)   The parties are bound by any usage to which they have agreed and by any practices which they have established between themselves.
(2)   The parties are bound by a usage that is widely known to and regularly observed in international trade by parties in the particular trade

concerned except where the application of such a usage would be unreasonable.

Article 1.9

(Notice)

(1) Where notice is required it may be given by any means appropriate to the circumstances.

(2) A notice is effective when it reaches the person to whom it is given.

(3) For the purpose of paragraph (2) a notice 'reaches' a person when given to that person orally or delivered at that person's place of business or mailing address.

(4) For the purpose of this article 'notice' includes a declaration, demand, request or any other communication of intention.

Article 1.10

(Definitions)

In these Principles

- 'court' includes an arbitral tribunal;
- where a party has more than one place of business the relevant 'place of business' is that which has the closest relationship to the contract and its performance, having regard to the circumstances known to or contemplated by the parties at any time before or at the conclusion of the contract;
- 'obligor' refers to the party who is to perform an obligation and 'obligee' refers to the party who is entitled to performance of that obligation;
- 'writing' means any mode of communication that preserves a record of the information contained therein and is capable of being reproduced in tangible form.

Chapter 2 – Formation

Article 2.1

(Manner of formation)

A contract may be concluded either by the acceptance of an offer or by conduct of the parties that is sufficient to show agreement.

Article 2.2

(Definition of offer)

A proposal for concluding a contract constitutes an offer if it is sufficiently definite and indicates the intention of the offeror to be bound in case of acceptance.

Article 2.3

(Withdrawal of offer)

(1)   An offer becomes effective when it reaches the offeree.
(2)   An offer, even if it is irrevocable, may be withdrawn if the withdrawal reaches the offeree before or at the same time as the offer.

Article 2.4

(Revocation of offer)

(1)   Until a contract is concluded an offer may be revoked if the revocation reaches the offeree before it has dispatched an acceptance.
(2)   However, an offer cannot be revoked
    (a)   if it indicates, whether by stating a fixed time for acceptance or otherwise, that it is irrevocable; or
    (b)   if it was reasonable for the offeree to rely on the offer as being irrevocable and the offeree has acted in reliance on the offer.

Article 2.5

(Rejection of offer)

An offer is terminated when a rejection reaches the offeror.

Article 2.6

(Mode of acceptance)

(1)   A statement made by or other conduct of the offeree indicating assent to an offer is an acceptance. Silence or inactivity does not in itself amount to acceptance.
(2)   An acceptance of an offer becomes effective when the indication of assent reaches the offeror.
(3)   However, if, by virtue of the offer or as a result of practices which the parties have established between themselves or of usage, the offeree

may indicate assent by performing an act without notice to the offeror, the acceptance is effective when the act is performed.

Article 2.7

(Time of acceptance)

An offer must be accepted within the time the offeror has fixed or, if no time is fixed, within a reasonable time having regard to the circumstances, including the rapidity of the means of communication employed by the offeror. An oral offer must be accepted immediately unless the circumstances indicate otherwise.

Article 2.8

(Acceptance within a fixed period of time)

(1) A period of time for acceptance fixed by the offeror in a telegram or a letter begins to run from the moment the telegram is handed in for dispatch or from the date shown on the letter or, if no such date is shown, from the date shown on the envelope. A period of time for acceptance fixed by the offeror's means of instantaneous communication begins to run from the moment that the offer reaches the offeree.

(2) Official holidays or non-business days occurring during the period for acceptance are included in calculating the period. However, if a notice of acceptance cannot be delivered at the address of the offeror on the last day of the period because that day falls on an official holiday or a non-business day at the place of business of the offeror, the period is extended until the first business day which follows.

Article 2.9

(Late acceptance, delay in transmission)

(1) A late acceptance is nevertheless effective as an acceptance if without undue delay the offeror so informs the offeree or gives notice to that effect.

(2) If a letter or other writing containing a late acceptance shows that it has been sent in such circumstances that if its transmission had been normal it would have reached the offeror in due time, the late acceptance is effective as an acceptance unless, without undue delay, the offeror informs the offeree that it considers the offer as having elapsed.

Article 2.10

(Withdrawal of acceptance)

An acceptance may be withdrawn if the withdrawal reaches the offeror before or at the same time as the acceptance would have become effective.

Article 2.11

(Modified acceptance)

(1)   A reply to an offer which purports to be an acceptance but contains additions, limitations or other modifications is a rejection of the offer and constitutes a counteroffer.

(2)   However, a reply to an offer which purports to be an acceptance but contains additional or different terms which do not materially alter the terms of the offer constitutes an acceptance, unless the offeror, without undue delay, objects to the discrepancy. If the offeror does not object, the terms of the contract are the terms of the offer with the modifications contained in the acceptance.

Article 2.12

(Writings in confirmation)

If a writing which is sent within a reasonable time after the conclusion of the contract and which purports to be a confirmation of the contract contains additional or different terms, such terms become part of the contract, unless they materially alter the contract or the recipient, without undue delay, objects to the discrepancy.

Article 2.13

(Conclusion of contract dependent on agreement on specific matters or in a specific form)

Where in the course of negotiations one of the parties insists that the contract is not concluded until there is agreement on specific matters or in a specific form, no contract is concluded before agreement is reached on those matters or in that form.

Article 2.14

(Contract with terms deliberately left open)

(1)   If the parties intend to conclude a contract, the fact that they intentionally leave a term to be agreed upon in further negotiations or to be determined by a third person does not prevent a contract from coming into existence.

(2) The existence of the contract is not affected by the fact that subsequently
    (a) the parties reach no agreement on the term; or
    (b) the third person does not determine the term,

provided that there is an alternative means of rendering the term definite that is reasonable in the circumstances, having regard to the intention of the parties.

Article 2.15

(Negotiations in bad faith)

(1) A party is free to negotiate and is not liable for failure to reach an agreement.
(2) However, a party who negotiates or breaks off negotiations in bad faith is liable for the losses caused to the other party.
(3) It is bad faith, in particular, for a party to enter into or continue negotiations when intending not to reach an agreement with the other party.

Article 2.16

(Duty of confidentiality)

Where information is given as confidential by one party in the course of negotiations, the other party is under a duty not to disclose that information or to use it improperly for its own purposes, whether or not a contract is subsequently concluded. Where appropriate, the remedy for breach of that duty may include compensation based on the benefit received by the other party.

Article 2.17

(Merger clauses)

A contract in writing which contains a clause indicating that the writing completely embodies the terms on which the parties have agreed cannot be contradicted or supplemented by evidence of prior statements or agreements. However, such statements or agreements may be used to interpret the writing.

Article 2.18

(Written modification clauses)

A contract in writing which contains a clause requiring any modification or termination by agreement to be in writing may not be otherwise modified or terminated. However, a party may be precluded by its conduct from asserting such a clause to the extent that the other party has acted in reliance on that conduct.

Article 2.19

(Contracting under standard terms)

(1)   Where one party or both parties use standard terms in concluding a contract, the general rules on formation apply, subject to Articles 2.20–2.22.

(2)   Standard terms are provisions which are prepared in advance for general and repeated use by one party and which are actually used without negotiations with the other party.

Article 2.20

(Surprising terms)

(1)   No term contained in standard terms which is of such character that the other party could not reasonably have expected it, is effective unless it has been expressly accepted by that party.

(2)   In determining whether a term is of such a character regard is to be had to its content, language and presentation.

Article 2.21

(Conflict between standard terms and non-standard terms)

In case of conflict between a standard term and a term which is not a standard term the latter prevails.

Article 2.22

(Battle of forms)

Where both parties use standard terms and reach agreement except on those terms, a contract is concluded on the basis of the agreed terms and of any standard terms which are common in substance unless one party clearly indicates in advance, or later and without undue delay informs the other party, that it does not intend to be bound by such a contract.

Chapter 3 – Validity

Article 3.1

(Matters not covered)

These Principles do not deal with invalidity arising from

(a)   lack of capacity;

(b) lack of authority;

(c) immorality or illegality.

Article 3.2

(Validity of mere agreement)

A contract is concluded, modified or terminated by the mere agreement of the parties, without any further requirement.

Article 3.3

(Initial impossibility)

(1) The mere fact that at the time of the conclusion of the contract the performance of the obligation assumed was impossible does not affect the validity of the contract.

(2) The mere fact that at the time of the conclusion of the contract a party was not entitled to dispose of the assets to which the contract relates does not affect the validity of the contract.

Article 3.4

(Definition of mistake)

Mistake is an erroneous assumption relating to facts or to law existing when the contract was concluded.

Article 3.5

(Relevant mistake)

(1) A party may only avoid the contract for mistake if, when the contract was concluded, the mistake was of such importance that a reasonable person in the same situation as the party in error would only have concluded the contract on materially different terms or would not have concluded it at all if the true state of affairs had been known, and

(a) the other party made the same mistake, or caused the mistake, or knew or ought to have known of the mistake and it was contrary to reasonable commercial standards of fair dealing to leave the mistaken party in error; or

(b) the other party had not at the time of avoidance acted in reliance on the contract.

(2) However, a party may not avoid the contract if

    (a) it was grossly negligent in committing the mistake; or

    (b) the mistake relates to a matter in regard to which the risk of mistake was assumed by or, having regard to the circumstances, should be borne by the mistaken party.

Article 3.6

(Error in expression or transmission)

An error occurring in the expression or transmission of a declaration is considered to be a mistake of the person from whom the declaration emanated.

Article 3.7

(Remedies for non-performance)

A party is not entitled to avoid the contract on the ground of mistake if the circumstances on which that party relies afford, or could have afforded, a remedy for non-performance.

Article 3.8

(Fraud)

A party may avoid the contract when it has been led to conclude the contract by the other party's fraudulent representation, including language or practices, or fraudulent non-disclosure of circumstances which, according to reasonable commercial standards of fair dealing, the latter party should have disclosed.

Article 3.9

(Threat)

A party may avoid the contract when it has been led to conclude the contract by the other party's unjustified threat which, having regard to the circumstances, is so imminent and serious as to leave the first party no reasonable alternative. In particular, a threat is unjustified if the act or omission with which a party has been threatened is wrongful in itself, or it is wrongful to use it as a means to obtain the conclusion of the contract.

Article 3.10

(Gross disparity)

(1) A party may avoid the contract or an individual term of it if, at the time of the conclusion of the contract, the contract or term unjustifiably

gave the other party an excessive advantage. Regard is to be had, among other factors, to

(a)   the fact that the other party has taken unfair advantage of the first party's dependence, economic distress or urgent needs, or of its improvidence, ignorance, inexperience or lack of bargaining skill; and

(b)   the nature and purpose of the contract.

(2)   Upon the request of the party entitled to avoidance, a court may adapt the contract or term in order to make it accord with reasonable commercial standards of fair dealing.

(3)   A court may also adapt the contract or term upon the request of the party receiving notice of avoidance, provided that party informs the other party of its request promptly after receiving such notice and before the other party has acted in reliance on it. The provisions of Article 3.13(2) apply accordingly.

Article 3.11

(Third persons)

(1)   Where fraud, threat, gross disparity or a party's mistake is imputable to, or is known or ought to be known by, a third person for whose acts the other party is responsible, the contract may be avoided under the same conditions as if the behaviour or knowledge had been that of the party itself.

(2)   Where fraud, threat or gross disparity is imputable to a third person for whose acts the other party is not responsible, the contract may be avoided if that party knew or ought to have known of the fraud, threat or disparity, or has not at the time of avoidance acted in reliance on the contract.

Article 3.12

(Confirmation)

If the party entitled to avoid the contract expressly or impliedly confirms the contract after the period of time for giving notice of avoidance has begun to run, avoidance of the contract is excluded.

Article 3.13

(Loss of right to avoid)

(1)   If a party is entitled to avoid the contract for mistake but the other party declares itself willing to perform or performs the contract as it was understood by the party entitled to avoidance, the contract is

considered to have been concluded as the latter party understood it. The other party must make such a declaration or render such performance promptly after having been informed of the manner in which the party entitled to avoidance had understood the contract and before that party has acted in reliance on a notice of avoidance.

(2) After such a declaration or performance the right to avoidance is lost and any earlier notice of avoidance is ineffective.

Article 3.14

(Notice of avoidance)

The right of a party to avoid the contract is exercised by notice to the other party.

Article 3.15

(Time limits)

(1) Notice of avoidance shall be given within a reasonable time, having regard to the circumstances, after the avoiding party knew or could not have been unaware of the relevant facts or became capable of acting freely.

(2) Where an individual term of the contract may be avoided by a party under Article 3.10, the period of time for giving notice of avoidance begins to run when that term is asserted by the other party.

Article 3.16

(Partial avoidance)

Where a ground of avoidance affects only individual terms of the contract, the effect of avoidance is limited to those terms unless, having regard to the circumstances, it is unreasonable to uphold the remaining contract.

Article 3.17

(Retroactive effect of avoidance)

(1) Avoidance takes effect retroactively.

(2) On avoidance either party may claim restitution of whatever it has supplied under the contract or the part of it avoided, provided that it concurrently makes restitution of whatever it has received under the contract or the part of it avoided or, if it cannot make restitution in kind, it makes an allowance for what it has received.

Article 3.18

(Damages)

Irrespective of whether or not the contract has been avoided, the party who knew or ought to have known of the ground for avoidance is liable for damages so as to put the other party in the same position in which it would have been if it had not concluded the contract.

Article 3.19

(Mandatory character of the provisions)

The provisions of this Chapter are mandatory, except insofar as they relate to the binding force of mere agreement, initial impossibility, or mistake.

Article 3.20

(Unilateral declarations)

The provisions of this Chapter apply with appropriate adaptations to any communication of intention addressed by one party to the other.

Chapter 4 – Interpretation

Article 4.1

(Intention of the parties)

(1)   A contract shall be interpreted according to the common intention of the parties.
(2)   If such an intention cannot be established, the contract shall be interpreted according to the meaning that reasonable persons of the same kind as the parties would give to it in the same circumstances.

Article 4.2

(Interpretation of statements and other conduct)

(1)   The statements and other conduct of a party shall be interpreted according to that party's intention if the other party knew or could not have been unaware of that intention.
(2)   If the preceding paragraph is not applicable, such statements and other conduct shall be interpreted according to the meaning that a

reasonable person of the same kind as the other party would give to it in the same circumstances.

Article 4.3

(Relevant circumstances)

In applying Articles 4.1 and 4.2, regard shall be had to all the circumstances, including

(a)   preliminary negotiations between the parties;
(b)   practices which the parties have established between themselves;
(c)   the conduct of the parties subsequent to the conclusion of the contract;
(d)   the nature and purpose of the contract;
(e)   the meaning commonly given to terms and expressions in the trade concerned;
(f)   usages.

Article 4.4

(Reference to contract or statement as a whole)

Terms and expressions shall be interpreted in the light of the whole contract or statement in which they appear.

Article 4.5

(All terms to be given effect)

Contract terms shall be interpreted so as to give effect to all the terms rather than to deprive some of them of effect.

Article 4.6

(Contra proferentem rule)

If contract terms supplied by one party are unclear, an interpretation against that party is preferred.

Article 4.7

(Linguistic discrepancies)

Where a contract is drawn up in two or more language versions which are equally authoritative there is, in case of discrepancy between the versions, a preference for the interpretation according to a version in which the contract was originally drawn up.

Article 4.8

(Supplying an omitted term)

(1) Where the parties to a contract have not agreed with respect to a term which is important for a determination of their rights and duties, a term which is appropriate in the circumstances shall be supplied.

(2) In determining what is an appropriate term regard shall be had, among other factors, to
   (a) the intention of the parties;
   (b) the nature and purpose of the contract;
   (c) good faith and fair dealing;
   (d) reasonableness.

Chapter 5 – Content

Article 5.1

(Express and implied obligations)

The contractual obligations of the parties may be express or implied.

Article 5.2

(Implied obligations)

Implied obligations stem from

   (a) the nature and purpose of the contract;
   (b) practices established between the parties and usages;
   (c) good faith and fair dealing;
   (d) reasonableness.

Article 5.3

(Co-operation between the parties)

Each party shall co-operate with the other party when such co-operation may reasonably be expected for the performance of that party's obligations.

Article 5.4

(Duty to achieve a specific result – duty of best efforts)

(1)   To the extent that an obligation of a party involves a duty to achieve a specific result, that party is bound to achieve that result.

(2)   To the extent that an obligation of a party involves a duty of best efforts in the performance of an activity, that party is bound to make such efforts as would be made by a reasonable person of the same kind in the same circumstances.

Article 5.5

(Determination of kind of duty involved)

In determining the extent to which an obligation of a party involves a duty of best efforts in the performance of any activity or a duty to achieve a specific result, regard shall be had, among other factors, to

(a)   the way in which the obligation is expressed in the contract;

(b)   the contractual price and other terms of the contract;

(c)   the degree of risk normally involved in achieving the expected result;

(d)   the ability of the other party to influence the performance of the obligation.

Article 5.6

(Determination of quality of performance)

Where the quality of performance is neither fixed by, nor determinable from, the contract a party is bound to render a performance of a quality that is reasonable and not less than average in the circumstances.

Article 5.7

(Price determination)

(1)   Where a contract does not fix or make provision for determining the price, the parties are considered, in the absence of any indication to the contrary, to have made reference to the price generally charged at the time of the conclusion of the contract for such performance in comparable circumstances in the trade concerned or, if no such price is available, to a reasonable price.

(2) Where the price is to be determined by one party and that determination is manifestly unreasonable, a reasonable price shall be substituted notwithstanding any contract term to the contrary.

(3) Where the price is to be fixed by a third person, and that person cannot or will not do so, the price shall be a reasonable price.

(4) Where the price is to be fixed by reference to factors which do not exist or have ceased to exist or to be accessible, the nearest equivalent factor shall be treated as a substitute.

Article 5.8

(Contract for an indefinite period)

A contract for an indefinite period may be ended by either party by giving notice a reasonable time in advance.

Chapter 6 – Performance

Section 1: Performance in General

Article 6.1.1

(Time of performance)

A party must perform its obligations:

(a) if a time is fixed by or determinable from the contract, at that time;

(b) if a period of time is fixed by or determinable from the contract, at any time within that period unless circumstances indicate that the other party is to choose a time;

(c) in any other case, within a reasonable time after the conclusion of the contract.

Article 6.1.2

(Performance at one time or in instalments)

In cases under Article 6.1(b) or (c), a party must perform its obligations at one time if that performance can be rendered at one time and the circumstances do not indicate otherwise.

Article 6.1.3

(Partial performance)

(1) The obligee may reject an offer to perform in part at the time performance is due, whether or not such offer is coupled with an

assurance as to the balance of the performance, unless the obligee has no legitimate interest in so doing.
(2) Additional expenses caused to the obligee by partial performance are to be borne by the obligor without prejudice to any other remedy.

Article 6.1.4

(Order of performance)

(1) To the extent that the performances of the parties can be rendered simultaneously, the parties are bound to render them simultaneously unless the circumstances indicate otherwise.
(2) To the extent that the performance of only one party requires a period of time, that party is bound to render its performance first, unless the circumstances indicate otherwise.

Article 6.1.5

(Earlier performance)

(1) The obligee may reject an earlier performance unless it has no legitimate interest in so doing.
(2) Acceptance by a party of an earlier performance does not affect the time for the performance of its own obligations if that time has been fixed irrespective of the performance of the other party's obligations.
(3) Additional expenses caused to the obligee by earlier performance are to be borne by the obligor, without regard to any other remedy.

Article 6.1.6

(Place of performance)

(1) If the place of performance is neither fixed by, nor determinable from, the contract, a party is to perform:
(a) a monetary obligation, at the obligee's place of business;
(b) any other obligation, at its own place of business.
(2) A party must bear any increase in the expenses incidental to performance which is caused by a change in its place of business subsequent to the conclusion of the contract.

Article 6.1.7

(Payment by cheque or other instrument)

(1) Payment may be made in any form used in the ordinary course of business at the place for payment.

(2) However, an obligee who accepts, either by virtue of paragraph (1) or voluntarily, a cheque, any other order to pay or a promise to pay, is presumed to do so only on condition that it will be honoured.

Article 6.1.8

(Payment by funds transfer)

(1) Unless the obligee has indicated a particular account, payment may be made by a transfer to any of the financial institutions in which the obligee has made it known that it has an account.

(2) In case of payment by a transfer the obligation of the obligor is discharged when the transfer to the obligee's financial institution becomes effective.

Article 6.1.9

(Currency of payment)

(1) If a monetary obligation is expressed in a currency other than that of the place for payment, it may be paid by the obligor in the currency of the place for payment unless
   (a) the currency is not freely convertible; or
   (b) the parties have agreed that payment should be made only in the currency in which the monetary obligation is expressed.

(2) If it is impossible for the obligor to make payment in the currency in which the monetary obligation is expressed, the obligee may require payment in the currency of the place for payment, even in the case referred to in paragraph (1)(b).

(3) Payment in the currency of the place for payment is to be made according to the applicable rate of exchange prevailing there when payment is due.

(4) However, if the obligor has not paid at the time when payment is due, the obligee may require payment according to the applicable rate of exchange prevailing either when payment is due or at the time of actual payment.

Article 6.1.10

(Currency not expressed)

Where a monetary obligation is not expressed in a particular currency, payment must be made in the currency of the place where payment is made.

Article 6.1.11

(Costs of performance)

Each party shall bear the costs of performance of its obligations.

Article 6.1.12

(Imputation of payments)

(1) An obligor owing several monetary obligations to the same obligee may specify at the time of payment the debt to which it intends the payment to be applied. However, the payment discharges first any expenses, then interest due and finally the principal.

(2) If the obligor makes no such specification, the obligee may, within a reasonable time after payment, declare to the obligor the obligation to which it imputes the payment, provided that the obligation is due and undisputed.

(3) In the absence of imputation under paragraphs (1) or (2), payment is imputed to that obligation which satisfies one of the following criteria and in the order indicated:

    (a) an obligation which is due or which is the first to fall due;
    (b) the obligation for which the obligee has least security;
    (c) the obligation which is the most burdensome for the obligor;
    (d) the obligation which has arisen first;

If none of the preceding criteria applies, payment is imputed to all the obligations proportionately.

Article 6.1.13

(Imputation of non-monetary obligations)

Article 6.1.12 applies with appropriate adaptations to the imputation of performance of non-monetary obligations.

Article 6.1.14

(Application for public permission)

Where the law of a State requires a public permission affecting the validity of the contract or its performance and neither that law nor the circumstances indicate otherwise

    (a) if only one party has its place of business in that State, that party shall take the measures necessary to obtain the permission;

(b)   in any other case the party whose performance requires permission
      shall take the necessary measures.

Article 6.1.15

(Procedure in applying for permission)

(1)   The party required to take the measures necessary to obtain the per-
      mission shall do so without undue delay and shall bear any expenses
      incurred.
(2)   That party shall whenever appropriate give the other party notice of
      the grant or refusal of such permission without undue delay.

Article 6.1.16

(Permission neither granted nor refused)

(1)   If, notwithstanding the fact that the party responsible has taken all
      measures required, permission is neither granted nor refused within
      an agreed period or, where no period has been agreed, within
      a reasonable time from the conclusion of the contract, either party is
      entitled to terminate the contract.
(2)   Where the permission affects some terms only, paragraph (1) does not
      apply if, having regard to the circumstances, it is reasonable to uphold
      the remaining contract even if the permission is refused.

Article 6.1.17

(Permission refused)

(1)   The refusal of a permission affecting the validity of the contract ren-
      ders the contract void. If the refusal affects the validity of some terms,
      only such terms are void if, having regard to the circumstances, it is
      reasonable to uphold the remaining contract.
(2)   Where the refusal of a permission renders the performance of the con-
      tract impossible in whole or in part, the rules on non-performance apply.

Section 2: Hardship

Article 6.2.1

(Contract to be observed)

Where the performance of a contract becomes more onerous for one of the
parties, the party is nevertheless bound to perform its obligations subject to
the following provisions on hardship.

Article 6.2.2

(Definition of hardship)

There is hardship where the occurrence of events fundamentally alters the equilibrium of the contract either because the cost of a party's performance has increased or because the value of the performance a party receives has diminished, andF

(a) the events occur or become known to the disadvantaged party after the conclusion of the contract;
(b) the events could not reasonably have been taken into account by the disadvantaged party at the time of the conclusion of the contract;
(c) the events are beyond the control of the disadvantaged party; and
(d) the risk of the events was not assumed by the disadvantaged party.

Article 6.2.3

(Effects of hardship)

(1) In case of hardship the disadvantaged party is entitled to request renegotiations. The request shall be made without undue delay and shall indicate the grounds on which it is based.
(2) The request for renegotiation does not in itself entitle the disadvantaged party to withhold performance.
(3) Upon failure to reach agreement within a reasonable time either party may resort to the court.
(4) If the court finds hardship it may, if reasonable,
    (a) terminate the contract at a date and on terms to be fixed; or
    (b) adapt the contract with a view to restoring its equilibrium.

Chapter 7 – Non-performance

Section 1: Non-Performance in General

Article 7.1.1

(Non-performance defined)

Non-performance is failure by a party to perform any of its obligations under the contract, including defective performance or late performance.

Article 7.1.2

(Interference by the other party)

A party may not rely on the non-performance of the other party to the extent that such non-performance was caused by the first party's act or omission or by another event as to which the first party bears the risk.

Article 7.1.3

(Withholding performance)

(1)   Where the parties are to perform simultaneously, either party may withhold performance until the other party tenders its performance.

(2)   Where the parties are to perform consecutively, the party that is to perform later may withhold its performance until the first party has performed.

Article 7.1.4

(Cure by non-performing party)

(1)   The non-performing party may, at its own expense, cure any non-performance, provided that
   (a)   without undue delay, it gives notice indicating the proposed manner and timing of the cure;
   (b)   cure is appropriate in the circumstances;
   (c)   the aggrieved party has no legitimate interest in refusing cure; and
   (d)   cure is effected promptly.

(2)   The right to cure is not precluded by notice of termination.

(3)   Upon effective notice of cure, rights of the aggrieved party that are inconsistent with the non-performing party's performance are suspended until the time for cure has expired.

(4)   The aggrieved party may withhold performance pending cure.

(5)   Notwithstanding cure, the aggrieved party retains the right to claim damages for delay as well as for any harm caused or not prevented by the cure.

Article 7.1.5

(Additional period for performance)

(1)   In a case of non-performance the aggrieved party may by notice to the other party allow an additional period of time for performance.

(2)   During the additional period the aggrieved party may withhold performance of its own reciprocal obligations and may claim damages but may not resort to any other remedy. If it receives notice from the other party that the latter will not perform within that period, of if upon expiry of that period due performance has not been made, the aggrieved party may resort to any of the remedies that may be available under this Chapter.

(3)   Where in a case of delay in performance which is not fundamental the aggrieved party has given notice allowing an additional period of time of reasonable length it may terminate the contract at the end of the period. If the additional period allowed is not of reasonable length, it shall be

extended to a reasonable length. The aggrieved party may in its notice provide that if the other party fails to perform within the period allowed by the notice the contract shall automatically terminate.

(4)　Paragraph (3) does not apply where the obligation which has not been performed is only a minor part of the contractual obligation of the non-performing party.

Article 7.1.6

(Exemption clause)

A clause which limits or excludes one party's liability for non-performance or which permits one party to render performance substantially different from what the other party reasonably expected may not be invoked if it would be grossly unfair to do so, having regard to the purpose of the contract.

Article 7.1.7

(Force majeure)

(1)　Non-performance by a party is excused if that party proves that the non-performance was due to an impediment beyond its control and that it could not reasonably be expected to have taken the impediment into account at the time of the conclusion of the contract or to have avoided or overcome it or its consequences.

(2)　When the impediment is only temporary, the excuse shall have effect for such period as is reasonable having regard to the effect of the impediment on the performance of the contract.

(3)　The party who fails to perform must give notice to the other party of the impediment and its effect on its ability to perform. If the notice is not received by the other party within a reasonable time after the party who fails to perform knew or ought to have known of the impediment, it is liable for damages resulting from such non-receipt.

(4)　Nothing in this article prevents a party from exercising a right to terminate the contract or to withhold performance or request interest on money due.

Section 2: Right to Performance

Article 7.2.1

(Performance of monetary obligation)

Where a party who is obliged to pay money does not do so, the other party may require payment.

Article 7.2.2

(Performance of non-monetary obligation)

Where a party who owes an obligation other than one to pay money does not perform, the other party may require performance, unless
- (a)   performance is impossible in law or in fact;
- (b)   performance or, where relevant, enforcement is unreasonably burdensome or expensive;
- (c)   the party entitled to performance may reasonably obtain performance from another source;
- (d)   performance is of an exclusively personal character; or
- (e)   the party entitled to performance does not require performance within a reasonable time after it has, or ought to have, become aware of the non-performance.

Article 7.2.3

(Repair and replacement of defective performance)

The right to performance includes in appropriate cases the right to require repair, replacement, or other cure of defective performance. The provisions of Articles 7.2.1 and 7.2.2 apply accordingly.

Article 7.2.4

(Judicial penalty)

- (1)   Where the court orders a party to perform, it may also direct that this party pay a penalty if it does not comply with the order.
- (2)   The penalty shall be paid to the aggrieved party unless mandatory provisions of the law of the forum provide otherwise. Payment of the penalty to the aggrieved party does not exclude any claim for damages.

Article 7.2.5

(Change of remedy)

- (1)   An aggrieved party who has required performance of a non-monetary obligation and who has not received performance within a period fixed or otherwise within a reasonable period of time may invoke any other remedy.
- (2)   Where the decision of a court for performance of a non-monetary obligation cannot be enforced, the aggrieved party may invoke any other remedy.

Section 3: Termination

Article 7.3.1

(Right to terminate the contract)

(1) A party may terminate the contract where the failure of the other party to perform an obligation under the contract amounts to a fundamental non-performance.

(2) In determining whether a failure to perform an obligation amounts to a fundamental non-performance regard shall be had, in particular, to whether

  (a) the non-performance substantially deprives the aggrieved party of what it was entitled to expect under the contract unless the other party did not foresee and could not have reasonably foreseen such result;

  (b) strict compliance with the obligation which has not been performed is of essence under the contract;

  (c) the non-performance is intentional or reckless;

  (d) the non-performance gives the aggrieved party reason to believe that it cannot rely on the other party's future performance;

  (e) the non-performing party will suffer disproportionate loss as a result of the preparation or performance if the contract is terminated.

(3) In the case of delay the aggrieved party may also terminate the contract if the other party fails to perform before the time allowed it under Article 7.1.5 has expired.

Article 7.3.2

(Notice of termination)

(1) The right of a party to terminate the contract is exercised by notice to the other party.

(2) If performance has been offered late or otherwise does not conform to the contract the aggrieved party will lose its right to terminate the contract unless it gives notice to the other party within a reasonable time after it has or ought to have become aware of the offer or of the non-conforming performance.

Article 7.3.3

(Anticipatory non-performance)

Where prior to the date for performance by one of the parties it is clear that there will be a fundamental non-performance by that party, the other party may terminate the contract.

Article 7.3.4

(Adequate assurance of due performance)

A party who reasonably believes that there will be a fundamental non-performance by the other party may demand adequate assurance of due performance and may meanwhile withhold its own performance. Where this assurance is not provided within a reasonable time the party demanding it may terminate the contract.

Article 7.3.5

(Effects of termination in general)

(1) Termination of the contract releases both parties from their obligation to effect and to receive future performance.
(2) Termination does not preclude a claim for damages for non-performance.
(3) Termination does not affect any provision in the contract for the settlement of disputes or any other term of the contract which is to operate even after termination.

Article 7.3.6

(Restitution)

(1) On termination of the contract either party may claim restitution of whatever it has supplied, provided that such party concurrently makes restitution of whatever it has received. If restitution in kind is not possible an appropriate allowance should be made in money whenever reasonable.
(2) However, if performance of the contract has extended over a period of time and the contract is divisible, such restitution can only be claimed for the period after termination has taken effect.

Section 4: Damages

Article 7.4.1

(Right to damages)

Any non-performance gives the aggrieved party a right to damages either exclusively or in conjunction with any other remedies except where the non-performance is excused under these Principles.

Article 7.4.2

(Full compensation)

(1) The aggrieved party is entitled to full compensation for harm sustained as a result of the non-performance. Such harm includes both any loss which it suffered and any gain of which it was deprived, taking into account any gain to the aggrieved party resulting from its avoidance of cost or harm.

(2) Such harm may be non-pecuniary and includes, for instance, physical suffering or emotional distress.

Article 7.4.3

(Certainty of harm)

(1) Compensation is due only for harm, including future harm, that is established with a degree of certainty.

(2) Compensation may be due for the loss of a chance in proportion to the probability of its occurrence.

(3) Where the amount of damages cannot be established with a sufficient degree of certainty, the assessment is at the discretion of the court.

Article 7.4.4

(Foreseeability of harm)

The non-performing party is liable only for harm which it foresaw or could reasonably have foreseen at the time of the conclusion of the contract as being likely to result from its non-performance.

Article 7.4.5

(Proof of harm in case of replacement transaction)

Where the aggrieved party has terminated the contract and has made a replacement transaction within a reasonable time and in a reasonable manner it may recover the difference between the contract price and the price of the replacement transaction as well as damages for any further harm.

Article 7.4.6

(Proof of harm by current price)

(1) Where the aggrieved party has terminated the contract and has not made a replacement transaction but there is a current price for the

performance contracted for, it may recover the difference between the contract price and the price current at the time the contract is terminated as well as damages for any further harm.

(2) Current price is the price generally charged for the goods delivered or services rendered in comparable circumstances at the place where the contract should have been performed or, if there is no current price at that place, the current price at such other place that appears reasonable to take as a reference.

Article 7.4.7

(Harm due in part to aggrieved party)

Where the harm is due in part to an act or omission of the aggrieved party or to another event as to which that party bears the risk, the amount of damages shall be reduced to the extent that these factors have contributed to the harm, having regard to the conduct of each of the parties.

Article 7.4.8

(Mitigation of harm)

(1) The non-performing party is not liable for harm suffered by the aggrieved party to the extent that the harm could have been reduced by the latter party's taking reasonable steps.

(2) The aggrieved party is entitled to recover any expenses reasonably incurred in attempting to reduce the harm.

Article 7.4.9

(Interest for failure to pay money)

(1) If a party does not pay a sum of money when it falls due the aggrieved party is entitled to interest upon that sum from the time when payment is due to the time of payment whether or not the non-payment is excused.

(2) The rate of interest shall be the average bank short-term lending rate to prime borrowers prevailing for the currency of payment at the place for payment, or where no such rate exists at that place, then the same rate in the State of the currency of payment. In the absence of such a rate at either place the rate of interest shall be the appropriate rate fixed by law of the State of the currency of payment.

(3) The aggrieved party is entitled to additional damages if the non-payment caused it a greater harm.

Article 7.4.10

(Interest on damages)

Unless otherwise agreed, interest on damages for non-performance of non-monetary obligations accrues as from the time of non-performance.

Article 7.4.11

(Manner of monetary redress)

(1)   Damages are to be paid in a lump sum. However, they may be payable in instalments where the nature of the harm makes this appropriate.

(2)   Damages to be paid in instalments may be indexed.

Article 7.4.12

(Currency in which to assess damages)

Damages are to be assessed either in the currency in which the monetary obligation was expressed or in the currency in which the harm was suffered, whichever is more appropriate.

Article 7.4.13

(Agreed payment for non-performance)

(1)   Where the contract provides that a party who does not perform is to pay a specified sum to the aggrieved party for such non-performance, the aggrieved party is entitled to that sum irrespective of its actual harm.

(2)   However, notwithstanding any agreement to the contrary the specified sum may be reduced to a reasonable amount where it is grossly excessive in relation to the harm resulting from the non-performance and to the other circumstances.

Academy of European Private Lawyers

EUROPEAN CONTRACT CODE
PRELIMINARY DRAFT

BOOK ONE(*) CONTRACTS IN GENERAL
CHAPTER I

PRELIMINARY PROVISIONS

Article 1.

Notion

1. A contract is the agreement of two or more parties to establish, regulate, alter or extinguish a legal relationship between said parties.IIt can also produce obligations or other effects on only one of the parties.
2. Except as provided for in the following provisions, a contract can also be created by concluding acts or omissions, following a previous statement of intent or according to custom or good faith.

Article 2.

Contractual autonomy

1. The parties can freely determine the contents of the contract, within the limits imposed by mandatory rules, morals and public policy, as established in the present Code, Community law or national laws of the Member States of the European Union, provided always that the parties thereby do not solely aim to harm others.
2. Within the limits imposed by the preceding paragraph, the parties may draw up contracts not regulated by the present Code, particularly by combining different legal types and connecting several acts.

Article 3.

General and specific rules relating to contracts

1. Contracts, whether or not specifically named in the present Code, are subject to the general rules contained in this book.

(*) The first translation from French into English of the preliminary draft was done by Dr John Coggan of Oxford. The final version was the result of revision by Prof Maria Letizia Ruffini Gandolfi of Milan and Prof Peter Stein of Cambridge.

2. Rules applicable to contracts specifically named in this Code also apply, by analogy, to contracts not so named.

Article 4.

Rules relating to unilateral acts

Unless otherwise provided for in this Code or Community Law or mandatory rules in force in European Union Member States, the following rules relating to contracts must be observed, insofar as they are compatible, for unilateral acts carried out for the drawing up of a contract or during the subsequent relationship, even if intended to extinguish or invalidate said contract.

Article 5.

Contractual capacity and essential requirements of contract

1. Unless otherwise provided, persons concluding a contract shall have completed their eighteenth year of age, or , if emancipated, shall have obtained the necessary authorizations required by their national laws.
2. A contract concluded by a non-emancipated minor, by a person declared legally incapable or, even temporarily, incapable of understanding or intending, can be annulled in accordance with Article 150 below.
3. The essential elements of a contract are:
   a) the agreement of the parties;
   b) the content.
4. A special form is not required, except in cases and for the purposes specified by the rules of the present Code.

CHAPTER II

FORMATION OF CONTRACT

Section 1

Pre-contractual negotiations

Article 6.

Obligation of good faith

1. Each of the parties is free to undertake negotiations with a view to concluding a contract without being held at all responsible if said contract is not drawn up, unless his behaviour is contrary to good faith.

2. To enter into or continue negotiations with no real intention of concluding a contract is contrary to good faith.

3. If in the course of negotiations the parties have already considered the essentials of the contract whose conclusion is predictable, either party who breaks off negotiations without justifiable grounds, having created reasonable confidence in the other, is acting contrary to good faith.

4. If the situations considered in the above paragraphs occur, the party who acted contrary to good faith shall be liable for the harm he has caused to the other party to the extent of the costs the latter had to incur while the contract was being negotiated. Loss of opportunities caused by the negotiations underway shall also be made good.

Article 7.

Obligation to inform

1. During negotiations each party who knows or should know any fact or right which would help the other party to appreciate the validity of the contract and the benefit of concluding it is under a duty to inform the other.

2. In the event of information being omitted or falsely or partially declared, if the contract has not been made or is void, that party who has acted contrary to good faith is responsible to the other party as stated in article 6, para. 4. If the contract has been concluded, the former party must return monies paid or indemnify the latter, in both cases the amount being determined on equitable grounds by the court, save the other party's right to annul the contract on grounds of mistake.

Article 8.

Duty of confidentiality

1. The parties are bound to handle with reserve any confidential information obtained during negotiations.

2. Whichever party does not perform this obligation shall compensate the other for any loss, and if the former has also drawn undue benefit from this confidential information he must indemnify the latter to the extent of said enrichment.

Article 9.

Negotiations with consumers off commercial premises

1. The dealer who proposes a contract to a consumer off commercial premises is bound to inform him in writing of his right to withdraw from said contract in the manner and time period specified in Art. 159.

2. In this Code the word consumer means an individual who acts for purposes which do not come within the scope of his professional activities.

3. Failure to inform a consumer of his right as indicated in para. 1 of this Article produces the consequences itemised in Art. 159 at the dealer's expense and in favour of the consumer.

Article 10.

Negotiations in international-intercontinental dealings

1. Unless agreed to the contrary, parties to international-intercontinental contract negotiations are bound by generally accepted trade practice which they know or should know about regarding similar contracts in that same commercial field.

2. Whichever party does not fulfil the obligations of paragraph 1 of this article is responsible to the other party as stated in the previous articles insofar as they are applicable.

Section 2

Conclusion of contract

Article 11.

Oral offer and acceptance

1. The oral offer to form a contract, even if accompanied by a document delivered personally to the offeree at the same moment, must be accepted promptly unless it appears otherwise from the negotiations or the circumstances.

2. If the offer can be accepted subsequently or is made by telephone, the contract is concluded at the place where and moment when the offeror has or must be deemed to have knowledge of the other party's acceptance.

Article 12.

Written offer and acceptance

1. When one of the parties by whatever means sends the other an offer to conclude a contract, the contract is formed at the place and time when the offeror has or must be deemed to have knowledge of the acceptance of the other party.

2. If the offer is addressed to several specific persons the contract is concluded at the place and time when the offeror has or must be

deemed to have knowledge of the acceptance of one of the other parties, unless specified in the offer or reasonably to be deduced therefrom or from the circumstances that the offer lapses unless accepted by all the offerees or a specific number thereof. In the latter case, the contract is concluded at the place and time when the offeror has or must be deemed to have knowledge of the last of the acceptances.

Article 13.

Offer and invitation to make an offer

1. A statement aiming to form a contract amounts to an offer if it contains all terms of the said contract or sufficient information concerning its content that such statement can be the object of an acceptance pure and simple, and if it states or at least implies the offeror's intention to be bound in case of acceptance.
2. A statement not fulfilling the conditions of the preceding paragraph or which, being addressed to no specific persons, is an advertising communication does not constitute an offer and cannot be accepted. It is an invitation to make an offer, unless it contains a promise in favour of a person carrying out a certain action or revealing the existence of a given situation; in such case it is a promise to the public according to Art. 23.

Article 14.

Effectiveness of offer

1. The offer is not effective until it is received by the party to whom it is directed and may therefore be revoked until that moment by the offeror even if the latter has stated in writing that the offer is irrevocable or must be considered as such under Art. 17.
2. The offer is effective until it is revoked, rejected or lapses.

Article 15.

Revocation, rejection or lapse of offer

1. The offer can be revoked until the person to whom it was directed has sent the acceptance.
2. The offer, even if irrevocable, ceases to be effective when a rejection reaches the offeror even if the rejection be accompanied by a counter-offer.

3. Except as provided in Art. 11 para. 1 and Art. 16 para. 5, an offer, even if irrevocable, lapses:
    a) by the expiry of the time set for its acceptance, unless said acceptance has taken place in the way and in the forms laid down in the offer or according to law and custom;
    b) if no time is indicated, after the expiry of a period which can be deemed reasonable, taking account of the nature of the transaction, custom, and the speed of the means of communication which have been used.
4. The delay with which the offer reaches the person to whom it is addressed, if said delay is imputable to the offeror, reasonably postpones the lapse of the offer.

Article 16.

Acceptance

1. Acceptance is a statement or conduct which expresses the clear intention to conclude the contract in accordance with the offer.
2. The acceptance is effective when the offeror has knowledge of it.
3. Silence and inactivity amount to acceptance only when:
    a) such has been agreed by the parties or may be inferred from relations which have been established between the parties, circumstances or usage;
    b) the offer is for the purpose of concluding a contract having binding effects solely on the offeror.
4. In the case of b) of the above para., the offeree can reject the offer within the time required by the nature of the transaction or usage. Without such rejection the contract is concluded.
5. If the offeror gives prompt confirmation to the other party, he can treat the contract as concluded though knowledge of the acceptance arrive after the time fixed in Art. 15 para. 3 or the acceptance be not in the terms and conditions or form required in the offer.
6. An acceptance that does not conform to the offer involves a rejection of the latter, and is a new offer except as provided for in the following paragraph.
7. If the acceptance contains clauses which are different from but do not materially alter the offer, in that they deal with aspects marginal to the relationship, and if the offeror does not promptly communicate his disagreement with such modifications, the contract is deemed to be formed according to the terms of acceptance.
8. The acceptance can be revoked provided that the revocation reaches the offeror before or at the same time as said acceptance.

Article 17.

Irrevocable offer

1. The offer is irrevocable if the offeror has expressly bound himself to keep it open for a certain period or if, based on previous relations between the parties, negotiations, clause content or usage, it must be reasonably deemed as such. Except as stated in Art. 14 para. 1, any revocation of an irrevocable offer is without effect.

2. The same applies if the offer is irrevocable following an agreement between the parties.

Article 18.

Death or incapacity

In the event of the death or supervening incapacity of either the offeror or the offeree, the offer or acceptance do not become ineffective unless so justified by the nature of the transaction, or the circumstances.

Article 19.

Adhesion of other parties to contract

If other parties can adhere to a contract and the manner of adhesion has not been determined, said adhesion must be directed to such body as may have been constituted for the performance of the contract or, in the absence thereof, to all the original contracting parties.

Article 20.

Unilateral acts

Declarations and unilateral acts which must be communicated to the addressee to be effective produce their effects according to law, usage and good faith as soon as they come to the knowledge of the party to whom they are directed and can be revoked until that moment, even if their author declares them irrevocable.

Article 21.

Presumption of knowledge

1. The offer, acceptance, their withdrawal and revocation as well as the withdrawal and revocation of any other declaration of intent, including

the acts mentioned in the previous article, are deemed to be known at the moment they are communicated orally or, if written, delivered by hand to the addressee or reach his place of business or of work residence, postal address, habitual abode, or elected domicile.

2. The addressee can prove that, without his fault, it was impossible for him to have notice of said statements.

Article 22.

Offer to public

1. An offer to the public, when it contains the essential terms of the contract towards whose formation it is directed, is effective as an offer, unless it appears otherwise from the circumstances or usage.

2. Revocation of the offer to public, if made in the same form as the offer or in equivalent form, is effective even as to one who has had no notice of it.

Article 23.

Promise to public

1. A promise to the public, as in Art. 13 para. 2, is binding on the promisor as soon as it is made public and lapses after the date specified or implied by its nature or purpose or one year after its issue if the event contemplated in it has not occurred.

2. A promise made to the public can be revoked before the expiration of the times mentioned in the previous paragraph in the same form as the promise. In such case the person revoking the promise must pay fair compensation to those who, in good faith, were induced by said promise to incur expenditure, unless he can prove that the expected outcome would not have been obtained.

Article 24.

Concluding acts

Except to the extent provided in the preceding provisions, a contract is formed by means of concluding acts when all the requisites of the contract result from such acts, considering also previous agreements and relations, publication, if any, of price catalogues, offers to the public, laws, regulations and usage.

CHAPTER III

CONTENT OF CONTRACT

Article 25.

Requisites of content

The content of the contract must be useful, possible, lawful, determined or determinable.

Article 26.

Useful content

The content of the contract is useful when it is in accord with even non patrimonial interests of one or more parties.

Article 27.

Possibility of content

The content is possible when the contract can be performed without objective obstacles, of material or legal nature, which would absolutely prevent the aim being realised.

Article 28.

Supervening possibility of content

In a contract subject to a suspensive condition or time limit the content is deemed possible which becomes so before fulfilment of the condition or expiration of the time limit.

Article 29.

Future things

The contract can involve performance with respect to future things, except when forbidden by the present code or by Community or national laws.

Article 30.

Lawful and non-abusive content

1. The content of a contract is lawful and non-abusive when it is not contrary to mandatory rules laid down in the present Code, in Community or national laws, nor to public policy or morals.

2. The content of the contract is unlawful when it is the means of evading a mandatory rule.

3. As provided for in article 156, any contract is rescindable by which one of the parties, abusing the situation of the other's danger, need, incapacity to understand or intend, inexperience, economic or moral subjection, gets the other to promise or deliver to the former or to a third party a performance or other patrimonial advantages which are clearly disproportionate to what said party has given or promised in exchange.

4. In the general contract conditions provided for in Art. 33, those clauses are ineffective, unless specifically approved in writing, which create in favour of the person who has prepared them in advance limitations on liability, the power of withdrawing from the contract, or of suspending its performance, or which impose time limits involving forfeitures on the other party, limitations on the power to raise exceptions, restrictions on contractual freedom in relations with third parties, the extension or tacit renewal of the contract, arbitration clauses or derogations of the competence of the courts.

5. In contracts drawn up between a professional and a consumer, apart from Community rules, those terms are ineffective which have not been individually negotiated, if they create a significant imbalance, to the detriment of the consumer, between the rights and obligations arising under the contract, even if the professional is in good faith.

Article 31.

Determination of content

1. The content of the contract is determined when the object and ways of performance as well as the relevant time limits can be implied from the agreement of the parties.

2. If determination of the content of a contract is referred to one of the contracting parties or to a third party, it must be deemed, if there is any doubt, that they shall proceed on an equitable basis.

3. If determination of the content of a contract referred to one of the contracting parties or to a third party is not made within a reasonable period of time or is manifestly inequitable or erroneous, the determination is made by the court.

4. A determination left to the sole discretion of the third party can be impugned, by proving his bad faith in order that said determination can then be requested from the court.

5. If the contract does not specify the quality of the performance nor how it should be determined, a party must tender performance of not less than average quality taking into account usages.

6. If neither the pecuniary amount of the debt nor the way in which its determination is to be made have been agreed, the amount to be paid shall be taken from the official price lists of the place where performance must be made or, failing that, from the price generally paid in that place.

Article 32.

Implied terms

1. In addition to the express terms, the contract shall be deemed to include terms which
    a) are imposed by this code or by Community or national laws, even in place of different clauses introduced by the parties;
    b) stem from the obligation of good faith;
    c) must be deemed tacitly intended by the parties on the basis of previous business dealings, negotiations, the circumstances, and general and local usage;
    d) must be deemed necessary in order that the contract can produce the effects intended by the parties.
2. Unless otherwise provided by provisions concerning form, those statements made to each other by any of the contracting parties during negotiations or the forming of the contract with respect to a situation or expectation, of fact or law, concerning the subjects, contents or aims of the contract, shall be effective between the parties, if those statements correspond substantially to the contractual text and if they can have determined the agreement of said parties; availability of the remedies in Art. 151 and 157 is excepted.
3. In international-intercontinental contracts it is presumed, unless otherwise agreed, that the parties to the contract under consideration have implicitly considered applicable general usage regarding contracts of the same type and the same commercial area, which the parties know or are deemed to know or ought to know.

Article 33.

Standard conditions of contract

General conditions of a contract drawn up by one of the parties in order to regulate numerous specified contractual relations in a uniform manner are effective as to the other party, if he has knowledge of said conditions or should have knowledge thereof by using normal due attention, excepting and unless the parties concerned have agreed to replace or not to apply those or any part of those conditions, or if said conditions must be deemed abusive under the provisions of this present code or of Community or national laws.

CHAPTER IV

FORM OF CONTRACT

Article 34.

Special form required for validity

1. When a contract requires a special form in order to be valid, the contracting parties must adopt this form when they manifest, even through non-simultaneous acts where permissible, their intent to agree on all the elements of the contract.
2. A real contract is completed by delivery of the object of the contract, unless it is deemed, because of usage or agreement by the parties, that the parties intended to make an a-typical consensual contract.

Article 35.

Contracts invalid if not in writing

1. Contracts that transfer ownership or transfer or constitute other real rights in immovables must be made by public act or private writing, under penalty of nullity.
2. The preceding paragraph applies also to corresponding preliminary contracts, unless otherwise stated by the laws of the State in which the immovables are situated.
3. Community laws concerning land as well as those of the States in which the immovables are situated, which are the object of the contract, are excepted.
4. A gift shall be made by public act under penalty of nullity, even if its object is movables, unless their value is moderate given the economic condition of the donor.

Article 36.

Special form for proof of contract

1. If a special form is required for proving a contract, the contract must be drawn up in that form even if no such act existed when the parties decided to conclude the contract.
2. For proving contracts whose value exceeds 5,000 Euros, said contracts must be in writing. To be set up against a third party the contract must be of certain date unless it is proved that the third party had knowledge of the contract.

3. Where a special form is required for proving the contract, Community laws and those of the member States of the European Union that admit proof by other means are excepted.

Article 37.

Form agreed upon for contract

Unless Community or national laws of the place where the contract is concluded provide otherwise, if the parties have agreed in writing to adopt a specific form for the future contract it is presumed that such form was intended for the validity of the contract.

Article 38.

Contracts made using set forms or formularies

1. In contracts made by subscribing to forms or formularies printed or in any case prepared for the purpose of regulating certain contractual relationships in a uniform manner, clauses added to such forms or formularies prevail over the original clauses of said forms or formularies when they are incompatible with them, even though the latter have not been struck out.
2. The provisions of Art. 30 paragraph 4 must also be applied.

CHAPTER V

INTERPRETATION OF CONTRACT

Article 39.

Analysis of contract and evaluation of extrinsic elements

1. When statements in the contract are of such a kind as to reveal clearly and univocally the intention of the contracting parties, the content of the contract must be deduced from the literal sense of the terms used, considering the contract as a whole and connecting the various parts of the contract one with the other.
2. In place of the meaning commonly given to the words used, the meaning expressly declared by the contracting parties shall prevail or, failing that, the different technical meaning or that current according to commercial use and custom which is in accordance with the nature of the contract.
3. In case of doubts arising on examination of the text which cannot be resolved by a comprehensive evaluation of the text, whether said doubts

be in connection with the behaviour of the contracting parties even after the conclusion of but compatible with the text of the contract, said contract shall be interpreted according to the common intent of the parties which can be ascertained by reference to extrinsic elements concerning the parties.

4. In any case, the interpretation of the contract shall in no way produce effects contrary to good faith or reasonableness.

Article 40.

Ambiguous expressions

1. When, despite an evaluation made in accordance with Art. 39 para. 3, it is not possible to give a univocal meaning to the terms used by the contracting parties, the following provisions must be observed in order.
2. In case of doubt, the contract or the individual clauses shall be interpreted in the sense in which they can have some effect, rather than in that according to which they would have none.
3. Any clauses prepared by one of the contracting parties and which have not been the subject of negotiation, shall be interpreted in the case of doubt against the party who supplied them.

Article 41.

Obscure expressions

When, notwithstanding the application of the preceding articles, the contract remains obscure, it shall be understood in the sense least burdensome for the debtor, if it is gratuitous, and in the case of a non-gratuitous contract, in the sense which equitably reconciles the interests of the parties.

CHAPTER VI

EFFECTS OF CONTRACT

SECTION 1

General provisions

Article 42.

Effects on parties and in favour of third persons

A contract has the force of law between the contracting parties and produces effects for the benefit of third parties as laid down in the rules contained in this chapter.

Article 43.

Alteration, dissolution and withdrawal

1. The contract can be altered, renegotiated or dissolved by mutual consent, or in the situations stated in this Code, or by national or Community laws.
2. Except as provided for in Art. 57, para. 2, the power of unilateral withdrawal may be granted to one of the contracting parties or to both by agreement between the parties within the limits stated in this code or in national or Community laws.

Article 44.

Integration of extra-agreement factors in the contract

The effects of a contract derive not only from agreements between the parties but also from the rules in this Code, national and Community laws, usage, good faith and equity.

Article 45.

Obligatory effects

1. A contract can oblige the contracting parties to give, do or not do something.
2. The obligation to deliver a specified thing includes the obligation to look after it until its delivery and to take all appropriate steps to keep it in the state in which it was when the contract was concluded, excepting performance of the obligations due from the party who is to receive it and excepting destruction of or damage to the thing due to act of God or force majeure.
3. Unless otherwise agreed, the obligation to deliver a thing includes delivery of the accessories and appurtenances considered as such when the contract was agreed, and also any ungathered fruits produced by the thing after the agreement, and all measures should be to taken to bring this to effect.
4. When the object of the obligation is the delivery of things specified only as to kind, the debtor shall deliver things of the same kind and not below average in quality.
5. That party who has well grounded reason to fear that the behaviour of the other party not in conformity with the obligations explicitly or implicitly stated in the foregoing paragraphs may affect his rights, can obtain, even before the expiry of time limit established for the performance, one of the measures provided for in Article 172.

6. One who has promised an act or an obligation of a third party is bound to indemnify the other contracting party if the third party refuses to bind himself or does not perform the promised act.

7. The same obligation to indemnify the other contracting party applies to one who has stated unequivocally in writing that a fact or situation has happened or was to happen when and if that situation has not or does not occur.

Article 46.

Real effects

1. Unless explicitly agreed to the contrary, a contract, concluded to transfer ownership of a movable thing or to create or transfer a real right with respect to that thing, has real effects on the contracting parties and on third parties from the moment of delivery to the entitled person or to one charged by that person to receive it or to the carrier who, according to an agreement, must provide for delivery.

2. In the situation provided for in the preceding paragraph, if the one who transfers by contract a movable thing or a real right with respect to that thing is not the owner of the thing or entitled to the right thereof, the other party to the contract becomes the owner or entitled to the right in accordance with said contract at the moment of delivery, provided he is in good faith.

3. For registered movables and immovables, the rules concerning real effects in force in the different States at the moment when this Code is adopted shall continue to apply. In any case, for registered movables and land real effects occur only when the rules concerning publicity existing in the area of the immovable thing or where the registered movable property is to be delivered to the entitled person have been fulfilled.

4. In the above situation, the destruction of or damage to the thing is at the risk of the entitled person from the moment when that person, or one charged by him to receive the thing or the carrier who is bound by contract to deliver it, has accepted delivery.

Article 47.

Conveyance of the same thing or personal right of enjoyment to several persons

1. If, by successive contracts, a person conveys ownership of a movable thing or a real right with respect to the same thing to more than one contracting party and in the contracts it is stated that real effects occur apart from delivery of the object, the one who in good faith has actually come into possession is preferred.

2. If successive contracts convey the personal right of enjoyment of the same thing to several contracting parties, the enjoyment belongs to the party who first obtained it. If none of the contracting parties has obtained enjoyment, the one who has the prior title of certain date is preferred.

Article 48.

Undertaking not to alienate or to change price

1. An engagement assumed by one party not to alienate the thing received from the other party is effective only between the contracting parties, independently of the good or bad faith of a third buyer. Such undertaking is not effective unless limited to an appropriate period of time and unless it responds to an actual interest of the alienating person.
2. The provisions of the above paragraph also apply if one of the parties has undertaken not to alienate the thing received at a price different from that determined in the agreement.

Section 2

Accessory clause affecting the operation of the contract

Article 49.

Suspensive condition

1. The parties can condition the effectiveness of the contract, or of any clause or clauses of the contract, upon a future and uncertain event happening or not happening.
2. In this case, the contract becomes effective when the condition is fulfilled, unless the contracting parties have expressly agreed that the contract shall take effect from the time when the contract was made and have agreed on the way said retroactive effects can operate in accordance with law and the interests of the parties.
3. Even if the parties have agreed on a retroactive effect of the condition, the fruits taken are only due from the day on which the condition is fulfilled.

Article 50.

Resolutive condition

1. The parties can condition the dissolution of the contract, or of any clause or clauses in the contract, upon a future and uncertain event happening or not happening.

2. The effects of fulfilment of the condition retroact to the time when the contract was made only if the parties have so agreed, as provided in para. 2 of Art. 49, subject to the application of para. 3 of the same article.

Article 51.

Pendent condition

During the pendency of a suspensive condition the contracting party who is under an obligation or has created or transferred a real right, shall act according to good faith in order to safeguard the interests of the other party, who can, if such is the case, judicially request one of the remedies provided for in Art. 172, without prejudice to the right to damages.

Article 52.

Fulfilment of condition

1. If no date is fixed for the fulfilment of the condition, the condition is considered not fulfilled at the moment when fulfilment is shown as clearly impossible.
2. A condition is considered fulfilled or not fulfilled when the interested contracting party causes or prevents its fulfilment.

Article 53.

Unlawful or impossible conditions

1. A contract to which a condition, whether suspensive or resolutive, is attached is void if such condition is contrary to mandatory rules, public policy, or morality.
2. An impossible condition makes the contract void if it is suspensive; if it is resolutive, it is treated as non-existent.
3. If an unlawful or impossible condition is attached to a single clause of the contract, the provisions of the preceding paragraphs apply as to the validity of such clause, except for the provisions of Art. 144 on partial nullity.

Article 54.

Merely potestative condition

1. A contract subject to a suspensive condition whose fulfilment is dependent on the mere will of one of the parties is void.

2. A merely potestative suspensive condition attached to a single clause of a contract makes the whole contract void, subject to the provisions of Art. 144.

Article 55.

Condition referring to past or present

The contracting parties may agree that a contract, or one or several of its clauses, can be effective in the case of an event happening or not happening, in the past or the present, which the parties are unaware of at the time when the contract is made.

Article 56.

Starting and concluding dates

The contracting parties may agree that a contract, or one or several of its clauses, can be effective from a certain date and until a given date. The parties may also refer to events which are certain to occur in the future even if the precise moment is not certain.

Article 57.

Beginning and end of contractual effect in the absence of specific times

1. In the absence of an initial time agreed between the parties, the contract becomes effective as soon as it is made, except and unless a different initial time can be inferred from the circumstances or usage.
2. In contracts for continuous or periodic performance and in the absence of a time limit agreed between the parties, either party can withdraw from the contract by giving notice to the other party according to the contract, usage, or good faith.

Article 58.

Computation of time

1. If the parties have agreed an initial time or a time-limit without indicating a starting date or a future event but referring to a period of a certain number of days, months or years, the following provisions are to apply.
2. The first day of the period indicated by the parties shall not be counted.
3. Months are calculated disregarding the number of days in each month and referring to the day that corresponds to the day of the starting month.

4. If the period in question is in years, reference is made to the day and month corresponding to those of the starting year.

Article 59.

Charge

1. Contracts concluded gratuitously can be encumbered by a charge. The beneficiary is bound to perform the charge up to the limit of the value of his benefit.
2. Performance of a charge which is in the public interest, can be requested even by the public authority, after the death of the interested party.
3. The provisions of the above paragraphs also apply in the case of contracts in favour of third parties, with regard to that third party.

Section 3

Representation

Article 60.

Contract entered into by representative

1. A contract made by a representative in the name and in the interest of the principal, within the limits of the powers conferred by the principal on the representative, produces effects directly as to the principal, provided that the third party to the contract is aware that he is a representative.
2. Unilateral declarations made by or to a representative duly authorised to make or receive them produce effects directly as to the principal.
3. Paragraphs 1 and 2 also apply when the power of representation is conferred by law or by the court.

Article 61.

Apparent representative

If a person lacks authority to act in the name and in the interest of another, but this latter acts in such a way as to lead the third contracting party to believe reasonably that the apparent representative has been granted authority, the contract is concluded between the apparent principal and the third party.

Article 62.

Grant of authority

1. Power of representation can be conferred by written or oral statement directly to the representative or to the third contracting party . In the first situation, the third party contracting with a representative can require that he present proof of his authority, and if the power of representation has been conferred in written form, that he be given a copy of the authority signed by the representative as authentication.
2. Power of representation must be conferred in the form prescribed for the contract which is to be made by the representative.

Article 63.

Revocation of authority

1. If the principal has expressly agreed that the authority be irrevocable, the revocation of the authority is not effective without prejudice to the right to damages of the third party who, without fault, had no knowledge of the irrevocability.
2. When an authority is conferred also in favour of the representative or a third party, it cannot be revoked without the consent of the interested party, unless there is just cause.
3. When the representative power is revoked or ceases for some other reason, the document evidencing said power must be returned to the principal.
4. Revocation of a power of representation or modification in the powers of a representative shall not become effective if they were not made known to the third parties with whom the representative has or will come into contact, unless it is proved that they knew of them when the contract was made. Other grounds for termination of representation conferred by the principal cannot be set up against third parties who, without fault, had no knowledge of them.

Article 64.

Representation without power

1. One who has contracted as a representative without having the power to do so, or in excess of the authority conferred on him, is liable for any damage suffered by the third contracting party, as a result of his having believed in good faith that he was concluding a valid contract with the presumed representative, unless said third party avails himself of the power to treat the contract as made with the unauthorised representative.

2. It the third party does not avail himself of the power to request performance of the representative without powers, compensation under the preceding paragraph is due, at the choice of the aggrieved party for the damage he would have avoided if the representative had had the authority or had not stated he had it.

Article 65.

Ratification

1. A person can take upon himself the effects of a contract concluded in his name by a representative lacking authority, by addressing to the third party a ratification made with the formalities prescribed for the formation of such contract. The ratification must be made within a reasonable time and the third party can ask said interested person to make his intention clear as to ratification, setting a time limit at the expiration of which, in the event of silence, ratification is deemed to be denied.
2. The ratification has retroactive effect, but the rights of third parties in good faith are unaffected.
3. The power of ratification descends to the heirs.

Article 66.

Capacity of representative and principal

When a power of representation is conferred by a principal, it is sufficient for the validity of a contract made by the representative that the mental faculties of the latter be not impaired by sickness, whereas the principal must be capable of contracting, as stated in article 5 of this present code, and the contract must not be one into which he is forbidden to enter.

Article 67.

Subjective conditions

1. A contract is voidable if the consent of the representative is defective. If such defect concerns matters predetermined by the principal, the contract is voidable only if the consent of the latter is defective.
2. In cases in which good or bad faith, knowledge or ignorance of certain circumstances are a relevant, reference is made to the representative, unless the matters at stake were predetermined by the principal.
3. In no case can a principal who is in bad faith take advantage of the ignorance or good faith of the representative.
4. The rules of this article and of Art. 66 do not apply to a person who is charged merely to transmit the will of another.

Article 68.

Contract with oneself and conflict of interests

1. A contract which the representative makes with himself, whether acting on his own behalf or as the representative of another party, is voidable, unless specifically authorised by the principal, or unless the content of the contract is established in such a way as to preclude the possibility of a conflict of interests.
2. Such a contract can be attacked only by the principal.
3. A contract made by a representative in conflict with the interest of the principal can be annulled by the principal, if the conflict was known or ought to have been known by the third person.

Article 69.

An entrepreneur's agents and attorneys

1. One who is permanently appointed for the operation of an enterprise or branch of it, and as such establishes contact with third parties, is deemed to be empowered to make the same contracts in the name and on behalf of the entrepreneur, concerning the enterprise's activity, as can be concluded by anyone exercising a similar function in the same area.
2. Employees of the persons mentioned in the above paragraph who are in contact with third parties are considered empowered to conclude contracts concerning goods they deliver directly and to collect payment on delivery, unless there is a cashier operating on the premises where they are working.
3. In the case referred to in the previous two paragraphs, a third party can always require that the person in charge or his employees present proof of their authority.

Section 4

Contracts for persons to be named

Article 70.

Nomination of contracting party reserved and manner of naming declaration

1. Until the contract is concluded, a party can reserve the power to subsequently name the person who is to acquire the rights and assume the obligations arising from said contract. This power does not apply to contracts which cannot be concluded by a representative or for which

the identification of the actual contracting parties is required at the moment of stipulation.

2. The naming declaration of the person who is to replace the contracting party must be communicated to the other party within eight days from the making of the contract, unless the parties have established a different time limit. The provisions of Art. 21 of the present Code apply.

3. The declaration contemplated in the preceding paragraph is not effective unless accompanied by the expressed acceptance of the person named or unless a power of representation earlier than the contract exists.

4. If the contract is made in a particular form, even if such form is not prescribed by law, the naming declaration or the acceptance of the person named, as also the power of representation, are without effect unless they follow the same form.

5. If national law of the place where the contract is made or is to be performed requires a particular form of publicity, said form applies to the acts in the previous paragraph. For contracts concerning real estate or registered movable property, Art. 46, para.3 of the present code must be applied with the effects contemplated therein.

Article 71.

Effects of naming declaration and effects of lack of same

1. When the naming declaration has been validly made, the named person acquires the exclusive rights and assumes the obligations arising from the contract, with effect from the date when the contract was made.

2. The provisions of Art. 67 of the present code apply to the named person and to the contracting party who nominated him.

3. If the naming declaration is not validly made within the time limit set by law or by the parties, the contract definitively produces its effects between the original contracting parties.

Section 5

Contracts in favour of third parties

Article 72.

Right attributed to third parties

1. Parties can make a contract in order to attribute a right to a third party, charging one of said parties to perform in favour of the third party.

2. The third person can be unidentified or not exist at the time the contract is made.

3. Unless otherwise agreed, the third person acquires the right against the promisor at the making of the contract without his acceptance being necessary. He can nonetheless refuse the right. In that case, the promisor is bound to performance, not in favour of the third party but of the stipulator, unless it appears otherwise from the intention of the parties or the nature of the relationship.

4. The parties can modify or dissolve the contract by mutual consent until the third person has declared to them that he intends to avail himself of the stipulation in his favour.

Article 73.

Powers attributed to third parties

1. The rights of the third party can be subject to the condition that the stipulator fulfils his contractual obligations to the promisor. The third party, can take any action against the promisor, in the event of omitted, delayed or inexact performance, as if he himself had made the contract. He can also avail himself of any exemption or limitation of liability clause contained in the contract.

2. The promisor can raise against the third party defences based on the invalidity or ineffectiveness of the contract, omitted, delayed or inexact performance of said contract, but not defences based on other relationships between the promisor and the stipulator.

Article 74.

Applicable provisions

1. National rules remain in force regarding revocation of gifts for ingratitude or reduction of gifts for the reinstatement of the shares reserved when the right has been conferred on the third party gratuitously. In this last case, Art. 59 of the present code also applies.

2. If the contract has been concluded to transfer ownership of some thing or to attribute rights over that thing to a third person, the provisions of Art. 46 of this code shall apply.

CHAPTER VII

PERFORMANCE OF CONTRACT

Section 1

General provisions

Article 75.

Modes of performance

1. Each of the parties is bound to perform exactly and completely all the obligations laid on him by the contract, without request from the entitled party being necessary. In rendering due performance the debtor must conform to what has been agreed by the parties, good faith and the diligence required in each specific case in accordance with the agreements, circumstances and usage.
2. In the performance of obligations inherent in the exercise of a professional or entrepreneurial activity the degree of due diligence depends also on the nature of the due performance.
3. When a contract requires performance of an obligation to do by a professional, the obligation is fulfilled when the debtor has with due diligence set in motion all the acts necessary for the expected result unless according to the agreement between the parties, or the circumstances or usage, it must be deemed that performance is satisfied only when the final result is completely obtained.
4. The expenses of performance and receipt are charged to the debtor.

Article 76.

Authorisation of creditor or third party

1. When performance of the obligation requires the availability, presence or co-operation of the entitled party, the debtor must first inform the latter of his readiness to perform and they must agree the method of performance according to contract provisions. If the entitled person fails to inform the debtor of his availability within a reasonable time, or they cannot agree on the matter, the debtor can formally offer performance in accordance with Art. 105.
2. If performance of the obligation requires the availability presence, or co-operation of a third person or the authorisation of a public body, the debtor shall, unless otherwise stipulated, make the necessary contact with the third person or obtain the due permission.

Article 77.

Partial performance

1. The creditor can reject partial performance, even though the performance is divisible, unless otherwise provided by the contract, law or usage.
2. However, if the debt is partly liquidated and partly non-liquidated, the debtor can make payment and the creditor can demand payment of the former part of the debt according to the terms of the contract or to this present code, without waiting for the latter to become liquidated.

Article 78.

Performance different from that due and with property the debtor cannot dispose of

1. The debtor cannot free himself from the obligation by a performance different from that which is due, even if of equal or superior value, unless the creditor consents. In the latter case, the obligation is extinguished when the different performance is carried out.
2. When the different performance consists in the assignment of credit the obligation is performed when said credit has been collected, unless the parties have expressed a different intention and except if collection failed because of the transferee's negligence.
3. If the debtor has paid with property of which he had no right to dispose, he cannot request the return of said property except by offering payment with property of which he has the right to dispose. The creditor who in good faith received payment with property the debtor had no right to dispose of can return said property and demand performance due, without prejudice to his right to damages, but he must so conduct himself as not to prejudice the rights of the property owner or of the person who can lawfully dispose of property used by the debtor.

Article 79.

Performance by third party

1. Unless the contract stipulates that an obligation must be performed personally by the debtor or the nature of the performance requires it, the obligation can be performed by a person charged by the debtor or by a third person even without the debtor being aware, but the creditor can refuse such performance if it is prejudicial to himself or if the debtor has notified him of his objection.

2. The third party who has performed the obligation, if he had guaranteed it or if he had a direct interest in the performance, is subrogated to the rights of the creditor. The latter, however, can expressly subrogate the third person in his own right when said creditor receives payment, unless the third party has performed the obligation without the debtor knowing.

Article 80.

Incapacity of debtor or creditor

1. Payment by a debtor lacking capacity cannot be impugned, unless performance was different from that due and consisted of an act of disposition of property of significant value, having regard to the economic situation of the debtor, and provided that the payment does not require of the debtor capacity to act or the debtor's legal representative to intervene. However, the creditor can object to a declaration of annulment by proving that the payment was not prejudicial to the debtor.
2. Payment to a creditor not legally capable of receiving it discharges the debtor only in so far as it benefits the creditor. The burden of proof lies with the debtor.

Article 81.

Person to whom payment must be made

1. Payment must be made to the creditor or his representative specified for the purpose, or to the person designated by the creditor, even if not mentioned in the contract, or authorised to receive it by law or by the judge. Payment made to a third party not entitled to receive it frees the debtor if the creditor ratifies it or in so far as the latter has benefited thereby.
2. The debtor who makes payment to a person who, on the basis of unequivocal circumstances, seems entitled, even if as an apparent representative, to receive it, is discharged if he proves he was in good faith. The person who receives the payment is bound to restore it to the true creditor.
3. Payment to a creditor not entitled to receive it because of the pendency of sequestration, expropriation or similar proceedings against him is ineffective.

Article 82.

Place of performance

1. Performance of contractual obligations shall be carried out at the place specified or implied in the contract, or, failing such provision,

according to usage and circumstances, given the nature of the performance required. If the place in which the performance is to be carried out is not specified in the contract, or cannot be inferred, from the aforesaid criteria, the following rules apply.

2. The obligation to deliver a certain and specified thing shall be performed at the place where the thing was situated when the obligation arose. If said obligation concerns goods produced by the debtor, they shall be delivered at the business premises of the debtor at the time the obligation matures.

3. The obligation having as its subject matter a sum of money shall be performed, at the debtor's risk, at the residence of the creditor, or if he is an entrepreneur, at the creditor's business premises, at the time the obligation matures. If the residence or business premises are different from those when the obligation arose, and if this fact makes performance more burdensome, the debtor, by informing the creditor in advance, has the right to make payment at his own residence.

4. In all other cases, the obligation shall be performed at the residence of the debtor at the time the obligation matures.

Article 83.

Time of performance

1. Contractual obligations shall be performed at the time indicated or implied in the contract or, failing such provision, according to usage and circumstances, given the nature of the performance required and the manner and place of performance. If no time of performance has been specified in the contract or cannot be determined on the basis of these criteria, and it is not reasonable to allow the debtor adequate time to prepare and render due performance, the obligation must be carried out immediately.

2. Unless otherwise agreed, performance must be made at a reasonable time and, if the creditor is an entrepreneur, during normal business hours.

3. If, in the contract, a time limit for performance is established or such can be determined on the basis of the above criteria, it is presumed to be in favour of the debtor who can carry out performance even before the expiry of the term, unless said term appears to have been established in favour of the creditor or of both. If the time limit is set for the benefit of the creditor, he can refuse performance before the term, unless it is not prejudicial to his interests.

4. If the time limit has not been fixed for the benefit of the creditor, he can demand performance before the expiry of the term, only if the debtor has become insolvent or, by his own act, has reduced the security he had furnished or has failed to furnish the security promised.

5. The debtor cannot seek reimbursement for payments made in advance due to not knowing the time limit.

6. Computation of the time limit for performance shall be made according to the provisions of Art. 58. Unless otherwise agreed, if the term expires on a non-working day, it is extended to the next working day, except where usage dictates otherwise.

Article 84.

Imputation of payment

1. A person who owes several debts of money or of the same kind of thing to the same person can declare at the time of payment which debt he intends to satisfy. The imputation can also concern obligations stemming from voidable and unenforceable contracts. It is binding on the creditor, in the absence of his refusal within reasonable time.

2. If the debtor does not indicate his intention, even by implication, to the creditor, the latter can, by issuing a receipt or later, declare to which debt he intends to impute the payment, provided the obligation is valid and enforceable; the creditor cannot subsequently change the imputation. The debtor cannot object said imputation, unless the creditor, for this own advantage, has resorted to subterfuges or unfairly availed himself of the circumstances.

3. If neither the debtor nor the creditor have expressed an imputation, the payment shall be imputed to the matured debt; among several matured debts, to that which has least security; among equally secured debts, to the one which is most burdensome to the debtor; among equally onerous debts, to the oldest. If these criteria do not help, imputation is made proportionally to the various debts.

Article 85.

Issue of receipt and release of securities

1. The creditor who receives payment shall, upon request from the debtor, issue a release in a form which the latter can legitimately claim. The expenses of issuing said release are, unless otherwise agreed, charged to the debtor.

2. The creditor shall make a notation on the instrument establishing the debt that the debt has been paid, even if the instrument is returned to the debtor, who is entitled to request it. If the creditor declares that he cannot return said document, the debtor is entitled to demand that a statement to that effect be added to the release form.

3. The creditor who has received payment shall return the movable property given as security, shall permit the release of other property from the real guarantees given for the credit and from any other encumbrance which may in any way restrict the right to dispose of the property.

Section 2

Performance of certain contractual obligations

Article 86.

Performance of pecuniary obligations

1. Pecuniary debts are discharged upon the debtor putting at the disposal of the creditor in the normally practised ways the total sum due, in money which is legal tender at the time and place of payment. Payments made via a bank or in similar form extinguish the debt without the creditor having to accept them, or, failing this, without their tender in accordance with Article 105.

2. If the sum due was indicated in money which is no longer legal tender or which is no longer acceptable or cannot be used at the moment of payment, the debt must be discharged in money which is legal tender, equal in value to the original money.

3. If a pecuniary debt is to be paid at some period after it was created the debtor shall, unless otherwise agreed, pay the creditor compensatory interest on the sum at the rate agreed in writing by the parties concerned; in the absence of an agreement, the provisions of Art. 169, para. 3, shall be applied. If, at the time of payment, the money has undergone over 50% depreciation in real value since the obligation was assumed, the debtor, unless otherwise agreed, shall pay the creditor, who is not delaying performance of the obligation, a supplementary amount over and above the nominal value of the debt. This re-evaluation shall be calculated according to Art. 169, para. 4.

4. Voluntary payment of interest at a higher rate than that indicated in the preceding paragraph, provided the rate is not usurious, does not give the right to reclaim the excess.

5. Unless otherwise agreed, the debtor who delays the payment of a pecuniary debt is responsible for any loss incurred by the creditor as a result of devaluation, even if the amount is inferior to that in paragraph 3 of this article, and following the provisions of Art. 169, para.4.

Article 87.

Performance of cumulative and alternative obligations

1. When a contractual obligation requires two or more performances, the debtor shall make all of them unless it results otherwise from the agreement of the contracting parties, the circumstances or usage.
2. The debtor of an alternative obligation is discharged by making one of the two or more performances contemplated in the obligation but cannot make part of one and part of the other or others.
3. Unless the parties have agreed otherwise, the election is for the debtor and becomes effective either upon declaration of his option or at the beginning of one of the performances.
4. If the party who is entitled to the election does not exercise his option within the stated time limit, election passes to the other person unless the latter intends to dissolve the contract and require payment of damages.
5. If one of the two performances becomes impossible, for a reason imputable to neither of the parties, the obligation is considered pure and simple. If the impossibility can be imputed to one party, the other can consider that the former is not fulfilling his obligation.

Article 88.

Performance of indivisible and in solido obligations

1. Save agreement to the contrary and always providing that the law does not state otherwise, when a contract requires performance of the same obligation from two or more debtors, the creditor can, at his choice, require of any one of the several debtors performance of the entire obligation; performance by any co-debtor extinguishes the debt.
2. The co-debtor who has totally or partially performed the obligation can claim from each of the other co-debtors that portion of the debt paid for which each was responsible. The shares of each are, unless otherwise agreed, presumed equal.
3. If a performance is due from one debtor to several creditors, each creditor can demand performance of the entire obligation only if the obligation is indivisible, or it has been so agreed, or the law so states; in such a case, the performance obtained by one creditor extinguishes the obligation towards all the others. In relations *inter se* the *in solido* obligation is divided among the various creditors in equal parts, unless otherwise agreed and unless it was contracted solely in the interest of one or some of them.
4. In the case at para. 1 of this Article, unless otherwise agreed, notice to perform and any other communication or declaration concerning the debt, even if intended to interrupt the limitation or to waive the credit, must be addressed to all the co-debtors, on pain of inefficacy, unless

said communications are to be effective only as to one co-debtor for his share of the obligation. In the case mentioned at para. 3 of this Article, any communication made to the debtor by one of the creditors is effective only for the communicator, unless otherwise agreed.

5. The provisions of this Article are applicable to obligations which are indivisible by law, convention or their nature.

CHAPTER VIII

NON-PERFORMANCE OF CONTRACT

Section 1

General Provisions

Article 89.

Non-performance

Subject to the following provisions, a contractual obligation is deemed not performed when one of the parties, his representatives or employees, behaves differently than as provided by the contract or there occurs a situation, of law or fact, different from what may be considered to have been promised.

Article 90.

Debtor who makes written declaration of non-performance

1. When the debtor has declared, in writing, to the creditor that he does not intend to perform the obligation, the latter may, in writing and without delay, and in any case within eight days, inform the former that, because of said declaration, he considers the obligation not performed. In the absence of such communication, the creditor cannot refuse a subsequent performance.

2. Within eight days of receipt of the communication provided for in the previous paragraph, the debtor can in writing contest the creditor's declaration of non-performance and, unless the creditor, within the subsequent eight days revises his position in writing, the debtor must apply to the court having jurisdiction within the subsequent 30 days. Failing this on the part of the debtor, the non-performance is deemed definitively ascertained.

3. Subject to a different agreement between the parties, the time limits indicated above and below are suspended by holidays and non-working days, and calculated according to Art. 58.

Article 91.

Debtor unable to perform

1. If, before the expiration of the time-limit there are reasonable grounds for believing that the debtor is not or has not been able to put himself in a position to perform the obligation or to perform it without significant defects, and this situation is not due to an act or omission by the creditor, the latter can invite the former in writing to give adequate guarantee, within a reasonable time, which shall be not less than fifteen days, that performance will follow and can declare that, failing guarantee, non-performance shall be deemed definitively ascertained.

2. A debtor who fails to give the requested guarantee can, in writing within eight days, contest the creditor's request and unless said creditor, within the subsequent eight days revises his position in writing, the debtor must apply to the court within the subsequent 30 days. Failing this on the part of the debtor, the non-performance is deemed definitively ascertained.

Article 92.

Failure to deliver a specific thing

An obligation to deliver a certain specific thing is deemed not performed if the thing is not delivered within the time limit or in the manner provided for or is delivered with defects or a thing is delivered which is or can be deemed different, unless, and without prejudice to compensation for loss,

a) the debtor obtains from the creditor an extension of the time or the court grants it on reasonable grounds;

b) the defects can be repaired and the creditor accepts repair at the debtor's expense, within reasonable time, or the court authorises repair;

c) the thing to be delivered is lost or has deteriorated without the debtor being responsible or the creditor accepts the delivery of a different thing or the court declares that on reasonable grounds it can be deemed that performance has taken place in such a way;

d) the creditor exercises his power of only making a payment in proportion to the lesser value of the thing received, the amount of which is to be fixed by the court failing prior agreement.

Article 93.

Non-delivery of a quantity of things specified only as to kind

The obligation to deliver a quantity of things specified only as to kind is deemed not performed if the things are not delivered within the time limit or in the manner provided for or are delivered in quantity or quality inferior or superior to that due or of different type, unless, without prejudice to compensation for loss,

a) the debtor obtains from the creditor an extension of the time for delivery of all the items or of those not yet delivered or a delay is granted by the court for reasonable grounds;

b) the creditor returns the surplus to the debtor or he does not return it and pays for it according to the price in the contract;

c) the creditor accepts the goods of inferior quality or quantity by paying proportionately less, the amount being fixed by the court failing agreement.

d) some or all of the goods due are lost or have deteriorated without the debtor being responsible, and the creditor accepts delivery of different goods or the replacement of some goods or the repair of those with defects or the court has reasonable grounds to consider the obligation performed by reason of the delivery of different or partially replaced or repaired goods.

Article 94.

Non-performance of an obligation to do

1. An obligation to do something is considered not performed when the work is not done within the contracted time limit, or it is partially or defectively done, or unsuitable things or materials are used, unless, in these cases, and without prejudice to compensation for loss, the creditor or court grants the debtor a period of time to finish the works or eliminate the defects or repair the damage or replace the inappropriate things and materials used, provided such repairs or replacements can be considered reasonable having regard to the contract, usage or good faith.

2. There is no non-performance if the debtor, without it being his responsibility, is unable to perform a personal obligation to do something, and the creditor or the court allows the debtor to have himself replaced by another competent person, all responsibility for the performance remaining with the debtor.

3. If the obligation is of the type provided for in Article 75, para.3, it is deemed not performed if the result is not satisfactory, unless the debtor can prove, that he is professionally qualified, when that is required, and that he has made timely use of the necessary techniques, means, tools, places and appropriate employees according to the circumstances.

Article 95.

Non-performance of a negative obligation

The obligation not to do something shall be deemed not performed every time an act is done in breach of it, unless said act is performed by representative or an employee who did not know of the agreement not to do it and said agreement was included in a wider contractual context and the creditor or the court allows the debtor a time limit for demolition or reinstatement and that this demolition or reinstatement duly occurs, in good time, without prejudice to compensation for loss.

Article 96.

Default of debtor

1. The debtor shall not be considered in default if
   a) no final date, nor time expressed in a period of days, months or years has been stipulated for performance, and the creditor has not, in advance, given the debtor notice in writing of performance being required within a reasonable time;
   b) the creditor or the judge have, in advance, extended the debtor's time limit for performance;
   c) in bilateral contracts, the creditor is delaying his performance and the term for it has already expired;
   d) the debtor has tendered in due time the entire performance to the creditor, requesting him to accept it, the effects of a possible default of the creditor remaining unaffected.

2. If the terms at letters a) and b) of this Article have expired and in the absence of the situations at c) and d) of this Article, the debtor is deemed in default. Consequently he is not discharged and is responsible– according to the provisions of Art. 162 ff. – for the damages, even if the loss of the due thing or the impossibility of performance cannot be imputed to the debtor, except when he proves that the thing or the matter of performance would also have failed if it had been in the care of the creditor. In this latter case, the debtor must give the creditor the sum obtained from the insurer or from the person responsible for the destruction or withdrawal of the thing due or for the non-performance of the work.

Article 97.

Obligations which cannot be considered non-performed

1. Even if the debtor delays in performing the obligation due or only renders it partially, said obligation cannot be considered not performed if

unforeseen extraordinary events have previously happened which made performance excessively onerous and which therefore give the debtor – as laid down by Art. 157 – the right to a re-negotiation of the contract. The debtor must, however, have served notice on the creditor of his intention to avail himself of this right, before the expiry of the term fixed for performance, or before the creditor has addressed to the debtor the notice provided for in Art. 96 letter a) above.

2. If after the contract is made the performance becomes objectively impossible, for reasons not imputable to the debtor, the obligation cannot be considered not performed; but if it can be deemed that the contract states or implies a guarantee that performance is possible, the debtor shall compensate the creditor for the damage incurred through the latter's belief in the possibility of performance.

Article 98.

Subsequent better offer

Non-performance occurs when the debtor fails to render due performance and alleges that he has received a better offer for the same performance from elsewhere, unless such possibility of withdrawal is stated or implied in the contract.

Article 99.

Non-performance of protection duties

In carrying out the due performance, the debtor must take all precautions necessary to ensure no damage occurs to the person of the creditor, his employees and property; in the event of failure to respect this duty, the obligation is considered not performed if damage occurs during or because of the performance and is an immediate, direct consequence thereof. Otherwise the debtor is liable in tort.

Article 100.

Non-performance due to the non-realisation of promised situations

1. The contractual obligation is non-performed if a certain event or state of fact or law which one of the contracting parties promised or assured – even without reward – would occur does or did not happen.
2. If in a declaration, which is not in the contract and is not the object of a promise or assurance, it is stated that an event has happened or not, or will happen or not, and that declaration is not in accordance with fact, the person who made the declaration can be responsible in tort to the one who suffered damage as a result of said declaration.

Article 101.

Early performance or in quantity superior to that due

The creditor may receive performance by the debtor in advance of the time fixed or in greater quantity than due. In this latter case, he shall pay a proportionally higher amount, though if he refuses he shall not be considered in default.

Article 102.

Performance without interest to creditor

A creditor cannot refuse an offered performance by claiming it is no longer useful to him and is of no benefit because of supervened circumstances, unless such right of refusal can be deduced, even implicitly, from the contract and the creditor has warned the debtor in due time of the supervening occurrence of said circumstances and in any case before the debtor has started preparing or undertaking performance.

Section 2

Default of creditor

Article 103.

Notion of creditor's default

The creditor is in default if, for no valid reason, he does not accept, or refuses, or prevents, or obstructs performance on the part of the debtor, or does not exercise the option provided for in Art. 87, para. 2, for an alternative credit if the other party does not intend to make the election himself, or does not obtain – when he is obliged – the presence of a third person or the permit or licence from the public authority prescribed in Art. 76, para. 2, or in any case, by action or inaction, prevents the debtor from performing.

Article 104.

Default of creditor which results in non-performance

1. In the situation of the preceding Article, the debtor can serve a written notice to the creditor to desist from his behaviour specifying which acts of commission or omission have prevented or hindered performance and indicating which acts or omissions must cease or which must be

performed by the creditor, within an appropriate time having regard to the nature of the obligation, usage and good faith. In any case such time cannot be less than 15 days.

2. When the time limit expires, unless the behaviour has ceased, the creditor shall be considered responsible for non-performance.

Article 105.

Actions required for discharge of debtor

1. In the situation of Art. 103, instead of establishing the creditor's non-performance, the debtor intending to release himself by performing the obligation due, must make to the creditor, in the appropriate place for performance, actual tender or tender by notice of the entire due performance including accessories, fruits and interest, in the appropriate form as prescribed, on application, by the court of First Instance having jurisdiction of the debtor, in the place where the tender must be made.

2. If it is impossible for the debtor to know the precise quantity of money or things due, he can, with the leave of the court, offer an amount or quantity based on his knowledge, promising to pay or provide the difference.

3. If the creditor accepts the tender and receives performance, the debtor is discharged. In the situation of para. 2 of this Article, discharge is subject to the debtor paying what is still due in accordance with a well-founded request of the creditor.

4. If the creditor refuses the offer of performance of an obligation to give, the debtor, in order to obtain discharge, must deliver what is due in the form prescribed by the court mentioned in para. 1 of this Article, to whom the debtor can make the pertinent request in the same application contemplated in the previous para 1. The regularity of the delivery and the discharge are determined by the court. If the obligation is one of doing, the debtor must perform as prescribed by the court who subsequently finds correct the debtor's performance and his discharge.

5. The tender alone is sufficient – and delivery or performance is unnecessary – when the performance cannot be made because of the absence or incapacity to receive it of the creditor or of his representative or there is doubt, without the debtor's responsibility, as to the person to whom performance must be made, or several people claim the right to the performance, or the document establishing said right has been lost, and these circumstances have been specified in the application contemplated in para. 1 of this Article.

Section 3

Effects of non-performance

Article 106.

Exoneration and limitation of liability clauses

1. Any agreement in advance limiting the debtor's liability for fraud or gross negligence is void.
2. Any agreement that one of the contracting parties can not raise exceptions in order to avoid or delay due performance is without effect as to exceptions for nullity, voidability and rescission of the contract. However, even in cases in which the agreement is effective, the court, recognising that there are serious reasons, can suspend judgment and, if that is the case, require security.
3. Except as provided in Article 30 on abusive clauses, an agreement limiting or excluding the debtor's liability for slight fault is without effect if the creditor made it while he was in the service of the debtor or the liability arises during professional or entrepreneurial activity exercised in a monopolistic regime under a licence from the authority.
4. The parties can make valid agreements concerning margins of tolerance in the performance or franchise in the compensation for loss which must be in accordance with usage or good faith, considering the status of the parties and the nature of the performance.
5. The parties can validly make agreements on mere presumptions of the fortuitousness of events which, in the situations contemplated, are normally due to fortuitous events.

Article 107.

Substantial non-performance

1. For the purposes of the following rules, non-performance is substantial if it concerns one of the main (not secondary) obligations in the contract, and also when, taking into account the qualities of the persons and the nature of the performance, non-performance inflicts harm on the creditor depriving him substantially of what he was entitled to expect under the contract.
2. Non-performance is considered substantial when
   a) it is total;
   b) it is partial but the creditor has objectively no further interest in complete performance.

3. Secondary obligations are those whose performance has slight importance with respect to the economics of the contractual relationship and the creditor's interest.

Article 108.

Creditor's right to suspend performance of bilateral contracts

1. In contracts providing for mutual counter-performance, if one of the parties fails to perform or offer to perform his obligation, regardless of the gravity of the non-performance, the creditor can suspend his own performance which is due at the same time or subsequently, unless such refusal to perform is contrary to good faith.
2. The refusal is deemed, in particular, contrary to good faith when:
   a) it creates excessively onerous consequences for the other party;
   b) the non-performance is not substantial and the creditor's refusal causes the extinguishing of his obligation;
   c) the refusal prejudices a basic right of the person.

Article 109.

Early performance or in greater quantity or after the expiry of the essential time limit

1. Subject to the provisions of Art. 101, the creditor has the right to refuse performance offered or made before the time limit, or in greater quantity than that due, provided his refusal is not contrary to good faith as understood in the preceding Article as far as applicable.
2. In any case the creditor has the right to refuse performance offered or made after the expiry of a time limit which has been agreed as essential.

Article 110.

Extension of time and allowance of instalment

1. If an extension of time is granted by creditor or judge to the debtor before the commencement of performance or when the contract is only partially performed, the creditor cannot have recourse to the remedies provided for in the following Articles until expiry of said term, but he can take precautionary measures or apply to the judge for an injunction, without prejudice to the right to compensation for loss.
2. If creditor or judge have granted the debtor an instalment payment of the debt, the debtor loses this benefit in case of default in the payment of only one instalment which exceeds one-eighth of the total debt.

Article 111.

Specific performance

1. The debtor not having yet performed the obligation, whatever the importance of non-performance may be, the creditor can obtain performance or completion in specific form, if this is objectively possible and, in any case subject to compensation for loss.

2. In particular, the creditor can:
   a) judicially obtain delivery of the due certain and specified thing or quantity of things specified only as to kind, and which the debtor can dispose of or has transferred to a third party in bad faith or by a simulated act;
   b) obtain the court's authorisation to acquire where possible and at the debtor's charge, the certain specific thing or quantity of things specified only as to kind which are due and which are at the disposal of third parties;
   c) obtain that where possible, the debtor be ordered to carry out or complete the due obligation; the creditor can also obtain judicial authorisation to carry out or complete himself said performance or to get a third party to do so at the expense of the debtor;
   d) obtain that the debtor be ordered to destroy what he has done in violation of an obligation not to do, or the creditor can obtain judicial authorisation personally to destroy what has been done in violation of an obligation not to do or to get a third party to destroy it, at the expense of the debtor;
   e) obtain a judgment producing the same legal effect of the contract which the debtor was bound to conclude by a preliminary contract he has not performed.

3. In order to induce the non-performing debtor to comply with the judgment requiring objectively possible, specific performance of the obligation, the court can also fine the debtor who does not comply or complies late up to three times the value of the performance due. This sum shall be divided between creditor and the State in the respective ratio of seventy percent to thirty percent. Said fine can be either a fixed sum producing interest in the amount fixed by the court or a sum for each day of delay, which shall be divided as stated above.

Article 112

Substitutions in specific form, and repairs

1. If the debtor has not fulfilled the obligation in whole or in part, the creditor is entitled to obtain where objectively and

subjectively possible and subject to compensation for loss, that the debtor:

a) shall deliver a different thing of which he can completely dispose or make a different performance – which can adequately satisfy the creditor's interest – against payment of an additional sum or the return of part of the sum already paid; in the absence of agreement between the parties the court shall fix the sums for the cases of greater or lesser value of the thing or performance;

b) shall provide for the repairs necessary to eliminate the defects or imperfections in the things delivered or in the work done;

c) shall, in the event of problems arising during installation or first functioning of the thing delivered and due to a defect thereof, arrange for its correct installation and first functioning and provide for technicians to explain its use and, where necessary, to be responsible for the maintenance required for its proper operation for a certain period;

2. The creditor can also obtain authorisation from the court to carry out or have carried out by a third party any necessary repairs at the expense of the debtor.

3. The creditor intending to exercise any of the above rights must, on discovery of the defects, promptly notify the debtor.

4. Before the creditor sends the notice provided for in para. 3, the debtor, upon previous notice to the creditor, can provide replacement, elimination of defects or completion of delivery at his own expense.

Article 113.

Reduction in price

1. The creditor who intends to accept delivery of a different thing of lower value or with imperfections, or a smaller quantity than due, or performance of an obligation to do something different from that agreed or with imperfections, has the right, after promptly giving notice to the debtor, to pay a lower price than that agreed. If that is the case, he can obtain the return of part of the sum paid in proportion fixed, in the absence of agreement between the parties, by the court.

2. If the performance offered or made is of superior value to that due, Art. 101 shall apply.

Article 114.

Right to dissolve the contract

1. Substantial non-performance as understood in Art. 107 above gives the creditor the right to dissolve the contract by serving notice on the debtor to perform within a reasonable time, which shall be not less

than fifteen days, and declaring that, if the time limit expires without performance, the contract shall be deemed automatically dissolved.

2.   If the contract contains a clause providing that one party has the right to dissolve the contract upon non-performance of a specified obligation by the other party, non-performance shall be considered in any case substantial according to Art. 107, and the contract shall be deemed dissolved when the interested party gives notice to the other that he intends to avail himself of the dissolution clause.

3.   After expiry of the time indicated in para 1 of this Article or when the debtor has received the notice provided for in para 2, the creditor cannot demand any more and can refuse performance of the contract and the debtor is not bound any more to fulfill it. In addition the creditor can exercise the rights provided in Art. 115 and Art.116.

4.   Partial dissolution of a contract is also possible if the creditor decides to accept what he has received, although the debtor has not performed the entire obligation, the creditor having the right to make a proportionally lesser payment as provided for in Art. 92 and Art. 93.

5.   If non-performance occurs during the course of a contract for periodic or continuous performance, the effect of dissolution does not extend to performance already made.

6.   The creditor has no right to dissolve a contract whose non-performance only depends on action or omission attributable to the him, subject to the application of Art. 103 and Art. 104. Neither has the creditor this right if he has made the other party convinced that dissolution would not be sought even in the case of substantial non-performance.

Article 115.

Obligation to return

Subject to Art. 114, para. 5, in consequence of the dissolution of the contract, the creditor has the right to the return from the non-performing debtor of what said creditor has already given for performance due or, in any case, because of the contract, saving the right to compensation for loss and the obligation to return what he has already received according to Art. 160.

Article 116.

Damages

1.   Subject to the provisions of the above Articles, in the event of non-performance, independently of its importance the creditor is entitled to compensation for loss according to Art. 162 ff.

2. This right can be exercised in addition to those provided for in the above Articles and as provided for in Art. 171.

Article 117.

Rights of third party in good faith

The exercise of the above rights by the creditor does not prejudice the rights acquired by third parties in good faith over the property of the creditor or over what is due to him, before said creditor, justifiably fearing non-performance, has notified the third persons in writing or, in the case of land or registered movable property, before the transcription of his judicial applications in public records, according to the laws of the State where provided. This applies except for the provisions of Art. 161.

CHAPTER IX

ASSIGNMENT OF CONTRACT AND OF RELATIONSHIPS ARISING THEREFROM

Section 1

Assignment of contract

Article 118.

Notion

1. In the relationships arising from a contract which has not exhausted its effect, each party can assign his position totally or partially, gratuitously or non-gratuitously to third person or persons, if the actual relationship permits.
2. In such an event the parties can alter the content of the contract assigned and can also agree and compromise on the rights and obligations already derived or which can derive from the contract or from its performance or non-performance.
3. Unless otherwise agreed, the arbitration clause in said contract is also transferred.
4. If the transfer of contractual position occurs not by agreement of the parties but by operation of law and between living persons or by succession on death, the rules of this section shall not apply but those existing in each of the European States, save for the application of the principles of private international law if necessary.

Article 119.

Modes of assignment

1. A contract can be transferred by agreement between the assignor and the assignee and the assignment becomes effective when notice is given to the original contracting party if this latter has previously consented or when said party gives notice of acceptance to the assignor and the assignee.

2. Assignment can also take place by means of a trilateral agreement between the assignor, the original contracting party and the assignee and must be made thus in the case considered in para. 2 of Art. 118. The agreement must define the position of all contracting parties, their respective rights and obligations and any time limits.

3. When the assignment requires the authorisation of a judicial or administrative body or of a third party, the transfer is effective after said authorisation.

4. If the clause 'to the order' or equivalent is inserted in a document containing all the elements of the contract, endorsement of the document causes the endorsee to take the place of the endorser in the contract.

5. For the assignment to be valid it must take the form required for the contract assigned. If the notice to the original contracting party, his acceptance, or the trilateral contract are of certified date, the assignment is effective toward third persons, unless it is proved that said persons had full knowledge thereof.

6. Rules in force in the member States of the European Union are unaffected which provide for particular forms for the contract establishing assignment, and the intervention therein of certain persons or bodies.

Article 120.

Rights and duties of parties

1. The assignor is released from his obligations to the original contracting party and the assignee becomes responsible for them from the time when the assignment becomes effective. However, the original contracting party when he in advance, simultaneously or subsequently consents to the substitution can declare that he does not release the assignor. In this case, he can sue the assignor if the assignee fails to perform the obligations assumed, provided the original contracting party has given notice to the assignor of the non-performance within fifteen days of discovery of said non-performance. In the absence of such notice the original contracting party is liable for compensation for loss.

2. The assignor must give the assignee all information and documents necessary for him to exercise the rights and perform the obligations

arising from the contract. Failure to carry out these obligations shall cause the application of Art. 7 para. 2 of this code.

3. If there are well-grounded doubts about the validity or effectiveness of a contract of assignment, each debtor can apply to the court in order to be authorised to make a deposit as to performance due, as per Art. 105.

4. The original contracting party can raise against the assignee all defences arising out of the contract but not those based on other relationships with the assignor, unless he expressly reserved a right thereto when in advance, simultaneously, or subsequently consenting to the substitution.

5. The responsibility of the assignor both as to the validity of the contract assigned and as to its performance depends on the nature of the contract of assignment and, in any case, the agreement of the parties concerned.

6. However, if the parties in making the assignment have not referred to any type of contract and this cannot be deduced from the content of the agreement by interpretation, the following rules apply, unless otherwise agreed. If the assignment is not gratuitous the assignor is responsible for the invalidity or ineffectiveness of the contract assigned. The assignor is equally responsible and as a guarantor, within the limits of what he received if in good faith, for the obligations of the original contracting party which already exist, unless the non-performance of these obligations depends on the assignee. If the assignment is gratuitous, the assignor guarantees only the validity of the contract assigned and is responsible for its performance only if he has so promised and is in good faith.

Section 2

Assignment of claims

Article 121.

Assignability of claims

1. A claim arising from a contract or its performance or non-performance can be assigned in totality or partially to a third party or parties even though future or not yet recoverable, provided that the claim does not have a strictly personal character and that the assignment is not excluded by law, by agreement between the parties, or by the nature of the contract.

2. If the claim is partially assigned, the court can, if necessary, decide that the assignor and assignee must act in joinder vis-à-vis the original debtor.

3. A future claim can be assigned if it is determined or able to be determined according to Art. 31 of this code. In such case the assignment becomes effective when the claim comes into being on the assignor.

4. Assignment can be forbidden by contract but the agreement is effective against the assignee if the original contracting party proves that the transferee knew of it at the moment of transfer; in this case the assignee is prevented from acquiring the right over the original contracting party but not as regards the assignor.

5. A claim is not assignable if for the nature of the contract the assignment would substantially alter the obligation which was due from the original contracting party.

6. Apart from the provisions of Art. 118, the assignor can agree with the assignee that the latter shall be responsible for the performance of certain obligations.

Article 122.

Methods and effects of assignment

1. To be valid, an assignment does not require the agreement of the debtor – except in the case of a contract which expressly or by its nature excludes said assignment – and can be made as provided for in the following paragraphs.

2. An assignor can make a contract with the assignee, gratuitously or non-gratuitously, which obliges the former to transfer his claim to the latter. In this case assignment occurs by means of a second, abstract contract of assignment between said parties which enables the original contracting party to oppose the invalidity or ineffectiveness of this latter contract but not of the previous causal contract.

3. The assignor can also make a gratuitous or non gratuitous contract with the assignee, through which a claim due to the former passes to the latter, so that assignment occurs on mere agreement. If there is doubt as to the mode adopted for the assignment, this paragraph shall apply.

4. In the cases of paras. 2 and 3 of this Art., the assignment becomes effective as to the debtor of the original contract when he is notified of it or accepts it. Before such notice or acceptance the original debtor who pays the assignor is not discharged if the assignee proves that said debtor had knowledge that the assignment had been made. The notice to the debtor can be concomitant with the demand for performance.

5. For the contracts, declarations and acts of notice and acceptance mentioned above, para. 2 of Art. 36 of this code shall apply as to the value of the transferred claim.

6. In the above two cases (paras. 2 and 3 of this Article), assignment can be raised against a third party when the contracts, subsequent notice and acceptance are in documents of certified date, unless it is proved that said third person had knowledge of the assignment. If the same

claim has been the subject of more than one assignment to different persons, the first assignment notified to or accepted by the debtor, by an instrument bearing a certified date, shall prevail.

7. Unless otherwise agreed, assignment of a claim also transfers all accessories except those which are strictly personal.

8. Claims assigned to banks or factoring enterprises are not covered by the above Articles; they are governed by the current laws or uniform rules of the pertinent economic sectors or, in the absence of such laws and rules, by usage.

Article 123.

Duties of parties

1. The assignor shall deliver to the assignee the documents evidencing the claim that are in his possession, or an authentic copy thereof if only part of the claim is assigned, and provide all information necessary to enforce the claim.

2. When the assignment is not gratuitous, the assignor in good faith, within the limits of what he has received, is bound to guarantee the existence of the claim at the time of assignment and must also guarantee the present – and future if specifically promised – solvency of the original debtor, unless non-performance by the latter is due to negligence by the assignee. If these guarantees are excluded by agreement, the assignor remains liable if, as a result of his own act, the claim fails.

3. If the assignment is gratuitous, the grantor in good faith is responsible for the existence of the claim and the solvency of the original debtor only if and within the limits in which he has undertaken to guarantee them.

4. The grantor in bad faith is in any case liable for loss which the assignee suffers, provided that non-performance is not due to the negligence of the latter.

5. The original debtor has the same obligations to the assignee as he had to the assignor.

Article 124.

Rights of parties

1. The assignee acquires the same rights as the assignor had.

2. The original debtor can raise all the defences against the assignee which he could have raised to the assignor before assignment; but if he has unreservedly accepted the assignment, set-off cannot be opposed. Apart from the provisions of Art. 122, para 2, he can also raise defences regarding the invalidity of the assignment and, unless he has agreed

thereto, those based on the agreement excluding assignment, within the limits laid down in Art. 121, para. 4.

3. If well-founded doubts exist as to whether performance is due to the assignee or the assignor, the original debtor can obtain court authorisation that he shall make deposit or provide as ordered by said court, according to Art. 105 above.

4. When the assignment of a claim occurs by operation of the law, in the absence of specific provisions those of this present chapter shall be applied. In any case, the person who has performed succeeds in the rights of the creditor in proportion to his payment, if the payment is of a debt for which he was responsible; if on the other hand, the debt paid was not his responsibility, he can, until the moment of payment, demand to be replaced and succeeds to the rights of the creditor within the limits of what he has paid by means of a unilateral simultaneous declaration from the creditor following the provisions of Art. 36, para. 2 above.

Section 3

Assignment of debt

Article 125.

Assignment by succession or novation

1. There are two modes of assigning a debt:
   a) by succession, when the obligation is transferred objectively intact to a third person who is joined to the original debtor or replaces the latter as indicated in Article 126 below;
   b) by conventional extinction of the original debt and the simultaneous setting-up of a new obligation with a different debtor.

2. In the first of the cases in para. 1, the new debtor is bound *in solido* with the original debtor unless the creditor expressly releases the latter.

3. A novation occurs only if expressly and unambiguously agreed by the parties in their trilateral agreement. In case of doubt the assignment is presumed to be made by succession.

4. Apart from the provisions of paras. 2 and 3 of this Article, the parties can make the assignment of debt in the manner they consider most suited to their interests, for example as in Art. 126 below.

5. The debt can be assigned to one or more new debtors.

6. When the assignment occurs by operation of the law or as an accessory of the transfer of a good or set of goods, the assignment is subject to the provisions of this Section, as far as applicable, failing other specific rules.

Article 126.

Modes of assignment

1. By an agreement between the debtor and a third person, this latter can promise to extinguish the original debt and can perform within the limits of Article 79 para. 1. Such agreement has effect only between the original debtor and the third party.

2. A debtor can make an agreement with a third party which obliges the latter to extinguish the original debt to the creditor thus binding the third person with the original debtor *in solido*, unless the creditor expressly releases the latter.

3. A third party on his own initiative can make an agreement with the creditor by which the former binds himself to perform the obligation and becomes bound *in solido* with the original debtor unless the creditor expressly releases said debtor. By expressing opposition when coming to knowledge of the agreement, the original debtor can make said agreement ineffective.

4. Transfer of a debt can also occur by means of a preliminary agreement followed by a subsequent act of transfer of the claim. The agreement and the subsequent act are made by the creditor (agreeing with the third party) or by the original debtor (agreeing with the third party) even though said debtor is not entitled thereto; the operation becomes effective if the creditor gives his consent. In these cases the third person cannot set up against the creditor any defences based on the preliminary agreement which is the basis for the subsequent act of transfer, unless what invalidates the former is also an obstacle to the validity of the latter. Once the third party has paid, he can be indemnified by the original debtor up to the limits within which said debtor benefited. In the event of doubt as to the mode adopted for the transfer, that appearing in para. 3 of this Article shall apply.

5. In the above situations the third party may or may not be in debt to the original debtor; if not, he is entitled to be repaid or indemnified by the latter in proportion to what he has really paid, unless otherwise agreed, but the original debtor can set up against the third party the defences which might have been set up against the creditor.

6. In a trilateral agreement setting up a subjective novation, the parties can agree that in order to request performance the creditor shall make or at least offer a counter performance.

7. For all agreements and declarations contemplated in this Article, Art. 36, para. 2 of this Code shall apply, with regard to the value of the debt transferred.

Article 127.

Rights and duties of parties

1. Excepting as at Art. 126 para 4 above, unless the transfer occurs by means of a novation, the new debtor can set up against the creditor the defences of the original debtor. In addition, if the latter has been released by the creditor, all guarantees attached to the claim are extinguished, unless the guarantors expressly agree to continue them.

2. In the case of para. 1 of this Article, a creditor who has accepted the obligation of a third party cannot pursue the original debtor without having previously requested performance from the third party, and if the creditor has released the original debtor, he has no action against the latter if the third party becomes insolvent unless said creditor has made an express reservation of it.

3. If the assignment is made by means of a novation, the creditor and the new debtor can respectively exercise only those rights and raise only those defences which arise from the novation, except as in the following para.

4. If the obligation assumed by the new debtor, according to para. 1 lett. a) of Art. 125 above, is void or is annulled, the creditor who had released the original debtor, can require performance from the latter, but cannot avail himself of the guarantees furnished by third parties. If the assignment occurs through a novation, according to para. 1, lett. b) of Art. 125 above, the provisions of Art. 130, para. 5 shall apply.

5. If relevant, the rule in Art. 79, para. 2, shall be applied.

CHAPTER X

EXTINCTION OF CONTRACT AND DERIVED RELATIONSHIPS

Section 1

Extinctive facts and facts leading to foreclosure

Article 128.

Extinctive facts and facts producing ineffectiveness

1. A contract is discharged or is devoid of effect:
   a) by performance – or actual tender or tender by notice – of all the obligations in the contract, in the modes provided for in chapters VII and VIII of this book, and by the realisation of the aims of both contracting parties;
   b) by fulfilment of a resolutive clause;

   c)   at the expiry of a time limit;

   d)   by death or supervening incapacity, in cases indicated by the law;

   e)   by novation;

   f)   by dissolution by mutual consent;

   g)   by unilateral withdrawal;

   h)   by total dissolution;

   i)   by nullity;

   j)   by annulment;

   k)   by rescission;

   l)   by any other cause indicated in law.

2.   If a contract is definitively discharged or is devoid of effect the parties cannot make claims based on said contract apart from derogation in multilateral contracts in favour of the other contracting parties and for the protection of third parties; also except for the effects of validation, conversion and ratification, and apart from claims for return of what was given for performance and for compensation for loss resulting contractually or extra-contractually during the formation, performance or non-performance of the contract.

3.   Contractual obligations are discharged:

   a)   by performance – or actual tender or tender by notice – as laid down in chapters VII and VIII of this code, as well as enforcement proceedings against the debtor;

   b)   by novation;

   c)   by remission;

   d)   by tacit waiver;

   e)   by compensation;

   f)   by merger;

   g)   by loss or serious deterioration of the thing due or supervening impossibility of performance which must not be imputable to the debtor, except as provided for in Article 162 below;

   h)   for any other cause indicated in law.

4.   The extinguishing of an obligation – if definitive – prevents the creditor from laying any claims in relation to it, except for due restitutions and damages for unlawful acts occurred on the occasion of the performance or non-performance of said obligation.

5.   This present chapter covers the cases which are not covered by other rules in this code. To said rules reference is made for cases not contemplated here.

Article 129.

Facts leading to closure

1.   Limitation leads to closure of all rights deriving from a contract.

2. Forfeiture leads to foreclosure on the issue of a declaration or the performance of an act.

Section 2

Ways of extinguishing besides performance

Article 130.

Novation

1. The novation is objective when the parties agree to replace the previous contract by a new one materially different from the former which has not been completely performed and is thereby extinguished. The novation also extinguishes all guarantees of the original contract and its accessories, including payment facilities unless they are expressly confirmed in the new contract.
2. The intention to create a novation must be expressed by both parties, in an unequivocal manner and can also result from the objective incompatibility of the first contract with the second.
3. If the two contracts are not objectively incompatible, their co-existence must result from the unequivocal agreement of each contracting party.
4. In the event of doubt, it must be deemed that the original contract survives modified.
5. Invalidity of the original contract does affect the validity of the new one, nor the invalidity of the novative or of the second contract can reinstate the validity of the old one; but the party who is not in good faith is responsible for the loss incurred by the other party.
6. The reproduction or the repetition or the writing of a contract do not constitute novation unless the conditions of paras. 1 and 2 of this Article are fulfilled. If there is discrepancy between the original form of expression and the subsequent one, the latter prevails in the event of doubt.
7. The novation can concern, with similar effects, one clause of a contract or a resulting obligation.
8. Agreements provided for under paras. 1 and 7 of this present Article are subject to Art. 36 para. 2 of this code as concerns the amount of the new contract or the new obligation.

Article 131.

Remission

1. The creditor can extinguish the obligation already arisen or which can arise from a contract by renouncing it in one of the following ways.

2. The creditor can unequivocally communicate his release of debt to the debtor, who can within a reasonable time, declare he does not intend to avail himself of it. Voluntary restitution, by the creditor to the debtor, of the original instrument, even after partial payment of the sum owed, has the same effect as the creditor's declaration to release the debt. The remission granted to the principal debtor discharges the sureties. The creditor's waiver of the guarantees of the obligation does not raise a presumption of remission of the debt.

3. The creditor can renounce his claim by a contract made with the debtor.

4. The creditor can also renounce his claim by means of a contract having obligatory effect followed by an abstract act renouncing the claim. In this case the nullity of the first contract does not affect the subsequent contract.

5. The contracting parties can extinguish a unilateral or bi-lateral contract by making a subsequent contract in which they mutually renounce all the rights they had or might have had from the previous contract.

6. As concerns the amount of the debt remitted, Art. 36, para. 2 of this Code shall apply to all the acts provided for in the preceding paragraphs, even if remission of the debt is not due to a compromise. If the remission is gratuitous or intended gratuitously, the form of gift is not required.

Article 132.

Set-off

1. A claim deriving from contract is discharged by set-off when the creditor, for whatever reason, is also bound to perform an obligation to the other party. The compensation, which can also be claimed by a surety, must occur as follows.

2. The reciprocal debts, both being liquidated and collectable, must co-exist at the same date. They must have as object a sum of money or a quantity of fungible things of the same kind or quality. They are extinguished to the extent of their corresponding amounts.

3. Set-off takes place when a creditor claims it by a declaration which cannot be subject to a condition or a time. Such declaration must be communicated to the other party or made in court before the end of the first oral hearing of the case. Said declaration takes effect from the moment it is communicated to the other party or delivered in court. The other party can raise objection within reasonable time, according to the following paragraphs.

4. Set-off does not take place, and it can be refused towards the person claiming it, if either claim derives from a tort, or has been previously and with reasonable grounds contested by one party, or if the claim concerns the restitution of things deposited or loaned for use, or in case of waiver of set-off in advance, or in any other case contemplated by law. Current accounts connected with commercial relationships are governed by usage. Consumer laws existing in the European Union and its Member States are unaffected.

5. When two reciprocal debts are contracted as payable in two different places the expenses connected with transportation to the place of payment shall be taken into account, unless the creditor opposes set-off having a reasonable interest that performance be made at the place fixed.

6. If the conditions envisaged by para. 2 of this Article are not fulfilled, the creditor has only the right of retention towards the other party, according to Art. 108 above. If one of the credits is not liquidated, but is susceptible of easy and prompt liquidation, the judge, at the creditor's instance, can suspend judgment against this latter for the debt he is responsible for until the amount of the credit claimed in set-off is ascertained. Set-off can take place by agreement of the two parties, even if the above conditions are not fulfilled.

7. Art. 36 para. 2 applies to the declarations covered by this Article regarding the amount of the credit claimed by set-off.

Article 133.

Merger

1. A contract-based claim is not enforceable if and during such time as the attributes of debtor and creditor are united in the same person.

2. If the attributes of creditor and debtor *in solido* are united in the same person, para. 1 of this Article takes effect, to the extent of the amount due by said debtor, in respect to the other debtors. If the attributes of creditor *in solido* and debtor are united in the same person, para. 1 of this Article takes effect to the extent of the amount due to said creditor. The same rules apply to indivisible obligations.

3. Merger does not operate to the prejudice of third parties and in any cases where laws in force in the European Union and its Member States exclude it for the benefit of third parties.

Section 3

Limitation and forfeiture

Article 134.

Limitation

1. In the absence of a legal prohibition, expiry of the time limit produces a definitive closure on an inactive creditor as to the exercise of a disposable right derived from a contract, as provided by the following rules.
2. A time limit for the limitation begins to run from the moment when the creditor can enforce his credit whose amount must be certain.
3. Limitation occurs when the debtor, one of his creditors or anybody who has a legitimate interest, expressly declares to the holder of the right, in court or extra-judicially his intention to avail himself of said limitation. If this declaration is not made in court para. 2, Art. 36 above shall apply.
4. All the rights arising from a contract are extinguished by limitation after the lapse of ten years unless a different time limit is provided for as regards certain types of contract or particular institutions. If there has been a court condemnation, ten years is the limit in every case, even if a different period is provided for in this code for the right recognised by the judgment.
5. The parties can by agreement reduce the limitation term of ten years indicated in para. 4 but not the periods established for different types of contract, except for relationships involving a consumer and then only in the consumer's favour. Any other agreement intended to modify the legal regulation of limitation is void. Community rules prevail in any case.
6. Limitation is interrupted if a creditor initiates legal proceedings to enforce his rights or if he issues an extra-judicial notice for the same purpose or if the debtor acknowledges in any case his own debt. A new limitation period begins as a result of interruption.
7. Limitation is suspended: between husband and wife; between the persons subject to parental authority, guardianship or similar forms of protection and assistance, like those in the various systems, and the persons in charge thereof; between persons whose property is subject to the administration of others and those who exercise such administration until final approval of the account; and in any other situation covered by law. Suspension can also occur by an agreement between creditor and debtor who have decided to negotiate with a view to an amicable settlement, and for the whole negotiating period. When the suspension ceases, the time of limitation begins to run again joining the time already elapsed before suspension.

8. Any other right or action provided for in this code is subject to limitation of ten years, unless a different time-limit is indicated for certain situations.

Article 135.

Forfeiture

1. The rules on interruption and suspension do not apply to forfeiture unless otherwise provided by the rules relating to different types of contract.
2. The time limits relating to forfeiture established for the issue of a declaration or the performance of an act for different types of contract can be altered by agreement of the parties, only to the extent that said performance is not rendered excessively difficult.

Article 136.

Computation of time-limits

Time limits of limitation and forfeiture are computed according to Art. 58 above.

CHAPTER XI

OTHER CONTRACTUAL ANOMALIES AND REMEDIES

Section 1

Anomalies

Article 137.

Non-existence

1. In the absence of a fact, an act, a declaration, a situation which can be externally recognized and referred to the social notion of agreement, no contract shall exist.
2. Specifically no contract exists
    a) unless and until such time as there is an addressee or person capable of accepting the offer or declaration which is intended to qualify as an act of private autonomy or unless there exists a potential future person such as a conceived child or a company before registration;

b) unless there exists an object of the offer or declaration made in order to carry out an act of private autonomy;

c) if the acceptance – apart from what is stated in Art. 16 paras. 6 and 7 – does not correspond with the offer because of the equivocal nature of the latter;

d) if the fact, act, declaration, or situation, while existing, are incomplete to such a point that they cannot be legally valid either as a different and reduced contractual scheme or in expectation of other elements that may possibly supervene.

3. If there is doubt, the contract shall be considered void rather than non-existent.

Article 138.

Consequences of non-existence

1. Non-existence produces the absolute lack of any contractual effect apart from the obligations to restitution in Art. 160 and responsibility in tort according to Art. 161.

2. The situation envisaged in paras. 1 and 2 of Art. 137 above occurs in the mere presence of the relevant conditions. No regularisation nor corrective is possible and any one who has an interest can take account of this without any limitation running. In order to avail himself of this situation, said person can also make known to the other party the situation of non-existence, by sending the latter a declaration containing all the necessary indications with regard to such situation; he can also apply for a judicial finding. This action cannot be brought until six (three) months after reception of said declaration, to enable the parties to settle the question out of court. The right of applying to the court for the urgent reliefs of Art. 172 below is unaffected.

Article 139.

Deleted clauses

The provisions of Art. 138 paras. 1 and 2 shall apply even when a rule states that a clause or expression in a contract is deemed not written.

Article 140.

Nullity

1. Unless the law states otherwise, a contract is void

a) if it is contrary to public policy or morals or a mandatory rule adopted for the protection of general interest or situations of primary importance for society;

b) if it is contrary to any other applicable mandatory rule;

c) if any of the essential elements indicated in Art. 5, paras. 3 and 4 above are lacking;

d) in the other cases indicated in this code and in relevant, applicable European Union and Member States' legislation;

e) in all other cases where this Code or an applicable law states that some element is necessary under penalty of nullity or for an act to be valid or when equivalent expressions exist.

2. Para. 1 of this Article also applies to the single clause of a contract which can be deemed valid as to the remaining part, in accordance with Art. 144.

3. If there is conflict between European Union rules and those of its Member States, the latter shall prevail if they are of national social utility and especially if they are in accordance with basic constitutional rules of any of the States and concerning equality, social solidarity and protection of human rights.

4. In the case of a penal prohibition concerning the contract as such, i.e. punishing the behaviour of both parties, in relation to it the contract is void. Therefore the contract is void whose conclusion is forbidden in the absence of a previous specific authorization to said conclusion by a public body.

5. If performance of contract forms part of an illegal activity, the contract is not deemed void for the party not involved in said activity. This party can request performance of the obligation due to him and have recourse to the remedies provided for non-performance, inexact performance, or delay.

6. Subject to Art. 137, para. 2, lett. d), a contract lacking one or other required element is not void if the law permits subsequent making of the act and if the already subsisting elements are legally sufficient with reference to the supervening of the others which are necessary for completion of the contract.

Article 141.

Effects of nullity of contract

1. Except the provisions of the following paragraphs, nullity renders a contract totally without contractual effect *ab initio*, apart from the obligation to restitution under Art. 160 and possible responsibility in tort under Art. 161.

2. For nullity to occur it is sufficient that the conditions for it be present but the party who intends to avail himself of it must let the other

person know said nullity by sending him a declaration, before the expiry of ten years after the contract was made , giving all necessary indications. To this declaration Art. 21 and Art. 36 para. 2 shall apply. Before the matured time limit, said party can apply for judicial finding on the subject, but action can be brought only after six (three) months after reception of the notice, in order to enable the parties to settle the question out of court. If the contract has not yet been carried out, limitation concerning a plea of nullity occurs at the same time as for the action for specific performance of the contract.

3. The right to request the court for the measures of Art. 172 to be applied in emergency is unaffected.

Article 142.

Supervening nullity

1. If independently of the will of the parties and because of some event subsequent to the making of the contract an essential element to its validity goes missing, the ensuing nullity is not retroactive.
2. Except as provided for in this para. 1, all rules regarding nullity apply to supervening nullity.

Article 143.

Validation of void contract

1. A contract void for the reasons stated in Art. 140, para. 1, lett. a) cannot be validated, treated as partially void, converted or rectified in any way.
2. Contracts void for reasons other than those indicated in para 1 of this Article can be validated. Validation is made by an act of the contracting parties who reproduce the void contract but remove the cause of nullity and undertake to make due restitutions and perform their respective obligations, as would have been the case if the contract had been valid *ab initio*. This act is subject to Art. 36, para. 2.
3. In order to make this validation the parties proceed according to Art. 12 ff.
4. The provisions of this Article apply also to single clauses of an otherwise valid contract, as provided in Art. 144 below.

Article 144.

Partial nullity

1. Excepting as provided in Art. 143, para. 1, if a single clause or part of a contract is void, the rest of the contract remains valid, provided this

part can autonomously exist and reasonably realize the purpose of the parties.

2. In connected or multilateral contracts, when the nullity affects only one contract or the obligation of only one of the parties, the principle of this first paragraph shall apply, unless the void contract or the obligation of one party is considered essential to the bargain as a whole.

3. The rule of para. 1 does not apply if a different intention emerges from the action of the parties or the circumstances.

4. For partial nullity to occur it is sufficient that the conditions for it be present; but the party who intends to avail himself of said nullity must send a written declaration to the other party before the expiry of limitation of three years after the contract was made, giving all necessary indications. Art. 21 and Art. 36 para. 2 shall apply. Before the matured time limit, said party can apply for judicial finding on the subject; but action can be brought only after six (three) months after reception of said declaration, in order to enable the parties to settle the question out of court. The right nevertheless of requesting the court for the measures of Art. 172 below to be applied in emergency is unaffected.

5. Partial nullity does not occur if, applying mandatory rule or in virtue of a conversion as in Art. 145 below, the void clause or part is substituted, by a different clause or part.

Article 145.

Conversion of void contract

1. Apart from the provisions of Art. 40, para. 2 and Art. 143, para 1, a void contract produces the effects of a different valid contract of which it has the requisites of substance and form whenever the latter enables the objective sought by the parties to be reasonably realized.

2. This rule in para. 1 applies also to single clauses of a contract.

3. Conversion cannot take place if the contract or the circumstances reveal a different intention of the parties.

4. For conversion to occur it is sufficient that the conditions for it be present; but the party who intends to avail himself of the conversion must convey a written declaration to the other person before the expiry of limitation of three years after the contract was made, giving all necessary indications. Art. 21 and Art. 36 para. 2 shall apply. Before the matured time limit, said party can apply for judicial finding on the subject; but action can be brought only after six (three) months after reception of said declaration, in order to enable the parties to settle the question out of court. The right to apply to the court for the measures of Art. 172 below to be applied in emergency is unaffected.

5. The rules in this Article apply also to an annulled contract. As to a contract without effect, the provisions of Art. 153, para. 5 shall be applied.

Article 146.

Voidability

1. Voidability occurs in the cases indicated in para. 2 and only the party legally entitled can avail himself of it.
2. The contract is voidable
   a) in the case of incapacity of one of the parties, as in Art. 150;
   b) in the case of vices of consent (Art. 151, 152);
   c) in the cases covered by Articles 67 and 68;
   d) in any other case expressly covered by law.
3. The present article also applies to single clauses of the contract or to engagement of single parties in a multilateral contract when one or other can autonomously exist as regards the bargain as a whole.

Article 147.

Effects of annulment

1. Annulment has retroactive effect destroying the contract from the moment of its conclusion and the parties are bound to reciprocal returns according to Art. 160.
2. The provisions of para. 1 do not apply if restitution is impossible or too onerous for the party bound to make it. In this case the annulment takes effect from the moment when the declaration is received according to Art. 148, and the rule at Art. 160 para. 4 shall be applied.
3. Annulment of the contract enables the aggrieved party to recover damages according to Art. 162 within the limits fixed by Art. 6 para. 4 for the loss caused by the party who by his act caused voidance, according to Art. 162.

Article 148.

Modes and time limits of annulment

1. In order to annul a contract the entitled party – or if incapable his legal representative – must address a declaration to the other party giving all necessary indications. Art. 21 and Art. 36 para. 2 shall be applied to said declaration.

2. No action can be brought until six (three) months after reception of the declaration in order to enable the parties to settle the question out of court. The right to apply to the court for the measures of Art. 172 below to be applied in emergency is unaffected.

3. A party unable to make the restitution required by Art. 147 paras. 1 and 2 cannot have the contract annulled, except to the extent provided for in Art. 150, para. 4 for the benefit of persons incapable.

4. The other party or anyone having an interest can give notice to the entitled party – or if incapable his legal representative – to declare within a period of not less than sixty days whether or not he intends to proceed with annulment of the contract. After the expiry in vain of this time limit the entitled party or the legal representative are deemed to have abandoned annulment. The notice is covered by the provisions of Articles 21 and 36 para 2.

5. Annulment of the contract is subject to a three-year limitation starting from the day in which incapacity or violence ceased or from when the mistake was discovered; in all other cases the delay runs from making the contract. However, the declaration of para 1 of this Article can be made and raised as a defence by the person requested to perform the contract even after said period of three years.

Article 149.

Preservation and validation of voidable contract

1. Annulment of a voidable contract shall not occur if, within the time limit indicated in the declaration of the party proceeding to it (or within reasonable time if the limit is not stated), the other party binds himself to perform in a manner which conforms to the substance and characteristics of the contract the first contracting party intended to conclude or to perform obligations agreed by the parties so that a substantially similar result or acceptable to the interested party can be assured.

2. A voidable contract can be validated and thus remains confirmed in all its effects if the entitled contracting party or his legal representative declares, respecting the provision of Art. 36 para. 2, his intention not to proceed with annulment or voluntarily perform the contract. Validation requires that said contracting party – or if incapable his legal representative – is in a condition to validly conclude a contract and is fully aware of the reason for voidability.

Article 150.

Contract made by incapable person

1. As indicated in Art. 5 para. 2 a contract made by

a) a non-emancipated minor;
b) a person declared legally incapable of contracting (and in the absence of his representative or of a person charged with his legal assistance);
c) a person who is, even temporarily, incapable of understanding or intending;
d) a person whose physical incapacity prevents communication of his will, such as a deaf mute who cannot write,

is voidable, as provided for by Art. 146 ff., unless said contract has only produced benefits for the person lacking capacity.

2. The contract is not voidable if a minor, by subterfuge, has concealed his minority or if the other contracting party was in good faith because the mental state of incapacity was not recognizable or the declared incapacity was not easily ascertainable.

3. Furthermore a contract made by an incapable person is not voidable, in the case contemplated by Art. 5 para. 1, provided that he has obtained the permits required by his national law and if the act is one of normal daily life involving small expense and performed with money or means deriving from work open to the incapable person or put lawfully at his free disposition.

4. If the contract is annulled, the incapable person is bound to make restitution of what he has received, according to Art. 161, to the extent to which it has benefited him.

5. Third party guarantors of the contract made by an incapable person are liable to the other contracting party under the terms of the contract even if it is annulled, while maintaining their right to claim, if that is the case, against the incapable person or his legal representative.

Article 151.

Contract defective by mistake

1. Unilateral mistake is cause for annulment of a contract under the following conditions
   a) when the mistake concerns a basic economic or legal element or aspect of the contract and is decisive of consent;
   b) when the mistake arises through the fraudulent representation or unjustified reticence of the other party or in any case, if said party realises the existence of mistake and its importance in determining the contract or should have realised it by using ordinary care.

2. In the case of third person's fraudulent representation known to the party who took advantage therefrom, the contract is voidable.

3. If the conditions of para. 1 above do not occur, and the mistake does not depend on the gross negligence of the mistaken party, said person

can annul the contract only if he has no interest whatever in it and if he indemnifies the other party for the loss suffered for believing in the validity of the contract and in its punctual performance.

4. If the conditions of para. 1 above occur, mistake does not render the contract voidable but permits the mistaken party to claim a rectification of the extent of performance due by him or compensation for loss when

a) the mistake was merely one of calculation, unless its magnitude indicates that it was decisive of consent,

b) the mistake concerns a secondary element or has had no decisive effect on consent, i.e. the contract would have been nevertheless made but with different terms.

5. The mistaken party cannot annul the contract if this is contrary to good faith. If said party nevertheless insists on voidance, even after a reasoned reply from the other party, the court, after evaluation of the circumstances, can order the mistaken party to pay to the other party an equitable compensation.

6. The above provisions apply even if the mistake occurs in the declaration or when such declaration is transmitted inexactly to the other party by the person or office charged with it.

7. Either party can annul the contract if both parties have made the same mistake, concerning: determinative circumstances, though not expressly mentioned, which both parties deemed existent when making the contract; or the objective impossibility of performance; or the forecast as to the realisation of a certain event, thought not expressly mentioned, which is of decisive importance in the contractual context.

Article 152.

Contract defective by threats

1. Apart from what is provided for in Article 30, para. 3, a contract is voidable if it is made because of intimidation or serious threats – which would impress any normal person – directed at the contracting party or his relatives by the other party, or also by a third person if it was known by the other party who took advantage from it.

2. A threat to enforce a right can be cause for annulment only when it is aimed at obtaining unjust benefits.

3. Excepting the provisions in Art. 156, reverential fear is cause for annulment of a contract only if it results from the circumstances that the person who exerted his influence on the other party knew of its decisive effect and took unjust benefits from it.

Article 153.

Ineffectiveness

1. A valid contract is ineffective – i.e. it temporarily or permanently fails to have the legal effects at which it was aimed - either by agreement of the parties or by law, according to the following paragraphs.
2. Ineffectiveness by agreement of the parties, occurs in:
   a) a simulated contract according to Art. 155, excepted what is provided for there-in,
   b) a contract with suspensive or resolutive conditions or time limits as to the beginning or the end, according to Art. 49 ff.,
   c) a contract whose effects the parties have decided must be dependent on authorisation by a public authority, the approval or co-operation of a third party, or a similar condition, before their occurrence.
3. A contract which is ineffective by agreement of the parties becomes immediately effective on the agreed revocation of the simulation, or the conditions or time-limits or the preliminary conditions at lett. c) of the preceding paragraph.
4. Ineffectiveness by law, apart from what is provided in Art. 140, paras 1, 4, and 6, occurs in the cases of:
   a) a contract or declaration made in good faith without the parties being aware that it is an act with legal effects,
   b) a contract for which the law requires, under penalty of ineffectiveness, and not of nullity, the issue of a permit from a public authority or approval from an individual or any similar preliminary condition before the permission, approval or condition obtain,
   c) a contract, regarding which this code or the laws of the Community or European Union Member States provide that it is to be 'without effect', 'or has no effect', or use other expressions with similar meaning.
5. A contract which is definitively ineffective, according to para 4, letts. b) and c), can be validated, made only partially ineffective, or converted, according to Arts. 143, 144 and 145.
6. Ineffectiveness exists simply when the conditions for it are present; but in the case of para. 4 lett. a) and c) of this Article anyone who has an interest in it and intends to avail himself of said ineffectiveness must address a declaration to the person who must take account of it before the expiry of limitation of three years, giving all necessary indications. Before the matured time limit, said party can also apply for judicial finding on the subject; but action can be brought only after six (three) months after reception of said declaration in order to enable the parties to settle the question out of court, saving the right to apply to the court for the measures of Art. 172 below to be applied in emergency.

Article 154.

Non-opposability

1. The following cannot be opposed to third parties or certain third persons:
    a) the underlying contract in case of simulation as contemplated in Art. 155, unless otherwise provided therein;
    b) apart from the provisions of Art. 140, para. 1 lett. a), contracts concluded either in violation of a ban aimed at protecting certain people or failing to observe provisions about form or publicity made to protect third parties,
    c) contracts drawn up between two persons with the intent – known to both parties – to defraud a creditor of one of them; in which case the creditor can retroactively assert said non-opposability by conveying notice to the two contracting parties before the expiry of limitation of three years after the contract was made.
    d) the situations and fact relationships underlying void contracts or created in order to put them into effect;
    e) contracts or acts referred to in this Code or the applicable laws of the Community or European Union Member States in terms which state that they are not opposable to third parties or certain third persons or using any analogous expressions.
2. Non-opposability exists simply when the conditions for it are present; but any interested party to avail himself of it must convey a declaration giving all necessary indications to the person who must take note of it before the expiry of limitation of three years after the contract was made. Before that time limit, said party can apply for judicial determination on the subject; but action can be brought only after six (three) months after receipt of said notice, in order to enable the parties to settle the question out of court. The power nevertheless remains unaffected to apply to the court for the measures of Art. 172 below to be applied in emergency.

Article 155.

Simulation and mental reserve

1. Unless otherwise provided by any applicable laws of the Community or the Member States of the European Union, if the parties conclude a simulated contract, i.e. one which is such only in appearance, said contract is without effect; and if the parties agree to make a different, underlying contract, this latter is effective between them provided all the necessary requisites of substance and form are present and provided the simulation was not made in fraud of a creditor or the law. In the last case, the simulated and the underlying contract are both void.

2. Third persons, in addition to objecting the non-opposability of the underlying contract, can declare they avail themselves of it according to their legitimate interests and there is no limit to proofs adduceable for this purpose,

3. In order to avail themselves of an underlying contract, after having given proper written notice with the necessary indications, to which notice the provisions of Articles 21 and 36 para. 2 apply, neither party can have recourse to testimonial evidence but only to documentary evidence. Testimonial evidence is admissible only to prove that the underlying contract is illegal or in any case void.

4. If one party provides the other with a declaration which differs from the intent of the former, the declaration binds the issuer as far as the receiver can understand it in good faith, unless the receiver is aware of mental reserve on the part of the other party; in which case the declaration has on the receiver and third parties the effects of a simulated contract, in accordance with the above paras.

Section 2

Remedies

Article 156.

Rescission for lesion

1. Apart from the provisions on usury in the applicable laws of the Community or European Union Member States, in the case provided for at Art. 30 para. 3, the party who intends to rescind the contract must convey written notice to the other party giving all necessary indications, to which declaration Art. 21 and Art. 36 para. 2 shall apply.

2. No action can be brought until after six (three) months have elapsed from receipt of said notice, in order to enable the parties to settle the question out of court. The power nevertheless remains unaffected to apply to the court for the measures of Art. 172 below to be applied in emergency.

3. The other party or anyone concerned can intimate to the entitled party – or if incapable his legal representative – to declare within a period of not less than sixty days whether he intends to proceed with rescission of the contract. This time limit having elapsed in vain, the entitled party or his legal representative are deemed to all purposes to have abandoned rescission. The above declaration is covered by the provisions of Articles 21 and 36 para. 2.

4. Rescission of the contract is subject to limitation of one year from the formation of the contract. The defence of rescindability is subject to the same limitation.

5. One party's intentional or any case conscious profiting from the other party's inferiority or inexperience can result from the circumstances; but said intention or consciousness must be excluded in aleatory contracts and when the other party has expressed his intention to pay a high price because of his affection for the object of the contract or when relationships between the parties lead to the deduction that they intended to form a mixed contract, both gratuitous and remunerative.

6. A rescindable contract cannot be validated but rescission does not occur if an equitable basis is restored by agreement between the parties or, by judicial ruling at the request of one of them.

Article 157.

Re-negotiation of contract

1. If extraordinary unforeseeable events occur, such as those in Art. 97 para. 1, the party who intends to avail himself of the right provided for therein must communicate to the other party a declaration with all necessary information specifying – under penalty of nullity – the different conditions that he proposes in order to keep the contract alive. The declaration is covered by the provisions of Articles 21 and 36 para 2.

2. No action can be brought until after six (three) months have elapsed from receipt of said declaration, in order to enable the parties to settle the question out of court. The right nevertheless is unaffected to apply to the court for the measures of Art. 172 below to be applied in emergency.

3. If the event covered by para. 1 occurs, the other party can intimate to the party entitled to exercise the power there set out notice to declare within a period of not less than sixty days whether he intends to claim renegotiation of the contract. After this time limit has elapsed in vain the party entitled is deemed to have abandoned renegotiation. The intimation is covered by the provisions of Articles 21 and 36 para 2.

4. If the parties are unable to agree within the time limit at para. 2, the person entitled must – within the subsequent sixty days on pain of forfeiture – present said request to the court according to the procedure applicable in the place where the contract is to be performed.

5. After evaluating the circumstances and taking into consideration the interests and requests of the parties, the judge, with possible expert

assistance, can alter or dissolve the contract as a whole or in its non-performed part and, if required, and it is the case, order return of goods or award damages for loss.

Article 158.

Judicial upholding or denial of contract dissolution

1. The notice provided for in Art. 114, paras. 1 and 2, can also be given to the other party by means of an application to the judge in proceedings in which restitution and damages can be claimed.

2. Apart from the case in the preceding paragraph, no action can be brought until after six (three) months have elapsed from receipt of the notice mentioned in Art. 114, paras. 1 and 2, in order to enable the parties to settle the controversy out of court. The right nevertheless remains unaffected to apply to the court for the provisions of Art. 172 below to be applied in emergency.

3. If the right to dissolution of a contract is to be examined by the court, this latter can exercise the power to evaluate and decide according to Art. 92 ff. and in particular, the judge:

    a) can simply confirm dissolution following the creditor's declaration and he can also order the other party to return what he has received and to pay compensation for loss as provided for in Art. 162 ff.;

    b) can deny dissolution of the contract if the conditions in Chapter VIII are not met, and declare, if that is the case, that the debtor can perform the obligation and the creditor must accept performance,

    c) can, in accordance with the above rules, grant the debtor delay of the time of performance, staggering of payments, reasonable time to eliminate defects in the thing delivered or to demolish and restore to its former state what was done unlawfully, or to deliver a different thing or to make a different performance, or to substitute things or materials used, or to repair damage done, or to send technicians to ensure correct functioning of the thing delivered, or to grant the debtor other benefits and the court can evaluate under the above provisions and declare that the contract is deemed dissolved only if the debtor fails to avail himself of these benefits within the time limit or fails to do so adequately. In all the above the court can award damages for loss.

    d) In addition, after full evaluation of the circumstances, taking into account the reasons for non-performance and the interests of the parties and applying the principle of good faith, the judge can declare partial dissolution or specify that the debtor is not liable to pay any damages for loss, or order the debtor to pay damages without declaring the contract dissolved, in the interest of the creditor.

Article 159.

Withdrawal by consumer

1. In the case at Art. 9, the unsatisfied consumer or one who has changed his mind has the right to repudiate the contract or his contractual offer by sending to the other party or the person who negotiated the contract written notice in which the consumer can merely express his intention to withdraw from the contract or offer.
2. Said notice, covered by Art. 21, must be sent in the required manner and particularly within the time limits laid down in Community provisions according to whether the consumer has or has not been fully informed of his right to withdraw. The time limits run from the dates indicated in said Community provisions.
3. As soon as the notice at para. 1 has been or is deemed to have been known by the addressee, the parties are discharged from their respective obligations, except as provided in para. 4 of this Article, and always saving the consumer's right to be compensated for the damage caused by the thing delivered according to Art. 162 ff. Other Community rules or those existing in Member States of the European Union are unaffected providing specific sanctions on the dealer who fails to inform the customer completely and precisely about his right to withdraw from the contract.
4. The consumer must return to the other party the things delivered in fulfilment of the cancelled contract, as provided for in Community rules. The other party must follow Community rules on time limits and procedures to return to the consumer any moneys paid.
5. A consumer cannot waive his right to repudiate or withdraw from the contract or his contractual offer and any agreement contrary to the provisions of this Article and Art. 9 is void according to Art. 140, para 1, lett. a)

Article 160.

Restitution

1. Saving the provisions of para. 9 below, the parties benefiting from performance of a non-existent, void, annulled, ineffective, dissolved, cancelled contract, or one withdrawn from, are bound mutually to return what they have received, as stated in this Article and a party can refuse to do so if the other party is unable or does not offer to return as above.

2. The request for restitution shall be conveyed to the bound party by serving notice, with necessary indications according to Art. 21 and Art. 36, para. 2. No action can be brought until six (three) months after reception of the notice, in order to enable the parties to settle the controversy out of court; always excepting the right to apply to the court for the measures of Art. 172 in case of emergency.

3. The restitution must normally be in kind unless this is materially or legally impossible or excessively onerous for the party who is to perform, taking into account the interest of the other party, or unless specific restitution is not convenient for the latter because of the state of conservation of the thing to be returned. In these cases, restitution shall be made by payment to the other party of a reasonable and equivalent sum, the amount of which, failing agreement between the parties, shall be fixed by the court, saving the possibility to operate equitable compensation between the obligations to return to which the parties are reciprocally bound.

4. Even if restitution in kind is possible, the party entitled to it still has the right to choose between that form of restitution and a pecuniary sum, calculated according to para. 3 above, unless the option is contrary to good faith.

5. If money is to be returned, interest must be added and, if that is the case, an additional sum for re-valuation, calculating from the day when the payment was made, if the receiving party was in bad faith, or from the day restitution was requested, if in good faith. If a thing is to be returned, also a sum of money shall be paid for its use and depreciation – to which a sum shall be added for interest and, if suitable, an additional sum for re-valuation – which, failing agreement between the parties, shall be fixed by the court.

6. Interest is due according to Art. 169, para. 3. Re-valuation shall be calculated according to Art. 169, para. 4.

7. If performance originally made was a lawful activity for benefit of the other party, the party who performed has the right to equitable remuneration which, failing agreement between the parties, shall be fixed by the court, saving the possibility to calculate by means of compensation as provided for in para. 3 above.

8. The incapable person is bound to return what he has received within the limits indicated in Art. 150 para. 4.

9. Parties who have performed contractual duties which constitute offences liable to prosecution or which are against morality or public policy – but not against economic public policy – and the party who has made performance for a purpose which even only as to himself presents those characteristics, have no right to any restitution under this Article. This rule shall not apply to performance by incapable persons, by persons who without fault were unaware of committing

an immoral act or one with the above characteristics, or by persons who performed under duress. Community provisions and those of European Member States, which provide in the above cases for confiscation of what has been delivered or made in order to perform the contract, are unaffected.

Article 161.

Protection of third parties rights

1. In all cases of non-existence, nullity, annulment, ineffectiveness, non-opposability, cancellation, withdrawal and dissolution, each party is liable for any damage caused through his conduct to third parties who have in good faith relied on the appearance of the contract, if this latter produces a different effect or no effect.
2. Compensation for loss is governed by the provisions of Art. 162 ff., to the extent compatible.

Article 162.

Contractual liability: conditions

1. The debtor who does not exactly render performance is liable for that loss which must be reasonably deemed the consequence of the omitted, delayed or defective performance. Excepting what is provided for at para. 3 of this Article, the debtor is exempted from liability if he proves that the non-performance, defective performance or delay was not attributable to his conduct but to an external unforeseeable and irresistible cause.
2. The principle enunciated in the foregoing paragraph also applies to any other fact or situation considered a source of liability for damages in the provisions of this Code.
3. In the cases contemplated in Art. 75, para. 3, first part, the debtor is not liable for damages if he proves he acted with appropriate care in the specific case, as indicated in the said provision, and if he provides the proof required by Art. 94, para. 3. The person who has rendered a professional performance – with the informed consent of the aggrieved party, or his relatives, or the person charged with his legal representative – in a field of scientific experimentation which has not yet reached conclusive results is liable only if his conduct was grossly negligent.
4. Unless the debtor acted with fraud or negligence, compensation is limited to the loss for which – according to the contract, the circumstances, good faith, and usage – it must be reasonably expected a normally

prudent person would have accepted responsibility at the time the obligation arose.

5. Unless agreed differently, the debtor is responsible in accordance with para. 1 of this Article, even if he has availed himself of the services of auxiliaries or third persons in performing the contract, always safeguarding, if that is the case, his right to claim from these latter.

6. Unless otherwise agreed, in the event of defective performance, non-performance or delay in a contract with several debtors, Art. 88 shall apply with regard to compensation of the resulting loss.

7. The existence of loss must be proved and its amount assessed or else quantifiable according to Art. 168, para. 1.

Article 163.

Patrimonial loss: recoverable damages

1. Damages are recoverable for:
   a) the loss sustained, and
   b) the profits lost which the creditor could reasonably have expected in the normal course of events given the particular circumstances and measures taken by him. Profits lost shall include loss of the a particular gain which can be deemed with reasonable certainty to have occurred and which must be evaluated with regard to the time of non performance or delay.

2. Indirect patrimonial loss sustained by anybody in credit with the victim of the damage can be compensated only in case of death or grievous bodily harm suffered by this latter.

Article 164.

Non-patrimonial loss

1. Damages are recoverable in cases of:
   a) serious psychic disturbance or emotional shock caused by bodily harm or injury to the feelings, also of a legal person, or to the memory of a deceased relative;
   b) physical pain as a condition of bodily suffering, even if without pathological, organic or functional change,
   c) injuries to health and in the other cases indicated in the relevant provisions.

2. Indirect non-patrimonial loss can be compensated only if suffered by the close relatives of the victim.

Article 165.

Future and possible damage

1. Future damage is reparable and calculable according to the provisions of Art. 168, para. 1, if it is reasonably certain that the non-performance or delay have not exhausted their consequences unless the victim of the prejudice reserves the right to make a claim, even separately, after the future damage occurs.

2. Possible damage, i.e. which is feared likely to occur in the future does not give right to compensation before the event but the court can take precautionary measures according to Art. 172.

Article 166.

Function and modes of reparation

1. Apart from the subsequent mitigating provisions, compensation must specifically aim to eliminate the harmful consequences of non-performance, defective performance, delay, or other situations in which, according to the provisions of this present code, reparation is due. Said reparation shall create, as a rule, the fact situation which would have existed if the aforementioned situations had not occurred.

2. Thus, if possible, reparation shall take the form of specific performance or restitution supplemented, if necessary, by a pecuniary indemnity. If the entire or partial restoring to the former state is not possible or is too onerous for the debtor, considering the interest of the creditor, and in any case if the latter so demands, suitable pecuniary compensation shall be paid.

3. Specifically, if not otherwise provided for in another rule of this code or if not otherwise required by the actual situation, the result of reparation must provide the creditor or, in the cases provided for, the third party, with

   a) satisfaction of his interest (positive) in that the contract bepunctually and exactly performed, also taking into account the expenses and costs incurred by him and which would have been covered by performance if the prejudice comes from omitted, delayed or defective performance;

   b) satisfaction of his interest (negative) in that the contract has not been made or compromised, in the other cases, and particularly when damage comes from the non-existence, nullity, annulment, ineffectiveness, rescission, non-conclusion of the contract and in similar cases.

4. The amount of damages however must be calculated considering of the benefits which in consequence of the contract have already been provided without reward by the debtor for the creditor who cannot nor intends to disclaim said benefit.

5. All provisions in this Code which provide for specific manners of reparation in particular circumstances are safeguarded.

Article 167.

Contributing conduct of creditor

1. No compensation is due for damage which would not have occurred if the creditor had adopted the necessary measures he should have taken before the damage occurred.
2. After the occurrence of the damage, no compensation is due for *post hoc* increase in damage which the creditor could have prevented by adopting necessary measures.
3. If an act or an omission of the creditor has contributed to causing the damage, compensation is reduced according to the extent of the resulting consequences.
4. Failure by the creditor to warn the debtor of specific risks, inherent in performance, which the former knew or should have known can be valued according to para. 3.

Article 168.

Equitable measure of damages

1. If loss is proved or, in any case, not disputed but it is impossible or exceptionally difficult even with expert help to assess its precise amount, the loss can be equitably estimated on the basis of partial proofs and reliable elements supplied by the parties, considering all the circumstances of the case according to the presumption method applied with particular care to probability and likelihood.
2. Considering the behaviour, interest and economic situation of the creditor, the judge can equitably limit the amount of damages:
    a) if complete compensation produces disproportionate results or creates manifestly unsustainable consequences for the debtor in view of his economic situation, and if the omitted, defective or delayed performance was not due to bad faith,
    b) in cases of the debtor's minor negligence, particularly in contracts where no reward for the debtor's performance is provided.

Article 169.

Damages in pecuniary obligations

1. Saving particular rules concerning commercial or insurance relationships the debtor of a pecuniary obligation in cases of omitted, defective or delayed performance, shall compensate the creditor without the

latter having to prove the existence of damage, and the former cannot invoke the exemption from liability provided for in Art. 162, para. 1.

2.   Such compensation is by payment of interest due in the amount at para. 3 of this Article, increased, where appropriate, by a sum for revaluation according to Art. 86, para. 5.

3.   Unless otherwise agreed, interest is due at the official rate, published from time to time by the European Central Bank, and relative to the average return rate of money for private individuals and the average cost of borrowing for businesses.

4.   Unless otherwise agreed, revaluation shall be calculated on the basis of the most recent Cost of Living Index, periodically published by Eurostat.

5.   All the above sums of money produce in their turn additional interest and can be re-valued using the same criteria.

6.   Any different agreement controls.

Article 170.

Penal clause

1.   Apart from the provision in para. 5, if the parties, when drawing up the contract, have agreed that in the event of omitted, inexact or delayed performance, a specified penalty shall be due by the debtor, this shall be considered the reparation due from the debtor in the above situations, unless compensation was agreed on for additional loss.

2.   The above perfomance is due without the creditor having to prove the existence and amount of damage.

3.   The creditor can demand both the principal performance and the penalty only if the latter has been stipulated for mere delay.

4.   The penalty can be equitably reduced by the judge, if the debtor has made partial performance which has not been refused by the creditor or if the amount of the penalty is clearly excessive, always taking into account the interest that the creditor had in the performance.

5.   In all consumer contracts, penal clauses charged to the consumer in the standard conditions are without effect.

Article 171.

Actionable remedies and their joinder

1.   After requesting compensation, giving necessary indications, and after the six (three) months (for the same reasons given in para. 2 of Art. 160), counting from receipt of said request, have elapsed – whilst retaining the right, in emergency, to request the court for execution of

the measures contemplated in Art. 172 – the aggrieved creditor has the right to establish judicial or arbitration proceedings for the ascertainment and the assessment of recoverable loss to recover, if such is the case, damages from sustained, in order the debtor. The creditor equally has the right to request such ascertainment, regardless of the possibility or suitability of obtaining compensation, provided this is for lawful purposes, among which the availability of said findings in accordance with Art. 132, and as indicators for the evaluation of the size of his estate, not only for tax purposes.

2. Not only in the case covered by Art. 165, para. 1, the aggrieved creditor can apply to the court or arbitrators in order to have the mere existence of loss ascertained, leaving its assessment to a later judgement or arbitration.

3. In addition the to specific redress provided for in Art. 166, para. 2, the various remedies are cumulative so that the reparation shall entirely fulfil its purpose, provided the cumulation does not benefit the victim beyond the prejudice suffered nor disadvantage the debtor beyond what he can bear.

Article 172.

Conservation measures and summary remedies

1. In the situations specified in this code and in all cases where the rights or reasonably justified expectations of one of the parties, without his responsibility, are about to be or have been threatened, or are jeopardized or hindered by acts, omissions or harmful facts which have already occurred or may reasonably be expected to occur, the judge, at said party's instance, may make the following enforceable orders, in accordance with procedural rules of the place where such orders are made:

   a) prohibitive injunction, by which he orders the other party to cease an act or omission undertaken or feared. The judge can, should the case arise, also order said party to provide adequate security for the damage already caused or feared, and fix a time limit within which the order shall be carried out; he can in addition, if necessary, subordinate compliance with the order to the furnishing of a guarantee by the applicant,

   b) mandatory injunction, by which he orders the other party specific performance of an obligation to deliver or to do something. The judge can, should the case arise, also order said party to provide adequate security for the damage already caused or feared, and fix a time limit within which the order shall be carried out; he can in addition, if necessary, subordinate compliance with the order to the furnishing of a guarantee by the applicant.

2. Saving compliance with the applicable Community and national provisions, the application must be made to the competent judge for urgent remedies at the place where the injunctions are to be carried out.

Article 173.

Arbitration

1. Apart from the provisions of para. 4 below, in the situations where this Code provides for judicial intervention, either party can apply for arbitration by three arbitrators, as provided for in this Article, the expenses of which arbitration shall be governed by provisions in force in the place where said procedure occurs.

2. Apart from the applicable Community and national rules, and unless otherwise agreed by the parties, arbitration shall occur in the place where the judge sits who would otherwise handle the case, and in order to establish it, the party taking the initiative shall convey written notice to the other party giving all necessary indications and stating that he intends to submit the controversy – already raised as provided in the relevant provisions – to arbitration, giving the name of his arbitrator and inviting the other party to give written notice to his opponent of the name of the other party's arbitrator within a time-limit of not less than thirty days. If the other party fails to nominate his arbitrator within said time limit, the first party can apply to the judge having jurisdiction, for the appointment of an arbitrator for the other party, following the law, of the European Member State in which arbitration is to take place. In the absence of specific provisions on the subject, application can be made to the President of the Court of Second Instance sitting in the place where arbitration is to occur. The third arbitrator is chosen by agreement of the two chosen arbitrators or, failing agreement, by the above-mentioned judge, on application of said arbitrators or one of the parties. The provisions of Art. 21 and Art. 36, para 2, shall apply to the notices mentioned in this paragraph.

3. If the attempted conciliation of the parties does not succeed, the controversy must be settled, unless otherwise agreed by the parties, on the basis of the provisions of this Code and any others applicable, by a written majority award granted from the arbitrators not more than six months after nomination of the last arbitrator. The award is effective under Art. 42 and, as soon as issued, enables the orders in Art. 172 to be made.

4. This Article does not apply:
   a) if mandatory provisions state that the controversy cannot be settled by arbitration;

b) if it is not a matter of deciding a controversy, but of granting prohibitive or mandatory injunction, fixing or extending a time limit, authorizing a deposit or adopting similar measures. In all these cases Art. 172 shall apply;

c) if arbitration procedure is excluded by the contract, or a different arbitration procedure is provided for;

d) when the controversy has already been brought before a court.

PRINCIPLES OF EUROPEAN TRUST LAW*

Article I

Main characteristics of the trust

(1) In a trust, a person called the 'trustee' owns assets segregated from his private patrimony and must deal with those assets (the 'trust fund') for the benefit of another person called the 'beneficiary' or for the furtherance of a purpose.

(2) There can be more than one trustee and more than one beneficiary; a trustee may himself be one of the beneficiaries.

(3) The separate existence of the trust fund entails its immunity from claims by the trustee's spouse, heirs and personal creditors.

(4) In respect of the separate trust fund a beneficiary has personal rights and may also have proprietary rights against the trustee and against third parties to whom any part of the fund has been wrongfully transferred.

Article II

Creation of the trust

The general rule is that in order to create a trust a person called the 'settlor' in his lifetime or on death must, with the intention of creating a segregated trust fund, transfer assets to the trustee. However, it may also be possible for a settlor to create a trust by making it clear that he is to be trustee of particular assets of his.

Article III

Trust fund

(1) The trust fund consists not only of the original assets and those subsequently added, but also of those assets from time to time representing the original or added assets.

(2) The trust fund is not available to satisfy claims made against the trustee in his personal capacity. Except to the extent that the settlor's creation of the trust contravenes laws protecting his creditors, spouse or heirs, the trust fund is available only for claims made by creditors dealing

* This text is published in D J Hayton, S C J J Kortmann, H L E Verhagen, *Principles of European Trust Law*, The Hague 1999.

with the trustee in his capacity as such and, subject thereto, for claims of the beneficiaries or the enforcer, who is an office holder entitled to enforce a trust for purposes.

(3) A trustee of several trusts must keep each trust fund not only segregated from his private patrimony but also from each of the other trust funds, except to the extent that the terms of the trusts otherwise permit.

Article IV

Trusts for beneficiaries or for enforceable purposes

(1) Upon creating a trust, the settlor must designate ascertained or ascertainable persons as beneficiaries to whom the trustee's obligations in respect of the trust fund are owed or will be owed, or must designate purposes in respect of which there is an enforcer.

(2) To the extent that the settlor fails to create rights affecting the whole of the trust fund the trustee will own the assets for the benefit of the settlor or his successors.

(3) Any beneficiary, or any enforcer of a trust for purposes, has a right to information needed to protect his interest and to ensure that the trustee accounts to him.

(4) Subject to the terms of the trust, a beneficiary can make a disposition of his rights.

(5) Any beneficiary, or any enforcer of a trust for purposes, has the right to seek judicial enforcement of the terms of the trust.

Article V

Trustees' duties and powers

(1) The trustee must exercise his rights as owner in accordance with the law and the terms of the trust.

(2) The fundamental duty of a trustee is to adhere to the terms of the trust, to take reasonable care of the trust assets and to act in the best interests of the beneficiaries or, in the case of a trust for purposes, the furtherance of those purposes.

(3) A trustee must keep separate and protect the trust assets, must maintain accurate accounts and must provide the beneficiaries and the enforcer with information requested to protect their interests.

(4) Except to the extent otherwise permitted by the terms of the trust or by law, a trustee must personally perform his functions. He must act honestly and he must avoid all conflicts of interest unless otherwise authorised.

(5)   A trustee is accountable for the trust fund, must personally make good any loss occasioned to the trust fund by his breach of trust and must personally augment such fund by the amount of any profits made by him in breach of his duty.

Article VI

Remedies against trustees for breach of trust

Remedies that the court can provide against a trustee for breach of trust include an order restraining particular conduct or removing the trustee from his office and replacing him or decreeing payment of compensation for losses or restitution of profits. The court may also have power to declare that particular assets of the trustee have always been part of the trust fund and never became part of his private patrimony or are to be regarded as security for satisfying his liability.

Article VII

Liabilities of third parties

Where a trustee wrongfully transfers part of the trust fund to a transferee who is not protected as a purchaser in good faith or otherwise, the transferee must make good the loss to the trust fund or may be ordered to hold the assets so transferred (or assets representing them) as part of the trust fund separate from his private patrimony or as security for satisfying his liability. This liability may extend to any subsequent transferee who is not protected as a purchaser in good faith or otherwise.

Article VIII

Termination of a trust

(1)   Notwithstanding the terms of the trust, where all the beneficiaries are in existence, have been ascertained, and are of full capacity, then, if all such beneficiaries are in agreement, they can require the trustee to terminate the trust and distribute the trust fund between themselves and their nominees as they direct. However, if some material purpose of the settlor remains to be served then the beneficiaries may not be permitted to terminate the trust.

(2)   A trust terminates (a) by virtue of all the trust fund having been distributed to beneficiaries or having been used for trust purposes or (b) by virtue of there being no beneficiaries and no person, whether or not then in existence, who can become a beneficiary in accordance with the terms of the trust, or (c) by virtue of a person exercising a power of termination.

(3)   At the close of the permitted period for the duration of the trust
      (subject to the trustee retaining sufficient assets to make reasonable
      provision for possible liabilities) the trust fund shall be distributed by
      the trustee as soon as reasonably practicable in accordance with any
      terms of the trust setting out how the trust fund should then be
      distributed. However, if there are no such terms then the trust fund
      shall be owned by the trustee for the benefit of the settlor or his
      successors.

(4)   In the case of a trust for purposes, where such purposes have been
      fulfilled so far as possible or cannot now be carried out, then the trust
      fund shall be owned by the trustee for the benefit of the settlor or his
      successors, unless the terms of the trust are varied or extended.